ENGLISH PUBLIC THEOLOGY

T&T Clark Enquiries in Theological Ethics

Series editors

Brian Brock
Susan F. Parsons

ENGLISH PUBLIC THEOLOGY

A Reformation Response to the Crisis of Natural Rights

Joan Lockwood O'Donovan

LONDON • NEW YORK • OXFORD • NEW DELHI • SYDNEY

T&T CLARK
Bloomsbury Publishing Plc
50 Bedford Square, London, WC1B 3DP, UK
1385 Broadway, New York, NY 10018, USA
29 Earlsfort Terrace, Dublin 2, Ireland

BLOOMSBURY, T&T CLARK and the T&T Clark logo are trademarks of
Bloomsbury Publishing Plc

First published in Great Britain 2024
Paperback edition published 2025

Copyright © Joan Lockwood O'Donovan, 2024

Joan Lockwood O'Donovan has asserted her right under the Copyright, Designs
and Patents Act, 1988, to be identified as Author of this work.

For legal purposes the Acknowledgments on p. x constitute an extension
of this copyright page

All rights reserved. No part of this publication may be reproduced or transmitted in
any form or by any means, electronic or mechanical, including photocopying, recording,
or any information storage or retrieval system, without prior permission in writing
from the publishers.

Bloomsbury Publishing Plc does not have any control over, or responsibility for, any
third-party websites referred to or in this book. All internet addresses given in this
book were correct at the time of going to press. The author and publisher regret any
inconvenience caused if addresses have changed or sites have ceased to exist,
but can accept no responsibility for any such changes.

A catalogue record for this book is available from the British Library.

Library of Congress Cataloging-in-Publication Data

Names: O'Donovan, Joan Lockwood, 1950- author.
Title: English public theology: a reformation response to the crisis of natural rights /
Joan Lockwood O'Donovan.
Description: London; New York: T&T Clark, 2024. | Series: T&T Clark enquiries in theological
ethics | Includes bibliographical references and index.
Identifiers: LCCN 2023022381 (print) | LCCN 2023022382 (ebook) | ISBN 9780567712516
(hb) | ISBN 9780567712561 (pbk) | ISBN 9780567712523 (epdf) | ISBN 9780567712554
(epub) | ISBN 9780567712530
Subjects: LCSH: Public theology–England. | Reformation–England. |
Natural law–England–History.
Classification: LCC BT83.63 .O43 2024 (print) | LCC BT83.63 (ebook) |
DDC 296.70942–dc23/eng/20230710
LC record available at https://lccn.loc.gov/2023022381
LC ebook record available at https://lccn.loc.gov/2023022382

ISBN: HB: 978-0-5677-1251-6
PB: 978-0-5677-1256-1
ePDF: 978-0-5677-1252-3
ePUB: 978-0-5677-1255-4

Series: T&T Clark Enquiries in Theological Ethics

Typeset by Deanta Global Publishing Services, Chennai, India

To find out more about our authors and books visit www.bloomsbury.com and
sign up for our newsletters.

*To Oliver, Matthew, and Paul,
and in memory of the late George Grant*

CONTENTS

Acknowledgments	x
List of Abbreviations	xi
INTRODUCTION	1
Theological Interpretation of Church Tradition	3
Contemporary Crisis of the English Reformation Tradition and of Liberal Rights Society	6
A Critical and Constructive Theological Alternative to Modern Liberal Rights	9

Chapter 1
THE REFORMATION FOUNDATIONS OF ENGLISH PUBLIC THEOLOGY	17
The Laws of Tudor Church Polity	18
Authorized English Bibles	23
Books of Common Prayer	27
Edwardian and Elizabethan Homilies	41
Forty-Two and Thirty-Nine Articles	48

Chapter 2
THE REFORMATION TRADITION IN CRISIS	51
The Church's Disengagement from the Reformation Tradition	52
Exclusion of the Reformation Tradition from Political Discussion	62
Challenges to the Public Status and Functioning of the Church of England	66
Conclusion	82

Chapter 3
DIAGNOSING THE LATE MODERN POLITY: THE DYNAMICS OF LIBERAL NATURAL RIGHTS	83
The Interrelated Contradictions of Late Modern Society	85
Clarifying the Contradictions via the History of Modern Natural Rights	87
Contemporary Political and Legal Ramifications of Liberal Natural Rights	94
The Scientific-Technological Trajectory of Liberal Natural Rights	97
The Juridical Cultural Trajectory of Liberal Natural Rights	101
Which Theological Alternative to Modern Liberal Natural Rights?	103

Chapter 4
CONTINUITIES OF THE PREMODERN AND MODERN NATURAL RIGHTS TRADITIONS — 107

- Canonist Construction of Subjective Natural Right and Permissive Natural Right — 107
- Juridical Ecclesiology: Imperial Papalism and Ecclesiastical Corporatism — 113
- Formative Rights Theories: Marsilius and Ockham — 116
- Evangelical and Naturalist Rights Theories: Wyclif and Gerson — 123
- Thematizing Control and Freedom: Summenhart — 125
- Toward Legal Assimilation and Overcoming of Natural Right — 126
- Political Construction on the Natural Right of Self-Defense — 130
- Critical Summary and Reformation Alternative — 132

Chapter 5
THE PRIORITY OF SOTERIOLOGY — 139

- A Soteriological Approach to the *Imago Dei* — 139
- God's Accomplished Work of Salvation — 142
- Resurrection and Creation, Justification, and Revelation — 148
- Toward a Dynamic, Relational, and Christological *Imago Dei* — 154

Chapter 6
GOD'S ONGOING WORK OF JUSTIFICATION: BRINGING SINNERS TO FAITH — 159

- Aspects of "A True and Lively Faith" — 159
- The Single Object of Faith — 160
- The Liveliness of Faith — 165
- The Certainty of Faith — 171
- Assurance, Election, and Predestination — 173
- Faith and Moral Action: Toward an Ethic of Dispossession and Repossession — 175

Chapter 7
SCRIPTURAL COMMUNICATION OF GOD'S WORD OF SALVATION — 179

- The Sufficiency and Authority of Scripture — 179
- The Textual Structure of Scriptural Sufficiency — 181
- The Divine and the Human Historical Genesis of the Text — 184
- Redemption of Historical Community: Scripture as Divine and Human Tradition — 189

Chapter 8
THE CHURCH'S COMMON WORSHIP INFORMING THE PRACTICE OF
   FAITH   193
   The Visible Church as Worshipping Community   193
   Liturgical Forms of Attending to God Speaking   195
   Corporate Worship as Archetypical Obedience to Christ's Rule   203
   The Sacraments as Faithful Action   205
   Corporate Worship and the Renewal of Faithful Action, Then and Now   214
   The Struggle of Spiritual Worship against Idolatry, Then and Now   216

Chapter 9
AUTHORITY IN THE CHURCH   221
   Spiritual and Political Authority in the Articles   222
   Tudor Ministerial Orders against Catholic Traditions   227
   Evangelical Ministries in the Liturgies of Ordering   232
   The Reformed Discipline against Tudor Ministerial Orders   239
   Overcoming the Public Hegemony of Political and Technological
      Rule: The Publicity of Nonjuridical Practices and Authorities   250

Chapter 10
POLITICAL JURISDICTION UNDER GOD'S JUDGMENT   255
   God's Ordination of Political Jurisdiction   256
   The Theological and Practical Insufficiency of Political Jurisdiction   260
   Political Authority and the Moral Priority of Obedience   264
   God's Appointment and Equipment of the Ruler   268
   The Human Constraints on Political Authority   275
   A Theological Alternative to the Western Natural Rights Political
      Tradition   281

Bibliography   293
Index   305

ACKNOWLEDGMENTS

I am grateful to my husband, Oliver, for patiently curbing my prolixity, to John Walker for his invaluable labors on the index, and to the series editors, Brian Brock and Susan Parsons, for their unstinting enthusiasm and support for publishing this work.

Of the more recent opportunities afforded me to develop a critique of natural rights in tandem with an apology for English Reformation public theology, I am especially grateful for the invitations to publish the following articles: "The Liberal Legacy of English Church Establishment: a contribution to the legal accommodation of religious pluralism in Europe," *Journal of Law, Philosophy and Culture* (ed. William Wagner) 6, no. 1 (2011): 17–45; "A Timely Contribution of the English Reformation to an Evangelical Public Theology of Law and Freedom," *Political Theology* 19, no. 4 (2018 Special Issue: *Reformation Political Theology*, ed. Bradford Littlejohn): 314–30; "Understanding Law and Constitutionalism in Modernity: The Critical Contribution of English Reformation Public Theology," in *Christianity and Constitutionalism*, ed. Nicholas Aroney and Ian Leigh (Oxford: Oxford University Press, 2022), 149–72.

ABBREVIATIONS

Full bibliographical details for each reference are found in the Bibliography.

BCP	*The Book of Common Prayer 1559*. Edited by John Booty.
CR	*Corpus Reformatorum*. Edited by Heinrich Ernst Bindseil *et. al.*
CS	*Certain Sermons or Homilies (1547)*. Edited by Ronald B. Bond.
DP	*Defensor pacis*. Translated by Alan Gewirth.
FSPB	*The First and Second Prayer Books of Edward VI.*
GH	*The Two Books of Homilies Appointed to be read in Churches*. Edited by John Griffiths.
HAL	*A History of Anglican Liturgy.* Geoffrey J. Cuming.
IG	*From Irenaeus to Grotius: A Sourcebook in Christian Political Thought*. Edited by Oliver O'Donovan *and* Joan Lockwood O'Donovan.
INR	*The Idea of Natural Rights: Studies on Natural Rights, Natural Law and Church Law 1150–1625*. Brian Tierney.
LFM	*William of Ockham: A Letter to the Friars Minor and Other Writings*. Edited and translated by Arther Stephen McGrade and John Kilcullen.
MWL	*Miscellaneous Writings and Letters of Thomas Cranmer*. Edited by John Edmund Cox.
OND	*Opus nonaginta dierum*. William of Ockham.
PG	*Patrologia cursus complete . . . Series graeca*. Edited by J.-P. Migne.
PL	*Patrologia cursus complete . . . Series prima [latina]*. Edited by J.-P. Migne.
SD	*A Short Discourse on Tyrannical Government*. Edited by A. S. McGrade.
ST	*Summa Theologiae*. Thomas Aquinas
STG	*The Second Treatise of Government: Two Treatises of Government*. John Locke, Edited by Peter Laslett.
TA	*On the Thirty-Nine Articles: Conversations with Tudor Christianity,* 2nd edn. Oliver O'Donovan.
TC	*The Tudor Constitution: Documents and Commentary,* 2nd edn. G. R. Elton.
VPW	*Francisco de Vitoria, Political Writings*. Edited by Anthony Pagden and Jeremy Lawrance.
WJW	*The Works of John Whitgift*. Edited by John Ayre.
WRH	*Of the Laws of Ecclesiastical Polity*. The Folger Library Edition of the Works of Richard Hooker.
WD	*Writings and Disputations of Thomas Cranmer Relative to the Sacrament of the Lord's Supper*. Edited by John Edmund Cox.

INTRODUCTION

This study brings together inquiries into two historical legacies that are rarely brought together in contemporary academic discussion: the legacies of English Reformation public theology and of Western natural rights.

The inquiries differ somewhat in form and objective. The first takes the form of a critical apology for the public theology of the English Reformation, commending it as a theoretical and practical resource in the face of contemporary indifference and hostility. By "public theology" I denote theology that is "public" in two senses long recognized in Western thought: it is embedded in orders of practice established in "public (governmental) law" and carrying society-wide authority, and it gives an account of "public authority" and its institutional modes of practice. The second inquiry is consistently critical, endeavoring to show the problematic character of Western natural rights theory from its early historical formulations and the destructive moral, political, and legal impact of its prevailing modern strand.[1] As these differences suggest, my analysis and assessment of Western rights is from a theological perspective heavily indebted to the public theology of the English Reformation. Deepening engagement with this theology over two decades has provided a systematic framework for my present critique of the evolving Western conceptuality of rights, which has allowed me to incorporate a spectrum of nontheological insights without, I hope, losing the argument's theological moorings.

The aim of this study, then, is to commend defining features of English Reformation public theology, both for their perennial ethical and political soundness and for their diagnostic and therapeutic relevance to the ethical and

---

1. My wedding of an apology for English Reformation public theology and a critique of natural rights theory has developed over two decades out of a succession of published articles, including "Rights, Law and Political Community: A Theological and Historical Perspective," *Transformation: An International Dialogue on Mission and Ethics* 20, no. 1 (2003): 30–8; "The Liberal Legacy of English Church Establishment: A Contribution to the Legal Accommodation of Religious Plurality in Europe," *Journal of Law, Philosophy and Culture* 6, no. 1 (2011): 17–45; "A Timely Contribution of the English Reformation to an Evangelical Public Theology of Law and Freedom," *Political Theology* 19, no. 4 (2018): 314–30; "Understanding Law and Constitutionalism in Modernity: The Critical Contribution of English Reformation Public Theology," in *Christianity and Constitutionalism*, ed. Nicholas Aroney and Ian Leigh (Oxford: Oxford University Press, 2022), 149–72.

political malady of late modern society. With this aim, my study swims against the current tide of scholarly ethical and political discussion which, outside of select Anglican circles, neglects the English Reformation as a critical and constructive theological resource. Admittedly, English Reformation thought, owing to its comparative obscurity, has not attracted the sustained criticism leveled at the magisterial continental reformers over the last sixty years by an assortment of theologians, ethicists, historians, political and social philosophers. Nevertheless, it has been negatively affected by the recent widespread detachment of Christian ethical and political thinking from dominant Reformation theological orientations, largely in favor of Aristotelian and Thomist virtue and natural law orientations, or syntheses of Reformation with scholastic or Renaissance traditions. Notably, the formative and influential critiques of modern political theory and practice produced by adherents of Aristotelian and/or Thomist thought have cast Reformation (especially Lutheran) theology as a key historical precursor and source of modern defects.[2]

Whatever may be the scholarly constituency of interest in my inquiries, their undertaking requires a theological justification. For their theological sights are narrowly focused on one church tradition of thought and practice, and that tradition itself requires that such narrowing of theological sights be justified. English Reformation public theology recognizes the paramount need of moral and political theology for wide-ranging, searching engagement with the Scriptural text and with the longer exegetical and theological inheritance attaching to the text, the theological task beginning and ending in faithful, informed, and disciplined reflection on the authoritative Scriptural witness to the Word of God spoken in Christ. However, the English reformers also recognize the vital contribution to the church's mission of the more modest task of interpreting the English church's reforming theology and practice to its sympathizers and its detractors, within it and outside it.

The present apology is undertaking this more modest task, in the mode of recollecting the English church's founding tradition of reforming thought and practice. The apology's recollective character does not distract from concern with the church's present mission, for its intelligibility as a communal mission with an enduring temporal identity depends on its present communal appropriation of a defining historical tradition. In that this defining tradition understands the church's

---

2. For example, Alasdair MacIntyre, *A Short History of Ethics: A History of Moral Philosophy from the Homeric Age to the Twentieth Century* (London: Routledge, 1966); John Milbank and Adrian Pabst, *The Politics of Virtue: Post-Liberalism and the Human Future* (London and New York: Rowman & Littlefield, 2016); Quentin Skinner, *The Foundations of Modern Political Thought, Vol. 2: The Age of Reformation* (Cambridge: Cambridge University Press, 1978); Eric Voegelin, *History of Political Ideas, Vol. IV: Renaissance and Reformation*. The Collected Works of Eric Voegelin, vol. 22 (Columbia: University of Missouri Press, 1998); Sheldon S. Wolin, *Politics and Vision: Continuity and Innovation in Western Political Thought* (Princeton: Princeton University Press, 1960, expanded 2004).

mission as communication of God's Word in Christ witnessed in the Scriptures, its recollection must be undertaken within the authoritative horizon of the written tradition of Scripture. As such, my recollection will be critical as well as apologetic: frank about the weaknesses as well the strengths of the Reformation inheritance. In addition, it will be both ecumenical and provincial: attuned to the tradition's familial resemblances with others sharing the Scriptural horizon, as well as to its distinctive features. Moreover, as my critique of Western natural rights draws on this Reformation inheritance, it must also be undertaken within the Scriptural horizon. I will briefly enlarge on the theological justification and coherence of these two undertakings before outlining their unfolding over successive chapters.

Theological Interpretation of Church Tradition

Theological recollection of a church's historical tradition recognizes two aspects of the grounding of this exercise in the writings of Scripture. The first is that the distinctive social and institutional identities of historical churches have, to a significant extent, been generated, defended, and developed over time by their exegetical and hermeneutical handling of the written traditions of ancient Israel and the apostolic writings; and, correspondingly, that diversity in handling the biblical canon and biblical texts has played a pivotal role in generating and sustaining the deeper differences among identifiable church traditions. In accepting their indebtedness to a particular church tradition, then, theologians inescapably confront the issue of the coherence and fidelity of their tradition's handling of the biblical witness. But how they approach this issue depends, in some part, on understandings within their tradition of the task and modes of Scriptural interpretation and the dynamic of epistemological authority involved. Resembling its continental counterparts, the English Reformation tradition stresses the supremely authoritative status of the written tradition of the canonical Scriptures as an independent, objective measure of the hermeneutical fidelity of subsequent church traditions, so that assessment of this fidelity takes the form of continually testing a tradition's interpretative judgments by the textual testimony of Scripture. Those responsible for such testing by virtue of their training in biblical and theological studies generally regard it as indispensable to the church's continuing theological energy and discipline deployed in internal ministries, discussions, and practices and in ecumenical and missionary outreach.

The second aspect is the Scriptural revelation of Christ's church as a historical and an eschatological community: a spatially and temporally bound mission of proclaiming the gospel of Jesus Christ and a communion of the faithful in the Spirit transcending spatial and temporal boundaries and participating in Christ's coming kingdom. The church's historical identity is given in the creatureliness of human beings as embodied souls, partaking in a single nature, a single way of being, which, nevertheless, is variegated in time and space by virtue of ethnic, cultural, geographical, social, economic, and political determinants. These determinants shape and are shaped by the ongoing mission of particular churches with their distinctive theological orientations, liturgical styles, and arrangement of ministries, which theological inquiry can never simply ignore or perfunctorily repudiate if it is to serve the local church's mission. For communal mission requires continuity with past thought and practice if it is to meet with integrity novel exigencies in the present.

At the same time the church as an eschatological community cannot simply accept tradition as the immanent-historical womb of its thinking and acting, so that thinking and acting are merely present appropriations of what is bequeathed; for tradition per se is not the concrete universal, the local matrix within which universality is given. Only the tradition of Scripture through which the trinitarian God is concretely revealed in history is that matrix, and only this tradition can demonstrate the falsely universalist claims of moral and political traditions. Theological inquiry, therefore, must aim at an engagement with the Scriptural tradition beyond the particular determinations of historical church tradition, even while fulfilling its obligation to understand and expound church tradition with grateful humility and critical discernment. For faithful appropriation of ecclesial tradition is a purifying appropriation, detecting in the light of the Scriptural measure the tradition's erroneous wanderings and sinful worldly collusions and having no other purpose than to render what is handed down an efficacious communication of the universal life and ministry of Christ's church.

Frequently complicating the task of recollecting church tradition are the rival claims of different strands of thought and practice to articulate most fully and effectively continuity with the church's defining legacy. In this situation, recollection can take one of several courses: it can prioritize one historical strand over another (or others) or undertake to synthesize the different strands or to focus on their shared historical foundation. Our recollection takes the third course, which, in the case of the Church of England, has an undeniable epistemological advantage: namely, the high degree of institutional and scholarly consensus concerning the historical foundation of the Anglican tradition. It is generally recognized to consist of public instruments produced in the reigns of Henry VIII, Edward VI, and Elizabeth I, intended to be definitive or constitutive of the thought and practice of the reformed church in England: namely, the reforming legal statutes, the authorized vernacular bibles, the Edwardian and Elizabethan prayer books and ordinals, doctrinal Articles of Religion, and official books of homilies. Excepting (in part) the homilies, these instruments have been presupposed by all strands of thought and practice within the Church of England over four centuries, and some continue to have legal force as church standards.

It is decisive for my apologetic and critical undertakings that the tradition constituted by these instruments is a tradition *both* of secular government and law *and* of spiritual ministry and worship. Precisely because the tradition's core theological components are "public" in respect of their legal authority and their substance, my apology has its completion in criticism of the prevailing public tradition of natural rights thought and practice. For it belongs to the apologetic genre to join battle with forces hostile to the apologist's "cause," and the prevailing natural rights tradition is hostile to this tradition of public theology. My apologetic campaign, therefore, has the objective not merely of dispelling ignorance and misconceptions about this tradition but of marshaling the tradition's critical acumen to challenge the intellectual orientations and canons of judgment of its contemporary despisers and opponents. Whatever the latter's precise theoretical perspectives, moral and political orientations, and communal allegiances, I shall argue that they share ideas progressively elaborated within the Western tradition of natural rights.

The public foundation of the English Reformation theological tradition, its historical profile as a tradition of church establishment, justifies my preponderant concern with the contemporary vicissitudes of this tradition in the English context, as distinct from the larger Anglican context within Britain and throughout the world. For legal establishment is the one feature of the Church of England that significantly distinguishes it from its Irish, Welsh, and Scottish progeny in Britain[3] and from most of its historical progeny outside Britain, which are either disestablished or nonestablished Anglican churches. A conspicuous irony of the Anglican Communion, comprising the mother church and her daughter churches, is that this core political dimension of the mother church's theological and institutional identity has had to be suppressed in the coming into being of independent daughter churches as self-standing, self-governing associations. Disestablished Anglican churches have divorced themselves from this political inheritance in accommodating changing political and legal, social, cultural, and geographical realities, whereas nonestablished Anglican churches are without this inheritance. Moreover, in the postcolonial world which the majority of Anglican churches inhabit—the world of state-building and political maturation, frequently of ethnic and religious strife, sometimes of political repression or persecution— the established Church of England carries the stigma of a discredited imperial past, an embarrassing conjunction of political and religious allegiance, and the legitimizing of state religious control.

It is not the case, however, that the Church of England's Reformation inheritance has no distinctive theological illumination and practical guidance to offer to its Anglican progeny today. Relevant are two considerations touching

---

3. The (Anglican) Church of Ireland, present today in both Northern Ireland and the Republic of Ireland, was disestablished by the Irish Church Act 1869 and the Church in Wales in 1920 under the Welsh Church Act 1914. The Scottish Episcopal Church was a nonestablished autonomous church from its inception in 1690. The framework of English church establishment must be distinguished from that of Presbyterian church establishment in Scotland, with its complex and turbulent history of multiple legislative foundations (1560, 1638, and 1690). Brought under British parliamentary jurisdiction by the Union Treaties and Acts of Union 1706 and subsequently torn apart by schisms over the issue of civil jurisdiction, the established church's modern constitutional settlement lies in the Church of Scotland Act 1921, which recognized the church's independent jurisdiction in matters of doctrine, worship, government, and discipline, and together with the Church of Scotland (Property and Endowment) Act 1925, provided the basis of reunification.

civil and ecclesiastical polities. Touching civil polity, the consideration is that many ex-British colonial territories have retained elements of the British civil political and legal tradition fashioned or refashioned within her Reformation inheritance. In the more politically and economically advanced of these territories, the reconstruction of these British traditions on a secular rights footing in the modern period, but most dramatically since the Second World War, is now reaping a similarly troubling social and political harvest as in Britain; and in the less advanced territories, their constitutional construction as secular rights states has in many respects not yielded the hoped-for harvest of social and political justice and stability, owing to the domestic and foreign agents of exploitation and upheaval. Thus, along the spectrum of ex-British colonial states, Christian political reflection may benefit from a fresh encounter with the Reformation theological underpinnings of English civil law and government in addressing urgent contemporary social and political issues.

Touching ecclesiastical polity, the consideration is that most Anglican churches display a considerable continuity of legal substance and culture with the mother church, despite their different histories of legal adaptation and revision; this continuity simultaneously reflects and reinforces their common inheritance of faith, ministry, and worship. One major continuity in Anglican church law is the attaching to church offices of positive duties founded on divine right and law; another is the legal authorization of a prayer book, and, in most churches, of liturgical variations on it. These common legal features carry with them understandings of the sources and purposes of law in the life of the church and the civil community, connecting contemporary Anglican churches with their patristic and medieval, as well as Reformation forebears. In recent years, heightened attention has been paid to the common Anglican legal legacy, as disruption of relations within and among Anglican churches by doctrinal, moral, and ecclesiological issues has prompted concern with the practical, institutional dimensions of Anglican identity and communion.

Contemporary Crisis of the English Reformation Tradition and of Liberal Rights Society

Although theoretical reflection and institutional practices are neither reducible to nor derivable from each other, they are interdependent in communal traditions and equally implicated in their vicissitudes: they invariably wax and wane together. In the last seventy years, central elements of English Reformation public theology and practice have lost ground in English ecclesiastical and civil life and in international fora where they have incurred opprobrium, or merely dismissal and neglect. On the ecclesiastical front, contemporary liturgical practice, theological reflection, and instruction of clergy and laity within the Church of England have shifted away from the church's Reformation doctrinal, theological, and liturgical foundations. On the political front, within and across national borders, prevailing academic and popular discussions of the church's role in political society have left little or no space for this Reformation tradition and have removed its elements outside the bounds of admissible considerations.

The critical state of the English Reformation tradition today renders my apologetic enterprise both more difficult and more timely. It renders my enterprise a labor of retrieving a distant and neglected historical inheritance rather than of sustaining the integrity of a vibrant tradition, and so presents fresh grounds for questioning its worth. Such questioning can only be met by demonstrating the persisting critical and constructive power of the tradition: its capacity to clarify current theoretical and practical issues and impasses and illuminate a way forward. These issues and impasses are of broad and urgent concern in our late modern societies, pertaining as they do to the prevailing understanding and outworking of human freedom, authority, power, and law in multiple institutional and practical spheres: political, economic, educational, scientific-technological, and religious.

To bring the resources of English Reformation public theology to bear on these current issues and impasses is to advance diagnostic analysis of the perilous situation in which not only this church tradition but other denominational and religious traditions in Britain and elsewhere currently find themselves owing to internal and external developments. Moreover, religious traditions are not exceptional in the degree to which they have suffered and are suffering attenuation. The contemporary crisis of tradition has been recognized in many quarters across the intellectual, professional, and vocational spectrum: within education, the arts, medicine, law, politics, commerce, finance, and the trades. Therefore, a resurgence of concern in theological circles with the recent vicissitudes of church traditions has relevance for the wider resurgence of concern in society with the loss of traditions. As with other accounts of this crisis, my account identifies the attenuation of certain beliefs, practical wisdom, and concrete practices composing a particular communal inheritance, and identifies a nexus of causes responsible in part for that attenuation, these being structural and dynamic aspects of contemporary society entrenched in interdependent theoretical and practical spheres. My undertaking is to interpret the current crisis of the English Reformation tradition within a broader moral, political, and cultural diagnostic analysis distinguished from other analyses by drawing on the tradition's foundational theology. This undertaking occupies the first four chapters of my study.

Chapter 1 sets the stage by briefly sketching the historical genesis and content of the Reformation documentary foundations of English public theology within their domestic and European context. The sketch is primarily intended to give readers unfamiliar with these documents an appreciation of their import, coherence, and tensions as a continuing program of reform, and their exhibition of the theological foci of continental Lutheran and Swiss reforming streams, largely transmitted through the theological and literary labors of Archbishop Thomas Cranmer. This appreciation should enhance readers' engagement with the study's apologetic and critical enterprise but is not essential to it; so readers, if inclined, may safely pass over the introductory material.

Chapter 2 gives an account of the diminished contemporary presence of this Reformation tradition and the continuing challenges to it from within and outside of the Church of England. As the external, national, and international challenges highlighted in Chapter 2 are posed by dominant ideological and institutional features of liberal democratic pluralism, including the codification and implementation of human rights in public law and policy making, the chapter prepares for the critical analysis to follow of the modern development and contemporary sociopolitical impact of the liberal tradition of natural rights, understood to be the prevailing theoretical tradition of rights in the modern period.

My critical analysis in Chapter 3 of the modern liberal rights tradition is indebted to English Reformation theology for illuminating certain resemblances or analogous traits of the modern political ethos and ethic and the late scholastic ethos and ethic of which the English reformers were critical. Key are: an individualistic and voluntarist conception of moral agency and action, an excessively regulative and juridical orientation to human relationships, and an anthropocentric concentration on human rather than on divine right, righteousness, judgment, and freedom. I am, therefore, aligning myself with the critical thrust of English Reformation theology in implicating these features in the central contradiction of contemporary liberal democracy between the maximizing of individual and group freedoms and the expanding modes of control in all spheres of individual and communal life.

The chapter aims to show that the interconnections of these deleterious features of our contemporary social, political, legal, and economic environment are most clearly brought to light by charting the prevailing liberal tradition of natural rights. For their fundamental connecting thread is the unifying core of this liberal tradition: namely, an economic and juridical concept of the individual agent as the independent proprietor of his life, powers, and actions, with the moral right to dispose of his personal property and to secure his self-proprietorship against other agents by means of juridical action. In charting the elaboration of this core concept in the modern liberal rights tradition, the chapter concentrates on the formative contributions of Hobbes and Locke, before exploring the tradition's current political, legal, economic, social-cultural, and ecological ramifications. My controlling argument here and in the next chapter, pivotal to my overall project, is that this unifying conceptual core manifests the inevitable tendency of all naturalistic and rationalist ethical and political thought, not sufficiently informed by an evangelical moral epistemology and anthropology, to take as normative the distorted and disrupted relationships of sinful human beings to their creator, to themselves, and to one another.

Chapter 4 extends my critical historical analysis of natural rights theory and practice backward to premodern and protomodern developments in which different streams of scholastic theology (Scotist, Thomist, Aristotelian, and Ockamist), drawing on canonist legal commentary, cross-fertilized and later intersected with strands of Renaissance ethical and legal humanism.[4] The

---

4. For the sources and contributions to natural rights political thought in the late medieval and early modern periods, see especially Brian Tierney, *The Idea of Natural Rights: Studies on Natural Rights, Natural Law and Church Law 1150–1625* (Atlanta: Scholars Press,1997).

rationale of this undertaking is to question whether these earlier developments offer a theological alternative to later ones, able to rescue the humanistic promise of Christian natural rights thought and practice from the modern debacle of unbounded freedom, agonistic social relations, institutional legalism, and technological manipulation. My historical analysis casts doubt on this possibility by drawing out the thematic continuities of scholastic theoretical developments with modern liberal rights theory. Central to my argument is that, in providing key conceptual planks of the moral and political edifice of modern liberal rights, scholastic developments weakened, even dismantled, key planks of the theocentric and Christocentric moral and political inheritance from the Church Fathers. Principally, they undermined the patristic portrayal of created human relationships as nonproprietary and nonjuridical, and corresponding assignment of proprietary and juridical relationships to the fallen condition of humanity. The chapter concludes by outlining the critical and constructive alternative to the Western development of natural rights offered by the English reformers' revival of the theocentric and Christocentric foci of the longer biblical tradition of moral and political theology. The following chapters explore the soteriological, epistemological, ecclesiological, and political elements of this alternative.

A Critical and Constructive Theological Alternative to Modern Liberal Rights

Chapters 5 and 6 seek to demonstrate that English Reformation moral and political theology, in giving priority to soteriology, offers a dynamic, relational, and trinitarian anthropology that stands in opposition to the naturalist, voluntarist, and essentialist anthropology of the modern natural rights tradition. While the latter locates the "dignity" or unique moral status of human creatures in their proprietary freedom and control as acting subjects, English public theology resisted the temptation to conceptualize the "image of God" in which humanity is created in terms of immanent, self-standing human structures, qualities, or capacities and instead emphasized the immediate and direct dependence of humankind's creaturely being, desiring, knowing, and acting on God's Word unceasingly communicated through the Holy Spirit.

This soteriological perspective of English reforming theology keeps attention fixed on God's work of salvation in Jesus Christ, determining the history of created humankind beyond the causal nexus of sinful human reasoning, volition, and action. As God's renewal of his image in the humanity of Jesus Christ was the means of reconciling sinful humankind to himself and the end for which he created human beings, Jesus Christ alone manifests the creaturely relation of human obedience to the Father's Word in the Spirit's power, enabling humanity to act efficaciously and authoritatively within and over the nonhuman creation. This relationship restored and perfected in the Incarnate Son's obedient knowledge and self-expending love of the Father and of his fellow creatures exposes as a sinful conceit the liberal natural rights' conception of the unique moral fabric of human life in terms of subjective proprietary rights of autonomous willing, reasoning, and acting, primarily ordered to self-production and self-protection. God's Incarnate Word reveals what the liberal rights tradition disregards: the created openness of human beings to the claim and power of the creator's righteous and loving will for their common life, their unity and freedom in surrendering themselves to God and to one another and knowing themselves to be constrained by an irresistible, transcendent, and immanent imperative.

Chapter 5 presents the English reformers' Augustinian rendering of the Pauline paradigm for God's historical work of salvation as the justification of sinners. According to this biblical paradigm, God fulfills perfect justice and perfect mercy in a condemning and justifying judgment of sinful humanity. Justly condemning humankind to the captivity of sin and death for transgressing his law of life and righteousness, the Father mercifully justifies humanity through the obedient self-sacrifice of his Incarnate Son on the Cross, representatively fulfilling the law of righteousness and making satisfaction for the law's transgression. Thus, in completely uniting divine justice and divine love, Jesus Christ's saving work both validates concepts, relations, and practices constitutive of sinful humanity's moral and political life—those of justice and mercy, of juridical authority and representation, of giving, keeping (or transgressing) the law, of right-doing and wrongdoing, merit and guilt, reward, punishment, and satisfaction—and overcomes their intrinsic moral limitations and contradictions. These contradictions were starkly displayed in Christ's execution, which revealed political jurisdiction, although divinely ordained, to be infected with sinful tendencies to usurp God's rule and tyrannously to dominate fellow creatures. The peculiar enmeshing of this communal practice in the fabric of disordered human relationships renders theologically problematic the attribution of generic natural (original or created) rights of freedom and self-preservation to individual and collective subjects, in view of the intrinsically legal and justiciable character of rights apparent throughout the historical development of natural rights theory and practice.

The English reformers highlight the immeasurable distance that separates the benefits to sinful humanity of God's rule of salvation from the benefits of coercive jurisdiction by interpreting the juridical logic of Christ's sacrificial satisfaction with motifs that break through the conceptual boundaries of human jurisdiction. These are motifs of purifying human spiritual life from sin's stain, of emancipating and rescuing God's creation from the tyranny of destructive and disintegrative forces, of vanquishing the demonic power over sin and death, and of opening up to faithful human beings participation in God's promise of eternal communion with himself and with one another, fulfilling his sovereign law of love. This rich soteriological fabric sets in sharp relief the negativities of sinful human existence which God has overcome in Christ, demolishing the barriers to human emancipation erected by immanent forms of human self-understanding.

Chapter 6 completes the presentation of soteriology by explicating the English reformers' public account of faith. Faith is the form of the union of sinners with Christ and their reception of the benefits of Christ's victory over sin, death, and the law's condemnation. Authoritatively laid out in Cranmer's 1549 homilies on salvation, faith, and good works, this account conveys his expansive understanding of faith, encompassing hope as its forward-looking dimension and love as its active fruition. Four aspects of "true and lively" faith in Cranmer's account, in their dynamic moments of possession, dispossession, and repossession, frame a theological alternative to the proprietary ethos and ethic of natural rights. The foremost aspect is the single focus of faith on the Father's merciful acceptance of unworthy sinners entirely for the sake of his beloved Son, and owing solely to his righteousness, "merits and deservings." Faith's single focus bifurcates into a double focus: in laying hold of Christ's righteousness, sinners are confronted with their own unrighteousness and self-inflicted impotence and futility in striving to possess God and the highest spiritual goods. Hence, the second aspect of faith is the passive and active reception by sinners of God's acceptance of them in Christ delivering them from their disordered selves. Possessed by the Father's reconciling Word through the Spirit's power, they possess God in Christ and the Spirit of Holiness; dispossessed of their sinful selves, they actively disown their sinful selves, so that faith and repentance are coterminous.

The third aspect of faith is the necessary production of "good works": of interior and exterior actions pleasing to God and to the neighbor. Although no part of the causal nexus of justification, good works are intrinsic to faith as its "fruit." Faith as such is "lively," informed by hope and love: the faithful, wholeheartedly responding to God's gracious countenance and emboldened by their Saviour's promise to impart the Spirit of Holiness, strive to serve God in contrite humility. Illuminated and empowered by the Spirit, the faithful walk in the way of God's law, authoritatively interpreted by Christ's teaching and works of love. The fourth aspect of faith, the self-conscious assurance or "certainty" of its truth and liveliness, involves the faithful in appraising their past interior and exterior acts. Discernment of an increase of obedient love in their acts is made possible by their abiding in Christ and proleptically participating in his own knowledge and love of the Father.

Repossessing themselves in the knowledge and love of Christ, the faithful are on the road to possessing anew their neighbors and the nonhuman creation in knowledge, wisdom, and love, delivered from the nest of proprietary strivings and relationships (acquisitive, competitive, defensive, dominative, and exploitative) defining the illusory existence of sinful humanity. Faith illuminates the complex moral landscape of human beings living together by revealing their participation along with nonhuman creatures in a single divine-human community of created, fallen, and restored truth and good, in which God's eternally active Word is the one divine-human measure, estimator, valuer, and judge.

Chapter 7 addresses the epistemological dependence of faith on Scriptural revelation by explicating the English reformers' presentation of the sufficiency and authority of the Holy Scripture for salvation. The reformers present Scripture as *the literary testimony* to God's historical communication to sinful humanity of his saving word in Jesus Christ. Its testimony unifies the distinct historical moments of God's past and present communication: from Israel's foreshadowing literary witness in its vast historical scope, richness, and diversity, to the supremely authoritative witness of the apostolic writings in the emerging church, to God's continuing communication to later generations through reading and interpretation of the Scriptural writings. The knowledge imparted through these writings is, at once, objective and subjective: its object, the history of God's speaking and acting in Jesus Christ, is independent of the knowing subject, yet the knowledge involves a dialogical encounter with Jesus Christ in which the subject is effectually addressed and transformed. The "sufficiency" of Scripture, then, does not merely denote a quality internal to the textual corpus but the relation of the text in its entirety and its parts to the transcending realities of God's speaking and acting in his creation and salvation of humankind and the world—a relation of participation and invocation as well as representation. At the same time, the reformers accept as divinely given the intelligible coherence of the literary witness, and ground in this coherence the faithful, rational, and scholarly enterprise of textual interpretation.

As a corpus of literature recording the history of God's salvation, the Holy Scripture is for the English reformers supremely authoritative and sufficient, human and divine communal tradition. It resembles every other human communal inheritance in that it originates and develops within and among determinate historical communities, shaping and energizing communal vision and action and providing a supportive and integrative framework for other less comprehensive traditions of imagination, thought, and practice. But it is uniquely the divine Spirit's historical communication of the Father's Incarnate Word of Truth, Goodness, and Life, renewing humanity within and beyond the perishing *saeculum*. As the universal matrix for human traditions, including church traditions, the tradition of Scripture is the measure of their truth, goodness, right, beauty, and freedom, revealing the defects of their communal dynamics, and enabling their cathartic refinement. As such, the tradition of Scripture exposes the late modern tradition of liberal natural rights to be anti-tradition: a false universalism that undermines tradition by wedding the universal of autonomous human freedom to the universal of scientific-technological rationality. The liberal rights ideology of technological emancipation of the individual and collective will from internal and external, natural and historical constraints construes the inheritance of the past as a bondage to be overcome. Only the Spirit's continual communication through the biblical inheritance of the participation of created human life in God's historical redemption and eschatological perfecting validates and renews the role of communal tradition in the human realization of truth, goodness, and beauty.

In examining the structure of Scriptural readings and recitation in reformed English worship, Chapter 7 anticipates the fuller presentation in Chapter 8 of Tudor practices of worship as modes of attending to and responding to God's saving word spoken in the Scriptures. Tudor theology portrays the fellowship of faith as continually generated, nourished, strengthened, and purified by the dialogical practices of the assembled community in which the Spirit of the resurrected and ascended Christ is preeminently at work, incorporating believers into Christ's resurrection life and communicating to them his spiritual benefits. The chapter's principal argument is that the English reformers recognize the practices of corporate worship to be paradigmatic or archetypal exemplars of faithful action, uniquely conveying or imparting its human and divine aspects as formed by God's Word of salvation.

Four constitutive aspects of faithful action are identified and their significance is explored through the Tudor treatment of the sacraments, focusing on Holy Communion. First is the communication of faith, of the free acceptance by sinful human agents of the Father's reconciling and renewing judgment of themselves in the death and resurrection of Jesus Christ as the only ground and possibility of their performing good acts. Second is the common agency of all who, united to Christ by his Spirit, know and love themselves and their neighbors as forgiven sinners, raised and exalted with Christ, and called to participate in his renewed humanity. Third is waiting upon God's present address by attending to his directive word in the Scriptures which both reveals the universal path of faithful human action and confronts particular agents with concrete commands and opportunities arising within the newness and singularity of their life situations, beyond their imagination, desires, and calculations. Fourth is conformity to the Spirit's interior communication of the present meaning of God's law, unifying its many demands and enabling the agent to participate in Christ's freedom and lordship over the law.

In summarizing the emancipatory import of the English reformers' public theology and practice of "spiritual worship" for liberal-technological society, the chapter includes a brief appraisal of the reformers' iconoclasm. While deploring its theoretical failings and practical excesses, the appraisal commends certain insights into the logic of idolatry and the need to subject the production and reception of images by the faithful to a theologically sound discipline, suggesting that these should invigorate critical theological reflection today on the unrestrained proliferation of images across public media in a society largely lacking the intellectual and practical disciplines of communal faith in Christ.

Continuing in the ecclesiological domain, Chapter 9 examines the English reformers' portrayal of the authority of the visible church's ordained ministries in and over the church's practices of communicating God's saving Word. This authority is exegetical, theological, catechetical, liturgical, sacramental, and pastoral: in short, it is evangelical or proclamatory. However, as representing the community of faith, ministerial authority is also political, making judgments on behalf of its members commanding their deference, about a range of matters pertaining to ministry and practice, such as the preparation and appointment of ministers, the definition of doctrine and the prescription of formal liturgies. In that the primary purpose and operation of this political authority, according to the reformers, is to maintain the stability and unity of the visible community of faith under the condition of human sinfulness, the authority is necessarily jurisdictional: designating, judging and punishing offenses against God's revealed judgments and the church's public judgments conforming to them.

In proximity to the ecclesiology of the early Luther and the Zwinglian Heinrich Bullinger, English Reformation public theology largely sustains a relationship of dialectical tension and interdependence between the defining evangelical authority and the necessary jurisdictional authority of the ordained ministry. These two universal authorities and practices, between them, determine human moral agency and action in their dual reality, as already restored by Christ's conquest of sin and death and awaiting his coming kingdom, and as still struggling under the wages of sin and subject to the law's condemnation. In that the church's authority and practices of proclamation are constituted by the saving judgment of God in Christ, who is both the judge and the judged, they are removed from the divinely appointed secular authority and practices of coercive human judgment. The English reformers see this contrariness reflected in God's providential investing of supreme jurisdictional authority over his people in lay rulers, so that the English clerical hierarchy holds jurisdictional authority from, and under, its faithful lay monarch.

To clarify the issues involved in relating jurisdictional authority to the apostolic and Christological authority of the church's ordained ministries, the chapter contrasts the Tudor account of ministerial authority, taken principally from the Edwardian and Elizabethan Ordinals, to two alternative accounts which unite the proclamatory and juridical elements of ministerial authority as essential components of its Christological and apostolic endowment: namely, the canonist-papalist and the English presbyterian accounts. While criticizing the tendency of these two legalistic and juridical portrayals of ministerial authority to conflate in the visible church epistemological and political authority, divine and human law, and the temporal operations of God's preserving and justifying word of judgment, the chapter also criticizes the tendency of English reformed theology to confine authority in the visible church to coercive jurisdiction and reserve proclamatory authority to the invisible church.

The chapter's concluding argument is that the church's proclamatory authority, along with the authority of other social (i.e., essentially nonjurisdictional) institutions and enterprises, should be considered "public" on the long-accepted secular ground of freely and representatively commanding the belief, affections, intentions, and actions of members of a community, independent of the public communal authority of coercive jurisdiction. Church denominations must resist the temptation of all social institutions and sectors in our late modern, liberal rights society, to concede a monopoly of public authority to political-legal institutions and to derive from them whatever public authority they may claim for themselves. In succumbing to this temptation, the church obscures the universal authority of Christ, acting through the Holy Spirit, to liberate all human spheres of cooperative activity from their sinful deflections, and to return them to their divinely bestowed, intrinsic goods, purposes, modes of authority, and practice. Only by illuminating the natural (prelapsarian) communicative goods, relationships, and practices of human society and their renewal through Christ's resurrection victory, does the church uphold their moral priority to the fallen political order and the corresponding subordination of political authority and practices to serve them.

Two insights from English Reformation public theology are indispensable to meeting the challenge of understanding and sustaining the public authority of all societal institutions and vocational spheres in a contemporary milieu pervaded by a proliferation of disparate, frequently conflicting and irrational public influences, on the one hand, and on the other, the homogenizing juridical ideology and practice of liberal, egalitarian rights. First, nonecclesial public authorities and practices require underpinning by the common ethos and ethic embodied in the suprajurisdictional authority and practices of the visible church. Second, the inevitable intersecting of the public authorities of proclamation and jurisdiction should uphold the distinct generic unity of each institution while ordering human jurisdiction to God's saving rule through the church's proclamation.

Chapter 10 completes this study by examining the public theology of coercive jurisdiction in the reforming Tudor reigns, drawing on legal and political sources as well as liturgical, homiletical, and doctrinal sources. It presents the Tudor reformers' elaboration, under indigenous and foreign influences, of the pivotal biblical themes of God's ordination of coercive political rule and his appointment of rulers. While critical of strands in their elaboration that inflate the purpose and authority of rulers by inappropriate applications of Israelite and Christological models of kingship, the chapter sets forth the reformers' sound theological conceptions of the purposes, practices, dependencies and deficiencies, authority, and structural constraints of coercive jurisdiction, drawing out their contributions to resolving the contradictions regarding coercive jurisdiction in the Western tradition of liberal natural rights.

Chief among these contributions is the reformers' conception of political jurisdiction as the practices of giving binding public judgment for the restraint, punishment, and correction of wrongdoing and the advancement and vindication of well-doing in human society. Called forth by the restraining commands of God's law on human waywardness, these practices serve God's condemnation of antihuman sin and his merciful preservation of the goods of created and redeemed human community against sin's ravages. As such, they comprise a partial, insufficient representation of God's truth, love, and law, dependent for fulfilling their proper service on God's fuller revelation of himself in the material and spiritual blessings of created and redeemed human community, which they presuppose and are ordained to protect. Moreover, they are necessarily implicated in the moral evils of domination, conflict, and economic greed, which they seek to suppress and remedy, and so are no more than an indirect and remote sign of God's reconciling and renewing purposes accomplished in Jesus Christ. Thus, the moral limitations of coercive jurisdiction are given by its divinely ordained purpose and by its unavoidable human deficiencies.

The objective right and law of God revealed in nature and in Scripture constrain the political agency and action of the ruler and subjects alike within common bonds of obligation. In the political sphere as elsewhere, human freedom is obedience, the active embrace of obligation. The mutual obligations of the ruler and of the community of the ruled define the structure of political authority. Rulers are obliged by God to exercise a discipline of just legal judgment, command, and sanction over the ruled, individually and collectively. The community of the ruled is obliged by God to assent to the necessity, the form, and the guiding principles of collective discipline; to recognize or elect rulers; and to uphold their sovereign jurisdiction by advising and confirming their policies, rulings, and laws, having regard to past rulings and laws of which the community is the repository. For both ruler and community, the divinely given obligation is the authorization of political agency and action.

The chapter acknowledges the justified aspirations of later generations for greater freedom, toleration, equality, and security in social, economic, and political relationships than Tudor thought and practice countenanced. Nevertheless, it argues that the political perspective of Tudor public theology, delivered from its idolatrous tendencies, offers a more consistent and forceful criticism of late modern liberal rights ideology and practice, and a more coherent alternative to it, than premodern and protomodern natural rights theories. Tudor political theology convincingly indicts and corrects the late modern tendency to absolutize human proprietary freedom and its political actualization in the juridical definition, arbitration, and institutional inculturation of natural rights, and to elevate rights into the highest good, right, and dignity of all members of society.

Chapter 1

THE REFORMATION FOUNDATIONS OF ENGLISH PUBLIC THEOLOGY

The emergence of the legal, liturgical, confessional, and homiletic documents constituting the Reformation foundations of English public theology spans three historical phases, separated by change of rulers, shifting social and political exigencies, and alteration of personnel in the higher civil and ecclesiastical posts. Throughout all three phases, the legal framework of Tudor church reform was being assembled, although the major constitutional innovations originated in the Henrician phase. To this phase also belongs the Great Bible, the most conspicuous evangelical legacy of Henry VIII's tempestuous doctrinal and ecclesiastical vacillations. The 1547 collection of homilies (revised in 1549), the 1549 and 1552 prayer books and the ordinals, and the Forty-Two Articles of 1553 chart the reforming progress of an increasingly powerful and confident evangelical party in government during the minority of King Edward VI. The prayer book and ordinal of 1559 and the second collection of homilies issued in 1563/71 along with the Thirty-nine Articles (1563/1571) express the direction of reform and preoccupations of Queen Elizabeth's church polity.

After 1547, the foundations exhibit continuities of a broadly reforming outlook, the common coinage of contemporary continental and English reformers who had decisively broken with the late-medieval papal church. The supreme authority and intelligibility of Scripture, the total bondage to sin of fallen humanity, the sinner's justification solely by the merits of Christ's unrepeatable self-sacrifice on the Cross, the unqualified dependence of good works on faith, the imperative of vernacular corporate worship, the idolatry and tyranny of "invented" Roman traditions, and the civil magistrate's divinely ordained, independent jurisdiction—these were unifying theological foci of the European "magisterial" reforming streams across political and generational boundaries. Other continuities such as the monarch's unitary juridical authority over civil and ecclesiastical polity evidence a longer indigenous English tradition of reforming theology and practice. Still others betoken the theological and literary presence of a single individual, namely, Thomas Cranmer, who was Archbishop of Canterbury for most of Henry VIII's and all of Edward VI's reigns.

Archbishop Thomas Cranmer has the best claim of all Tudor figures to be considered the Reformation founder of the English church's public theological tradition, in view of his contribution to its constitutive documents. Well before his elevation to the See of Canterbury in 1533, Cranmer contributed prominently to King Henry's divorce campaign, gathering historical and theological arguments supportive of future moves in the king's constitutional revolution, while, after his appointment as archbishop, he was intimately involved with the progression of legal church reform until his deposition by Queen Mary in 1553. A driving force behind Edwardian ecclesiastical injunctions and legislation, he is, by scholarly consensus, the author of the preface to the Great Bible of 1540; the architect of the 1549 and 1552 prayer books and ordinals, and the Forty-Two Articles of 1553; and the author (or chief author) of three of the four pivotal homilies of the 1547 collection, and most probably of the fourth. Extending over three decades, Cranmer's archiepiscopal labors shaped the successive phases of Tudor church reform and, moreover, were deeply implicated in later controversies besetting the Elizabethan, Jacobean, and Caroline churches, which have fed perennial divisions within the national church, and sectarian fragmentation of it. For Cranmer's legacy was not wholly uniform, but encompassed an earlier more conservative (Catholic) Lutheran profile and a later more radical (Swiss) Reformed profile, giving rise to an ecclesiastical history of continual wrestling among a spectrum of positions largely circumscribed by the two profiles.

The Laws of Tudor Church Polity

Over the middle years of the long "Reformation Parliament" which met from 1529 to 1536, the English church and realm were entirely removed from papal jurisdiction in its legislative, judicial, and administrative aspects and made wholly subject to royal jurisdiction. Henry VIII's consorting with factional lay ambitions in the Parliament to curb the inflated privileges and powers of priests and prelates had the outcome of inaugurating a bold enterprise of constitutional reconstruction through a succession of parliamentary acts. The Submission of the Clergy in 1532, bringing clerical legislation entirely under royal control and a degree of lay oversight,[1] was completed by the 1533 Act in Restraint of Appeals, which wholly domesticated juridical processes and the court system, civil and ecclesiastical, under the monarch's sovereign jurisdiction, thereby enabling the desired settlement of

---

1. The "Act for the submission of the clergy . . ." (1534: 25 Henry VIII, *c.* 19) gave statutory embodiment to the 1532 accession of the ecclesiastical Convocations of Canterbury and York to the king's unprecedented demands that the clergy make no legislation without a royal license and submit existing church canons for approval by a royal commission of mixed lay and clerical composition. G. R. Elton, *The Tudor Constitution: Documents and Commentary*, 2nd edn. (Cambridge: Cambridge University Press, 1982), 348–50. Hereafter *TC*.

Henry's legendary suit for annulment of his marriage to Catherine of Aragon.[2] Its much-celebrated preamble pronounced the king's divine institution and equipment with "plenary, whole and entire power . . . and jurisdiction" to "render and yield justice and final determination" to "all manner of folk" within his realm "in all causes, matters, debates and contentions . . . without restraint or provocation to any foreign princes or potentates." Although leaving largely unaltered the existing provincial and diocesan structure of church courts, the act was revolutionary in unifying under a single lay *imperium* the archiepiscopal provinces of Canterbury and York, which, from the establishment of diocesan organization throughout England, had been separate and unconnected ecclesiastical jurisdictions.

The reconstruction of ecclesiastical jurisdiction proceeded apace through the passing of three more statutes in 1534: the Act in Restraint of Annates, the Dispensations Act, and the Act of Supremacy. Together, the first two transferred from the papacy to the Crown administration of the church's revenues, higher clerical appointments, and dispensations (licenses to depart from canon law), terminating all payments outside the realm to Rome.[3] The Act of Supremacy gave separate statutory acknowledgment of the king's supreme headship over the church in England, and assigned to the Crown the authority "to visit, repress, redress, reform . . . restrain and amend" clerical "errors, heresies, abuses, offences," both for "the increase of virtue in Christ's religion, and for the conservation of the peace, unity and tranquillity of this realm"—the twofold spiritual and temporal

---

2. 1533: 24 Henry VIII, *c.* 12: *TC*, 353–8. The structure of appeal in ecclesiastical suits was now from the archdeacon's to the diocesan bishop's court and then to the archiepiscopal court, except in causes touching "the King, his heirs or successors," where the appeal was directly to the Upper House of Convocation—an arrangement superseded by the establishment in 1534 of the royal Court of Delegates, in which laymen could sit, as the realm's highest ecclesiastical court.

3. The Act in Restraint of Annates (1534: 25 Henry VIII, *c.* 20: *TC*, 358–60) stopped payment to Rome of annates or first fruits by those presented to bishoprics and archbishoprics within "the King's dominions" and prohibited the King's subjects from procuring papal bulls for episcopal consecrations. It also established that in any episcopal or abbatial vacancy, the electing dean and chapter, or prior and convent, were obliged to elect the person nominated by the king in the "letter missive" accompanying the royal *congé d'élire* (license to elect). A companion statute (1534: 26 Henry VIII, *c.* 3: *TC*, 53–6) granted to the Crown the first fruits of all ecclesiastical "dignities, benefices and promotions," and as well, an annual "pension" of one-tenth of the church's total revenue. The Dispensations Act (1534: 25 Henry VIII, *c.* 21: *TC*, 360–4) put a final and complete termination to payments to Rome and provided that all dispensations be obtained from the Archbishop of Canterbury "for causes not being contrary or repugnant to the Holy Scriptures and laws of God." To guard against extortionate charges and unreasonable refusals of dispensations by Canterbury officials, the act provided for a public schedule of fees and authorized the Lord Chancellor to review and reverse archiepiscopal decisions.

ends of earthly rule.[4] The statute's reach was reinforced by the harsh Treason Act of the same year, intended to secure all aspects of the king's legislative revolution by making it high treason to utter or write seditious words against the King, Queen, or heir apparent.[5] By the close of 1534, the civil ruler was legally established as sovereign over the church in his territories with pontifical powers of administering its political and economic affairs, paving the way for the regime's relieving the church of about two-thirds of her property, including, most notoriously, the assets of dissolved monastic establishments.[6]

Henry VIII's assumption of sovereign ecclesiastical jurisdiction by parliamentary statutes set up constitutional tensions that were sustained throughout his reign by his conduct of government policy. On the one hand, the statutes derived his supremacy from divine appointment and institution alone, and not from parliamentary consent; whenever expedient, Henry exercised his supremacy without reference to Parliament, acting through his archbishops, appointed commissioners, or (from 1535 to 1540) his omnicompetent ecclesiastical vicegerent, Thomas Cromwell.[7] On the other hand, parliamentary statutes were indispensable to the enforcement of royal policies in the common law courts, for statutes alone created the requisite new offenses and punishments. For many reasons, the king could not ignore the various and conflicting interests represented in Parliament, even while assigning Parliament an enforcing and auxiliary role. By contrast, Henry's constitutional revolution set up no corresponding tensions between the Crown and the clerical Convocations, but simply undermined their governing authority in church affairs. Since the king, in designing his ecclesiastical policies, preferred to be advised by select committees of bishops and theologians rather than by the larger assemblies of higher clergy, the Convocations increasingly became merely assenting chambers.[8]

---

4. 1534: 26 Henry VIII, *c.* 1: *TC*, 364–5. While not explicitly extending the royal plenitude beyond the sphere of external church polity to encompass priestly sacramental power, it opened the door to royal regulation and correction of the whole range of clerical doctrine and practice.

5. 1534: 26 Henry VIII, *c.* 13: *TC*, 62–3.

6. The monarch's ecclesiastical *imperium* now far exceeded in scope his traditional feudal claim to be the sovereign liege lord of the clerical and lay estates of his realm and primary donor of the church's lands and goods, and as such, entitled to a range of ecclesiastical "dues" and the exercise of patronage in senior church appointments.

7. From the mid-thirties onward, almost all Henry's instruments for establishing the doctrine, worship, ministry, and finances of the English church rested on his authority as supreme head, in consultation with his spiritual counselors, whether or not legislated by Parliament. A notable exception was the enabling by parliamentary statute of the king's founding of six new dioceses and reestablishing of eight cathedral churches.

8. Felicity Heal, *Reformation in Britain and Ireland* (Oxford: Oxford University Press, 2003), 184–5.

After the Reformation Parliament, however, there remained theological ambiguity surrounding the status of episcopal jurisdiction: whether it derived from the royal imperium or independently from Christ, or from both. While the parliamentary acts implied its derivation from the royal plenitude, the doctrinal and catechetical compendium of 1537 entitled *The Institution of a Christian Man* (commonly called "the Bishops' Book") accorded to "priests and bishops" on Scriptural warrant an apostolic "spiritual jurisdiction" to be exercised *under* the lay monarch's sovereign jurisdiction, encompassing the powers of admitting or rejecting candidates for the priesthood, ordaining "rules or canons" concerning the church's worship and ministry, and verbally disciplining those "under their cure," even to the point of excommunication.[9] Significantly, much of the clerical exercise of jurisdiction in the church courts lay outside of the apostolic remit, being derived from, as well as exercised under, the royal imperium. In censuring offenders against church law and order with the imposition of temporal punishments (e.g., monetary fines, confiscation of property, and imprisonment), the clerical judges *always* acted as the king's ministers, even though much of the law they administered predated the Henrician reforming statutes.[10]

The constitutional tensions of Henry VIII's reign continued through the reigns of his Tudor successors, but with a shift of balance in the direction of Parliament. In the minority of Edward VI, the personal supremacy of the monarch could not carry its former weight, so the government, in prosecuting its agenda of church reform, made somewhat more use of Parliament and gave more explicit acknowledgment to parliamentary authority. A sequence of parliamentary statutes permitted communion in both kinds to clergy and laity; repealed the Henrician heresy laws; suppressed chantries, fraternities, guilds, and other pious trusts (vesting their property in the Crown); permitted priests to marry; authorized the abolition of images from places of worship; and established the centerpieces of Edwardian liturgical reform: the first and second vernacular prayer books of 1549 and 1552 and corresponding rites for the ordination of deacons, priests,

---

9. See "Corrections of the Institution by Henry VIII with Cranmer's Annotations," in *Miscellaneous Writings and Letters of Thomas Cranmer*, ed. John Edmund Cox for The Parker Society (Cambridge: University Press, 1846), 96–8. Hereafter *MWL*; Also, *A Necessary Doctrine and Erudition for Any Christian Man . . . The King's Book, 1543*, intro. T. A. Lacey (London: R. Browning, 1895).

10. The persistence in force of a good deal of medieval church law throughout Henry's reign, and far beyond it, resulted from the miscarriage of successive plans for church law reform: initially for the pruning of existing canon law and provincial constitutions and subsequently for the creation of a new ecclesiastical code. The 1533 Act providing for the appointment of a law-reforming commission prescribed that, until the commission to be established had completed its work, all existing Canons, Constitutions, Ordinances and Synodals Provincial "not contrariant or repugnant to the law, statutes and customs of this realm, nor to the damage or hurt of the King's prerogative" were to remain in force. Mark Hill, *Ecclesiastical Law*, 2nd edn. (Oxford: Oxford University Press, 2001), 7.

and bishops (1550, 1552). The 1552 Act of Uniformity rested both the 1549 and 1552 orders of worship on parliamentary authority. Moreover, as the reform agenda took an overtly evangelical and iconoclastic course, licensing unprecedented levels of violence against church fabric and ornaments, its promoters among Edward's counselors found Parliament convenient for circumventing resistance in the clerical Convocations. Nevertheless, while making extensive use of statute, Cranmer led reforming voices in deriving episcopal jurisdiction from the royal plenitude.[11]

Paradoxically, Queen Mary's 1554 repeal and abrogation by statute of all the Henrician and Edwardian Acts against papal jurisdiction reinforced parliamentary rather than royal authority;[12] but Queen Elizabeth's Act of Supremacy (1559) revived the constitutional tension by proposing to restore "the [ancient] rights, jurisdictions and pre-eminences appertaining to the imperial crown."[13] The tension was not significantly lessened by the Act's substitution of the royal title "supreme governor" for that of "supreme head" of the realm's two estates, for the concession to theological objections did not diminish the political content of the monarch's supremacy.

Although a key feature of Elizabeth's ecclesiastical settlement—namely, the slightly revised 1552 prayer book as the order of worship—was rapidly established on parliamentary authority by the 1559 Act of Uniformity,[14] the Queen proceeded to assert her independent governance of the church. Most notably, after carefully reviewing (and possibly altering) the draft formulary of thirty-nine doctrinal articles, passed by the two clerical Convocations in 1563, Elizabeth imposed them by royal authority without parliamentary approval and, in 1566, intervened in the House of Lords to prevent Parliament sanctioning them. Only with their reissue in 1571 did the Queen reluctantly assent to statutory sanction in an Act requiring clerical subscription to them.[15] Throughout her reign Elizabeth retained

---

11. Cranmer's abortive *Reformatio legum ecclesiasticarum* of 1553, in line with the original Henrician draft of reformed canons (1535), pronounced unequivocally that "all jurisdiction, both ecclesiastical and secular, is derived from [the King] as from one and the same source," and the Forty-Two Articles of Religion, following on its heels, nowhere declared an independent Christological and apostolic origin and form of episcopal jurisdiction. The 1552 liturgy of episcopal consecration, however, presents a more complicated picture, as we shall see.

12. An Act for the repeal of certain statutes made in the time of the reign of King Edward VI 1553: 1 Mary, st. 2, *c.* 2: *TC*, 408-9. An Act repealing all statutes . . . made against the see apostolic of Rome since the 20th year of King Henry VIII, and also for the establishment of all spiritual and ecclesiastical possessions and hereditaments conveyed to the laity 1554: 1 & 2 Philip and Mary, *c.* 8: *TC*, 368-72.

13. 1559: 1 Eliz. I, *c.* 1: *TC*, 372-7. Also on Parliament's authority was the repeal of the Marian legislation establishing the papal "usurpation."

14. 1559: 1 Eliz. I, *c.* 2: *TC*, 410-13.

15. 1571: 13 Eliz. I, *c.* 12: *TC*, 398 n. 113.

her father's strong sense of the monarch's separate relations with his temporal and spiritual estates, and a succession of ecclesiastical disputes increased her unease about challenges from the Commons to the authority of her higher clergy in Convocation.

The full constitutional impact of all these Tudor statutes depended on the territorial extension of the monarch's ecclesiastical jurisdiction beyond the English realm to the royal "dominions and marches," including Wales, Calais, the Channel Islands, the Isle of Man, and Ireland, with their distinct forms of government under the Crown. For most or all of the Reformation period, these territorial churches (with the exception of Ireland) were absorbed in either dioceses or provinces of the *Anglicana Ecclesia*.[16] Nevertheless, the practical force of Tudor statutes, as of other instruments of Tudor church policy, varied according to such factors as the overall security of English jurisdiction in these territories, the overcoming of cultural and linguistic barriers, and the strength of liturgical and doctrinal traditionalism.[17]

Authorized English Bibles

In the Tudor reigns, the reforming divines regarded access of the people to the Scriptures in the vernacular as essential to their personal faith and their corporate unity in its spiritual and political modalities. The corporate unity of the church's faith, on which the moral and political unity of society rested, issued from the communication of God's Word spoken in Jesus Christ through the written testimony of Scripture, which testimony could only be read and heard in the common tongue. The church's practices of publicly disseminating the Scriptural witness in the vernacular necessarily interwove divine authority and human epistemological and political authority, that is, the epistemological authority of communally recognized translators and interpreters of the canonical text, and the political authority of rulers to give binding settlement to socially disruptive disagreements over the Scriptural witness.

Given Henry VIII's pontifical tendency to unite political and epistemological authority in his royal person, and given the divisions within his territorial church over Scriptural translation and interpretation and Henry's strongly partisan,

---

16. The Welsh episcopal sees were incorporated in the southern province, Calais in the Canterbury diocese, the Channel Islands in the Winchester diocese, the Isles of Man see in the province of Canterbury and, subsequently, York (1541).

17. For example, in Wales, the Henrician reformation received effective backing from the gentry, whose local authority had been enhanced by the English government's abolition of Welsh lordships and imposition of the shire system; but in Ireland, where the jurisdictional claims of the English Crown depended historically on papal lordship, perpetual rebellions against English rule ensured that the English monarch's writ never ran beyond the pale and marches of Ireland, and the local Irish magnates were frequently lethargic in securing parallel enactment of English statutes in the Dublin Parliament.

if shifting, allegiances, vernacular Bibles required royal authorization for their public distribution and liturgical use within the kingdom. Thus, the most significant Henrician Bible became known as "The Great Bible" by virtue of its public eminence: exhibiting royal grandeur, bearing a preface by the Archbishop of Canterbury, and authorized for nationwide ecclesiastical distribution. First printed in 1539 and reprinted in 1540 with Cranmer's preface, it appeared more than 150 years after the earliest complete English translations of the Scriptures— the Wyclif/Lollard translations of 1380-4 and *c.* 1388—and was preceded in Henry's reign by William Tyndale's 1526 New Testament translation and by two complete English Bibles produced by Miles Coverdale (1535) and John Rogers (1537), both of which were heavily dependent on Tyndale's translations, not only of the New Testament but also of the five books of the Pentateuch, the Book of Jonah, and the Old Testament historical books.

To Tyndale, then, belongs the distinction of being the Tudor progenitor of the English Bible, having furnished his contemporaries with translations from the Hebrew and Greek in clear, compelling, and vivid English prose, demonstrating a masterful range of styles to match the stylistic kaleidoscope of the biblical literature.[18] However, their Lutheran overtones and accompanying theological glosses earned them condemnation as pestiferous heresy by the conservative Henrician establishment, together with Tyndale's polemical Lutheran tracts. While gratified by Tyndale's soundness on the topics of royal and papal power, Henry VIII otherwise loathed his Lutheran theological leanings and frowned on his independent, foreign publishing initiatives. Similarly, educated Henrician conservatives such as Stephen Gardiner and Thomas More, although concurring with the objectives of Renaissance biblical scholarship and admiring Erasmus's labors to establish the Greek and Hebrew texts, still associated unauthorized Bible translation and circulation with the English church's heretical undercurrents, downstream from Lollardy.

Nevertheless, within a year of Tyndale's death at the stake, Coverdale's complete English Bible (with Apocrypha) was printed in England. While his own translation work was frequently inferior to Tyndale's, being hampered by ignorance of Hebrew and Greek, he generally followed Tyndale quite closely, incorporating much of his revisionist New Testament scholarship shorn of its polemical annotations.[19] Moreover, his handling of the poetic and prophetic books, not reached by Tyndale, afforded displays of considerable theological and literary skill, the masterpiece being his translation of the Psalter. Coverdale's acute sensitivity to both "Hebrew parallelism and congregational singing" rendered his Psalter a treasured and enduring component of the Church of England's liturgical tradition for over four

---

18. See David Daniell's appreciative appraisal of Tyndale's translations in *The Bible in English* (New Haven and London: Yale University Press, 2003), 136–9.

19. Scholarly evidence suggests that about half of Coverdale's annotations are from Luther's 1536 Bible. Daniell, *The Bible in English*, 181.

and a half centuries. In addition, his Bible offered impressive organizational and production values that enhanced the ease, pleasure, and instruction of reading it.[20]

The "Matthew Bible," so called from its pseudonymous translator, Thomas Matthew (most probably John Rogers), succeeded in remedying some of the translation defects of Coverdale's work and in incorporating Tyndale's whole corpus of printed Bible translations. The superior scholarship demonstrated in its translation of Hebrew and Greek texts, its prolific marginal notes and cross-references,[21] commended it so highly to Thomas Cromwell, the king's ecclesiastical vicegerent, that he secured a royal dedication and license for it, and subsequently arranged for Coverdale to revise it, with the objective of installing it in every parish church.[22] Thanks to Cranmer's strenuous exertions, national distribution of Coverdale's revision, "the Great Bible," was not long delayed by Cromwell's rapid fall from power and execution in 1540 but was even assisted by royal imposition of a financial penalty on noncomplying parishes in 1541.

The price of this unprecedented nationwide distribution of the vernacular Scriptures was admission by the king's subjects of the monarch's unbounded authority to mediate "the word of God" by overseeing translation, distribution, and interpretation of the biblical text. This admission is graphically portrayed on the Great Bible's title page, depicting the towering figure of Henry VIII distributing copies of the "*VERBUM DEI*" to both estates of his realm via the supreme clerical and lay governors of his church. Most notably, King Henry sits under a diminutive divine sovereign but not under the biblical text itself; nor is there any other visible spokesman for the text to inform or to challenge his manner of mediating it.[23]

Nevertheless, once past the title page, the intelligent clerical or lay reader of the vernacular Bible, aided by tolerably well-informed annotations, was now able to encounter (with a clear political conscience!) a multitude of arresting and revelatory passages, especially in the New Testament, that challenged prevailing traditions erected on Jerome's Vulgate and its medieval glosses. Moreover, Cranmer's preface provided readers with pastoral and epistemological guidance, clarifying the reciprocal relationship between Scriptural and ecclesial authority and steering readers away from the opposite pitfalls of timid or lazy reluctance to read, on the one hand, and, on the other, overconfident and pugilistic assaulting of

---

20. Among them, a clear page layout, sustained decoration and engaging illustrations; prefatory, chapter by chapter summaries to each book; repeated book titles and chapter headings at the top of every page; and assembling the apocryphal books after the Old Testament, following Luther, rather than leaving them scattered among the Old Testament Writings, as did the Vulgate, following the Septuagint.

21. Unlike Coverdale, Rogers drew on the reforming scholarship of the contemporary French Bible translations: Lefèvre (1530, 1534) and Olivétan (1535).

22. Coverdale's revision strengthened Tyndale's translating and scholarly achievements in both Testaments and his own previous work, in the light of improved Hebrew scholarship.

23. For the title page, Diarmaid MacCulloch, *Thomas Cranmer* (New Haven and London: Yale University Press, 1996), 239.

the text. Partly owing to its invocation of patristic authorities, Cranmer's preface retained a programmatic importance for the English reforming establishment throughout the sixteenth century.

The Great Bible circulated for twenty-five years without further revision: Cranmer's revising ambitions were thwarted by episcopal and royal reluctance during the remainder of Henry's reign and were sidelined by more urgent church reforms during Edward VI's minority. Nevertheless, an exponential increase in new editions of existing Bible translations accompanied the quickened pace of Edwardian reform, partially stimulated by popular demand,[24] so that when the revision of the Great Bible was eventually undertaken in 1566-7, Bible reading in the vernacular had become a central shaping force of English ecclesiastical, moral, political, and linguistic culture.[25]

Significantly contributing to this development in Queen Elizabeth's first decade were the New Testament and complete Bible translations produced in Geneva in 1557 and 1560, by English émigrés equipped with the latest Reformed scholarship.[26] The rapid and sustained popularity among English speakers of the 1660 Geneva Bible was largely due to the quality of its translations and generally unrivalled scholarly apparatus, combined with its compact size and excellences of production and organization.[27] However, the loosely Calvinist cast of its scholarly pedagogy raised contentious issues for Queen Elizabeth's more traditional church establishment in the areas of ministerial orders and government, worship, and sacraments, prompting her Archbishop of Canterbury, Matthew Parker, together with episcopal colleagues, to undertake the production of an official rival, in the form of a revised Great Bible.

---

24. Forty separate editions of the complete Scriptures or the New Testament appeared in the six years of Edward's reign. Daniell, *The Bible in English*, 245.

25. See Ian Robinson, *The Establishment of Modern English Prose in the Reformation and the Enlightenment* (Cambridge: Cambridge University Press, 1998); Orlaith O'Sullivan, ed., *The Bible as Book: The Reformation* (London: British Library and New Castle: Oak Knoll Press, 2000).

26. The English translators were Calvinist-leaning theologians and biblical scholars who had fled the persecutions of Mary's reign. Most had relocated to Geneva from Frankfurt, in the wake of quarrels within the English refugee congregation at Frankfurt over Anglican orders and worship. Chief among their ranks were William Whittingham, Christopher Goodman, Thomas Sampson, Miles Coverdale, William Cole, William Kethe, and John Baron.

27. The Geneva translators further improved upon Coverdale's revisions of the Old Testament and Apocryphal texts, using Hebrew and Septuagint sources, and managed to retain "the ambiguities, obscurities, and ellipses" of the Hebrew texts, accompanying them with copious explanatory notes. Gerald Hammond, *The Making of the English Bible* (Manchester: Carcanet Press, 1982), 106. In addition, the numbering of verses facilitated the introduction of tables, concordances, variant readings, and cross-references.

Working to guidelines requiring the revisers to confine their labors essentially to correction and to avoid controversial "determinations," the bishops did not produce a worthy competitor to the Geneva Bible. Rather, the accomplishment of the Bishops' Bible, royally authorized in 1572 after further revision, was to ensure that enough of the English reforming legacy of Bible translation, up to and including the Geneva Bible, continued to be aligned with the national church into the next century.

The Bishops' Bible became the base text for the corporate work of translation that produced the historic "King James Version" (KJV) or "Authorized Version" (AV) of 1611. Liberally interpreting their similarly restrictive guidelines and drawing on a host of current scholarly editions,[28] the translators managed to deliver a text of singular distinction, and unforeseeable historical longevity and cultural impact.[29] Notwithstanding its scholarly and literary shortcomings,[30] their text largely succeeded in retaining the literary and theological strengths of its predecessors, complementing them with phrases of "lapidary beauty," spiritual intensity, and a Latin resonance that conveys centuries of faithful Christian tradition and preserves a "worshipful distance" from its subject matter.[31]

Books of Common Prayer

The most imposing legacy of evangelical reform from the Edwardian period, the prayer books of 1549 and 1552 and their progeny, together with the authorized vernacular Bibles, comprised the central pillars of the established English church throughout successive reigns until the civil war and after the Restoration of 1662. Moreover, of all the Edwardian reforming enterprises, the production of the two prayer books and ordinals did most in their day to attract the attention of continental reformers and to give the English church standing within the European circle of reforming churches. By Edward's reign, most of the significant reformers had tried their hand at liturgical production, and some, like Luther, Bucer, and Osiander, were prolific liturgists of immense stature, whose liturgical work offered important source material for the English liturgies.[32]

---

28. These included current Latin versions and the Rheims New Testament of 1582, translated for English Catholics from the Vulgate.

29. The KJV held sway in the English-speaking world until the mid-twentieth century.

30. They include inaccurate and muddled renderings, occasional pomposity, and a tendency to "flatten" stylistically diverse literature to "the same sonorous level." Daniell, *The Bible in English*, 441.

31. Ibid., 429, 440–2.

32. The most important contemporary liturgical sources for the 1549 prayer book were: Luther's liturgies produced between 1526 and 1540, the 1533 *Kirchenordnung* for the Principality of Brandenburg and the Free City of Nuremberg compiled by Johann Brenz and Andreas Osiander, and the eclectic revision of the Brandenburg-Nuremberg Order

While the 1549 and 1552 prayer books were, to a significant degree, collaborative and consultative enterprises of bishops and other learned churchmen, the guiding hand behind both books was that of Thomas Cranmer, whose literary, organizing, negotiating, and scholarly labors largely determined the selection and use of sources. Cranmer provided much of the draft material for the 1548 committee responsible for producing the new English rite, and he gathered the critical responses to the 1549 prayer book that would steer its subsequent revision. Cranmer could play this constructive and mediating role by drawing on his extensive theological/doctrinal and liturgical work over the previous decade, much of which was already in the public domain. His sense of what was theologically desirable and achievable in 1547–8 had been fashioned by copious experience in designing public instruments for promoting ecclesiastical uniformity of belief, requiring him to mediate intellectually and diplomatically between the more reforming evangelical and more conservative Catholic positions of his episcopal colleagues, and his royal master.[33]

Cranmer's liturgical accomplishments over this decade were also prolific. They included: devising a scheme for reducing the Daily Office or Hours to the two services of Matins and Vespers (*c.* 1538–9),[34] producing an English adaptation of the Latin Litany (1544),[35] laboring on an official English Primer (1545),[36]

---

prepared by Martin Bucer for the prince-archbishop of Cologne, Hermann von Wied, published in German in 1544, and in a widely circulated Latin translation (*Simplex ac Pia Deliberatio*) in 1545. Of comparable liturgical influence was a revision of the Breviary in two Latin recensions by Cardinal Francesco de Quiñones in 1535/6, on commission from Pope Paul III. For a more detailed description of these services and orders, G. J. Cuming, *A History of Anglican Liturgy* (London: Macmillan, 1969), 32–48. Hereafter *HAL*.

33. Such instruments as the Ten Articles of 1536, The Bishops' Book of 1537, and its Catholic revision of 1543 (The King's Book) concerned a wide spectrum of theological matters, from justification, faith, and good works to the number, authority, and reality of the sacraments, to the use of images, ceremonies, and veneration of saints and prayers to them.

34. The Office or Hours were the eight services of communal prayer, praise and Scripture reading at regular intervals comprising monastic worship, primarily. Cranmer's scheme of reduction, probably undertaken during Anglo-German negotiations on doctrinal and ecclesiastical issues, made use of a Lutheran morning service as well as Cardinal Quiñones' Breviary revisions, whereas his later scheme, reflecting the conservative swing of King and Council in the early 1540s, retained all the Hours and followed Quiñones' format more closely. For analysis and dating of the two schemes, Geoffrey Cuming, *The Godly Order: Texts and Studies relating to the Book of Common Prayer* (London: Alcuin Club, SPCK, 1983), 1–23.

35. The Latin Litany was a processional service of penitential intercessions traditionally used in times of national emergency. The occasion for Cranmer's English adaptation was King Henry's imminent invasion of France.

36. *The King's Primer* presented English translations of the traditional material of these popular devotional-catechetical manuals, with some reforming omissions and additions,

conducting (with Nicholas Ridley) a largely English mass for the opening of the 1547 Parliament, and overseeing the production of an English liturgy for lay reception of "communion in both kinds" (1548).³⁷ Thus, by the time he presented a draft of the vernacular prayer book to the 1548 committee, "practically every word of Matins and Evensong was already in print in English," as were the liturgical Epistles and Gospels, "while the Litany and The Order of the Communion needed little revision."³⁸

1549 Prayer Book

On the continental spectrum of vernacular orders of worship, the 1549 Book of Common Prayer legislated by Edward VI's First Act of Uniformity was toward the traditionalist end, but unmistakably evangelical in its reforming thrust. Its distinctive mediation of tradition and reform is exhibited in the intentions and principles guiding the selection and organization of its material, as set forth in the title, in Cranmer's preface and in his appended essay "Of Ceremonies, Why Some Be Abolished and Some Retained," which together comprise something of a programmatic framework for the book's liturgical content.³⁹

The lengthy title, *The Book of the Common Prayer and Administration of the Sacraments, and Other Rites and Ceremonies of the Church After the Use of the Church of England*, announces the book's liturgical comprehensiveness and exclusivity within the realm. Its collected services replace those contained in a plethora of separate books⁴⁰ and comprise a uniform liturgical order intended to overcome the existing diversity of local liturgical usages.⁴¹ In addition, the title indicates comprehensiveness in the sense of catholicity, declaring that the collected services

---

drawing on earlier English Primers and other Catholic humanist and evangelical reforming sources. *HAL*, 49–51; MacCulloch, *Thomas Cranmer*, 334–6.

37. For source analysis of the 1548 Order of the Communion, Cuming, *The Godly Order*, 75–80; also, *HAL*, 61–5.

38. *HAL*, 68.

39. Translated from Cranmer's earlier scheme for revising the Breviary, and heavily indebted to Quiñones, the Preface has reference principally to the Daily Office. His short, appended essay likewise originated in the English-Lutheran discussions of 1538 and enlarged on two of the articles produced by them.

40. Chiefly, the Missal, the Breviary, the Processional, the Manual, and the Pontifical. For a summary of their contents, *HAL*, 28–30.

41. *The First and Second Prayer Books of Edward VI*, intro. Douglas Harrison (London: Dent, 1910; repr. 1968), Preface, 4. Hereafter *FSPB*. The collected English services include the daily offices of Matins and Evensong, the Litany, the Ministration of Holy Communion, public and private Baptism, Confirmation, Solemnization of Matrimony, Visitation and Communion of the Sick, Burial of the Dead, Purification (Churching) of Women after Childbirth, and Commination against Sinners. The Ordering of Deacons and Priests and Consecration of Bishops was issued under separate cover until 1552.

belong to "The Church" (Universal) and are continuous with its most venerable traditions. This claim to catholicity is reflected in the volume and the scope of the prayer book's traditional material from the apostolic period onward, in Cranmer's use of the prevailing Latin rite of England (i.e., Sarum)[42] as the baseline for his liturgical reconstruction, and in the ecumenical and geographical breadth of his borrowings from contemporary reformed liturgies.

Cranmer's preface recognizes as an enduring liturgical standard the subapostolic and patristic churches' order for "common prayers" or "divine worship," entailing the thorough, sequential, and almost uninterrupted reading and reciting of the Scriptural text in the popular tongue, and it praises the order's nurturing of "godly" and Scripturally informed clergy and laity, desirous of reading, hearing and digesting "the very pure word of God."[43] Conversely, the preface laments the cumulative secretion into common prayers of superfluous and unedifying extra-biblical material,[44] disrupting and curtailing the disciplined, coherent encounter of worshippers with the Scriptural text. The accompanying proliferation of "ceremonies" in worship is decried in Cranmer's essay "Of Ceremonies" as unedifying and "unprofitable," liable to superstitious abuse and avaricious exploitation, obscuring of God's glory in Christ, and in their excessive multitude, converting Christ's gospel of spiritual freedom into a "Ceremonial Law," in "bondage of the figure or shadow."[45] The controlling ambition of liturgical reform is, then, to reverse the spiral of English ecclesial corruption by restoring the ancient order and recovering its long-dissipated benefits.

This restoration is impressively achieved in Cranmer's revision of the daily services of Matins and Evensong, the lynchpin of which is his design of the Lectionary (the table of Psalms and Lessons), providing for parallel cycles of sequential readings from both Testaments.[46] Shorn of extra-biblical interpolations, the remaining sequence of Psalm(s), Lesson (reading), Canticle (biblical or ecclesiatical song), Lesson, Canticle presents an almost continuous reading and

---

42. The Sarum Rite, i.e., the Use of Salisbury Cathedral, was a variant of the Roman Rite.

43. *FSPB*, 3–4.

44. "uncertain stories, Legends, Responds, Verses, vain repetitions, Commemorations…" *FSPB*, 3.

45. *FSPB*, 286–7.

46. Following the civil calendar, Cranmer's scheme provides for the sequential reading through of the psalms every month, of the Old Testament once a year (omitting the "least edifying" books and chapters, and with minor additions from the Apocrapha), and of the New Testament three times a year (excepting the Apocalypse, read only on occasional feasts), both Testaments being read at the rate of one chapter per lesson. The scheme entails the radical reduction of commemorations in the church's calendar to those of New Testament saints and All Saints.

reciting of Scripture.[47] Cranmer's overriding intention of enhancing attentiveness to God's speaking through the Scriptures was served not only by these revisions but by all his evident principles and methods of liturgical revision throughout the prayer book: abbreviating elaborate and repetitive sequences of prayers, pruning back ceremonial, simplifying complicated rules and procedures of practice, and ensuring intelligibility in all speaking, singing, and acting. For Cranmer, the Scriptural revelation of "Christ's Gospel" judged every element of received tradition, determining whether its effect be to "confound and darken" or to "declare and set forth Christ's benefits unto us."[48]

Inevitably, the vernacular Communion service proved to be the most controversial feature of the 1549 prayer book, as it continues to be in scholarly debates over its theological intentions, compromises, and influences.[49] Although structurally less innovative than the new Daily Office, it traversed more theological minefields and so offered more grounds for offense to various parties. In combining the Sarum rite with the 1548 order for reception in both kinds, it seriously modified the traditional Latin service, as signaled by the nomenclature "Supper of the Lord and The Holy Communion." In the pre-sermon portion of the service closely following Sarum,[50] Cranmer's revising hand is most pronounced in the vernacular "collects" (set prayers): in the introduction of two (alternative) prayers for the monarch, and in the "seasonal collects" traditionally forming a liturgical triad with the assigned Epistle and Gospel readings.[51] Of the eighty-four seasonal collects, two-thirds are his translations and adaptations of Latin originals and one-third are entirely new creations, largely replacing prayers containing intercessory invocations of saints. Freely rendering the Latin texts, Cranmer's translations and adaptations frequently display his stylistic adeptness at transforming elegant Latin into elegant English cadences with a

---

47. The Psalms and Lessons at Matins and Evensong are contained within parallel liturgical frameworks, drawn, respectively, from the medieval Hours of Matins, Lauds and Prime, and from the Hours of Vespers and Compline. The regular canticles of Matins—*Venite* (Ps. 95), *Te Deum Laudamus, Benedictus* (Lk. 1:68-79) and those of Evensong—*Magnificat* (Lk. 1:46-55) and *Nunc Dimittis* (Lk. 2:29-32), are translations taken either from The Great Bible or *The King's Primer*. FSPB, 21–5.

48. *FSPB*, 287.

49. Cranmer's own eucharistic theology took shape through his grappling with the range of possibilities offered him by the recently arrived émigrés, Martin Bucer, Peter Martyr (Pietro Martire Vermigli), Bernardino Ochino, and Jan Laski (John à Lasco), and by his episcopal colleagues, Nicholas Ridley and John Hooper.

50. The liturgy retained the Introit, *Kyrie, Gloria,* collects, Epistle, Gospel, and Creed in the traditional order.

51. The lessons (readings) are practically identical with Sarum, but now in the Great Bible translation.

heightening of expressive power and beauty, and his theological adeptness at introducing subtle, yet precise, reforming nuances of intellectual and emotional depth; while his original compositions bring, in addition, a wealth of Scriptural borrowings. The more striking and significant post-sermon innovations are the following. 1. Two (alternative) exhortations taken from the 1548 Order urge communicants to come to the sacrament with repentance, faith, obedience, charity, humility, and thankfulness, and warn the impenitent, faithless, and malicious not to partake to their destruction. Both stress that spiritual feeding on Christ is given to those spiritually prepared to receive Him.[52] 2. The Offertory no longer entails the offering of bread and wine upon the altar as the people's gift to God, in preparation for the sacrifice, but only the offering of alms deposited into the "poor men's box." 3. Alterations are made to the "Canon" of the Mass[53] intended to eliminate any suggestion of performing a meritorious sacrificial offering or oblation for the living and the dead, re-presenting (in the sense of repeating) Christ's redemptive sacrifice on the Cross; and, as well, intended to undermine the doctrine of "transubstantiation," of the substantial conversion of bread and wine into Christ's sacrificed body and blood. These have given rise to centuries of debate over whether the 1549 Canon accommodates belief in the local, substantive (corporeal) presence of Christ's sacrificed body and blood in (or "under" or "with") the consecrated elements. 4. Figuring prominently in the Canon's conclusion and in the remaining preparation for reception of the sacrament is the worshippers' confession of unworthiness to receive Christ's benefits by partaking of his flesh and blood, and petition for assurance of the Father's merciful acceptance of their service.[54] 5. Rubrics controlling clerical dress and ceremonial reinforce the verbal innovations.[55]

The 1549 revision of the medieval baptismal service entailed a more concerted pruning away of "dark" and "dumb" ceremonial, to display its gospel core. Nevertheless, the service retains the two-part structure of the Sarum rite, with Exorcism at the church door and Baptism at the font, and half of the traditional ceremonies belonging to both parts. The Baptism is heavily indebted to contemporary Lutheran liturgies,

---

52. The second also emphasizes diligence in frequent reception.

53. The medieval Canon comprised the central sequence of eucharistic prayers of thanksgiving and consecration which only the 1549 Communion service, among the reformed, evangelical liturgies, loosely retained.

54. These figure especially in the "general Confession" and Absolution, the "comfortable words" from the New Testament, and in the so-called "Prayer of Humble Access." *FSPB*, 224–5.

55. Reinforcing the theological shift away from the sacrificial mass and transubstantiation to an interpretation centered on corporate reception of the benefits of Christ's passion are the celebrant's "plain" white alb and cope, the ceremonial neglect of "fraction" and "conmixture," the use of unprinted wafers, the requirement of at least one noncelebrating communicant, and the remaining of communicants in the "quire" after the offertory and departure of noncommunicants.

especially its expository and exhortatory portions, with their theological stress on the public and corporate nature of the sacrament and the centrality of the congregation's and the godparents' faith in the Father's "good will" declared by his Son toward the infant candidates.[56] Overall, the service presents a balance of emphasis on the mystical washing away of sins and spiritual regeneration within the body of Christ.[57]

Of the occasional services, the Solemnization of Matrimony follows the familiar Sarum liturgy most closely, notwithstanding notable modifications;[58] whereas Burial forcefully displays the reforming agenda of the Communion and the Litany: curtailing or suppressing ceremonial processions, petitions for the dead, and the mass as propitiatory sacrifice.[59] While drawing extensively on the Latin burial rite,[60] its prayers make no concessions to the doctrines of purgatorial punishment and the benefits accruing to the deceased from celebration of the Eucharist.[61] The prevailing theme from 1 Cor. 15 is the confidence of faith that those who have died to sin in Christ shall be raised to incorruptible and immortal life in him.

---

56. This includes the preface and opening address, the "Flood-prayer," the choice and exposition of the Gospel (from Mark 10), and the charges to the godparents.

57. Against the dominant reforming trend, the 1549 prayer book retains the Confirmation service (*FSPB*, 247-51, 404-9) but now precedes it with an explanatory introduction and a catechism. The service's explicit rationale—that children of an age of discretion should ratify their baptismal promises before the church—renders the catechetical examination intrinsic to it; and accordingly, tailors the catechism's theological scope to fulfilling the service's rationale. In the confirmation liturgy, which is an extended prayer for the regenerating gifts of the Holy Spirit, the episcopal laying on of hands has replaced the older ceremony of anointing.

58. *FSPB*, 252-8, 410-16. Centrally, the service retains the pre-Reformation English wording of the plighting of troth and giving the ring. Modifications include an evangelical expansion of the opening exhortation and a reformulation of the third "cause" of matrimony; blessing of the couple replacing blessing of the ring; the insertion of two texts, "Those whom God has joined together..." and the declaration of marriage, both borrowed from Luther's rite.

59. *FSPB*, 269-77, 424-7.

60. For example, for Scriptural sentences during the procession and committal, for the words of committal and the four psalms and suffrages of the church service. Even its most Lutheran feature, the Sequence of the committal, *Media Vita in Morte Sumus*, echoes Luther's German paraphrase of a Lenten antiphon from Compline, translated by Coverdale into English meter, and converted by Cranmer into solemn prose. *HAL*, 89; MacCulloch, *Thomas Cranmer*, 331.

61. While the masses for the dead in the Roman Sacramentaries (the Western mass books from the eighth to the thirteenth centuries) and the Sarum Missal, heavily dependent on the Sacramentaries, show almost no trace of the "popular belief" in "a purgatorial fire of discipline and punishment," they do contain phrases construing the eucharistic offering as a "sacrifice of propitiation." James H. Scrawley, "The Holy Communion Service," in *Liturgy and Worship: A Companion to the Prayer Books of the Anglican Communion*, ed. W. K. Lowther Clarke (London: SPCK, 1933), 368-9.

1550 Ordinal

Although compiled by a committee appointed under a parliamentary act, evidence suggests that Cranmer produced the services in the course of 1549, drawing on a recently completed treatise on ordination by Martin Bucer.[62] Cranmer transformed Bucer's proposal of a single form of ordination nuanced for the different ministries into three distinct services[63] and introduced differences among them supportive of retaining, against the Reformed trend, the venerable ecclesial tradition of the three orders.[64] Cranmer's preface supplies the rationale of the rites of ordering by setting forth the twofold form of admission into the historic ministries of the reformed English church: first, the calling, testing, and examining of candidates to determine whether they are adequately erudite in Latin and in Scripture, and virtuous in conduct and "conversation"; and second, the admission and approval "by public prayer, with imposition of hands." Common to all three services (besides the Communion) are the Litany, the Oath of the King's Supremacy, presentation and questioning of the candidate(s), laying on of hands and commissioning, presentation with the "instruments" of office, and exhortation concerning the duties of the ministry. The prayers, exhortations, and questioning in each service reflect the content of the assigned Epistles and Gospels.

The services convey the particularities of each ministry in its relation to the others. Deacons have an auxiliary liturgical and pedagogical ministry—chiefly, assisting at the celebration of Communion, reading aloud the Scriptures and Homilies, and instructing youth in the Catechism—and an administrative ministry in distributing alms. Priests have the primary evangelical and pastoral ministries in their congregations: preaching and teaching God's word; celebrating the dominical sacraments; and gathering in, nurturing, and admonishing Christ's flock to bring it to oneness and maturity of faith. Bishops are preeminently governors in Christ's church, maintaining and promoting obedience to him in faith and practice through teaching and exhortation, the laying on of hands, correction, and punishment.

---

62. Bucer's treatise, *De ordinatione legitima ministrorum ecclesiarum revocanda*, appears basically to describe the Strasbourg ordination rite. For the Latin text and English translation, Edward Charles Whitaker, *Martin Bucer and the Book of Common Prayer* (Alcuin Club; Great Awakening: Mayhew-McCrimmon, 1974), 176-83. Also for Bucer's contribution, Constantin Hopf, *Martin Bucer and the English Reformation* (Oxford: Blackwell, 1946), 88-94. For discussion of the sources and later development of the ordinal texts, Frederick Edward Brightman, *The English Rite: Being a Synopsis of the Sources and Revisions of the Book of Common Prayer*, 2 vols (London: Rivingtons, 1915), 2:928-1017.

63. However, he designed each service to be inserted into the Communion in such a manner as to allow the conferring of all three orders in a single compounded service.

64. With studied imprecision, Cranmer's preface traces the orders back to "the Apostles time" on the combined witness of "holy scripture and ancient authors." *FSPB*, 292. While the differences introduced among them ran along both evangelical and traditional lines, the traditional differences (in prayers, vestments worn, ceremonial formulae, and "instruments" of office) were the more incompatible with Bucer's proposal.

While the liturgies recognize differences in dignity, responsibility, and spiritual equipment among the orders,[65] their dominant and unifying theme is the duty of all orders to increase their knowledge and understanding of God's word through prayerful, assiduous, and unceasing study of the Scriptures, as testified by the "instruments" delivered.[66]

1552 Prayer Book

Apart from the ambitions of Cranmer and his like-minded associates for further liturgical reform, a number of factors conspired to make revision desirable and possible. The ferocity and extent of popular resistance to the vernacular liturgies, principally from Catholic conservatism in the southwest counties, swayed the king's evangelical councilors toward more aggressive liturgical reform, consonant with the iconoclastic campaign underway; their accrual of power within the Council, combined with the steady ascent of reforming stalwarts to senior bishoprics, gave political plausibility to this policy. Concurrently, critical reactions to the "papist" residue of the 1549 prayer book from eminent divines at home and abroad[67] were building up a reforming momentum, especially around ceremonial, clerical garb, and church furnishings, and impressing upon the Archbishop and others the ecumenical benefit of bringing English worship into closer alignment with continental practices. The undertaking of Cranmer's inveterate Catholic adversary, Stephen Gardiner, to demonstrate the compatibility of the vernacular Communion liturgy with traditional Catholic eucharistic doctrine increased this momentum and resolved Cranmer to ensure the prayer book service against mischievous misinterpretation.[68]

---

65. These are more noticeable between the diaconal and priestly ministries than between the priestly and episcopal ministries.

66. Deacons receive the New Testament; priests the Bible, together with the chalice and bread; and bishops (following tradition) have the Bible laid on their necks, and a pastoral staff placed in their hands. The medieval traditions of bestowing eucharistic vestments on deacons and priests and investing bishops with ring and mitre have been discarded.

67. Key was Bucer's detailed critical review of the prayer book with recommendations (known as *The Censura*), produced in 1550 at Cranmer's invitation and followed by Vermigli's supplement. The Latin text and English translation of *The Censura* is provided in Whitaker, *Martin Bucer and the Book of Common Prayer*, 9–174. Other influential criticisms came from Calvin, Bullinger, Jan Laski (émigré superintendent of the London "Stranger Church"), and Bullinger's English disciple, Bishop John Hooper.

68. Stephen Gardiner's *Explication and assertion of the Catholic Faith touching the most blessed sacrament of the altar* . . . comprised a refutation of Cranmer's defence of the reformed eucharistic theology of the prayer book, to which Cranmer responded with the furious counter-refutation, *An Answer to a crafty and sophistical cavillation devised by Stephen Gardiner*.

The menace of mischievous misinterpretation proved useful, when the parliamentary Act of Uniformity authorizing the revised book addressed the delicate task of justifying changes to the existing book, described as "a very goodly order . . . agreeable to the Word of God and the primitive Church, very comfortable to all good people."[69] Accordingly, the revision, broadly speaking, endeavored to reduce the prayer book's compromising Catholic content and to inhibit compromising traditionalist uses while clarifying and expanding its evangelical and reformed content and uses. To begin with, the revisers sought to encourage lay attendance at the daily services of Morning and Evening Prayer by summoning with bells and to enhance lay participation in worship by increasing congregational speaking and by largely replacing the individual "I" with the corporate "we" as the pronominal voice of congregational speech. The corporate voice is prominent in the beautifully crafted penitential introduction with which both services were now provided, comprising biblical sentences, an invitation to confession, confession, and absolution.[70]

Predictably, the Communion service invited the most drastic remodeling, involving several structural, verbal, and ceremonial changes. The service now opens with a recitation of the Ten Commandments, interleaved with a congregational refrain beseeching God's mercy for transgression of his law.[71] It has dismantled the 1549 eucharistic Canon with its three components (intercession for the church, consecration, and oblation) and introduced strategic alterations of wording, to preclude interpretation of the Eucharist as a propitiatory sacrifice for the whole church, living and dead,[72] entailing transubstantiation of the elements.[73]

---

69. The Act observed that "divers doubts" had arisen respecting "the fashion and manner" of "ministration" of "the common service." Although arising "rather by the curiosity of the minister and mistakers rather than of any other worthy cause," these doubts gave occasion for "the more plain and manifest explanation hereof" and, as well, "the more perfection of the said order of common service" to render it "in some places . . . more earnest and fit to stir Christian people to the true honouring of Almighty God." 1552: 5 & 6 edn. VI, *c.* 1: *TC*, 407.

70. For the introduction's borrowing from Calvin's Strasbourg liturgy, see Martin Davie, "Calvin's Influence on the Theology of the English Reformation," *Ecclesiology* 6, no. 3 (2010): 319.

71. *FSPB*, 377–9. Placing of the recitation follows Bucer, Calvin, and Poullain at Strasbourg, and the refrain recalls Luther and Calvin's metrical version.

72. The intercession for the church, now directly following the offertory, is separated from the prayer of consecration by the exhortations to worthy reception and the penitential preparation, and its petitions are confined to "the church militant" on earth. See 287 n. 503. In addition, the worshippers' oblation is repositioned, along with the *Gloria in excelsis*, at the end of the service. *FSPB*, 382, 390–1.

73. The Prayer of Humble Access is repositioned from just before distribution of the sacrament to before the Prayer of Institution, to avoid misinterpretations of its references to eating Christ's flesh and drinking his blood. Also undermining corporeal presence and

Conversely, these changes accentuate the sacramental power of the Eucharist as the church's recollection (not recapitulation) of Christ's "once for all" saving sacrifice, to make spiritually (not locally or corporeally) present to faithful communicants Christ's sacrificed body and blood,[74] and thereby to bring forth their sacrificial offering (oblation) of themselves, their "souls and bodies" with their "praise and thanksgiving."[75] The changes are again reinforced by rubrical alterations to clerical vestments and liturgical performance.[76]

Although less heatedly divisive, revision of baptism involved further pruning back of "superstitious" ceremonies and refocusing of the sacrament's transformative efficacy on the dynamic social-spiritual action rather than on the physical elements.[77] The action and prayers give more development than previously to the significance of baptism as the opening act of the believer's incorporation

---

transubstantiation are omission of the *Benedictus* after the *Sanctus*, the *Epiklesis* from the Prayer of Institution, and the *Agnus Dei* during the Communion. Most dramatically, in administering the bread and wine to the communicants, the "minister" (not "priest") no longer says: "The body [similarly "The blood..."] of our Lord Jesus Christ which was given for thee, preserve thy body and soul unto everlasting life." *FSPB*, 388–9.

74. The Prayer of Institution (no longer, obviously, of consecration) comes immediately before the Communion of priest and congregation, coordinating in one unbroken movement Christ's act of self-giving and the church's act of receiving. In delivering the bread and wine the minister says, "Take and eat this [similarly "Drink this"] in remembrance that Christ died for thee and feed on him in thy heart by faith, with thanksgiving." *FSPB*, 388–9.

75. The concluding sequence of the worshippers' oblation and the *Gloria* provide a post-communion climax of corporate exultation.

76. The rubrics further simplify clerical dress, specify a white linen covering for the communion table, and the sacramental use of ordinary, good quality white bread. They require the minister to stand at the north side of the Communion table and to distribute the bread into the communicants' hands (not mouths), and they allow him private use of any remaining elements. The notorious "black rubric" (so called because appearing in black rather than red ink as a late addition to the first printed 1552 prayer books) theologically justifies kneeling to receive the Communion as a practice signifying "humble and grateful acknowledging" of Christ's benefits and, thereby, avoiding "profanation and disorder," without inviting adoration of the bread and wine or implying "any real and essential presence ... of Christ's natural flesh and blood." The elements remain in their "natural substances," so cannot be adored without idolatry; and our Saviour's "natural body and blood ... are in heaven and not here," occupying only one place at one time. *FSPB*, 392–3.

77. Jettisoned were the ceremonies of exorcism, anointing the baptized, bestowing the chrism, and blessing the font; although retaining the affirmation that Christ's baptism "didst sanctify the flood Jordan and all other waters, to the mystical washing away of sin" protected the symbolic efficacy of washing in water as a vehicle of the Holy Spirit's cleansing action. *FSPB*, 395.

into the fellowship of faith and discipleship, that is, Christ's body.[78] Reflecting more severe disapproval of intercession for the dead, or even liturgical attention to them, the 1552 Burial is a vestigial service of procession to, and committal at, the graveside, retaining only the Scriptural sentences, the *Media Vita* sequence, the act of committal, and the lesson from 1 Corinthians 15, concluding with the Lord's Prayer and two other prayers. Finally, ceremonial changes to the Ordinal, now included in the prayer book, further reinforce the evangelical character of the church's official ministry.[79]

1559 Prayer Book

Within six months of Elizabeth's succeeding to the throne, her first Parliament passed the Act of Uniformity authorizing the 1552 prayer book, with some few, but important modifications. While the factors giving rise to this settlement of the church's worship still attract vigorous debate, the following situational elements are well established: the conservative religious sympathies of a large segment of Elizabeth's subjects; the country's important international Catholic alliances; the Cranmerian reforming stripe of Elizabeth's Principal Secretary, William Cecil, and his powerful associates on her Council; the more traditionalist (pre-1552) features of worship retained by the Queen in her private chapel; the significant opposing factions within Parliament of episcopal and lay traditionalists in the House of Lords and determined reformers in the House of Commons; and the rapid post-settlement promotion to senior episcopal posts of English continental exiles from Queen Mary's persecution who were keen promoters of the 1552 prayer book. In the light of the above, it seems likely that Cecil and his inner circle prepared the liturgical settlement and piloted it through the shoals of parliamentary debate, having persuaded the Queen of its overall desirability.[80]

Not surprisingly, the prayer book's important modifications were all eucharistic concessions to more conservative Catholic orientations. They consisted in restoring to the administration of the bread and wine the 1549 words allowing for Christ's

---

78. Signing with the cross now follows baptismal washing and is accompanied by reception of the baptized "into the congregation of Christ's flock," and a congregational attestation of the signing to be a token of the infant's future faith and discipleship. In addition, the faith of the godparents, as promising for the infant, is highlighted by the minister's addressing the interrogations directly to them (and not to the infant). *FSPB*, 397-9.

79. In line with Bucer and Hooper's criticisms and preferences, wearing of albs by deacons and priests, and of surplices and copes by bishops, is discontinued, as is the handing over of chalice and paten to priests, and the pastoral staff to bishops. Bibles are delivered to all three orders, without ceremonial distinguishing of the episcopal office.

80. Heal, *Reformation in Britain and Ireland*, 357-62. Winthrop S. Hudson, *The Cambridge Connection and the Elizabethan Settlement of 1559* (Durham: Duke University Press,1980); Norman L. Jones, Faith by Statute: *Parliament and the Settlement of Religion 1559* (London: Royal Historical Society, 1982).

"real" or "corporal" presence (n. 79) and pairing them with the memorialist, spiritual-presence formula of 1552 (n. 80); omitting the contentious "Black rubric" on kneeling (n. 82); and introducing a rubric on church "ornaments" intended to restore eucharistic vestments, but with lamentably ambiguous wording.[81] While these concessions, reinforced by a few more modest ones,[82] achieved greater theological comprehensiveness than the 1549 rite, they similarly failed to pacify rigorists on either side of the battle lines.

Various ecclesiastical directives filled out the prayer book settlement, commencing with the injunctions for the royal visitation of 1559. These required clergy who were licensed to preach to deliver a sermon to their congregations at least once a month (reduced to once a quarter by the bishops' *Interpretations* of 1560–1), to read the official homilies in the other weeks, and to catechize "the youth of the parish" on "every second Sunday."[83] Correspondingly, they required all parishioners on "Sundays and holy days" to attend during "the whole time of the godly service," consisting of Morning Prayer, the Litany, and the Holy Communion.[84] Most dramatically, they directed the removal of "all shrines . . . tables, candlesticks . . . pictures, paintings, and all other monuments of feigned miracles, pilgrimages, idolatry, and superstition," thereby sanctioning the revival of large-scale iconoclastic destruction.[85]

Apart from the beauty and power of prayer book prose, the single compensation for the austere visual aesthetic of Elizabethan worship was the cautious revival of liturgical instrumental and vocal music from its Edwardian attenuation, supported by a royal injunction of 1559.[86] Besides enjoining the maintenance of existing

---

81. Prefixed to Morning Prayer, the rubric directs that the vestments to be used by clergy "at all times in their ministration" shall be those legislated by Parliament's authority "in the Second year of the reign of King Edward the Sixth," whereas the Act of Uniformity authorizing the 1549 prayer book fell in King Edward's third year. Although probably a mere chronological error, the repetition of this wording in the 1662 prayer book ensured that it would become a historical battleground between "high" and "low" churchmen.

82. For example, withdrawal from the Litany of the reference to "the tyranny of the Bishop of Rome and all his detestable enormities" (*FSPB*, 362) and provision of Proper First Lessons for Sundays. *HAL*, 122.

83. Henry Gee and William John Hardy, eds., *Documents Illustrative of English Church History* (London: Macmillan, 1896), 420, 430, 434.

84. Ibid., 434.

85. Ibid., 428. A Royal Order of 1561 required that the "rood" (crucifix) of the "rood screen" should be removed, but the screen retained, topped by a suitable "crest"—usually the royal arms, and that the Ten Commandments should hang on the wall above the simply covered communion table, which was to replace the altar at the east end, when not positioned in the body of the chancel for the celebration of Communion.

86. In the Edwardian prayer book liturgies, the reduction of the number of psalms, canticles, antiphons, responds, and so on had reduced the sheer volume of music, while the jettisoning of polyphony had diminished musical complexity and sublimity. Nevertheless,

choral foundations in collegiate and parish churches (assuming the maintenance of cathedral choral establishments), the injunction directed that "a modest and distinct song" be used throughout the church's "common prayers," enabling them to be "plainly understood," and also allowed for the more elaborate musical setting of "an hymn or suchlike song" at the beginning or end of daily services.[87] This royal endorsement of liturgical music encouraged leading English composers to produce part settings for the canticles and occasional festival psalms at Morning and Evening Prayer, for other Scriptural texts to be sung as "Anthems"[88] and for segments or the whole congregational portion of the Communion service. Organ solos became common during the offertory, and short voluntaries sometimes appeared between lessons and canticles. The radiating hub of these developments was the large and distinguished musical establishment of Elizabeth's chapel royal from which outstanding composers gave new impetus to English cathedral music.[89] Too meagerly resourced to benefit greatly from this impetus and having no tradition of Lutheran hymns and chorales, most parish churches remained under the Edwardian diet of somewhat monochrome service settings.[90] Consequently, parish music increasingly came under the sway of the Genevan tradition of metrical psalms,[91] as represented by the regularly revised editions of Sternhold and Hopkins, *Psalms Collected in English Metre*, which gained nationwide popularity

---

large portions of the revised rites were either intended or allowed to be sung, as the rubrics made clear, in the "plain tones" which Cranmer judged seemly for corporate devotions and accessible to the musically untutored.

87. Gee and Hardy, *Documents*, 435.

88. The Anglicized form of "antiphon," the English "anthem" was an important development of antiphonal liturgical music, thanks to the pioneering compositions of William Byrd and his pupils, Thomas Morley and Orlando Gibbons, alternating accompanied solo voices and chorus. Anthem texts were often drawn from the Collect, Gospel, or Epistle of the day, or a psalm. Horton Davies, *Worship and Theology in England: From Cranmer to Baxter and Fox, 1534–1690*, combined edn. (Grand Rapids: Eerdmans, 1996), I:400–2.

89. Elizabeth's musical establishment employed sixty musicians, singers and instrumentalists, and included the most celebrated Catholic composers of polyphony, Thomas Tallis and William Byrd, and a number of distinguished colleagues taught and inspired by them. For discussion of the works of English Reformation composers and their successors, Andrew Gant, *O Sing unto the Lord: A History of English Church Music* (London: Profile, 2015); Peter Le Huray, *Music and the Reformation in England 1549–1660* (repr. with corrections, Cambridge: Cambridge University Press, 1978).

90. Cranmer's liturgical preference for syllabic musical settings (one note per syllable) was met by John Merbecke's simple Gregorian-style arrangements for unaccompanied, unison voices, covering Matins, Evensong, Communion, and Burial (with Communion).

91. During the early 1540s, Clément Marot, at Calvin's instigation, metricized a good number of the psalms. Marot's superb poetry, together with their masterful musical settings by Bourgeois, Greiter, and Franc, made the psalms a great national and international success, in private (family) devotions as in public worship.

with congregations, and set the tone of English parish worship and popular piety for many generations.[92]

Throughout Elizabeth I's long reign, the 1559 prayer book and accompanying Ordinal met with continuous resistance from both Catholic and Puritan quarters. Harsh official suppression ensured that Catholic resistance took the form of recusant worship, covert mission, and occasional attempts on the queen's life. By contrast, Puritan dissent was vociferously vocal and often overtly disobedient, being strongly represented in its Presbyterian form within the ranks of Elizabeth's clergy and parliamentarians.[93] Despite its considerable influence, Puritan (Presbyterian, Genevan) resistance failed to elicit significant modifications of worship and ministry from Elizabeth's government, or from that of her Stuart successor, James I. Most importantly, following the restoration of the monarchy in 1660, it was an expanded version of the 1559/1604 (Jacobean) prayer book that the 1662 Act of Uniformity legislated. Conceding little ground to opposing Laudian (Catholicizing) and Puritan agendas for prayer book revision,[94] this version would comprise Anglican worship in the royal dominions and colonies for the next three centuries.

Edwardian and Elizabethan Homilies

Throughout the Tudor and Stuart churches, the official homilies were primarily intended to serve two purposes: to compensate for poorly equipped clergy with

---

92. Thomas Sternhold's published edition of nineteen English metrical psalms (*c.* 1548) was expanded to thirty-seven psalms by John Hopkins and publish posthumously in 1549. A further expanded edition was first published with music in Geneva in 1556 for use by the reformed community of English Marian refugees. Their ministers, Christopher Goodman and William Whittingham, with others produced the *Whole Book of Psalms Collected into English Metre*, published under royal license by John Day in 1562. This collection, known as Sternhold and Hopkins, underwent sixty-five editions before the end of the century, outstripping superior rivals. Gant, *O Sing Unto The Lord*, 109–13; Daniell, *The Bible in English*, 322–30.

93. The fringe revolt of more radical Separatists, increasingly beyond the pale of Elizabeth's church establishment, was more harshly and summarily suppressed.

94. The opposing agendas proved mutually frustrating in the official consultations for revision, the Savoy conference and the 1661 meeting of the Convocations. The "Laudian" party comprised bishops formerly in King Charles I's episcopal establishment led by Archbishop William Laud, which had produced in 1637 a major prayer book revision in the direction of 1549, intended by the king to be the official Scottish rite, with cataclysmic effect! By 1662 such Laudian divines as John Cosin, Matthew Wren, and William Sandcroft were ready with draft proposals for a restoration prayer book, heavily indebted to the 1549 and 1637 predecessors. The presbyterian program was put before the Savoy Conference in two forms: a complete liturgical order produced by Richard Baxter and a list of criticisms under the title, *Exceptions*, drawn up by a committee. *HAL*, 149–59; Geoffrey J. Cuming, *The Durham Book* (Oxford: Oxford University Press, 1961).

insufficient natural and educational endowment and to ensure some degree of uniformity in preaching. These purposes were closely linked in the Edwardian and earlier Elizabethan years when ignorance of the central theological tenets of reformed faith and practice and their biblical foundation was widespread and seemingly intractable in certain geographical areas, and a constant dose of reliably evangelical and biblical teaching was needed to overcome the traditional habits of the majority. But from the second decade of Elizabeth's reign onward, the prevailing purpose of the official homilies was to curtail clerical preaching of a more biblically and theologically informed outlook which deviated from or assaulted the prayer book settlement. However, the designers and promoters of the prescribed homilies always hoped to build up a truly common mind among believers, to persuade uncertain and recalcitrant clergy and laity on contentious matters and not merely to achieve outward restraint, being themselves convinced of the interdependence of spiritual communion and social peace and order.

The official Tudor homilies lay outside the mainstream of patristic and medieval homilies in two respects: their thematic organization and their extensive argumentative, apologetic, and polemical material. As dilations on topics or themes rather than biblical passages, their selection owed more to circumstantial factors than to the intrinsic logic and parameters of biblical texts. Consequently, they neither provided the cumulative biblical education of sermonic commentary on chapters and books of the Bible, nor were they consistently integrated into the liturgical cycle of Bible readings. Nevertheless, they were prodigal in their use of Scripture, being almost catenae of Scriptural quotations, paraphrases, and allusions, interspersed with quotations and paraphrases of the Church Fathers, cited after the Scriptures to demonstrate the fidelity of Tudor church reform to authoritative Christian tradition. As many of the official homilies dealt with topics of inflamed controversy, they kept in their sights the surrounding terrain of dissenting arguments and practices: Catholic, Presbyterian, Anabaptist, and Separatist. In expounding doctrines, defending practices, and delivering exhortations, they attempted maximal demolition of inimical positions, typically devoting a section to refuting objections and counterarguments. Relying on neither classical rhetorical nor scholarly embellishment, they sought to persuade through "cumulative and reiterative" argumentation, in "sober" and "lucid" speech, employing direct, pithy, and vivid language.[95]

The first collection of homilies, issued promptly upon Edward's taking the throne, was the timely completion of Cranmer's earlier frustrated enterprise to disseminate through preaching the core evangelical content of such formularies as the Ten Articles (1536) and the Bishops' Book.[96] Publication of the collection

---

95. Ronald B. Bond, ed., *Certain Sermons or Homilies (1547) and A Homily against Disobedience and Wilful Rebellion (1570): A Critical Edition* (Toronto: University of Toronto Press, 1987). Hereafter *CS*.

96. With good reason, Bond views these formularies as closer historical antecedents of the Edwardian homilies than Richard Taverner's *Postils on the Epistles and Gospels* (1540),

in 1547,[97] with a preface in the king's name, claiming royal and Privy Council authorization, was accompanied by an injunction requiring all parishes to obtain a copy. This state of affairs was presupposed by the 1549 prayer book rubric directing that after the Creed "shall follow the Sermon or Homily, or some portion of one of the Homilies."[98] Crucial to the emerging status of the homilies as a "benchmark of reformed belief" were their fulsome endorsements by the Forty-Two Articles of 1552.[99]

The collection consists (after the preface) of twelve sermons grouped into broadly doctrinal and moral topics, beginning with an exhortation to the reading of Scripture forming an epistemological introduction. The doctrinal topics display an obvious theological sequence, beginning with the miserable state of sinful humanity and passing to accounts of salvation, faith, good works, and Christian love and charity. The last two provide the theological framework for the moral topics to follow: swearing and perjury, "declining from God," fear of death, civil obedience, whoredom and adultery, and strife and contention.

Although the homilies were published anonymously, the authorship of six of them is well attested and universally accepted by scholars. Beyond dispute is Cranmer's authorship of the three pivotal sermons on salvation, faith, and good works,[100] presenting the consecutive planks of a synthetic evangelical soteriology; and, as well, his responsibility for the collection's polemical preface, which, anticipatory of the prayer book's preface, sets out the pedagogical and pastoral task of the homilies against the eclipsing of God's word and corruption of faith and morals by the papal tradition. The two homilies flanking Cranmer's central contribution, those on the misery and condemnation of sinful humankind and on Christian charity, are known to have been written by two staunch Catholic traditionalists, John Harpsfield and Edmond Bonner, by virtue (ironically) of their republication with signatures in the 1555 Marian collection.[101] Of considerable interest is that both Harpsfield's depiction of the wretchedness of frail human creatures consumed by sin and Bonner's presentation of the Christ-centered love

---

comprising simple, evangelical Scriptural expositions following the liturgical calendar, even though two of Taverner's postils appeared in the Elizabethan collection. CS, 4.

97. Its full title is *Certain Sermons or Homilies, Appointed by the King's Majesty to be Declared and Read by All Persons, Vicars, or Curates, Every Sunday in Their Churches Where They Have Cure.*

98. *FSPB*, 214.

99. *CS*, 5. Article 34 prescribes the homilies as "godly and wholesome, containing doctrine to be received of all men" and Article 11 on justification entirely defers to the topic's homiletic treatment.

100. Cranmer's authorship is attested in writing by his contemporaries, John Bale and John Gardiner, and by the Elizabethan bishop, John Woolton (1576), and as well, by material in the Archbishop's "Notes on Justification." See *MWL*, 128; also, *CS*, 26.

101. Bonner was an Henrician bishop who had occupied the see of London since 1540, and Harpsfield was his chaplain.

of God and neighbor provide a sympathetic and illuminating frame for Cranmer's evangelical manifesto, although Cranmer's scandalous innovations were unknown to these worthies at the time of writing!

In the absence of conclusive historical evidence, Cranmer has been widely favored as the most probable author of the opening exhortation to Scripture reading, with its unequivocal evangelical epistemology.[102] His association with "An Exhortation against the Fear of Death," although more flimsy on historical grounds,[103] is credible on theological grounds, given the homily's affecting contrast between the tormenting fears surrounding death for the "carnal man" and the "assured trust" and joyful expectation surrounding it for those whose hope rests wholly in Christ's merits. Of the homilies on moral topics, "Against Whoredom and Adultery," confidently assigned to Thomas Becon,[104] is a revealing indictment of the time's prevailing sexual laxity. The sermon "Against Swearing and Perjury," stressing the distinction between the unlawful taking of God's name in vain and the lawful invocation of God's name in public oaths, declarations, and promises, suggests the perceived extent of Anabaptist influence and encourages us to discern in the homily, "Of the Declining from God" an attack on Anabaptist antinomianism, and in "An Exhortation to Obedience," an attack on Anabaptist political separatism and rebellion. However, the latter homily, of unknown authorship and date, may have been responding primarily, or entirely, to the English rebellions of 1536 and their sequel, given its denunciation of the pope's political usurpation. Finally, the sermon "Against Contention and Brawling," of long (but unconfirmed) association with Bishop Hugh Latimer, appears to be an attempt to subdue the quarrelsome and rancorous relations surfacing within the Edwardian church polity around its deep doctrinal and liturgical divisions.

A royal injunction gave undisguised expression to the homilies' intended function of regulating the preaching of bishops and of clergy licensed to preach,[105] and the failure of this measure to control the pulpit resulted in the government's resort in 1548 to revoking a good number of preaching licenses and, subsequently, to prohibiting all sermons for an indeterminate period. In 1549, the government adopted the alternative tactic of rendering the homilies more palatable to resisting clergy and laity by dividing them into smaller portions for congregational delivery

---

102. Apart from the loose structural continuities of its argument with Cranmer's 1540 preface to the Great Bible, its five corroborating patristic citations also appear in his "commonplaces" under the heading "Sacrae Scripturae intellectus et utilitas." John Griffiths, *The Two Books of Homilies Appointed to be Read in Churches* (Oxford: Oxford University Press, 1859), Preface, xxvii. Hereafter *GH*.

103. *CS*, 28.

104. Becon was Cranmer's evangelical chaplain and a prebendary preacher at Canterbury Cathedral. *CS*, 28.

105. W. H. Frere and W. M. Kennedy, eds., *Visitation Articles and Injunctions of the Period of the Reformation*, 3 vols (London: Longmans, Green, 1910), 2:132.

(as the prayer book rubric advertised).[106] The centrality of the homilies to Cranmer's reforming strategy may be gauged by his concluding the 1547 collection with a list of topics for a future collection.

Cranmer's ambition remained unfulfilled until Queen Elizabeth, after expeditiously issuing a new edition of the Edwardian homilies in 1559, set in motion plans for a second collection of homilies to incorporate previously contemplated and additional topics, their production being distributed among the bishops. The collection finally published in 1563 was neither as large nor as varied in authorship as had been projected. Even so, its mere twenty homilies were two-and-one-half times longer than the original twelve, and they would be considerably enlarged in 1571 by the sermon "Against Disobedience and Wilful Rebellion" composed in the wake of the northern Catholic uprising. Nearly half of the sermons, according to their nineteenth-century editor, John Griffiths, show sufficient stylistic continuities to indicate a single authorship, for which the most likely candidate is Bishop John Jewel, long suspected of being the collection's editor.[107]

The Queen's own editorial interference in the collection[108] presaged her continuing, heavy reliance on the homilies over forty years as her chief instrument for reining in, even suppressing, the preaching of her Presbyterian-leaning clergy primarily. These remained unreconciled to the compulsory substitution of officially censored homilies, judged to be riven with theological errors, for timely and inspired expositions of freely chosen biblical texts. Not even the staunchest defenders of Elizabeth's church settlement among her senior churchmen, including her archbishops, could muster enthusiasm for her prolonging a device suitable only as a short-term expedient, a pis aller. Yet mandatory use of the homilies proved irresistible even to James I, who, despite his early sympathy with Puritan ambitions for an educated preaching ministry, came to use the collections as indispensable standards and boundaries for preaching, authorizing publication in 1623 of an amended edition uniting the collections. Although no later editions bore the imprint of public authority, the homilies retained wide theological influence over Caroline clergy and continued to have their defenders and admirers even into the Restoration period and beyond.[109]

While the arrangement of homilies in the 1563/71 collection lacks the theological coherence of its Edwardian predecessor, their topics loosely fall into three groups: theological and soteriological, concerning the manifold gifts of God, the saving work of Christ and the Holy Spirit, repentance, and biblical authority; ecclesiological, concerning worship and the sacraments; and moral, concerning

---

106. *FSPB*, 214.

107. *GH*, Preface, xvii.

108. Manuscript evidence suggests that Elizabeth delayed publication of the volume after its approval by the Houses of Convocation, to make her own changes in the copy submitted for royal assent.

109. Millar MacLure, *The Paul's Cross Sermons 1534–1642* (Toronto: University of Toronto Press, 1958), 170.

obedience and disobedience to God's commandments. In the soteriological group, the four Christological sermons—on the Nativity, the Passion (two sermons), and the Resurrection—were intended for Christmas Day, Good Friday, and Easter Day.[110] "Of the Nativity" gives a full account of Christ's person and saving work within a covenantal framework; the passion sermons are penitential meditations on Christ's self-sacrifice on the Cross; and the Easter sermon expounds the resurrection as the "ground and foundation" of the church's faith. The homily, "That all Good Things Cometh from God," for use in Rogation Week, has three parts devoted to the seasonal themes of God's infinite goodness and generosity in ordering the whole nonhuman creation for the "use and comfort" of humankind, the absolute dependence of humankind on God's continuing bounty, and the mediation of the Father's material and spiritual blessings by Jesus Christ and the Holy Spirit.[111] The sermon "Of Repentance and of True Reconciliation unto God" expounds the necessity of constant repentance, its great benefits and its constituent parts, implicitly correcting perceived errors of sectarian perfectionism and Catholic penitential theology.[112] More aggressively apologetic, "An Information for Them Which Take Offence at Certain Places of the Holy Scripture" counters conservative Catholic arguments for restricting hearing and reading of the Scriptures.

The second group of homilies concerning worship and the sacraments, cautiously attributed by Griffiths to Bishop Jewel, includes the first three in the collection, indicating the weightiness and urgency of the issues which they address. The opening sermon, "Of the Right Use of the Church," is primarily an exhortation to attendance at divine service, in the face of "great slackness and negligence." It follows the prayer book in presenting the components of common worship and stresses the imperative of worship being coordinated *listening*, speaking, and assenting rather than uncoordinated private devotions. Immediately following is the voluminous "Against Peril of Idolatry and Superfluous Decking of Churches," a theological-historical justification of comprehensive iconoclasm drawing on a 1539 treatise of Jewel's intimate acquaintance, Heinrich Bullinger.[113] From Scriptural and patristic sources, it argues that all images of the Trinity or its Persons, whether painted, embossed, or sculpted, are dishonoring and deceiving representations,

---

110. The first passion homily and the homily on the resurrection were taken from Taverner's *Postils* (n. 102) but edited by different hands.

111. These three parts, composing one discourse, apparently conflate sermons on different texts. A fourth part relates to the Rogation ceremony of "beating the bounds," the customary liturgical perambulation around the town (parish) boundaries, and is followed by an Exhortation for use during the perambulation.

112. Largely translated from the sixth homily on the prophet Joel (focusing on 2:12-13) of the Zurich theologian, Rudolf Gwalther, the homily expounds the parts of repentance as "contrition of the heart," "unfeigned confession of our sins unto God," faith in God's promises "touching . . . forgiveness of our sins," and "amendment of life." *GH*, 527-9.

113. The author both extracts material directly from Bullinger's "De Origine Erroris in Divorum et Simulacrorum Cultu" and makes use of an existing abridgement of it. *GH*, xxxi.

violating the second commandment, and that the historical proliferation and use of images in Christendom has exhibited an inner pagan dynamic in the inexorable transition from their mere presence in places of worship to their becoming objects of worship. Ironically, the next homily on church upkeep addresses the evidently serious problem of careless neglect of church fabric maintenance by clergy and parishioners, largely reflecting the popular anger and disaffection occasioned by the Edwardian and Elizabethan iconoclastic campaigns.[114]

The later sermons "Concerning Prayer," "Of the Place and Time of Prayer," and "That Common Prayer and Sacraments Ought to be Ministered in a Tongue that is Understood of the Hearers" give an abridged airing to the theological motifs of the collection's opening homily. The first is an exposition of and exhortation to petitionary prayer, which stresses that it must always be directed to God the Father and Christ the only mediator, never to angels or saints, and that its proper objects are the living, not the dead; the second chastises congregations for their attachment to the frivolous and idolatrous elements of Catholic worship; and the third seeks to demonstrate why common prayer and the (dominical) sacraments, from their very nature, must be ministered in the vernacular tongue. Enlarging upon this demonstration, the homily "Of the Worthy Receiving and Reverent Esteeming of the Sacrament of the Body and Blood of Christ" argues that effectual partaking of the sacrament requires that the communicant properly understand Christ's intention and commands concerning it and have a firm faith in the pledge and seal of redemption contained therein.

While remaining in an evangelical, reforming mold, the moral homilies of 1563 are generally less polemical than the ecclesiological ones. Among these, "Of the State of Matrimony" stands out as a significant theological complement to the Cranmerian marriage liturgy.[115] Contrasting in tone is the 1570 homily "Against Disobedience and Wilful Rebellion."[116] Responding to the northern Catholic insurgence and on its heels, the papal bull excommunicating and deposing the Queen, the sermon is a haranguing tirade on the evils of rebellion against civil rulers and the prolific vices of rebels, completed by a history of papal political usurpation. Despite its belligerent style, it constitutes a valuable Tudor presentation of the biblical theology of political jurisdiction, further developing key structural and thematic aspects of its more concise Edwardian predecessor. The homily's excessive length and tediously protracted polemic support other literary evidence of its production by John Jewel, author of the equally long-winded "Against Peril of Idolatry."[117]

---

114. Heal, *Reformation in Britain and Ireland*, 443.

115. The first half of the homily is translated from an address of the Lutheran preacher, Veit Dietrich (Theodor) of Nuremberg, and the second half from a homily of Chrysostom.

116. Originally intended for northern pulpits, it was included in the national sermon collection by Convocation in 1571.

117. *GH*, xxxvii–xxxviii; 570 n. 1.

Forty-Two and Thirty-Nine Articles

The Edwardian and Elizabethan Articles stand in a succession of Tudor church formularies post-dating Henry VIII's break with Rome and designed to establish a broad unity of understanding of the English church's faith and practice. Like the 1559 prayer book, the Elizabethan Articles of 1571 are heavily dependent on their Cranmerian forerunner, and the Cranmerian Articles of 1553 follow an ecumenical reforming trajectory provided by the draft Anglo-German doctrinal statement of 1538 (never formally agreed) and its Lutheran template, the Confession of Augsburg. For Cranmer, the ecumenical dimension was always central, never incidental, to the confessional project. But its centrality was magnified by the growing need in the early 1550s for a united evangelical response to the flood of Tridentine canons. Evidence of Cranmer's aspiration to spearhead an international doctrinal agreement was his endeavor to engage Bullinger, Calvin, and Melanchthon in a consultation over his project of English canon law revision, encompassing doctrinal formulations. Only after a disappointing response to his high-level invitations and the irrecoverable parliamentary defeat of his completed law revision did the Articles come before a committee for final revision in 1553.[118] However, postponement of the Articles' final revision and publication may also, or instead, have resulted from the decision to publish them jointly with a new catechism.

The ecumenical interest is most pronounced in those articles exhibiting verbal correspondences with the Anglo-German statement and/or the Confession of Augsburg—namely, on the Trinity (I), the Incarnate Son (II), the Resurrection (IV), the official ministry (XXIV), the sacraments (XXVI), and church traditions (XXXIV). However, taking the articles altogether, the polemical interest in confuting a string of Roman and Anabaptist "errors" appears to be more determinative of their content.[119] Nevertheless, the Forty-Two Articles are not a list

---

118. MacCulloch, *Thomas Cranmer*, 501–4. According to MacCulloch, the hypothesis that Cranmer did not want to produce an English church formulary when a truly ecumenical confession was a live possibility may also account for the interval between his production of doctrinal articles for limited clerical subscription in 1549 and the national issuing of the articles in 1553.

119. In the Roman camp, the Articles chiefly target errors concerning justification and meritorious works (XI, XII, XIII), *grace ex opere operato* (XXVI), purgatory (XXIII), the sacrificial mass and transubstantiation (XXIX, XXX), worship in an unknown tongue (XXV), the infallibility and universal authority of Roman church tradition vis-à-vis Scripture (XX, XXI, XXII, XXXIII), clerical celibacy (XXXI), and the grounds and extent of papal and civil jurisdiction (XXXV, XXXVI). In the Anabaptist camp, the Articles target trinitarian and Christological heresies (I–IV, VII), Pelagianism (VIII–XII, XVII), perfectionism and antinomianism (XIV, XV, XVIII, XIX), millenarianism, universalism, and other errors concerning the resurrection of the dead (XXXIX–XLII), community of property/possession (XXXVII), the ordination and holiness of ministers (XXIV, XXVII), the authority of church

of anathemas, but a reasonably consistent and coherently ordered set of doctrinal affirmations covering the Scriptural and creedal rule of faith, individual faith and salvation in Christ, corporate faith and salvation (the nature and authority of the church, her ministry, sacraments, and discipline), and civil rule and polity. They present the considered positions of Archbishop Cranmer and leading Edwardian churchmen, whose emphases, judgments, and discriminations, in responding to prevailing issues and pressures, give them a distinctive theological shape and direction. Moreover, the polemical edge of their positions is frequently offset by an irenic and inclusive intention, expressed in the deliberate minimizing of their contentious theological content.

The Articles' shape and direction were somewhat altered by the Elizabethan revision led by Archbishop Parker.[120] The revisers retained the Cranmerian order and the same number of articles, but by removing four and adding four, and Convocation's review of the Articles removed three more, reducing the number to the familiar thirty-nine. In preparing the draft, Parker injected a second dose of official Lutheranism into the English formulary by drawing on the Confession of Württemberg for two new articles—on the Holy Spirit (V) and on good works (XII), and for expanded articles on the Incarnate Son (II), the sufficiency, integrity and canon of Scripture (VI, VII), free will (X), and justification (XII).

The addition of Article V and expansion of Articles II and X exemplify one type of revision, namely, enlargement for the sake of doctrinal clarity and completeness. Another type of revision aimed at modulating the official response to erroneous doctrines according to the perceived level of danger they currently posed: for example, the revisers omitted Articles XXXIX–XLII concerning "the last things" that chiefly refuted Anabaptist "errors" no longer considered a formidable danger. A third type combines these purposes by introducing, strengthening, or extending articles to counter what were perceived to be increasingly virulent doctrinal threats from Catholic or Puritan positions. For example, against the Tridentine decree of 1546 (fourth session) that juxtaposed the writings of Scripture and unwritten apostolic traditions as equal sources of "saving truth and moral discipline," and received Apocryphal books into the Scriptural canon, the revised Article VI gives a more pointed statement of the sufficiency of Scripture and upholds the superior authority for the church of the Old Testament over the Apocrypha, precisely listing both canonical and Apocryphal books. Similarly, against the 1547 canon (seventh session) asserting Christ's institution of all seven sacraments, the revised Article XXVI (now XXV) explicitly confines to two the sacraments of the gospel commanded by Christ. Among other articles displaying heightened resistance

tradition and discipline (XX, XXXII–XXXV); refusal of infant baptism (XXVIII); oath-taking (XXXVIII); and civil jurisdiction over the regenerate (XXXV). See E. J. Bicknell, *A Theological Introduction to the Thirty-Nine Articles of the Church of England* 3rd edn., rev. H. J. Carpenter (London: Longmans, Green, 1955), 15–19.

120. With Bishop Guest of Rochester, Parker prepared a revised edition for discussion by the Convocations meeting in 1563.

to Catholic pressure is the fresh assertion in Article XXXIII (now XXXIV) of the authority of the "particular or national" church over humanly ordained "ceremonies or rites." Undoubtedly, this assertion also targeted Puritan dissent against the queen's ecclesiastical powers, while other revisions defining moderate reformed positions—for example, on the scope of Christ's atoning work (I) and predestination and election (XVII)—were intended to exclude Puritan (Calvinist) extremes. Finally, a fourth type of revision aimed at bringing earlier Edwardian theological language and judgments into line with current royal and episcopal thinking on such matters as Christ's eucharistic presence (XXIX, now XXVIII), the objectivity of sacramental grace (XXVI, now XXV), and the nature and limits of the monarch's government of the church (XXXVI, now XXXVII).

The ultimate revision of the Articles in 1571 produced no significant modifications, but a parliamentary Act extended compulsory subscription to them to include all beneficed clergy, and not only members of Convocation. While the Act circumvented Puritan objections by requiring subscription only to the doctrinal (as distinct from the disciplinary) articles, Convocation proceeded on its own authority to require comprehensive subscription. Subsequent forms of subscription in 1583 and 1604 required clerical candidates to "believe all the Articles" (as well as the whole Book of Common Prayer) "to be agreeable to the Word of God," thus establishing the formula for almost three centuries.

Chapter 2

THE REFORMATION TRADITION IN CRISIS

The English Reformation tradition of public theology, as a tradition of both political and ecclesiastical thought and practice, was central to English Christian society for over four centuries. Although its political, legal, liturgical, and doctrinal components were never entirely free of controversy and dissent, calling forth pastoral and juridical responses of accommodation and restraint, the unifying force of this tradition was, nevertheless, discernible within England's ecclesiastical and civil polity. However, the last seventy years have seen an unprecedented disengagement from this inheritance in the Church of England's worship and doctrine and in its political framework and setting.

In the church's worship and doctrine, abandonment of the use of the 1662 Book of Common Prayer and Ordinal has been pivotal to this disengagement. In that the 1662 prayer book's use was (and is still) required by parliamentary law,[1] that it enshrined the King James Version of 1611 in Bible readings[2] and was regularly published under one cover with the Thirty-Nine Articles of Religion, it gathered the biblical, liturgical, doctrinal, and political strands of the English Reformation's public legacy and conveyed the legacy's coherence. Thus, the Church of England's detachment from the 1662 prayer book has been accompanied by detachment from the translation tradition of the King James Version and from the pedagogical and disciplinary roles of the Thirty-Nine Articles of Religion. Initiated and managed by the church's theological, liturgical, and pastoral authorities, this disengagement has affected all aspects of its ministry, from clerical and lay ministerial training to congregational worship and education to undertakings of evangelical and social "outreach." Moreover, the disengagement has been conducted and received among church members with a degree of confidence or acquiescence in its historical necessity and inevitability that has undermined the normative status of the Reformation tradition.

The Reformation tradition has, likewise, lost ground within Britain's civil and political life, particularly in the appearance of various political and legal challenges

---

1. The 1662 *Book of Common Prayer* was a schedule attached to the 1662 Act of Uniformity.

2. The exception were the Psalms taken from Coverdale's translation in the 1539 Great Bible.

to the public status and functioning of the Church of England. These challenges have not preponderantly arisen from theologically rooted objections to church establishment, either within the Church of England or within other churches and religious communities; but rather, from a nontheological conception of liberal, democratic, pluralistic political society that has little or no room for the public recognition of religious institutions. This conception constitutes the controlling political matrix in Britain today, where a dwindling proportion of the population have Christian church membership, and barely half profess vaguer forms of religious belief.[3]

The Church's Disengagement from the Reformation Tradition

Disengagement from the 1662 Prayer Book

Nowhere have reservations about the Reformation legacy been more dramatically expressed than in the transformations undergone by the church's worship since the 1960s. These transformations have unsettled the historical identity of the English church and her progeny more than any others, loosening the centuries-old bond of common worship among congregations within the Church of England and within the international fellowship of churches emerging from Britain's past imperial, commercial, and missionary enterprises.

Prior to the postwar period, the official standing of the prayer book's 1662 edition as the legally prescribed liturgical order for all worship of the national church insured a degree of institutional prominence to its enduring theological content, whatever the objections to it and practical deviations from it in some Anglican circles. Even its 1928 revision by church authorities was sufficiently modest and unpopular not to supplant this liturgical legacy.[4] It was not merely long habituation to liturgical uniformity that inclined English churchmen and women to look to prayer book worship for the church's outward unity rather than to formal, confessional standards: it was also the intrinsic intellectual and affective power of the prayer book's liturgies.

---

3. Christianity in the UK (2005–20). https://faithsurvey.co.uk/uk-christianity.html

4. In the 1920s the church's governing bodies (the Convocations of Canterbury and York and the church's National Assembly) produced a Revised Prayer Book, largely in response to the long-running theological protest of Anglo-Catholics and the chaotic state of worship resulting from their unofficial liturgical experimentation and proliferating practices. The relatively modest and uninspired liturgical revisions of this book received a disappointing reception among church members, antagonizing the more extreme Anglo-Catholics, their evangelical opponents, and all enthusiasts of the existing order. Although the proposed book was twice rejected by Parliament (1927 and 1928), suffering two defeats in the Commons, its use was widely introduced by diocesan bishops on the grounds of assumed administrative discretion.

2. The Reformation Tradition in Crisis

Throughout its history, the Church of England has typically responded to liturgical controversies by officially comprehending a degree of plurality within the prayer book order: in the positioning of verbal material and the use of vestments and ceremonial practices. Although this strategy of limiting disunity periodically extended to unauthorized toleration of illicit deviation, it remained that of preserving as much unity in corporate worship as was credible and beneficial in the circumstances. The outcome of the strategy was, for the most part, to enrich prayer book worship for all, and not only for the discontents, with adornments of architecture, furnishings, art, ceremonial, and music that enhanced the spiritual impact of the inherited liturgies. We can scarcely contemplate how impoverished the tradition would have been without the eighteenth-century hymnody of Charles Wesley and the Anglo-Catholic psalm chants and hymnody of the following century! This venerable policy of "comprehension" has been invoked as affording a precedent for the postwar deviation from the church's tradition. But the invocation of this precedent lacks plausibility because it ignores the novelty of the postwar liturgical outworking of the principle of plurality, namely, disregard for the goods of historical continuity, stability, and commonality in the church's corporate worship.

To begin, the overarching structural change to worship has been the loss to most parish churches of the Sunday services of Morning and Evening Prayer, leaving Holy Communion as the exclusive Sunday diet of most congregations. This has inevitably meant a reduction in public reading, reciting, and expounding of the Scriptural text—the Cranmerian rationale of Morning and Evening Prayer. Although partly attributable to the diminished congregational appetite for attending multiple Sunday services and weekday services, their demise has also reflected a waning of clerical enthusiasm for their continuance, influenced by trends in the scholarly field of liturgics and in the broader cultural and social environment.

In recent decades, liturgical scholarship and production has become an international academic and practical specialism, involving interdenominational cross-fertilization among scholars and practitioners, with the resulting concentration on joint interests. A major impetus was the formidable labor of Catholic liturgists, post-Vatican II (from 1965), to provide accessible, vernacular masses. Infusing their work and its trans-denominational reception was a common devotion to renewing the church's mission across society, indebted to the Council's fresh evangelical and progressive positions. In Anglican circles, this liturgical ecumenism and its missionary spirit broadly reinforced the Anglo-Catholic focus on, and interpretation of eucharistic worship, with further reinforcement coming from churches in the Anglican Communion that historically used a more Catholic rendition of the Book of Common Prayer.[5] Besides encouraging eucharistic

---

5. The earliest were the Episcopal Churches of Scotland and of the United States. The Scottish tradition originated in the 1637 prayer book revision that King Charles I injudiciously attempted to impose on the Scottish church, provoking a Presbyterian

monism in Anglican worship, international liturgics has encouraged acceptance of liturgical revision as a continuous scholarly and creative revitalizing of the church's worship. Thus, throughout Anglicanism, liturgical revision has flowed outward from its eucharistic center to encompass all regular and occasional services, strongly embracing the principle of comprehending plurality. Successive rounds of liturgical revision in the Church of England and its daughter churches have multiplied the liturgical options for every service and, as well, devised additional services and liturgies, catering not only to the diverse festivals and seasons of the church's worship but to differing liturgical and pastoral leanings and needs of clergy and congregations.

Comparison of the successive rounds of liturgical revision in the Church of England, producing *The Alternative Service Book* (1980) and *Common Worship* (2000), reveals an intensifying preoccupation with structural units as the framework for multiplying optional forms and prayers.[6] This preoccupation exhibits the mutating debt of liturgical revision to Dom Gregory Dix's magisterial work, *The Shape of the Liturgy*. Consolidating previous decades of scholarly investigations into early Christian liturgies, it sought to demonstrate that the liturgical unity of the early churches consisted in an invariable structural sequence of practices rather than words, the structural units frequently displaying variable verbal content; and, moreover, that this sequence was (and is) intrinsic to the unity and power of the church's eschatological action.[7]

Although Dix's disparaging assessment of the Cranmerian eucharistic liturgies as structurally deficient was not universally accepted by Anglican liturgists, his structural approach to liturgical analysis met with near-universal endorsement: perhaps predictably, as it perfectly suited a missionary outreach in tune with the populist, pluralistic, anti-uniformity, and anti-elitist sentiments of the times. His

rebellion against the episcopal establishment. Closely aligned with Cranmer's 1549 prayer book, this revision continued to be favored by the Nonjuring Scottish bishops who formed the (nonestablished) Episcopal Church of Scotland, becoming the baseline for the officially adopted 1764 Episcopal prayer book. The impact of the 1764 Scottish book on the American Episcopal liturgical tradition was owing to the twin need of the Anglican churches in postrevolutionary America for a domestic episcopate and a revised prayer book. Barred from receiving consecration from English bishops, the first American episcopal candidate—Samuel Seabury, bishop-elect of Connecticut—was consecrated by bishops in the Episcopal Church of Scotland on the understanding that churches in his charge would adhere closely to the eucharistic liturgy of the 1764 book. Through Seabury the Scottish liturgy heavily influenced subsequent American Episcopal prayer book revision.

6. The controlling role given to structures in devising liturgies by the 1989 and 1995 publications, *Patterns of Worship*, is even more pronounced in the liturgical rationale of Common Worship, as explicated by one of its devisors, Jeremy Fletcher, in *Communion in Common Worship: The Shape of Orders One and Two*, Grove Worship Series 159 (Cambridge: Grove Books, 2000).

7. Dom Gregory Dix, *The Shape of the Liturgy* (London: A&C Black, 1945), 247–67.

analytical and axiological emphasis on structural rather than linguistic uniformity gave liturgists everywhere the rationale for both maximal liturgical flexibility and unceasing liturgical revision, sensitive to congregational diversity and shifting linguistic and social trends. It precipitated the dramatic transformation in the church's conception of an authorized liturgical order: from an authorized collection of printed services, with alternative and additional liturgical texts, to an authorized collection of liturgical resource materials, directives, and advice, with some mandatory texts.[8] The Statement on Liturgy produced by the 1988 Lambeth Conference of Anglican Communion bishops conveyed this transformation with blinding clarity:[9]

> Whilst a set liturgy properly provides a ground-plan structure and the text of central prayers, yet nowadays it can and should often provide for material written for the occasion, for extemporary contributions, and for singing of items . . . chosen spontaneously. Provinces should be ready to have basic authorized forms for the central parts of certain rites such as the Eucharist, and for those forms to give a substantial part to the congregation. But they should also provide outline structures into which a choice of materials, already existent or written for the occasion, can be fitted. And we look for further openness still which will encourage the truly spontaneous contributions of spiritually alive congregations.

Unsurprisingly, the increasing complexity of locating and using liturgical options in the official compilations, combined with the continuing appearance of supplementary material, has resulted in churches abandoning the use of even semipermanent books in congregational worship, in favor of centrally or locally produced pamphlets for repeated use, once-off service sheets, and/or overhead or video projection, thereby lending a fleeting, deracinated, and discontinuous quality to regular corporate acts of worship, and rendering them prey to passing social preoccupations and clerical enthusiasms.

It is somewhat paradoxical, then, that the capacity of liturgical structuralism to accommodate variety has not extended to variety of eucharistic interpretation, for nearly all the revised eucharistic options available in the books of 1980 and 2000 have adhered to an ecumenical interpretation of the Eucharist as the church's sacrifice of her service taken up into Christ's sacrifice on the Cross. This interpretation and the eucharistic sequence in which it is embedded differs significantly from the Cranmerian interpretation and sequence from 1552 to 1662, as Dix well understood. In that all the prayer book services from 1552 to 1662 are verbal and structural expressions of an identifiable Reformation soteriology, anthropology,

---

8. For discussion of this transformation, Alan Jacobs, *The Book of Common Prayer: A Biography* (Princeton: Princeton University Press, 2019), 189–92.

9. Lambeth 1988 Statement on Liturgy, Section 168: Flexibility in Rites, in *Lambeth and Liturgy 1988*, Grove Worship 106, edn. with intro. and comm. Colin Buchanan (Nottingham: Grove Books, 1988), 12.

and ecclesiology, it is inevitable that other revised liturgical options, including those for ordination services, should exhibit departures from their predecessor's distinctive theological positions and emphases.[10]

While Anglican evangelical circles have also contributed to the rounds of liturgical revision, favoring liturgical flexibility as congenial to congregational initiative, they have, as well, shown a marked tendency toward less formality, charismatic enthusiasm, and the semiabandonment of set liturgy, under Pentecostalist and other Protestant influences. Parishes and educational institutions of evangelical persuasion have enthusiastically embraced populist, youth-oriented, technologically au fait, cultural trends in spoken, visual, and musical communication, convinced that this is what missionary outreach requires. Frequently encountered in evangelical services is a dissonance between their central acts of Scripture reading and exposition and the multicentered, multimedia worship experience surrounding them, conducive to collective and individual self-absorption.

Contributing to this dissonance is the strong preference for worship led musically by "the worship band" featuring acoustic instruments and the heavy syncopated rhythm of amplified rock. The historical irony has not gone unnoticed: that the strand of Anglican ecclesiology traditionally most averse to the domination of worship by musical performance has come to embrace exactly that, in "the worship leader with a microphone, facing the 'audience,' his backing musicians behind him, like any other gig."[11] The appetite for the "pop," "folk," and "rock" genres of "praise songs," with or without band, has spread well beyond evangelical and charismatic circles, resulting in lesser or greater displacement of the older musical traditions of parish worship, from the Anglican repertoire of responses, psalm chants, and easier four-part anthems suited to parish choirs and congregations to the cumulative wealth of Anglican hymnody garnered from Lutheran, Reformed, Anglo-Catholic, and Wesleyan sources.[12] While not inseparable from the regular prayer book liturgies, this older musical inheritance complemented their corporate solemnity, theological and spiritual depth, rhetorical beauty, and disciplined pathos.

Across the board, then, published liturgical material and actual parochial practice testify that the Church of England's disengagement from the prayer book tradition is everywhere well-advanced. At the same time, some appreciation has surfaced of the incongruity of the established church's disengagement from the one uniform national order of worship. In the 1990s rising insecurity of clergy and laity over this incongruity prompted a synodical decision to incorporate the prayer book liturgies

---

10. For example, the ordination liturgies in *Common Worship*, with their various options, send out mixed ecclesiological signals in which evangelical and sacramental orientations to ministry vie for attention. See Colin Buchanan, *Ordination Rites in Common Worship*, Grove Worship 186 (Cambridge: Grove Books, 2006).

11. Gant, *O Sing Unto The Lord*, 360.

12. The more challenging musical settings from every period have largely remained the monopoly of highly trained choirs attached to cathedral, collegiate, and royal churches.

with all other currently authorized services and prayers under the one cover of *Common Worship*. This incorporation is welcome, in that it practically facilitates a revival of clerical and congregational engagement with the prayer book tradition as, at least, one core strand of congregational worship. However, such a revival depends on a wide-ranging desire for it, and for the program of clerical and lay reeducation it would entail. Thus far, the signs of this materializing are fairly meager in number, but promising where they occur, especially where they capture youthful enthusiasm.

Disengagement from the King James Bible

Throughout the Tudor Reformation, the royally commissioned and/or authorized publication and distribution of vernacular Bible translations, incorporating key benefits of Renaissance textual scholarship, were critical to the advancement of church reform: invigorating, interpreting, and vindicating its political, liturgical, and doctrinal aspects. The constant use in daily and weekly public worship of a single official edition enhanced the contribution of Bible reading to the creation of an English linguistic, ecclesiastical, social, and political culture, and rendered the authorized English Bible the possession of a national community. Therefore, in adopting the King James Bible for all liturgical use, the Anglican restoration of 1662 consolidated for future generations the integral relationship of an official vernacular Bible to the national church and a national linguistic culture.

The virtues of the King James translation of sonorous beauty, gravity, felicitous cadences, expressive intensity, and elevating grandeur made it a fitting complement of the 1662 prayer book liturgies. It was inevitable, then, that dissatisfaction with the language of the liturgies and with the King James translation would go hand in hand. This ground of dissatisfaction must be distinguished from such grounds as the translation's occasional glaring confusions in rendering passages and the obvious inaccuracies revealed by philological and textual scholarship. The latter inadequacies had been addressed in works of revision undertaken in the late nineteenth century by English and American scholars, producing the Revised Version (1885) and the American Standard Version (1901), which aimed at improving the accuracy and intelligibility of the text with relatively minimal disturbance of the KJV's language. Production in America of the 1952 Revised Standard Version (RSV) both culminated and transformed the conservative translation enterprise, for it aimed at preserving the theological and literary virtues of the "Tyndale-King James tradition" with a view to contemporary English diction. While assiduously replacing archaic, obsolete, and potentially confusing vocabulary and forms of expression, the revision committee renounced any intention of producing a new translation in today's language and stressed the suitability of this revised version "for use in public and private worship" and "not merely for reading and instruction."[13]

---

13. Preface to the Revised Standard Version 1952, in *The Oxford Annotated Bible*, Revised Standard Version, ed. H. G. May and B. M. Metzger (Oxford: Oxford University Press, 1962), xvi.

Despite the insensitivity of the RSV revisers to any liturgical role for archaism, their occasional hypersensitivity to verbal obsolescence, and inevitable failure always to preserve the literary virtues of the KJV, the RSV achieved a mediation of the English translation tradition in the contemporary scholarly and linguistic context that has not been rivaled and has scarcely been pursued! since. In the last fifty years, none of the major, reputable, widely circulated English translations have had an interest in perpetuating "the Tyndale-King James tradition."[14] These have been products of ecumenical, frequently international, interdisciplinary, and increasingly specialized scholarship, typically intended for a socially, culturally, and linguistically diverse global readership and for use as study Bibles equipped with the latest scholarly and pedagogical apparatus. The translators' overriding concern with accuracy, clarity, and accessibility of translation has much more frequently been combined with attention to cultural and sexual inclusivity or theological probity than to linguistic beauty and richness connected with liturgical use. The almost total disregard of the KJV tradition within the contemporary industry of Bible translation has abetted its virtual abandonment by Anglican churches in favor of a plurality of contemporary versions for both liturgical and study purpose, thereby depriving the Church of England and other Anglican churches of a significant linguistic and spiritual unifying thread. At the broader cultural level, in Great Britain and throughout the English-speaking world, vast ignorance of the historical literary heritage of the KJV is lamentable, but fairly insignificant in view of the massive popular ignorance of the Bible in any vernacular translation.

Disengagement from the Thirty-Nine Articles of Religion

While the Thirty-Nine Articles have never exercised as pervasive an influence throughout the Church of England as the *Book of Common Prayer*, they have comprised an accessible confessional standard for church members, being bound with the 1662 edition of the prayer book over many generations. More importantly, they have remained a legal authority for Church of England deacons, clergy, and bishops, who have been required to give a form of public assent to them (along with the prayer book and ordinal) at the time of their ordination or taking up of ministerial office. Consequently, their direct impact as a tool of theological pedagogy and discipline has principally been on members of the church's ministerial orders, but not exclusively, as the larger church membership has also quite regularly benefited from their exposition as a form of Anglican catechesis.

While periodically throughout their past, the Articles have met with theological criticism and lax interpretation and the requirement of public assent with bitter

---

14. These include the Jerusalem Bible (1966), the New English Bible (1970), the New American Bible (1970), the Good News Bible (1976), the New International Version (1978), and their sequels, the New Jerusalem Bible (1985), the Revised English Bible (1989), the fully revised Good News Bible (1994), and the New International Reader's Version (1997).

opposition, they have in recent years been subject to persistent institutional and clerical indifference and neglect, at least respecting their pedagogical and disciplinary roles. Subscription to them has continued to be secured only by progressively more accommodating revisions of the wording of the Declaration of Assent, the most recent of which (1975) allows ministerial candidates to evade serious intellectual engagement with them.[15] Other incentives for engagement have not been widely forthcoming from Church of England theological colleges which, over the last sixty years, have largely abandoned theological dialogue with the Articles, despite the contemporary availability of published theological and scholarly discussions of them.[16] Here again, forces of academic internationalism, specialism, and pluralism in theological education have intersected with the ascendancy of liberal theological orientations to reinforce clerical indifference to the Anglican identity embodied by the Articles. Thus, in virtually removing the Articles' disciplinary role, and with it, their potential for causing offense and division, the church has also undermined their unifying theological potential.

By contrast, in the arena of the Church of England's authoritative corporate doctrine and policy and its institutional relations and exchanges with external civil and ecclesial bodies, domestic and international, the Articles have continued to carry historical, constitutional weight. Admittedly, their status in ecumenical relations in the postwar decades generally exceeded their somewhat demoted status within the Anglican Communion,[17] prior to the outbreak of discord among

---

15. The Preface to the Declaration (read publicly by the ordaining bishop) presents it as an affirmation of the candidate's loyalty to the Church of England's "inheritance of faith," including its "historic formularies," as "your inspiration and guidance under God in bringing the grace and truth of Christ to this generation," following which the candidate declares his belief "in the faith revealed in the Scriptures and set forth in the catholic creeds and to which the historic formularies of the Church of England bear witness." The Canons of the Church of England (promulgated by the Convocations of Canterbury and York in 1964 and 1969 and by the General Synod of the Church of England from 1970), Canon C 15 in Hill, *Ecclesiastical Law*, 280. Compare with an earlier canon, A2 Of The Thirty-Nine Articles: "The Thirty-nine Articles are agreeable to the Word of God and may be assented unto with a good conscience by all members of the Church of England" (249).

16. For example, Gerald Bray, *The Faith We Profess: An Exposition of the Thirty-Nine Articles* (London: Latimer Trust, 2009); Oliver O'Donovan, *On the Thirty-Nine Articles: A Conversation with Tudor Christianity*, 2nd edn. (London: SCM Press, 2011); James I. Packer and Roger T. Beckwith, *The Thirty-nine Articles: Their Place and Use Today* (London: Latimer Trust, 1984).

17. Although the majority of Communion Churches have institutionally adopted the Articles in some form (by incorporation into a legal constitution, approval of them by canon, annexation to the prayer book, the requirement of clerical subscription, and examination of ordinands on their teaching), the chief collegial instrument of the Communion, the Lambeth Conference of Anglican Bishops, passed an ill-thought-out resolution (43) in 1968 that conveyed the dispensability of the Articles to the basis of Anglican unity. It suggested

and within Communion churches over issues of women's ministry, sexual ethics, and marriage doctrine. The spiritual and institutional depth of division over these issues has occasioned some fresh attention by official Communion organs to the historical legal and doctrinal instruments of Anglican unity, as illustrated by The Anglican Communion Covenant (2006)[18] and *The Principles of Canon Law Common to the Churches of the Anglican Communion* (2008).[19] This recourse to the traditional formularies is key to the historical, institutional integrity of the Church of England and her progeny within the universal catholic and apostolic church, and may presage a more coherent theological dialogue with the Articles in coming years.

Disengagement from Reformation Public Theology

Lest the preceding portrayal of the Church of England's detachment from its foundational Reformation elements appear at points to assume a hypercritical, traditionalist tone, it is important to clarify its intention with the following disclaimers. Its intention is not to deny that the church's clergy and laity should be discriminating in their reception of the tradition, critically differentiating modes and degrees of authority within its elements, sensitive to the requirements of effective mission for adaptation and fresh impetus in variable social and cultural contexts, earnestly open to opportunities for furthering ecumenical communion, flexible and realistic in institutionally addressing discordant interpretations and assessments of the tradition. Nor is its intention to deny that the Church of England throughout these years has always benefited from some discerning and responsible clerical and lay reflection, deliberation, and action on all these fronts. Rather, it is to propose that the church's institutional disengagement from its Reformation liturgical and doctrinal foundations in recent times has hampered collective appropriation of, and building on, its Reformation inheritance of ecclesial practice and theological thought. Consequently, Church of England clergy and laity have been deprived of valuable theological resources for resisting the doubtful assaults

---

that Churches consider: whether the Articles need be bound up with the Prayer Book; that assent to the Articles should no longer be required of ordinands; that subscription, if required, should place the Articles and other elements of Anglican tradition within the full "inheritance of faith" and within their historical context. David Broughton Knox, *Thirty-Nine Articles: The Historic Basis of Anglican Faith* (London: Hodder and Stoughton, 1967), 10–11; Packer and Beckwith, *The Thirty-Nine Articles*, 29–30.

18. Proposed by the Windsor Report Of The Lambeth Commission in 2004 and drafted by a working group of the Archbishop of Canterbury, in the hope that the Covenant would be an accepted instrument of Communion unity. See Anglican Communion Covenants 1.1.2.

19. A compendium of the common principles of canon law constituting a historical legal underpinning of Anglican unity, published by the Anglican Consultative Council. See Principles 49 and 50.

of the Zeitgeist on the church's particular tradition of Christian mission and formulating a constructive intellectual response to them in continuity with her past.

Without doubt, this loss to the church of theological assets has both reflected and increased the impact on its mission of the seismic cultural shifts of our times: shifts toward fascination with novelty and future possibility (especially technological), with individuality, subjectivity, and uninhibited freedom, with spontaneity and expressive authenticity; and on the other, shifts away from receptivity to objective and enduring frames of reference, common goods and loyalties, common authorities, and dependences. With other Christian churches in Britain and throughout the West, the Church of England has neither given much impetus to these seismic shifts, in contrast to contemporary philosophy, scholarship, and research in the humanities and the social and physical sciences, nor has it managed to counter with exemplary effectiveness their damaging effects on its corporate disciplines of ministry and practice.

Among these damaging effects aggravated by the loss of Reformation theological assets is the polarization of church members in contemporary controversies: most notably those over the vexatious issues of women's ministry and sexuality, with their attendant hostility and mistrust. Such recent initiatives as the Communion Covenant and Common Canon Law express an awareness that disregard of the traditional theological and practical moorings of Anglican churches has made it more difficult for the contending parties to chart a faithful, discerning, and charitable course through the complex tangle of disagreements. This disregard is implicated in another controversy within the Church of England: over the church's legal establishment or disestablishment. Shelved rather than resolved since the mid-nineties, upstaged by the momentous issue of women's ministry,[20] this recurring debate inevitably weakens the church's credibility and equipment for conducting a nationwide Christian mission on a reliably unified institutional basis. Both sides of the argument could have benefited, and could continue to benefit, from greater familiarity with the Reformation theological rationale of church establishment.

It should be conceded that the more thoughtful arguments in favor of church establishment[21] have been loosely aligned with the Cranmerian tradition, in setting forth the ecclesiological and political benefits, including witness to the divine ordination of the state and its responsibilities, to the grounding of human law in a universal moral order and to the social centrality of the church's faith and

---

20. The General Synod in its 1994 meeting "set its face against reopening the question of establishment and even against reviewing the relationship between church and state." Paul Avis, *Church, State and Establishment* (London: SPCK, 2001), 34. The synod's decision came in the wake of parliamentary ratification of the church measure for the ordination of women as presbyters.

21. These arguments amount to more than intrenched traditionalism, an instinctive reverence for the continuity of a social form over time that never critically appropriates the perceived intrinsic good(s) which the form reliably embodies and confers.

worship (and indirectly, of all communal religious belief and practice). Supporters of church establishment have recognized the tradition's contribution to creating and sustaining moral community by nourishing "common values," including the value of individual and collective moral freedom, particularly through the church's role in public education. They have supported the platform given by establishment to the church's "prophetic" address to political society, and the obligation placed on the church to undertake a geographically and socially inclusive evangelical and pastoral mission, together with the historical endowments making the mission possible.

It should also be conceded that the weightier ecclesiological and missiological arguments for disestablishment, expressing both widely shared concerns and the long-standing priorities of different constituencies, have not always or entirely been antipathetic to the Cranmerian tradition. Evangelicals and Anglo-Catholics have primarily been concerned about the threat to the purity of individual and corporate faith and holiness of life posed by the worldly objectives and contrivances of secular government. Both have emphasized the threat of secular authority to the spiritual rule of Christ in his Church, evangelicals focusing his rule in Scriptural revelation, and the Anglo-Catholics in apostolic episcopacy and longer sacramental traditions. Contemporary liberals, by contrast, have particularly feared the loss of the church's critical distance from power elites in matters of political and social justice. Church members of different persuasions have shared concern about the impediments to ecumenical progress (whether in Protestant or Roman Catholic directions) raised by the public privileges and restraints of church establishment, and disapproval of the current anomaly of largely "unchurched" politicians overseeing church affairs, as well as frustration with the cumbersome procedures of parliamentary ratification of synodical measures.[22]

However, no parties to the discussion have sufficiently engaged all the theological contours of the Cranmerian logic of church establishment inhering in the complex interface of ecclesial and political authority and practice, which are germane to determining and weighing the legitimate concerns and considerations wrapped up in this central issue for the Church of England's faithful mission.

Exclusion of the Reformation Tradition from Political Discussion

Reservations about church establishment within the Church of England have been reinforced by the exclusion of this Reformation tradition from the prevailing

---

22. For these arguments, Colin Buchanan, *Cut the Connexion: Disestablishment and the Church of England* (London: Darton, Longman and Todd, 1994); V. Pitt, "The Protection of Faith," in *Church, State and Religious Minorities*, ed. Tariq Modood (London: Policy Studies Institute, 1997), 36–9; Theo Hobson, *Against Establishment: An Anglican Polemic* (London: Darton, Longman and Todd, 2003).

national and international discussion about the role of religion in public life. In the postwar period, this discussion has been heavily influenced both by the American scholarly debate in this area and by the proliferation of international and national human rights declarations and conventions. Granted that the latter influence has been independent of the former with respect to its multiple and diverse political and social sources, multiplying with every decade; nevertheless, there has been a discernible interplay between the two.

The more obvious interplay has come from the direct pressure exerted by an American foreign diplomacy, informed by the domestic conversation, on the constitutional provisions and legal functioning of other polities. The more subtle interplay lies in the various interfaces of the American debate with the plethora of rights documents, in which the American debate furnishes rival hermeneutical approaches to them. This twofold interplay of influences will be illustrated later in this chapter in our glance at European rights policies, conventions, legislation, and adjudication; but our immediate concern is with the observable tendency of scholarly discussions of religion and public life outside of the United States to transpose the terms of the American debate into foreign national settings, so that they amount to reactive adaptations of American positions rather than genuinely indigenous discussions.

Such adaptations are unlikely to do justice to the theoretical resources of other nations' domestic historical traditions because the terms of the American debate reflect theological and philosophical positions long nurtured on American soil and historically foundational for the American polity, but which are quite alien, even inimical, to the theological and philosophical foundations of many other contemporary polities boasting liberal democratic institutions or aspiring to them. Great Britain is the paradigmatic case of such a polity, in that theological and philosophical dissent to the Church of England loomed large in the historical foundations and early development of American political society. Against the public theology of English church establishment, Puritan and Separatist dissenters pitted an antagonistic soteriological, ecclesiological, and political vision, the covenantal, voluntarist, perfectionist, and individualist elements of which were reflected in the American constitutional settlement of the eighteenth century.

Historically considered, it is logical that the parameters of the American debate should continue to be given by the religious "rights and liberties" enshrined in the First Amendment religion clauses of the American Constitution and in many state constitutions. This continuity is illuminated by John Witte's perspicacious account of the "forging" of the First Amendment clauses and the history of their jurisprudence in *Religion and the American Constitutional Experiment: Essential Rights and Liberties* (2000). Witte's study identifies six principles on which the architects of the clauses concurred: 1. liberty of conscience—foremost, the inalienable right of individual judgment in matters of religious belief and practice; 2. free exercise of religion—"the right to act publicly on one's conscientious beliefs" without encroaching upon "the rights of others," disturbing "the public peace," or otherwise breaching criminal laws;[23] 3. religious pluralism—the good and right of maintaining and accommodating "a plurality of forms of religious expression and organization in the community";[24] 4. religious equality—the equality of "all peaceable religions before the law," prohibiting the legal attaching of "preferential benefits" or "discriminatory burdens" to individual religious choices;[25] 5. separation of church and state—prohibiting chiefly the intermingling of ecclesiastical and civil jurisdictions, powers, and institutions; 6. disestablishment of religion—prohibiting coercive civil establishment of "mandatory forms of religious belief, doctrine, and practice."[26]

While mindful of the latitude with which individual founding fathers interpreted these principles,[27] Witte presents them approvingly as the enduring central imperatives of the American constitutional order and fundamental axioms of the American logic of religious liberty. Moreover, he views the vacillating and contradictory Supreme Court interpretations and applications of the religion clauses, especially in the last seventy years, as symptomatic of the court's failure to pursue a balanced and coherent integration of these six principles.

Comparing the scholarly debate about religion in the American public realm with First Amendment jurisprudence in the last seventy years, we can readily see that the various positions in the debate, whether philosophical, theological, or social scientific, loosely align with different jurisprudential positions in their interpretation and weighting of the six principles, and in the degree of balance and coherence among them achieved. So, on Witte's normative analysis, the strongly secularist stances of American liberal political argument, intent upon banishing religion from the realms of public discourse, law, and services, resemble the virulently secularist jurisprudential strands in their unbalanced hermeneutic of the six constitutional principles; whereas arguments for accommodating public religious pluralism on a platform of equal rights within a secular civil polity resemble the egalitarian religion-accommodating jurisprudential strands in their more balanced integration of the constitutional principles.[28]

---

23. *Religion and the American Constitutional Experiment*, revised and expanded 4th edn., coauthored with Joel A. Nichols (New York: Oxford University Press, 2016), 45.

24. Ibid., 47.

25. Ibid., 49.

26. Ibid., 59.

27. For example, "religion" could mean "Christianity" or "Protestantism," and "disestablishment" might even accommodate "mild and equitable establishment." Ibid., 39.

28. The secularist end of the American scholarly political continuum has, perhaps, had a preponderant international impact via the influence of John Rawls's writings, particularly *A Theory of Justice* (Oxford: Clarendon Press, 1972), which argues that establishing the principles of public justice and public policy in liberal, democratic, and pluralistic society

My central observation is this: all these principles are in varying degrees antipathetic to the theology and practice of English church establishment in so far as it has remained continuous with its foundations, with the consequence that the establishment tradition has elicited disregard and contempt from the interlocutors in the American discussion, and from British and continental thinkers who have appropriated its terms. However, two clarifications of this observation are necessary. First, it admits the possibility of interpreting both English church establishment and at least some of these principles to render them compatible. The changing face of religious freedom in England since the seventeenth century speaks not only of pragmatic compromise dictated by political necessity but also of a steady and mutually influential exchange between the Reformation inheritance of church establishment and domestic antiestablishment ecclesiastical and political traditions: for example, those of Protestant covenanting and independent evangelical churches, and from the mid-nineteenth century, post-Tridentine Catholicism. Second, the broadly voluntarist, covenanting ecclesial and political culture of nonconformity which, along with Enlightenment rationalism and civic republicanism, generated the American constitutional principles, has been an indigenous English tradition ever since the more radical Puritan "Separatists" of the later sixteenth century rejected the Elizabethan church establishment in toto. Thus, contemporary thinkers in the English dissenting traditions largely recognize as their own tradition the developed principles of the transatlantic discussion.

The adaptability as well as broad attractiveness of these principles, alike appealing to vulnerable religious minorities and anti-religious atheists and skeptics, has often induced defenders of English church establishment to construct their apologies as demonstrations of the support rendered by contemporary church establishment to the smooth social and political functioning of these principles in the culture of liberal, democratic, rights pluralism. Such flattering apologies succumb to the almost irresistible, universal logic of the contemporary debate: namely, the teleological ordering of the life of the church to the life of political society—an inversion of the Reformation logic. Thus, the urgent challenge for the apologist of the Reformation tradition today is not to bring it into line with the

should appeal only to a nonreligious, nonteleological, "thin" conception of the good. However critical some American political thinkers have been of his Kantian secularist constraints on public discussion and deliberations about justice, their own applications of the principles of liberty, equality, and plurality in the sphere of religious rights preclude the unequal alignment of public policy with one or more religious institutions in the manner entailed by church establishment. Apart from Witte's extensive publications on religious rights, see relevant writings of Robert Bellah, Patrick McKinley Brennan, W. Cole Durham, Richard Mouw, Richard Neuhaus, James Skillen, David Hollenbach and Nicholas Wolterstorff.

controlling principles of the contemporary political discussion but to bring its theological insights to bear on this discussion, critically and constructively.

Challenges to the Public Status and Functioning of the Church of England

The last seventy years in Britain have witnessed a series of concrete challenges to the legal status and practical functioning of the Church of England, the elements of which may be summarized as follows.

The monarch is the "Supreme Governor" of the Church of England under oath to "defend" it, and with his or her consort is required by law to "join in communion" with it. The king has the executive prerogative to appoint to senior ecclesiastical posts[29] on a Prime Ministerial nomination originating in a national church committee.[30] This prerogative expresses the jurisdictional sovereignty of the king-in-Parliament over all persons and estates in his kingdom, and the derivation from the Crown of episcopal jurisdiction in the church's external polity. The Crown allocates episcopal sees, determining their territorial and demographic boundaries, and delegates to bishops legal authority enforceable in the ecclesiastical courts operating under the High Court. In addition, the Sovereign has direct jurisdiction over certain churches, referred to as "royal peculiars." The Archbishop of Canterbury has the legal duty of crowning the Sovereign and officiating at the royal coronation service, and at all services connected to important state and royal occasions. He also has the duty of periodically visiting the Sovereign, ministering to the members of the royal family, and attending various state and royal celebrations as the king's "first subject." All worship on state occasions is under the aegis of the Church of England, with liturgical accommodations when appropriate.

The principal sources of Church of England public law are legislation by Measure and Canon issuing from its supreme legislative body, the General Synod, comprising the three Houses of Bishops, Clergy, and Laity. Measures passed by

---

29. These include bishoprics, deanships of cathedrals and "royal peculiars," and some cathedral canonries. The Crown has not appointed to offices in the Church of Scotland since the termination of episcopal government in 1690, nor does it appoint to the disestablished churches of Ireland and Wales.

30. In recent times episcopal appointments have proceeded by the prime minister submitting to the queen one of two nominations put forward by the Crown Nominations Commission in consultation with the Archbishop of Canterbury's and the Prime Minister's Appointment Secretaries. However, in 2007, the Labour Government of Prime Minister Gordon Brown proposed in a White Paper presented to Parliament (CM7172) that the prime minister "should not play an active role in the selection of individual candidates" for senior ecclesiastical posts, and so requested that only one name be submitted for recommendation to the queen. (The current Crown Nomination Committee is composed of the Archbishops of Canterbury and York, clerical and lay representatives of the General Synod, and representatives of the diocese's Vacancy-in-See Committee.)

Synod have the legal status of "primary legislation," or parliamentary statute law, once they have been accepted by both Houses of Parliament and have gained the Royal Assent.[31] Parliamentary ratification is usually, but not always, pro forma[32] and depends on the initial decision of Parliament's Ecclesiastical Committee to introduce the Measure to the two Houses.[33] Unlike Measures, Canons passed by the General Synod are not submitted to the Parliament but directly submitted to the monarch via the Home Secretary.[34] The General Synod, along with a substructure of diocesan and deanery synods, was created by an Act of Parliament in 1969 to replace an older law-generating body (the Church Assembly of 1919)[35] and to assume most of the powers until then retained by the Convocations of York and Canterbury.

Twenty-six senior bishops (Lords Spiritual) continue to sit in the unelected upper chamber of Parliament along with lay hereditary and life peers (Lords Temporal). Although a tiny minority (3 percent) of the House's members, they make a disproportionately weighty contribution to debates about legislation of a morally significant or controversial nature or affecting religious institutions; and the two archbishops are expected to speak on major national issues of whatever kind.[36] In addition, the "Lords Spiritual" have been the primary route by which

---

31. Synodical Government Measure 1969, s2(1). Hill, *Ecclesiastical Law*, 10. See also Norman Doe, *The Legal Framework of the Church of England*, 2nd edn. (Oxford: Oxford University Press, 1996), 55–66.

32. Three controversial measures regarding vacation of church benefices, episcopal appointment, and clerical ordination were rejected by Parliament between 1975 and 1989. House of Commons Information Office, *Church of England Measures*, Factsheet L10 (2010).

33. The Ecclesiastical Committee established in 1919 is composed of thirty members appointed equally from the Commons and the Lords, who serve for one entire Parliament. Its members scrutinize draft Measures submitted by General Synod's Legislative Committee, and report back, recommending amendment(s). When satisfied, it presents the Measure along with its final Report for the approval of both Houses of Parliament. Factsheet L10 (2010).

34. A "parent Measure may render lawful the making of particular provision by Canon": for example, the Priests (Ordination of Women) Measure 1993 permitted the promulgating of Canon C4B. Similarly, all Secondary Legislation comprises "statutory instruments made pursuant to primary legislation." Hill, *Ecclesiastical Law*, 12–15.

35. The Church of England Assembly (Powers) Act 1919: 9 & 10 George 5, c. 76.

36. According to Francis Brown's study of the role of the bishops in the House of Lords from 1979 to 1987, they contributed more to general debate on legislation than to its scrutiny and revision. Their contribution to scrutiny was most influential when the bill was one in which the church was recognized to have "a special and proper interest," the bishops were undivided, and supported by other groups in the House, such as the Roman Catholic peers. "Influencing the House of Lords: The Role of the Lords Spiritual 1979–1987," *Political Studies* 42, no. 1 (1994): 110–14. Gavin Drewry and Jenny Brock show that the bishops have most often addressed, among nonreligious matters, those concerning foreign policy, physical and

religious minority communities bring their concerns to the attention of a parliamentary committee.

Committees oversee the property and finances of the Church of England, which is legally structured as a public network of corporate and individual persons and property. The Church of England's historic assets are managed by thirty-three Church Commissioners,[37] including six ex officio (inactive) state office holders and nine members jointly appointed by the Crown and the two archbishops. Supplying about one-fifth of the church's ongoing financial needs from investment income, they are accountable to both Parliament and the Church of England's General Synod. Unusually for an established church, the Church of England neither receives direct government funding nor benefits from legally compulsory tithes (abolished in the late nineteenth century). The vast expense of maintaining and renewing the fabric of its ancient buildings, largely borne by parishes, is only offset by grants available under various public schemes for preserving historic edifices.[38]

In respect of its ministries, some special powers awarded to the Church of England by public law are outweighed by the nationwide obligations imposed on it. Historical establishment has invested the church with parochial ministries (including responsibility for baptism, marriage, and burial) unique in their territorial comprehensiveness, churches being found in every center of human habitation, from the smallest village to the largest city.[39] This has meant a more pervasive social and architectural presence than nonestablished churches have either achieved or desired. In addition, the Church of England has been extensively engaged in nonparochial, national ministries, including chaplaincies to a multiplicity of state-run or state-subsidized institutions—the armed forces, prisons, hospitals, lower and upper schools, and colleges; the founding and running of public and private church educational institutions at every level; and charitable

---

mental health, offender management and prisons, and immigration and asylum. "Prelates in Parliament," *Parliamentary Affairs* 24, no. 3 (1971): 222–4. This finding was repeated for the 2006–7 Session, as reported in Anna Harlow, Frank Cranmer and Norman Doe, "Bishops in the House of Lords: A Critical Analysis," *Public Law* (Autumn 2008): 490–509. Generally, relevant studies (including Francis Brown's) have drawn attention to the limitations on the bishops' contribution to the House arising from their episodic and variable attendance, owing to heavy diocesan obligations. Andrew Partington and Paul Bickley, *Coming Off The Bench: The Past, Present and Future of Religious Representation in the House of Lords* (London: Theos, 2007).

37. The Church Commissioners were formed in 1948 from the merging of two older bodies, Queen Anne's Bounty and the Ecclesiastical Commissioners.

38. For a summary of Church of England financing, R. M. Morris, ed., *Church and State in 21st Century Britain: The Future of Church Establishment* (London: University College, The Constitution Unit, 2009), 61–75.

39. The territorial ministry of the Church of England comprehends about 20,000 parish churches and chapels and forty-three cathedrals (forty-four including Gibraltar). Church of England, Research and Statistics, Ministry Statistics 2017.

enterprises, such as almshouses, hospitals, and orphanages. In the nineteenth century, the government significantly opened up these nonparochial ministries in England and Wales to Roman Catholicism, the Free Churches, and the Jewish community, with the established church retaining a *prima inter pares* role.

The more recent challenges to this historical residue of church establishment have emanated from a variety of sources: the ongoing saga of House of Lords reform, religious initiatives of government departments, other Christian denominations and non-Christian religious communities, European international law affecting religious freedom, and given domestic effect primarily through the provisions of the (British) Human Rights Act (1998/2000).

Of domestic political challenges, the most conspicuous is the seemingly interminable, if sporadic, project of reconstructing the British Parliament's unelected upper chamber. While the bishops' historic legislative role has made some would-be parliamentary reformers hesitate to remove any or all of them from the House of Lords, their parliamentary future is, at this juncture, undecided, as is the occasionally mooted prospect of introducing formal representation of other denominations and religious communities into the upper chamber, should the whole chamber or a portion remain appointed. In recent years, the constitutional issue of Lord's reform has been sidelined by the more pressing constitutional issues entailed in the UK's future relation to the European Union, and, to date, the constitutional connection between the juridical office of bishops under the Crown and their place in the House of Lords remains intact.[40]

Should this connection be severed, however, the whole complex of constitutional links between the Church of England and the Sovereign would inevitably be

---

40. The Royal Commission of 1999 ("the Wakeham Commission") produced a proposal to reduce the episcopal representation in the House to sixteen, and to allocate places to other Christian denominations in England (five), Scotland, Wales, and Northern Ireland (five), and to non-Christian religious communities (five). Royal Commission on the Reform of the House of Lords, *A House for the Future*, Cm 4534 (January 2000), paras. 15.15–15.19. Subsequently, two Joint Committee Reports of the Houses of Parliament (December 2002, April 2003) and a Government consultation paper (September 2003) on reform of the Upper House opted to defer the question of religious representation, the latter paper favoring the status quo; while a subsequent proposal of a cross-party group of senior politicians favored a reduced episcopal contingent without *formal* representation of other denominations and religious communities (Kenneth Clarke et al., *Reforming the House of Lords: Breaking the Deadlock* (London: University College, The Constitution Unit, 2005). In 2011–12 the Conservative-Liberal Democratic Coalition Government published a paper and introduced a draft bill proposing a largely or wholly elected House of Lords with an episcopal component reduced from twenty-six to twelve bishops over a fifteen-year period, but it eventually withdrew the bill. Most recently, the 2015 Lords Spiritual Act required that vacancies of Lords Spiritual be filled until 2025 by women bishops, excepting the "great sees" of Canterbury, York, London, Durham, and Winchester. See Julian Rivers, *The Law of Organized Religions: Between Establishment and Secularism* (Oxford: Oxford University Press, 2010), 292–6.

weakened, undermining the rationale both for the Crown appointment of bishops and for the parliamentary passing of Church of England law. The Crown appointment of bishops has already been weakened from the unilateral initiative of Prime Minister Gordon Brown to refrain from using "the royal prerogative to exercise choice" in selecting individual candidates for senior ecclesiastical posts,[41] so demonstrating the indifference of Her Majesty's Government in principle to senior church appointments. Severing of these legal and political links would also disrupt the public ceremonial links between the monarch and the church. As a result, the historic Christian foundations of the British constitution would be deprived of weighty public occasions of national visibility. This would further undermine the national public status of the Archbishops of Canterbury and York, and the status of Church of England bishops within their dioceses, significantly engaged in extra-ecclesiastical undertakings of communal responsibility and trust.

A second, less visible but more pervasive, political undermining of historic church establishment in the last two decades has been the proliferating initiatives of government departments and organizations to launch multilateral relations of consultation and cooperation with diverse "faith communities" in the provision of public religious ministries and charitable services. These multilateral relations, in which the Church of England is one among equals, are increasingly superseding the long-standing bilateral relations in which the church has functioned since the nineteenth century as broker and gatekeeper, enabling other Christian denominations and religious communities to access state resources in developing and sustaining their public ministries. To a considerable extent, these initiatives have been driven by crises over the social and cultural "integration" of immigrant religious minorities (Muslims most urgently) and over social failures and financial constraints in welfare provision, particularly in the inner cities. The multilateral "partnerships" envisioned have been largely designed to meet bureaucratic and ideological objectives of a social, political, and economic kind, formulated principally by social scientists. As such, although promising social benefits, they pose a host of relatively novel dangers to the practical integrity of the religious communities involved and to their peaceful coexistence.[42]

Chaplaincies in public institutions (more notably in prisons and hospitals than in the more conservative armed forces) exemplify the recent shift from statutory and administrative frameworks recognizing the primacy of the Church of England in accommodating other denominations and religions to a reforming agenda of implementing religious diversity and equality. Entailing the formation of "multi-faith" advisory and administrative bodies and the production of diversity-

---

41. p. 95 notes 153 and 154.

42. Luke Bretherton adroitly sets out these dangers in *Christianity and Contemporary Politics: The Conditions and Possibilities of Faithful Witness* (Chichester: Wiley-Blackwell, 2010), 33–45.

inclusive rather than "faith-specific" operational guidelines,⁴³ this agenda has professionalized chaplaincies within nontheological frameworks and subjected them to more intrusive governmental and quasi-governmental regulation, both developments contributing to the severing of their traditionally close relations with local churches and the parochial ministry. A similar detachment of service provision from its theological and institutional bases is observable across the range of government partnerships with Christian, and more recently non-Christian, religious charitable agencies providing welfare services.⁴⁴ Moreover, these developments have occurred within a political drive to foster "social cohesion" and "social capital" through the multiplication of processes of consultation, dialogue, and cooperative action among religious groups, and between them and every governmental level.⁴⁵ In regard to interreligious communication and cooperation, it is reasonable to suspect that consultative institutions initiated by the religious groups themselves, apart from a conspicuously functional, sociopolitical governmental agenda, are more likely to provide substantial spiritual, social, and political benefits.

It is instructive to observe the somewhat different course that accommodating religious plurality has taken in the sphere of primary and secondary education. Nineteenth-century divisions within Anglican and nonconformist churches over government funding of denominational versus nondenominational Christian education led to a legal distinction in 1902 of "government-provided" and "government-maintained" or "aided" schools: the former to be nondenominational in their appointments, governance, Christian instruction, and worship (with a parental opt out of instruction and worship); the latter to be denominational in these areas, as set by their trust deeds and their relationship to ecclesiastical authorities,

---

43. For example, the central administrative body for prison chaplaincy, while still having a Church of England Chaplain-General, is a multi-faith body with a remit that is not "faith-specific," and the official "inclusive" manual (Prison Service Order 4550) sets out copious details for the accommodation of eight recognized religions. See James A. Beckford and Sophie Gilliat, *Religion in Prisons: "Equal Rites" in a Multi-Faith Society* (Cambridge: Cambridge University Press, 1998). Similarly, the nondenominational professional body for hospital chaplaincy set up in 1992 was superseded in 2005 by the Multi-faith Group for Healthcare Chaplaincy; and the trajectory of NHS healthcare chaplaincy in the twenty-first century, set out in the updated NHS England Chaplaincy Guidelines 2015, is clearly toward increasing professionalism and specialism of services, developing uniform standards for religious and nonreligious "spiritual care," and aligning practice with equality, diversity, and rights obligations. https://www.england.nhs.uk/wp-content/uploads/2015/03/nhs-chaplaincy-guidelines-2015. Also Christopher Swift, *Hospital Chaplaincy in the Twenty-first Century: the Crisis of Spiritual Care on the NHS* (London: Routledge, 2009).

44. See River's legal review of "faith-based" charities in Great Britain's postwar welfare state. *The Law of Organized Religions*, 268–88.

45. See River's overview of "new consultation processes" in *The Law of Organized Religions*, 296–305. Also, Morris, *Church and State in 21st Century Britain*, 230–4.

after the model of the venerable Church of England grammar schools and their pre-Reformation predecessors.[46] A further legal distinction was introduced in 1944 between "voluntary-controlled" and "voluntary-aided" schools, to allow impoverished church schools to receive more generous government funding, but at the price of closer approximation to "government-provided" schools.[47] Given the Church of England's educational burden, about half of her schools became "voluntary controlled," while, by contrast, all Roman Catholic schools retained their "voluntary-aided" status. In addition to these persisting legal categories, a broader legal category of "faith-designated" schools[48] now includes such recent arrivals as faith-based Academies, and the voluntary-aided sector has become modestly multireligious, including a small number of Muslim, Hindu, and Sikh schools.[49] The significant point here is that the legal extension of the established Anglican educational model to cover other denominational and religious schools (in the category of voluntary-aided) has accommodated a plurality of largely independent, largely state-funded, religious educational foundations.

The Church of England's continuing educational burden is one aspect of the enormous practical challenge of sustaining a national ministry in the face of increasingly insupportable strains on its human and financial resources. The church struggles with the typical problems of clerical recruitment and a steady decline in voluntary church attendance and giving, while lacking the typical financial benefits of established churches elsewhere, of compulsory church rates and continuous civil upkeep of ancient church fabric. Its national burdens generate complaints from congregations about onerous financial obligations to diocesan and national church bodies, fuelling "congregationalist" ecclesiological leanings. In addition, they are a considerable drag on the church undertaking ambitious evangelizing and pastoral initiatives at various levels.

Turning to the challenge to Anglican establishment from other Christian denominations and non-Christian communities, the interreligious relationships comprise a mixed picture. While communities across the English religious spectrum have appreciated the capacity of Anglican establishment to accommodate a religious plurality in the public realm protective of their institutional independence, they have, nevertheless, entertained disparate appraisals of the legitimacy and appropriateness of Anglican establishment. Nonconformist

---

46. Education Act 1902: 2 Edward 2. Jewish schools, having received indirect public aid in the mid-nineteenth century, became wholly funded by subscription and fees.

47. Education Act 1944: 7 & 8 George 6.

48. This categorization followed in the wake of the *School Standards and Framework Act 1988*, *c.* 31, which clarified the legal basis for faith schools in the grant-maintained sector.

49. According to a House of Commons Briefing Paper of June 6, 2018 (No. 06972), faith-based schools make up 37 percent of state-funded primary education and 19 percent of state-funded secondary education. As of 2019, the non-Christian sector of state-funded schools includes thirty-one Muslim, twelve Sikh, and seven Hindu schools, as well as forty-nine Jewish schools.

churches are, in principle, opposed to interference by the civil government with churches' corporate freedom and government; but some, such as the Free Church and, preeminently, the Methodist Church, have more readily endorsed and taken advantage of the political recognition and support of Christian ministries historically entrenched in the establishment tradition.[50] The Roman Catholic Church harbors lingering resentment about legal exclusion of a Catholic monarch and, in addition, is debarred from episcopal representation in the House of Lords by its canonical requirement of juridical independence; but it retains a strong interest in England's Christian national identity and in the state recognition and support of its public ministries won and sustained within the establishment regime. Within non-Christian religious communities in Britain, there has been continued support for an Anglican establishment that gives public representation to minority religious voices and increasingly shares public space with them. Notable authorities and personages from the Jewish, Muslim, Hindu, and Sikh communities have favored the constitutional "umbrella" of the Church of England as a historically coherent, politically effective, and morally acceptable manner of relating religious minorities to public governance in Britain, tempering claims of civil equality with those of national historical identity and religious tradition.[51] Nevertheless, there are burgeoning demands within minority communities for a more rigorously pluralistic, egalitarian religious establishment of civil recognition and partnership, without Anglican primacy.

Leading thinkers and representatives of ethnoreligious minorities in England view these demands as expressing, on the one hand, the healthy political and social maturation of their communities, and on the other, growing anxiety about perceived external threats to, and assaults on the dignity, integrity, spiritual, and material welfare of their members. While these threats and assaults involve multiple societal spheres and multiple forms of inequity and offense, they are widely regarded within these communities as being intimately connected with the secularist tendencies of the overwhelming majority of British citizens (about 80 percent!) without active membership in any religious organization. Community members increasingly suspect that, in today's pervasive environment

---

50. In the historical stream of Wesleyan Methodism, the Methodist Conference has never rejected Anglican establishment in principle and has pursued unity negotiations with the Church of England since the 1960s according to a model of ecclesiastical self-government to which Anglican establishment today effectively conforms. Avis, *Church, State and Establishment*, 69–71.

51. See, for example, the essays of Bhikhu Parekh, Sylvia Rothchild, Ramindar Singh, and Daoud Rosser-Owen, as well as Tariq Modood's introductory essay, in *Church, State and Religious Minorities*, ed. Modood; Jonathan Sacks, *The Persistence of Faith: Religion, Morality and Society in a Secular Age* (London: Bloomsbury Continuum, 1991). Modood has developed and nuanced this position in multiple books and articles, including "Religious Pluralism in the United States and Britain: Its Implications for Muslims and Nationhood," *Social Compass* 62, no. 4 (2015): 526–40.

of detachment from organized religious faith and practice, the social and political template of "religious pluralism" and "multiculturalism" is, in fact, one of "secular assimilationism."[52]

Thus, it comes as no surprise to these members that the most aggressive and persistent campaigning for disestablishment of the Church of England in the postwar period has been pursued by irreligious liberal secularists who regard organized religious belief and practice as frequently illiberal and always divisive in the public realm.[53] Such secularists advance their case via an exaggerated account of the religious and cultural diversity of contemporary English society requiring the protection of constitutional and other legal reforms. Resisting their case, however, is the well-founded view crossing denominational and religious boundaries that free and equitable relations among both religious and nonreligious groups in the public sphere are not best served by discarding the culture and legal framework of Anglican establishment for the culture and legal framework of egalitarian rights, given that the former, not the latter, has long shaped (with other forces) the principles and practices of religious freedom in British society valued by believers of diverse stripes.

It is important, nevertheless, to stress the irresistible impact of the liberal culture and discourse of egalitarian rights across all denominational and religious divides in Britain, and on all approaches to the issue of church establishment/ disestablishment. It has become the lingua franca of discussion about public religious freedom and justice and has permeated the fabric of social and legal practice, from which members of religious groups cannot afford to stand aloof. Perhaps the strongest pressure toward embracing unreservedly the political and legal framework of egalitarian-rights pluralism, felt by all religious communities in Britain today, but especially the Muslim community, comes from too close an association in liberal sentiment of conservative objections to the political and legal impact of the rights culture with the wholesale vilification of Western religious, moral, and political culture by fanatically intolerant terrorist groups and political regimes. This association reinforces the secularist version of the rights framework and casts all religious reservations about this framework under suspicion of illiberal, even despotic, sympathies and designs.

The progressive elaboration of political policy and law respecting religious rights, equality rights, and discrimination in Europe and in Britain over the last fifty years, particularly the last two decades, has presented continuing challenges to English church establishment. The paramount sources of this elaboration have

---

52. T. Modood, "Establishment, Multiculturalism and British Citizenship," *The Political Quarterly* 65, no. 1 (1994): 62.

53. This campaigning peaked in the early 1990s, with the Liberal Democratic Conference (1990) passing a motion calling for church disestablishment, followed by the same proposal in Tony Benn's *Commonwealth of Britain Bill* presented to Parliament in 1991, and the total absence of church establishment in a constitutional document published that year by the influential Institute of Public Policy Research.

been the Council of Europe, the Organization for Security and Cooperation in Europe (OSCE), and the European Union. Its legal framework was given by the provisions of the European Convention for the Protection of Human Rights and Fundamental Freedoms (1950/53) and its subsequent Protocols, binding on all signatory member states in the Council of Europe, and enforced by the European Court of Human Rights in Strasbourg (ECtHR). From their inception, these legal instruments, together with the European Social Charter (1961 revised 1996) and its monitoring committee, have had the purpose of ensuring that the legal administrations of signatory states progressively comply with comprehensive standards of human rights protection. For European Union member states, this purpose has considerably been taken over by the 2009 Charter of Fundamental Rights interpreted by the Court of Justice of the European Union.[54]

Consequently, there are now a plethora of NGOs and European agencies, many under the auspices of the OSCE's Office for Democratic Institutions and Human Rights (ODIHR) and the Council of Europe, working to bring the legal provision in European states in line with the ever-growing body of European rights, nondiscrimination, and employment law. In more recent years, much of the attention of rights surveillance bodies has been focused on the postcommunist states that either have acceded, or are aspiring to accede, to the European Union, a number of which have historical traditions of Orthodox church establishment or Roman Catholic hegemony,[55] and have previously lacked the ethos and mechanisms of effective rights protection. It is largely through the ODIHR and the OSCE that American positions on religious rights and their embodiment in political culture, policy, legislation, and adjudication have exerted their weight. American influence is observable in the close alignment of the European Convention with the following concepts and principles: the individual is the primary subject (bearer) of religious rights, and the community the secondary and derivative subject; there is equality among individual and collective subjects of religious rights; collective subjects of religious rights are creations of individual choice; the social-legal reality of a religious right is universal and invariable, detached from the particular and

---

54. The Charter of Fundamental Rights came into effect with the Lisbon Treaty (2009).

55. In contrast to civil regimes of national church government, as found historically in Great Britain, the Scandinavian Lutheran states, and Eastern Orthodox countries, the Roman Catholic Church from 1850 to 1960 grounded the special forms of its public legal recognition, protection, privilege, and responsibility in the concordat agreements between the Holy See and separate states, as between two sovereign governments and societies with different (spiritual and temporal) competences. Post-Vatican II, the church, in its agreements and concordats with numerous states, has grounded the public civil protection of its independent activities in corporate religious rights derived from the universal religious rights of its individual members in those polities. For a concise review of the history of concordats, R. Minnerath, "The Position of the Catholic Church Regarding Concordats from a Doctrinal and Pragmatic Perspective," *Catholic University Law Review* 47, no. 2 (1998): 467–76.

variable beliefs and practices of communal bearers; and religious rights-bearers are private rather than public.[56]

Admittedly, this egalitarian individualism is offset to a degree by the Convention's recognition of "necessary" legal limitations to the manifestation of individual religious freedom "in the interests of public safety, for the protection of public order, health or morals, or . . . the rights and freedoms of others."[57] Taken together with the "margin of appreciation" doctrine that accords to national authorities "a reasonable margin" to interpret Convention rights and freedoms, adapting them to the relevant domestic law, the Convention can be read as offering more than sufficient latitude to national forms of church establishment. However, over several decades, both ODIHR guidelines for reviewing national legislation and ECtHR adjudication of cases brought before it have stressed governmental obligations to neutrality, impartiality, and nondiscrimination in the treatment of religious communities; and after 2000, governmental obligations to promote interreligious tolerance, dialogue, equality, and partnership.[58] While moderately successful in preventing and rectifying civil and political injustice and aggression against religious minority groups and their members, this egalitarian legal trajectory encourages a heavier-handed state regulation of religious freedom, sometimes tending toward the secularist agenda of suppressing the active public presence and integrity of religious communities, whether or not established: for example, ECtHR judgments upholding restrictions on conspicuous religious dress and disciplinary measures for noncompliance in the state educational systems of

---

56. The provisions of the European Convention pertaining to religious (and all other) rights have a markedly individualistic orientation. Article 9 (protecting the "right to freedom of thought, conscience and religion") casts religious freedom as an aspect of the individual's freedom of conscientious choice to believe, think, and act. Article 14 sets forth the principle of individual equality in the enjoyment of all Convention rights and freedoms, prohibiting discrimination on various grounds, including religion. Article 11 recognizes the individual's "right to freedom of peaceful assembly and to freedom of association with others." Only Article 2 of the First Protocol (1952) departs marginally from the individualistic paradigm by requiring that state involvement with education "respect the right of parents to ensure [for their children] such education and teaching in conformity with their own religious and philosophical convictions." Ian Brownlie, ed., *Basic Documents on Human Rights,* 2nd edn. (Oxford: Oxford University Press, 1981), 246–7, 257–8.

57. Article 9.2. Ibid., 246.

58. The Guidelines for Review of Legislation Pertaining to Religion or Belief 2004 sets out the principles of government neutrality, impartiality, and nondiscrimination vis-à-vis religious communities. Rivers, *The Law of Organized Religions,* 47–9. Summarizing a decade of case law on ECHR Article 9 that recognizes a range of collective religious rights, Rivers points to the Court's consistent emphasis on state neutrality and impartiality in exercising "regulative power" over religious communities, especially 53–4 n. 92.

Turkey[59] and France[60] and declaring against the crucifixes in Italian public school classrooms,[61] all on the grounds of the state's obligation to practice and to protect secular neutrality and pluralism in religious matters.

For two decades now, the matrix of rights "guaranteed under the European Convention" has been given legal effect within Britain primarily through the provisions of the Human Rights Act (1998). A key issue arising from the Act has been whether the unique legal status of the established church renders her organizations more vulnerable than other religious organizations to be treated under § 6 of the Act as "public [=governmental] authorities" liable for violations of the Convention rights of individuals, rather than as "private" [=nongovernmental] bodies considered to be collective recipients of their members' Convention rights under § 7. Although ECHR jurisprudence has consistently treated public law religious institutions as nongovernmental (=private law) entities for Convention purposes, defining these bodies by their character or "function" rather than by their domestic legal status,[62] the ambiguity in the Human Rights Act over the equation of "public authority" (§ 6) with "governmental organization" (§ 7) makes this treatment less obvious.[63]

59. *Leyla Şahin v Turkey*, App no. 44774/98 (ECtHR, November 10, 2005).

60. *Aktas v France*, App no. 43563/08 (ECtHR, June 30, 2009); *Bayrak v France*, App no. 14308/08 (ECtHR, June 30, 2009); *Gamaleddyn v France*, App no. 18527/08 (ECtHR, June 30, 2009); *Ghazal v France*, App no. 21934/08 (ECtHR, June 30, 2009); *Jazvir Singh v France*, App no. 25463/08 (ECtHR, June 30, 2009); *Ranjit Singh v France*, App no. 27561/08 (ECtHR, June 30, 2009).

61. Lautsi *v.* Italy (No. 30814/06) Eur. Ct. H.R. § 55 (November 3, 2009). The Italian crucifixes case is noteworthy for demonstrating both the pervasiveness of secularist reasoning and the unified strength of European opposition to a court-imposed suppression of the Christian identity of European nations and their church establishments. The Italian government's appeal of the ECHR ruling was supported by the governments of Lithuana, Slovakia, and Poland and had official expressions of support from twenty other countries. Ironically, however, the appeal was largely singing from the same song-sheet as the European Court ruling. It argued, for example, that the "cross" displayed in schools gave a predominantly "humanist message" of generally shared values independent of "its religious dimension," and so was "perfectly compatible with secularism and accessible to non-Christians and non-believers." Moreover, in overturning the ruling of the lower Chamber in 2011, the court's Grand Chamber accepted only the weakest of the Italian appeal arguments: that the "cross" was an "essentially passive symbol" of insignificant pedagogical influence. Lautsi *v.* Italy (No. 30814/06) Eur. Ct. H.R. (March 18, 2011) §§ 71–2.

62. For example, discussion of the paradigmatic Court decision, Holy Monasteries *v.* Greece (No. 13092/87; 13984/88) Eur. Ct. H.R. (1994) in Ian Leigh, "Freedom of Religion: Public/Private, Rights/Wrongs," in *Religious Liberty and Human Rights*, ed. Mark Hill (Cardiff: University of Wales Press, 2002), 137–9.

63. https://ww.legislation.gov.uk/ukpga/1998/42/section/6

While the Church of England has domestic legal confirmation that it will not be treated as a "public authority" under the Act in respect of the doctrinal, liturgical, and parochial activities of its bodies,[64] its courts, being inferior courts of law[65] (fortunately, seldom used), are to be treated under the Act as "public authorities" and may be open to challenge in such areas as their composition and procedures.[66] Church laws (i.e., Measures of the General Synod) have the advantage of being primary legislation that cannot simply be set aside by the courts; but like all other primary legislation they may be invalidated by judicial declaration of their incompatibility with some article(s) of the Human Rights Act. Moreover, all courts and tribunals are obliged under the Act (§ 3) to interpret their provisions, as far as possible, in conformity with the Convention rights of individuals. Finally, church-based or linked educational institutions are liable to be treated as public authorities on account of their statutory basis and state funding, but with only limited impact, owing to the clear and detailed primary legislation covering them.[67]

It is debatable whether the Church of England's unique status straddling the public-private institutional divide under the Human Rights Act renders it better or worse placed than are other denominations and religious communities, to resist the vexatious interference with evangelistic and charitable activities and the conditions of ministries resulting from the burgeoning of UK nondiscrimination and equality law within the legal framework and culture of the European Convention and the Human Rights Act.[68] On the one hand, since

---

64. See discussion by Leigh of the Court of Appeal's conclusion in the case of Aston Cantlow and Wilmcote with Billesley Parochial Church Council *v.* Wallbank, 3 WLR 1323 (2001) and of the House of Lord's reasoning in its reversal in 2003 of the Court of Appeal's holding. "Freedom of Religion," 149–52.

65. As inferior courts, they are under High Court control via judicial review.

66. Leigh, "Freedom of Religion," 153–5.

67. Ibid., 143.

68. The expansion of European law to protect a wider range of personal characteristics began with Article 13 of the Treaty of Amsterdam, empowering the Community to "take appropriate action to combat discrimination based on sex, racial or ethnic origin, religion or belief, disability, age or sexual orientation." Treaty of Amsterdam Art. 13, October 2, 1997. European antidiscrimination law now extends to such additional protected characteristics as gender reassignment and marital and civil partnership status. In the UK, the Equality Act 2010 codifies, harmonizes, and extends the regimes over the last decade of antidiscrimination legislation relating to protected characteristics. https://www.equalityhumanrights.com/en/equality-act/protected-characteristics. The negative impact of the antidiscrimination and equality legislation on religious organizations in the UK has been aggravated by recent changes to charity law denying religious organizations preferential treatment by removing the existing legal presumption of public benefit attaching to the registration of places of public worship. Charities Act 2006, *c.*, 50 §3(2). For the impact on religious bodies of nondiscrimination standards in the areas of employment and occupation, Lucy Vickers, *Religious Freedom, Religious Discrimination and the Workplace* (Oxford: Hart Publishing,

2000, a plethora of laws have undermined the public authority of the Church of England's doctrine and law respecting sexual relationships and marriage. The Civil Partnership Act 2004 contains provisions enabling the government to amend and even preempt other legislation, including ecclesiastical measures, in order to give full effect to the purposes of the Act.[69] The Equality Act 2010, having included "sexual orientation," "gender reassignment," and "marriage and civil partnership" among the "protected characteristics" of persons,[70] requires "public authorities" in the exercise of their functions to "have due regard to the need to . . . eliminate discrimination, harassment, victimization" and to "advance equality of opportunity" and "foster good relations" between persons who "share" and "persons who do not share" a "relevant protected characteristic." This entails a further need to "remove or minimize disadvantages suffered by persons who share a relevant protected characteristic," "take steps" to accommodate them and to "encourage" their participation "in public life."[71] The imposition on public authorities of a duty to promote an ill-defined and contentious equality among such diverse categories of persons is highly liable in intention and practice to promote a normative ranking of protected characteristics and society-wide ideological conformity to it. Finally, the Marriage (Same-Sex Couples) Act 2013, opening the legal status of marriage to same-sex couples, potentially brings the Church of England's canon law on marriage[72] into conflict with the law of the realm—a conflict prohibited by both parliamentary statute law and synodical measure,[73] and challenges the public status of the church's solemnization of marriage. However, the Act explicitly avoids this conflict[74] and also explicitly states that the public duty of clergy in the Church of England and the semiestablished Church of Wales to solemnize marriages (of residents in their parishes) does not extend to marriages of same-sex couples.[75] In addition, it provides that no religious organization or minister can be compelled to marry

---

2008; 2nd fully revised edition, 2016). For the implications for religious organizations of the Charity Act 2006, Rivers, *The Law of Organized Religion*, 158–80; Cathy Chan, "The Advancement of Religion as a Charitable Purpose in an Age of Religious Neutrality," *Oxford Journal of Law and Religion* 6, no. 1 (2017): 112–36. For the implications for faith-based welfare charities, Antony Lester and Paola Uccellari, "Extending the Equality Duty to Religion, Conscience and Belief: Proceed with Caution," *European Human Rights Law Review* 5 (2008): 567–73.

69. Civil Partnership Act 2004 c. 33, §§ 255, 259.
70. Equality Act 2010, s 4.
71. Ibid. s 149 (1) and (3).
72. Canons Ecclesiastical 1964 and 1969 B30 (1), revising the 1603 Code.
73. The Submission of Clergy Act 1533, s 3, as applied by the Synodical Government Measure 1969, s 1.
74. cl 1 (3).
75. cl 1 (4) (5).

same-sex couples or to permit this to happen on their premises, or be required expressly to "opt in" to marrying same-sex couples.[76]

The protection of religious freedom afforded by this latter provision to private religious institutions and their members is significant, as they, too, are in danger of their social identities and activities being undermined by the expanding horizontal application of "equality rights" from public to private, governmental to nongovernmental actors. Although British and ECtHR case law largely continues to protect the internal authority and freedom of private religious institutions to determine corporate matters of doctrine, worship, discipline, and staff employment,[77] the public religious freedom of their members has not been so well served, in some cases illustrating the influence of the governmental agenda of equality promotion on court decisions that unduly restrict the public expression of religious freedom. A notable example is *Ladele v Islington*,[78] in which the UK Court of Appeal allowed Islington Borough Council's "dignity for all" policy to override its (nondiscrimination) duty to accommodate the conscientious objection of a registrar from Christian convictions to officiating at civil partnership ceremonies, even though accepting that a practical accommodation could be found, consistent with the Council's offering a nondiscriminatory public service to same-sex couples entering civil partnerships. In this case, observed Julian Rivers, "promoting equality" meant requiring every employee to adopt the authority's conception of equality that "preferred protecting same-sex partners from the presence of others who disapproved of their lifestyle over finding ways to accommodate the religiously motivated convictions of those others."[79]

Most important, then, for the protection of religious freedom in the present legal environment is the witness of the historic constitutional position of the Church of England to the singular claim of publicity and authority embodied by *the church*, among primarily or essentially nongovernmental human institutions, communities, and associations. For this claim is not facilely detachable from the entire English legal tradition of protecting individual and communal freedom.

---

76. ss 2–5. For a critical assessment of claims that the British state's recognition of same-sex marriage is legally incompatible with religious liberty and church establishment, Javier Garcia Oliva and Helen Hall, "Same-Sex Marriage: An Inevitable Challenge to Religious Liberty and Establishment," *Oxford Journal of Law and Religion* 3, no. 1 (2014): 25–56.

77. See Ian Leigh, "Balancing Religious Autonomy and Other Human Rights under the European Convention," *Oxford Journal of Law and Religion* 1, no. 1 (2012): 109–26.

78. *LBV* [2010] 1 WLR 995.

79. Julian Rivers, "Promoting Religious Equality," *Oxford Journal of Law and Religion* 1, no. 2 (2012): 387. Rivers's wider critique dovetails at points with that of Christopher McCrudden's critical legal analysis and broader reflections in "The *Gay Cake* Case: What the Supreme Court Did, and Didn't Decide in *Ashers*," *Oxford Journal of Law and Religion* 9, no. 2 (2020): 238–70.

For over a decade, discontent with European and British legislation and adjudication of human rights fueled the British appetite for exiting the European Union, so beholden was EU treaty law to the European Convention and the ECtHR. However, despite continuing enthusiasm within Conservative party ranks for amending or replacing the British Human Rights Act and weakening the attention paid by UK courts to ECtHR jurisprudence,[80] Britain's exit from the EU has not so far brought about these developments (although the Withdrawal Bill of 2020 did exclude the EU Charter of Fundamental Rights from domestication in British law).[81] Moreover, negotiating them would be exceedingly difficult, given that the EU-UK Trade Agreement specifically commits the UK and EU to respecting the ECHR and to giving domestic effect to "the rights and freedoms" contained in it.[82] In any case, such developments would not necessarily mitigate the current political and legal pressures on English church establishment, given that political and legal thought and practice in Britain has already, to an extent, reconstructed itself on the foundation of egalitarian-rights pluralism, largely assumed to be intrinsic to liberal democratic polity, public justice, and the constitutional rule of law.

It is noteworthy that, when Britain domesticated the European Convention in the 1998 Human Rights Act, political and legal conservatives hoped that British legal traditions (constitutional, statute, and common law) could constructively absorb the Convention's systemic conceptuality of rights and the European jurisprudence flowing from it. This hope was nourished by the prudent decisions of the British government not to invest the Human Rights Act with constitutional authority, nor to admit Strasbourg court rulings as binding ipso facto on the British courts. However, more than twenty years later, it is clear that the English legal profession has undergone a massive reeducation and reorientation, with significant shifts in the judiciary's constitutional self-understanding, as evidenced by its enthusiastic welcoming of the Supreme Court and the regime of judicial review. From a historical-theological perspective, this reorientation is the latest episode in the long modern saga in which the British political elite—politicians, the political intelligentsia, and the legal profession—have largely eliminated theological and ecclesiastical elements from their constitutional understanding, conveniently forgetting that the English and British political identities historically took shape as theological and ecclesiastical identities.

---

80. The Conservative Party's commitment to replacing the HRA in its 2010 election platform was scuppered by the postelection Coalition with the Liberal Democrats, only to be revived in the 2014 Conservative proposals for a British Bill of Rights.

81. https://www.legislation.gov.uk/ukpga/2020/1/section/5/enacted. EU Withdrawal Agreement Bill 2020, clause 5 (4).

82. Article LAW.GEN.3.

Conclusion

Our overview in this chapter of the multiple dimensions of the present crisis affecting the Reformation tradition of English public theology and practice has attempted to convey how central this tradition is to the integrity of the Church of England's historical mission and to the integrity of the political society served by that mission. It has presented the attenuation of the Reformation tradition in the Church of England's life and in Britain's civil and political life as a dilemma in which both the church and political society lack the resources to understand and resist the destructive developments in which they are caught up. In outlining the civil/political dimensions of this crisis, the ideology of liberal egalitarian-rights pluralism has occupied center stage, as the lingua franca of discussion about public religious freedom and justice within and across national boundaries, as foundational for national constitutional law, for domestic and international legislation and adjudication, and for governmental policy formulation. Thus, the way has been prepared for our critical analysis of the modern and premodern historical development and the contemporary impact of natural rights theory and practice.

Chapter 3

DIAGNOSING THE LATE MODERN POLITY
THE DYNAMICS OF LIBERAL NATURAL RIGHTS

In recent generations, reflections on modern moral and political thought have regularly been informed by historical-theoretical narratives that discern key moments in the past as having dramatic and persisting effects in the present. The Protestant Reformation has often featured prominently among these moments. Notably, Quentin Skinner, Eric Voegelin, and Sheldon Wolin have integrated formidable critiques of modern theory and practice with a detailed historical indictment of Lutheran and Calvinist theology for paving the way to modern voluntarism, individualism, and statism by assaulting Christian Aristotelian ethical and political humanism.[1] With their impressive narratives, indicting, by implication, much English Reformation thought, this study is somewhat at odds.

My critique of late modernity has benefited greatly from the insights of these historical philosophers and others—most especially George Grant, C. B. Macpherson, Leo Strauss, and Ian Shapiro—whose works, together, have illuminated the influential contributions to the modern liberal contractarian tradition of natural rights by such figures as Thomas Hobbes, John Locke, and Richard Overton in the seventeenth century; Rousseau, Kant, and the apologists of the American and French Revolutions in the eighteenth; and the contemporary contractarians, John Rawls and Robert Nozick. Nonetheless, my critique has not adopted tout court their theoretical postures and historical narratives. Rather, my use of their accounts to diagnose the late modern predicament has been decisively shaped by the ethical and political insights of English Reformation theology, illuminating certain resemblances between the modern political ethos and ethic and the ethos and ethic to which the English reformers critically responded. This is the place to expand on our introductory summary of these resemblances.[2]

The features of the scholastic moral and political theological landscape of which the English reformers and their continental mentors were critical were all expressions of a shift of focus from divine to human judgment, willing and acting.

---

1. See Introduction, p. 2 n. 2.
2. Intro., 13.

Theologically appraised, this shift entailed inadequate acknowledgment of both the priority and the Christological unity of God's dealings with his human creature revealed in the Scriptures. Anthropologically appraised, the shift underestimated the immediate dependency of created and fallen human moral agency and action on the Father's saving work in Christ through the Holy Spirit. Chiefly concerned with the soteriological and ecclesiological dynamics of this shift, the reformers stressed that union with Christ by faith was a precondition for the performance of "good works," and the church's foremost mission was to bring sinners to faith by communicating God's saving word and work.

Coordinately, the reformers criticized two deviations of the late scholastic ecclesial tradition from the church's core evangelical mission. One was the centrality given to promulgating church law, combined with the tendency to conflate human and divine law, which subjected believers to an excessive number of compulsory disciplines and exactions. The other was the centrality of juridical practices in both the "spiritual" and "political" spheres of the church's ministry unified by the sacramental discipline of private penance. Sacramental penance accentuated the efficacy of these practices in regenerating the moral agency and action of individual believers, reinforcing the individualistic orientation of the juridical-ecclesial approach to communal sanctification.

A somewhat contrasting strand of moral individualism in late scholasticism criticized by the English reformers consisted of confidence in the individual's natural moral freedom, that is, the individual's rational capacity, bestowed by nature and persisting in the sinful condition, to know, will, and act in conformity with the universal moral law, both apart from and aided by Scriptural revelation. This strand underwent development in political theories of natural law, natural right, and natural rights, in which individuals, grasping the universal principles of natural justice, conceived largely in terms of the universal rights of human moral subjects, compacted to form communities of public rule and law protective of the rational moral order. Although English Reformation public theology took no explicit notice of these rationalist and voluntarist political theories, confining its critical attention to scholastic conceptions of the relationship of individual moral freedom to God's justifying grace in the soteriological-ecclesial realm, the Cranmerian depiction of public rule and law drawn from the Old and New Testaments stood sharply opposed at points to these late scholastic political elaborations.

Finally, the English reformers viewed the legalistic and juridical profile of contemporary Catholic ministry to express the sinful human will to dominate and control not only individual believers but God's past and present saving word to his human creatures. They situated the jurisdictional practices of the scholastic church within the more encompassing project of replacing the rule of God's creative and saving acts and judgments recorded in Scripture with the rule of human acts and judgments established in church tradition. Here also, they did not critically attend to the emerging forms of domination and control in the legalistic-juridical logic of scholastic "natural-rights" theories of secular political society and rule.

The Interrelated Contradictions of Late Modern Society

These targets of English Reformation criticism direct us to analogous targets in the late modern moral and political landscape: those of moral and political individualism and voluntarism, a legalistic and excessively juridical public culture, and mechanisms of regulation and control corrosive of moral freedom. English Reformation criticism also furnishes a persuasive theological diagnosis of these analogous features as symptoms of the practical and theoretical disengagement of human agency and action from God's righteousness, judgment, and freedom revealed in Jesus Christ. If these analogies between the scholastic and late modern environments appear somewhat loosely drawn and needing qualification, Chapter 4 should provide what is missing.

The frustrating and perplexing contradictions presented by these features of our contemporary moral and political landscape are widely experienced and sometimes observed, but only dimly understood by people. In the popular media and in more academic discussion, one or another contradiction regularly surfaces, but is inadequately addressed, because it is conceived to be a contingent incompatibility of means and ends largely susceptible of rectification. There is a failure to grasp the specific contradiction as an aspect of the generic contradiction of late modern society insuperable on its own terms, between the pursuit of freedom and the pursuit of control. For the last seventy years, a broad consensus has reigned: that the principal, unifying aim of liberal, democratic polity is to maximize the freedom of the plurality of individuals and groups composing society, freedom being generally understood as the power of individuals primarily, and of groups derivatively, to determine themselves through the exercise of choice. Such freedom has been widely conceived as emancipation from manifold external and internal constraints: physical, psychological, social, economic, cultural, and political. There has been a corresponding acceptance that the pursuit of freedom requires expanding forms of human control over the human and nonhuman world: methods of overcoming the uncertainty and unpredictability of natural action and the inherent limitations of natural organisms. It is commonly recognized that the regulative and productive forms taken by scientific-technological control necessarily penetrate every internal and external sphere of individual and communal human life.

These modes of control have gained broad acceptance as necessary means for achieving the aspirations of liberal democratic pluralism; and public controversies have largely concerned the serviceability of particular means and their compatibility with other means: whether these be biological technologies, social welfare programs, fiscal measures, educational policies, internet applications, or human rights legislation and adjudication. Although certain controversies have been thought by some to reveal perennial and endemic tensions (e.g., between the "negative" and the "positive," the "active" and the "passive" elements of human freedom), and even irreconcilable oppositions, admitting of no mediation, the intellectual mainstream has inclined toward a synthetic, mediating position, seeking to balance contentious, but potentially compatible, means. The prevailing conviction, or at least the hope, has been that rational and purposive human beings are, and will continue to be, capable of ensuring that these means remain in the service of human ends, rendering some benefit, however marginal, to sustaining and increasing human freedom. Today, however, we are witnessing among Western populations and their intelligentsia an unprecedented rupture of this hope, betokening a pervasive sapping of confidence in the coherence of inherited social and political aspirations. The more notable causes of this rupture include the following. Accumulating evidence of the destructive impact of Western technologies on the natural conditions of human freedom has called into question the dependence of liberal society on the inherent dynamic of technological development. The universally recognized contribution of modern industrial technologies to global warming and its ecological consequences; the demonstrably damaging outcomes of what many people consider morally repellent practices, from the industrial farming of crops, livestock, and fish, to the extravagant consumption of consumer goods and accompanying production of waste (especially toxic and nondegradable); and the known and imagined dangers, and controversial existing uses, of a broad spectrum of fast-developing technologies (reproductive, genetic, nano, electronic, nuclear, etc.)—all these have cast a shroud of suspicion over the technological ambition of "exploiting" nature in the service of human emancipation. Increasingly it appears that the technological enterprise of harnessing the predictable processes of nature to specified human purposes has brought into sharper focus the terrifying unpredictability of the material world.

In addition to the technological assault on the natural conditions of freedom, our generation is experiencing a direct assault on human freedom from the liberal democratic pursuit of an equality of freedom in society. Ordinary people are increasingly oppressed in all social spheres by manipulative techniques and strategies of influence, combined with externally imposed rules and regulations that stifle their proper freedom of judgment, speech, and action, and inappropriately subject them to the critical judgment of others. Across the vocational spectrum, this generalized subjection of persons to conformist pressures, legal regulation, and juridical procedures is the pervasive social form taken by contemporary bureaucracy. Although largely produced by technical applications of social-scientific rationality, contemporary bureaucracy is politically driven, deriving impetus from excessive governmental regulation of institutions, organizations, and agencies, the objective of which is to display and to secure the maximizing and equalizing of individual and collective freedom.

Outside of the bureaucratic vocational context, the role of social surveillance has progressively been diffused throughout the popular communications media. For many decades now, professional journalism has been fixated on its self-assigned role of relentlessly inspecting and assessing the orientations and conduct of public and private individuals and enterprises, exposing various misdemeanors, including failures of support and provision for individual and group rights. More recently, however, its dominance has been undercut by the arrival of a plethora of vast social media platforms, causing uncontrolled, large-scale democratic dispersal of the activities of social surveillance and public exposure, with similarly uncontrolled effects. While the incessant media revelations of personal and organizational failures and scandals have occasionally had some beneficial effect, they have also, by inducing anger and despair in their recipients, contributed to the tide of socially destructive passions and lawlessness corrosive of freedom.

The tide of disordered passions and conduct is nowhere more apparent than in the threatened and actual damages inflicted by the functioning of capitalist market economies on the economic, social, and political welfare of individuals and communities, quite apart from environmental degradation. It is widely perceived in popular and professional circles that excessive corporate profit and inflated managerial salaries flout the democratic ethos of social equality, that the coercive features of market exchange diminish the economic freedom of weaker players, and that the influencing of governmental policy, as well as its cunning evasion, by powerful financial and commercial interests, threaten the commanding role of the democratic majority. Indeed, there is a mounting sense among democratic populations that the global flow of investment capital seeking larger profit margins, favorable tax benefits, and speculative gains is robbing the majority of the world's citizens of effective political controls over their economic and social futures.

Finally, the arbitrary limits to inclusive pluralism within contemporary liberal democratic society are increasingly contested by individuals and groups who refuse to assent to society's nonnegotiable principle of equal individual self-determination in its reigning version(s). The reluctance of conservative religious believers and nonbelievers to endorse morally or religiously indiscriminate applications of this principle, or its educational indoctrination among the young, poses the question of whether pluralistic liberal democracy may, in fact, be an homogenizing political ideology and culture unaccommodating of dissenting traditions of belief, rationality, and practice.

Clarifying the Contradictions via the History of Modern Natural Rights

In the present social and political situation of lost confidence, anxious questioning, angry disaffection, confrontational ideological posturing, and bellicose public discourse, there is an urgent need for coherent theoretical clarification of the interconnections among these perplexing contradictions within liberal democratic ends and means, purposes, and practices. My undertaking of this clarification by charting the modern liberal tradition of natural rights in its political, economic, social, and ecological dimensions, is a condensed narrative sketch of quite well-traversed material, limited in both historical detail and scholarly sources. Importantly, however, my narrative sketch is also, from the theological perspective elaborated in later chapters, tracing the modern theoretical disengagement of human moral agency and action from God's freedom, judgment, and action revealed in Jesus Christ.

The Proprietary and Juridical Aspects of Liberal Natural Rights: Formative Elaborations

Throughout all developments of the liberal contractarian tradition of natural rights, there persists an identifiable conceptual core. This core is an economic and juridical anthropology: an understanding of human beings as naturally self-owning individuals, as proprietors with exclusive powers of disposal over their spiritual and corporeal capacities and acts. The individual's proprietary power of self-disposing in acts of choice is the original, natural right of human freedom, of self-determination; and the equality of individual human beings resides fundamentally in their equal proprietary freedom.

A most perspicacious account of the proprietary subject of natural rights has come from Richard Overton, leading pamphleteer of the English Leveller movement, writing in 1646:[3]

> To every individual in nature is given an individual property by nature, not to be invaded or usurped by any. For every one, as he is himself, so he hath a self propriety, else could he not be himself; and on this no second may presume to deprive any of without manifest violation and affront to the very principles of nature, and of the rules of equity and justice between man and man. Mine and thine cannot be, except this be. No man hath power over my rights and liberties, and I over no man's.... For by natural birth all men are equally and alike born to like propriety, liberty and freedom; and as we are delivered of God by the hand of nature into this world, every one with a natural, innate freedom and propriety—as it were writ in the table of every man's heart, never to be obliterated—even so are we to live, every one equally and alike to enjoy his Birthright and privilege; even all whereof God by nature has made him free.

Clearly, Overton conceived the individual's property in himself and in his energies and capacities as *full ownership*, an exclusive power of disposal effective against all other human beings (although not against the creator's sovereign proprietary right in his creatures), and that he identified the individual's total self-possession, his freedom from others, with the essential humanity belonging universally and equally to every person. Consequently, as C. B. Macpherson argued, for Overton and the Levellers, the individual's proprietary right of freedom underpinned all further claims for specific civil, religious, economic, and political rights and freedoms.[4]

From its seventeenth-century formulations, the modern tradition of natural rights recognized that free, self-disposing proprietors are also driven by passions, by primary and compelling desires to protect and augment their personal property.

---

3. *An Arrow against all Tyrants* 1646 (Early English Books Online Text Creation Partnership). https://quod.lib.umich.edu/e/eebo2/A90228.0001.001.

4. *The Political Theory of Possessive Individualism: Hobbes to Locke* (Oxford: Oxford University Press, 1962), 140–3.

Simultaneously, they are creatures of physical and psychological instincts conceived by materialistic science on a mechanistic or organic evolutionary model, and they are transcending, controlling subjects who magisterially direct or canalize these instincts, as owners use their possessions, in autonomous acts of rational choice. Individual wills are conceived as occupying an Archimedean point outside of the causalities of the material cosmos and outside of, in the sense of prior to, the ordering institutions of political society; and common human impulses are conceived as divorced (partially or completely) from an independently given, intelligible order of beings, goods, and ends.

Crucially, the free pursuit by individuals of self-preservation and self-augmentation undergirds their natural right to appropriate worldly things for their exclusive use, that is, exclusive of others using these things without their permission. In appropriating worldly things, vital and nonvital, for private use, individual or collective subjects take them into their orbits of power primarily in order more effectively to handle, manipulate, alter, and even destroy them, as it serves their self-interested purposes. Hobbes and Locke offered rival paradigms of how the natural right of appropriation is related to the right of private property in external things and, as well, to the juridical securing of the individual's personal property and its free development.

In *Leviathan* (1651), Hobbes conceived the individual's natural right as radically prior to natural law or social obligation, defining it as the unrestrained liberty "to use his own power, as he will himself, for the preservation . . . of his own life"; and to do whatever "in his own judgement and reason" is "the aptest means thereunto."[5] In their natural condition of virtually equal physical and mental powers and of rival desires and strivings, Hobbes's individuals have the unlimited right to use everything, including one another's bodies, unbounded by obligations of natural justice.[6] Only the intolerable insecurity of natural liberty and self-preservation in this condition necessitates the prudential stratagems for peace known as "laws of nature." These stratagems include the "mutual transferring of right" by individuals[7] via a voluntary contract to a sovereign civil power (excepting the right to preserve and defend their lives and bodies), with the objective of securing a sphere of limited civil rights, including the right of private property.

For Hobbes, then, property right presumes civil law and is a civil and not a natural right. Nevertheless, like all rights created by the sovereign civil power, property right remains an articulation of the natural proprietary freedom of contracting individuals, reflecting the structure of exclusive self-ownership. "Propriety" or ownership is for Hobbes the paradigmatic civil right, inseparable from justice understood both as the reliable performance by individuals of their voluntary

---

5. *Leviathan* 14.1, ed. J. C. A Gaskin (Oxford: Oxford University Press, 1996), 86.

6. *Leviathan* 13.1–3, 14.4: 82–3, 86–7. In the natural condition of war, says Hobbes, "nothing can be unjust. The notions of right and wrong, justice and injustice have no place. Where there is no common power, there is no law: where no law, no injustice" (13.13: 85).

7. *Leviathan* 14.9: 89.

covenants, and as "the constant will of giving to every man his own"—that is, of recognizing his lawful "propriety."[8] Although the sovereign ruler determines the private property of individual subjects through an original distribution of property right, through the legal forms of transferring property, and through public exactions on private wealth, the ultimate purpose of these determinations is to establish and secure over time a terrain for the unregulated liberty of individuals, defensible against interference by others, to dispose of their powers, acts, and external wealth according to their own judgments of what is most profitable: for example, in buying, selling, entering into contracts, and choosing their trades and abodes.[9] Moreover, as moral and legal constraint on private economic exchanges is confined to the performance of contracts, "the value of all things contracted for is measured [solely] by the appetite of the contractors," so that the just value is simply "that which they be contented to give"—in contemporary parlance, it equates with "demand."[10]

Diverging from Hobbes, Locke in his *Second Treatise of Government* (1689) presented natural right as coterminous with divinely given and rationally accessible natural obligation. On his account, the original "perfect freedom" of individuals to "order their actions and dispose of their possessions and persons as they think fit . . . without asking leave, or depending upon the will of any other man" is bounded by the natural obligation to preserve themselves, and when their "own preservation comes not into competition," to "preserve the rest of mankind."[11] The obligation of human individuals neither to "destroy" themselves nor to harm others in their "life, health, liberty or possessions" is imposed by their omnipotent Maker and sovereign Master, whose "workmanship" and "property" they all are, equal in their common "nature" and "faculties."[12]

Significantly, the individual's natural freedom, bounded by the natural duty of self-preservation, is for Locke inseparable from the natural right to acquire "possessions," that is, to appropriate the earth's bounty for private use, and the corresponding obligation to respect the possessions of others. These coordinate sets of rights and duties are inseparably connected with a third set: namely, the individual's right and obligation to prosecute offenses against the law of nature. Both the proprietary scope and the juridical scope of the individual's natural freedom in Locke's thought have defined the modern liberal rights tradition.

In the economic sphere, Locke's paradigm of property acquisition furnished a moral foundation for indefinite wealth accumulation in a free-market, money economy. From the individual's ownership of the "work of his hands," Locke argued that private appropriation of the earth's resources through human labor

---

8. *Leviathan* 15.3: 95–6.

9. *Leviathan* 21.6, 24.10, 11: 141, 166–7.

10. *Leviathan* 15.14: 100.

11. *The Second Treatise of Government* 2.4: *Two Treatises of Government*, ed. Peter Laslett (Cambridge: Cambridge University Press, 1988), 269–71. Hereafter *STG*.

12. *STG* 2.6: 271.

is their naturally just, lawful, and efficient use. His theory is that individual labor, by mixing something privately owned with the naturally common, assimilates the common to the sphere of private use and simultaneously invests it with value or usefulness.[13] Locke recognizes that "the law of nature," in articulating the equality of self-owing individuals, limits property acquisition to the amount which the individual can use before it spoils, thus leaving "as good and as large a possession" for others to appropriate through labor.[14] Nevertheless, the progression of Locke's argument makes abundantly clear that the proscription of waste places virtually no moral obstacle in the way of wealth accumulation through enterprise in a money economy, where currency accumulates rather than perishable goods, and where higher productivity is supposed to increase the availability of natural resources to the industrious.[15]

Thus, the individual's natural freedom and right of acquiring possessions through virtuous industry, serving the equal freedom and right of others, places no intrinsic moral limits on the individual's acquisitive activity. Wedded to the freedom and right of acquisition, the individual's natural pursuit in Locke is not of bare subsistence, but of "commodious" or "comfortable" self-preservation—a practical end which does not support a sharp distinction between the welfare needs and the superfluous wants of human beings. The commodious self-preservation of individuals encompasses their delight in, and enjoyment of, an abundance and variety of goods, the value and utility of which almost entirely comes from inventive and efficient human production, so that, with rising productivity, commerce, and international trade, the "needs" and "wants" of individuals become increasingly indistinguishable.[16] And should grave inequalities of wealth result

---

13. *STG* 5.25–30, 39: 285–90, 296. Ian Shapiro is rightly critical of James Tully's Thomistic reading of Locke's theory as propounding a concept of "common property" divinely given in creation, which all human beings have a proprietary right to use (*ius ad rem*) and from which "private property" (*ius in re*) is derived by individual labor. Tully, *A Discourse on Property: John Locke and His Adversaries* (Cambridge: Cambridge University Press, 1980), 64–79ff. Rather, as Shapiro contends, Locke does not view "the world" given by God "to men in common" as "common property," but as the common "natural" (i.e., nonproprietary) basis for property right established by just and efficient labor. *The Evolution of Rights in Liberal Theory* (Cambridge: Cambridge University, 1986), 89–92.

14. "The measure of property Nature well set, by the extent of men's labour and the conveniency of life. No man's labour could subdue or appropriate all, nor could his enjoyment consume more than a small part; so that it was impossible for any man, this way, to entrench upon the right of another or acquire to himself a property to the prejudice of his neighbor, who would still have room for as good and as large a possession (after the other had taken out his) as before it was appropriated" (2.5.36; 292).

15. *STG* 5.36–50: 292–302.

16. *STG* 5.42–3, 48: 297–8, 301.

from the inequalities of productive capacity among individuals, the indigent can always voluntarily contract to sell their labor.[17]

Thus, Locke's theory of property put in place enduring elements of what we know today as free-market capitalist ideology, despite his failure to recognize the central principles of scarcity and competition. These elements include the original or "natural" character of property rights, or rights of exclusive dominion; the validity of unlimited acquisition of property through voluntary exchange; the inseparability of needs and potentially infinite wants in the functioning of (what is now called) effective market demand; the equation of the value of goods in exchange with their "usefulness" or "utility"; and the functioning of alienable labor as an exchangeable commodity in the economic market. While all these elements, excepting the first, could be extracted from Hobbes's formulations,[18] they were developed schematically in Locke's writing.

These elements would prove susceptible of political elaboration in both libertarian and social welfare directions.[19] Libertarian thought would emphasize the persisting inviolability within civil society of the individual's natural rights of exclusive dominion (of property in both personal and external goods), the minimal protective role assigned to coercive rule by contracting individuals, and the general applicability of market principles to the political arena. By contrast, the theory of late welfare capitalism would limit the natural rights of individuals in scarce external goods (economic or social) by the principle of equality, derive principles of civil justice from this pre-political basis, and admit some governmental management of market processes of competition, production, and demand and some equalizing redistribution of property in civil society. Either way, the core would remain the acquisitive, competitive individual seeking to maximize his freedom through the accumulation of property.

Intimately connected with the natural property right of individuals in Locke is their equal right to judge infractions of the natural law, whether injuries to themselves or to others, and to inflict punishment on malefactors proportionate to their transgressions, so as "may serve for reparation and restraint."[20] Significantly, Locke presents the individual's right of judgment as vindicating the rational maxims of social conduct divinely given for the "mutual security" of all, and not

---

17. Shapiro argues, against Tully's objections, that Locke's economic thought supports the concept of a voluntary wage-labor contract. *The Evolution of Rights*, 139–43.

18. Notable is Hobbes's recognition of human labor to be a source of value and an alienable, marketable commodity: "The value, or worth of a man, is as of all other things, his price; that is to say, so much as would be given for the use of his power: and therefore is not absolute; but a thing dependent on the need and judgement of another." *Leviathan* 10.16: 59.

19. For an illustration, see Shapiro's discussions of Robert Nozick's "neoclassical" libertarianism and John Rawls's Keynesian liberalism.

20. *STG* 2.7, 8: 271–2.

just the rights of injured parties,[21] while attributing to injured parties a separate natural right to take reparation (satisfaction) from the offending party. By contrast, Hobbes's rational stratagems for curbing the individual's natural right of unrestrained appropriation and aggression against his equals reserve the right of coercive judgment to the civil power, on the grounds that no one, being partial to his own benefit, is "a fit arbitrator in his own cause."[22]

Locke's conception of the continuing primacy in civil society of the natural juridical right of individuals is a core component of the liberal contractarian legacy. Notably, under the civil contract (compact), injured parties retain to themselves and do not entrust to the communal magistrate their natural right to demand reparation from the offender.[23] More importantly, civil society, as the repository of the judicial rights of its compacted members, retains the residual or final power of public judgment. While Locke concedes that individuals are ill-equipped to judge and punish equitably in their own cause and, equally, that civil government is the divinely ordained and "proper remedy" for lawless violence,[24] he, nevertheless, argues that were civil society to entrust the powers of public judgment to deputies (i.e., governors) who prove less fitted for the task than its individual members acting independently, it would be entitled to withdraw the powers of public judgment from those agents and invest them in others. This could be done either peacefully (by constitutional procedure) or, where necessary, by cooperative revolutionary action (closely resembling coercive judgment in the state of nature).[25]

A century after Locke's *Second Treatise*, the project of reconstructing the political contract along the lines of a market exchange of rights would occupy a prominent stream of American Revolutionary thought. Addressing the question of which natural rights are alienable in the civil contract and which inalienable, Thomas Paine proposed that each individual retains those natural rights "in which the power to execute is as perfect in the individual as the right itself" and "deposits ... in the common stock of society" those in which "though the right is perfect in the individual, the power to execute them is defective." To inalienable rights Paine assigns "all the intellectual rights, along with rights of acting for one's own "comfort and happiness ... not injurious to the natural rights of others"; to alienable rights he assigns paradigmatically the "right to judge in [one's] own cause," which is imperfect in practice "without the power to redress."[26] Most strikingly, his analogy of the joint stock company, in which "every man is a proprietor in society, and draws on the capital as a matter of right," has the effect of accentuating the superior

21. *STG* 2.8: 272.
22. *Leviathan* 15.30, 31: 103–4.
23. *STG* 2.11: 273–4.
24. *STG* 2.13: 275–6.
25. *STG* 19.211–42: 406–28.
26. *The Rights of Man, Being an Answer to Mr. Burke's Attack on the French Revolution* (London: J. Watson, 1848), 25.

bargaining position and adjudicating power of the contracting individuals and as well the dominant role of calculative rationality in setting the terms of the civil contract.

The continuing predominance of property right within the "negative" libertarian tradition is readily intelligible; for property right in personal and external goods secures and enlarges the individual's primary right of freedom as a power of acting which he possesses and which entails an obligation of noninterference on the part of all other subjects, and especially, of government. The influence of property right on the more recent development of "positive" or welfare rights is less obvious. For welfare rights are entitlements or claim rights of subjects to goods or opportunities that others alone or in part provide—for example, nourishment, housing, education, medical care, employment, and voting opportunity. However, the claim right of subjects to these benefits derives fundamentally from the claimant's self-propriety, which generates the obligation on the part of others to provide the benefits. The logic of this derivation is that individual self-proprietors have the natural right to use and develop their powers and capacities freely and, therefore, are entitled to the external goods necessary to exercising their proprietary freedom: which goods other self-proprietors have an obligation to provide, if able to do so, and the goods are otherwise unavailable. In advanced liberal democracies, the obligation of providing these goods falls on governments as representing all members of civil society. Where the obligation of governmental provision is a constitutional obligation, it reflects the assumed or stated terms of the political contract through which the equal natural rights and derivative obligations of individuals are translated into the rights and obligations of citizens and of their governmental organ for securing and advancing individual and (derivative) collective freedom.

Contemporary Political and Legal Ramifications of Liberal Natural Rights

The prevalence in late modern polities of a liberal ideology, which derives individual and communal obligations from the universal proprietary rights of individuals, has ramifications for political and legal theory and practice. The most prominent is that constitutional law articulates the normative rationale of political and legal practice as the protection and fulfillment of individual and collective rights. Constitutional law is dominated by the continuous production of an intentionally comprehensive codification of universal human rights to function as the encompassing conceptual framework for enacting, implementing, and adjudicating law. These codified and largely justiciable rights comprise the controlling language of public justice, of political and legal relationships, to which more traditional concepts of public authority, objective right, obligation, equity, and competence are subordinated or assimilated.

The constitutional codification of justiciable rights feeds the tendency of political theorists and politicians to adopt the logic and principles of market economics. Influential political theorists, enamored of neoclassical economics, conceive the state as a "business run by entrepreneurs," political parties as "firms trying to maximize votes," and "voting preferences as utility functions"; while politicians "sell a commodity as entrepreneurs," employ agencies to "package their products for advertising, and gear those products to what they believe the market demands."[27] Correspondingly, citizens, in their dealings with politicians and government, are consumer-conscious, seeking in return for their political support and compliance the best possible protection and provision for an expanding range of freedoms and entitlements. Legal codification of their freedoms and entitlements fosters consumer consciousness by increasing the incentives and opportunities for individuals and groups to demand legal redress of failures of governmental and public agencies to furnish the promised goods and services. Further extending the opportunities for legal redress is the horizontal application of rights from public to private, governmental to nongovernmental, actors (individuals and organizations). The overall effect is toward recasting public law in the mold of private law, and the common good as the aggregation of private goods.

The modeling of political relationships on market economics reinforces other trends in legal theory and practice that accentuate the difference between law-making and law adjudicating. One trend is toward bureaucratizing adjudication, to remove it from the uncertainty and unpredictability of law-making. Bureaucratizing involves subjecting adjudication to the norm of generating consistent, rationally transparent outcomes through strict compliance with an internal system of precise rules governing practice. This enterprise expresses the modern liberal aspiration to secure with scientific predictability the rights of autonomous subjects by means of rational, methodological conformity. It fails to fulfill the aspiration, however, as its strategy for achieving consistent outcomes in court decisions is undermined, all too predictably, by the failure to eradicate the operation of judicial discretion in construing the "facts" of particular cases and interpreting and applying legal sources, including discordant rules reflecting diverse political and social orientations and other contextual factors—a failure widely canvassed in the contemporary jurisprudential schools of natural law, legal realism, post-realism (policy science and legal process), and deconstructive critical studies.[28]

A contrary trend within political and judicial thought under a constitutional rights charter is to present legal adjudication as superior to law-making, in

---

27. Shapiro, *The Evolution of Liberal Rights Theory*, 197–8. Shapiro interprets the libertarian political theory of Robert Nozick in *Anarchy, State and Utopia* (Oxford: Blackwell, 1974) and *Philosophical Explanations* (Cambridge, MA: Harvard University Press, 1981) as firmly anchored in the American "public choice" tradition, as developed in Antony Downs, *An Economic Theory of Democracy* (1957), James Buchanan and Gordon Tullock, *The Calculus of Consent: Logical Foundations of Constitutional Democracy* (1962), and Kenneth J. Arrow, *Social Choice and Individual Values* (1963).

28. For discussion of these schools, Dennis Patterson, ed., *A Companion to Philosophy of Law and Legal Theory*, Part 2 (Oxford: Blackwell, 1999).

providing a less partisan, more balanced legal articulation of the value consensus of liberal, democratic, and pluralistic polity, taken to be the standard of law-ruled polity. As guardian of constitutional justice, the judiciary is considered best situated to elaborate the legal substance of this value consensus, namely universal rights, and the role of rights in rationally organizing the legal field in theory and practice. Rather than reinforcing the rational stability of judicial process, however, the conceptuality of liberal-egalitarian human rights is prone to undermine it by encouraging a progressivist creativity in court decisions (shadowing that of rights-based social ethics), which regularly enlarges the category of justiciable rights and extends the judicial application of the equality principle. As Nigel Biggar astutely argues in *What's Wrong with Rights?* (2020), constitutional charters that include abstract, unconditional, and indeterminate rights allow judges to exercise excessive philosophical discretion in judging cases and to cast themselves as "developers" rather than "interpreters" of law, "responsible for keeping it abreast of social mores."[29] Untroubled by the inherent limitations of case law and its relative public unaccountability compared to statute law, the judiciary is in the forefront of contemporary strivings to expand the directive, pedagogical, and regulative functioning of public law.

The controlling influence of the juridical discourse of universal and equal rights extends beyond political and legal institutions to all institutional spheres of late modern societies. The discourse has demonstrated its power to assimilate to the political, juridical realm, common human goods and right relationships which the longer Western traditions of thought and practice have portrayed as pre-political/pre-juridical and trans-political/trans-juridical, the theological tradition having assigned them to the orders of original creation, redemption, and sanctification. Thus, the rights discourse tends to suppress the foundational and determining import for human society of social, communicative goods, and relationships that are not intrinsically political/juridical and proprietary. These include life and the natural activities sustaining it, marital and family relationships, language, communication of knowledge, collaborative skills and work, common moral and aesthetics sensibilities, judgments and practices, and above all, fellowship in faith and worship of God. Moreover, the discourse suppresses the dependence of the political/juridical order on, and in key respects, its teleological ordering to, these goods and relationships which give positive substance and form to human freedom.

The previous chapter has indicated some of the obstacles to sustaining effective legal protection of the public right of religious freedom in its communal and institutional dimensions within a juridical culture of egalitarian rights. The preponderant political pressure is either toward privatizing the authority and practice of religious institutions or toward intrusive legal regulation of their

---

29. Nigel Biggar, *What's Wrong with Rights?* (Oxford: Oxford University Press, 2020); Abstract of Chapter 11. https://academic-oup-com.ezproxy.is.ed.ac.uk/book/33698/chapter/288287199

institutional practices occupying public space; for the modern template of legal protection of religious freedom is protection of the maximal equal freedom of religious and moral choice for individuals and not protection of social traditions of faith and worship in which the reality of freedom cannot be separated from its concrete communal substance. Within the ideology of egalitarian civil rights deriving collective from individual freedom, legal and social concessions made to historical traditions of public religious faith and practice are without robust theoretical justification.

To obtain a fuller understanding of the ramifications of modern liberal rights within and beyond the political and legal spheres, it is necessary to investigate further the scientific-technological trajectory of the proprietary rights tradition.

The Scientific-Technological Trajectory of Liberal Natural Rights

Throughout the modern evolution of liberal natural rights, the proprietary freedom of individuals has entailed the domination of nonhuman and human nature through science and technologies. Locke's economic theory depicted the individual's relationship to the nonhuman natural environment as one of domination, control, and creation of utility and value through productive labor, use, and exchange; conversely, it depicted the natural terrain prior to human appropriation for productive use as "waste land" or "wilderness" of negligible utility and value.[30] His depiction was congruent with the model of natural science wedded to the pursuit of human technical progress disseminated in the writings of Francis Bacon and René Descartes. Their nontheological and nonteleological scientific method objectified the natural world as an immanent system of efficient causal relationships among elements deprived of meaning and worth apart from their utility for the productive and inventive activity of free human beings, striving to fulfill their proprietary and defensive needs and wants.

Since the eighteenth century, the relentless development of scientific technologies, with their infinitely inventive capabilities, has exponentially increased the ease and the range of human acquisition and use of worldly things, whether natural or artificial. Physical and social-scientific technologies have together conspired to produce the absorption of human interest, energy, and imagination in the activities of acquiring, using, and consuming property. However, the ordering of experimental science to humankind's technological use of "natural resources" runs deeper than its various extrinsic objectives: it is intrinsic to the method of much scientific inquiry and its analytical concepts. To pursue knowledge of natural processes through experimental practices of manipulation and control rather than through inactive observation and contemplation is to pursue knowledge of natural

---

30. STG 5.36–46: 292–300.

relations of force, susceptible of mathematical representation.[31] The "making" or "production" entailed in experimental discovery leads seamlessly to the "making" or "production" of practical and technical application, as otherwise, the natural dynamics experimentally discovered have little interest or value. Modern technologies can harness natural energies to human uses because the experimental method is itself technology (from *techné* and *logos*): that is, a "co-penetration" of making and knowing. Simultaneously, the experimental method is the offspring of mathematical physics which, as a purely theoretical mode of representing, already "pursues and entraps nature as a calculable coherence of forces."[32]

In Hobbes's and Locke's political and economic elaboration of the self-owning and self-disposing subject of rights, it is apparent why the subjugation and devaluation of nonhuman nature goes hand in hand with the subjugation and devaluation of human nature. It is because human nature, conceived as the physical, appetitive, emotional, and cognitive powers and dispositions of individuals, becomes the object of manipulation and control by a calculating rationality that is at once detached from, and instrumental to, the individual proprietary will. For Hobbes and Locke, the calculations of reason generate political devices—the political contract, the order of public laws, the power (Hobbes) or powers (Locke) of law-making, adjudication, and enforcement—to overcome the natural deficiencies of individual actors by constraining and channeling, as well as expressing and facilitating, their proprietary freedom. For both thinkers, these political devices produce an objective unification of diverse, rival individual wills, providing the common framework for the fulfillment by individuals of their private ambitions and passions.

Hobbes's political devices appear to be more coercively manipulative than Locke's in that, unlike Locke, he explicitly aspires to recast political philosophy on

---

31. Hans Jonas's account of modern scientific analysis in *The Phenomenon of Life: Toward a Philosophical Biology* is worthy of lengthy quotation: "Analysis has been the distinctive feature of physical inquiry since the seventeenth century: analysis of *working* nature into its simplest dynamic factors. These factors are framed in such identical quantitative terms as can be entered, combined, and transformed in equations.... Once left to deal with the residual products of this [reduction of nature] or rather, with their measured values, mathematics proceeds to reconstruct from them the complexity of phenomena in a way which can lead beyond the data of the initial experience to facts unobserved, or still to come, or to be brought about." (Evanston: Northwestern University Press, 2001), 200. In his philosophical essay, "Knowing and Making" (1975), George Grant explores the "co-penetration" of "knowing" and "making" in the dominant modern scientific-technological paradigm of knowledge. *The George Grant Reader*, ed. William Christian and Sheila Grant (Toronto: University of Toronto Press, 1998), 407–17.

32. Martin Heidegger, "Die Frage nach der Technik," in *Vorträge und Aufsätze* (Pfullingen: Günther Neske, 1954), 25; "The Question Concerning Technology," in *The Question Concerning Technology and Other Essays*, trans. William Lovitt (New York: Harper and Row, 1977), 21.

the model of mathematical physics, imitating its clear and certain, mathematically formulated laws of force among material objects. Consequently, his acting individuals in the state of nature, devoid of mediating social bonds, are analogous to intersecting vortexes of mobile force, or colliding atoms of uniform mass, requiring channeling by public rules into lanes of noncolliding action. By contrast, the mediating social rationality of Locke's individuals in the state of nature, their common recognition of obligations to respect one another's equal freedom and property rights, renders the political devices to remedy the deficiencies of natural society less arbitrary, coercive, and manipulative. Nevertheless, as Shapiro argues, Locke's theoretical progression from the naturally knowable proprietary freedom and property rights of individuals to rationally and divinely given laws protecting objective (intersubjective) human interests, to the civil securing of these rational givens by the strategy of compact, also conforms to the paradigm of a clear and certain science, "proceeding with mathematical rigour, from self-evident premises via incontrovertible chains of reasoning to apodictic conclusions."[33]

The subsequent development of economic, social, and political inquiry as scientific disciplines with empirical research methods has revealed the persisting legacy of Hobbes's and Locke's political theories to be the endeavor of a calculating and detached human reason to overcome the deficiencies of human nature in the service of the individual's proprietary freedom. Within that endeavor, economic theories have displayed varying degrees of confidence that individual freedom is best advanced by the rational subjection of political society to the intrinsic laws of market processes, combined with political regulation and intervention. Likewise, sociological theories have displayed varying degrees of confidence that individual freedom is best advanced by the discovery and employment of social "facts," "relations," and "laws" to bring social structures and processes into line with rational principles of efficiency, productivity, harmony, and stability. What has prevailed in all the human sciences, however, is rational objectification of the individual and communal life of human beings, including its moral and religious aspects, within a predictive causal system involving the mathematical representation of individual and collective action, which enables the production of desired outcomes through manipulative techniques.

The techniques of manipulation issuing from these sciences are legion, from targeted advertising to create and sustain demand for commodities and services, to managerial strategies for corporate growth and commercial competitive edge, to the money-generating devices of banking, to educational methods designed to increase learning, to psychosocial therapies for preventing and resolving conflicts, to governmental projects and regulations to bring about specific outcomes in any and every societal sphere.

The most pervasive technique in both social intensity and extent is that of the bureaucratic organization and administration of collective undertakings. A century ago, Max Weber definitively summarized its constitutive features as: a fixed, stable

---

33. Shapiro, *The Evolution of Rights*, 123.

jurisdictional area and structure of command; assignment of regular, defined activities to qualified persons; their detailed regulation by explicit rules devised for the achievement of specified, calculable results; and the regular monitoring of performances for their conformity and achievement. Adoption of this universally applicable "technique of techniques" by institutions, organizations, and businesses has encouraged the technical, procedural formulation of practices, and thereby has homogenized and rigidified the activity and relationships of individual practitioners, degrading their moral richness, and depriving practitioners of opportunities to exhibit practical discernment, imagination, subtlety, and versatility.

The outcome, currently attested across society, is individual frustration, alienation, and eventually flight from work. Especially in the public services, with their close political regulation and surveillance, practitioners are exhausted and exasperated by their subjection to excessive, constantly changing, inappropriate and counterproductive procedures, rules and measures of rationality, efficiency, transparency, and justice. Today, a predictable complaint of distressed practitioners within and without the public services is that invasive bureaucratic impositions inhibit their acquisition and use of mature practical wisdom and skills, and do not accommodate the inescapable contingencies, ambiguities, and tensions of their daily occupations. The effect of these impositions is to disrupt and render less fruitful the cooperative pursuit of substantive goods through traditions of common practice.

It is, therefore, lamentable and perplexing that current concern in professional, academic, and journalistic circles with the degrading of individual and common action by bureaucratic and other technologies has resulted in so little practical amelioration, has proved scarcely capable of slowing, not to speak of arresting, the dynamo of technique. This is especially puzzling, as sociological, philosophical, and theological criticism of the totalitarian drive for cultural and practical conformity in the bureaucratic liberal state has had a variegated and often distinguished history from the postwar period to the present.[34] The practical inefficacy of such informed concern may be owing in part to its inadequate penetration of the symbiotic relationship between the growing culture of technical control and the juridical ethos of the liberal rights culture.[35] In turn, this inadequacy may, to an extent, reflect the current aversion to imputing any *intrinsically* anti-liberal dimensions or

---

34. Originally rooted in Durkheimian and Marxist social analysis, influential criticism of the totalitarian, homogenizing project of the liberal bureaucratic state was developed over the postwar decades by social and political philosophers of the Frankfurt School (*Frankfurter Schule*)—notably Theodore Adorno, Max Horkheimer, Herbert Marcuse, and Jürgen Habermas—by the French theologian and philosopher Jacques Ellul, and more recently by Paul Edward Gottfried, *After Liberalism: Mass Democracy in the Managerial State* (Princeton: Princeton University Press, 2001), among others.

35. An admirable exception is Onora O'Neill's analysis of the interconnection of the bureaucratic degradation of work and the political primacy of rights in "The Dark Side of

implications to the hegemonic ethic of egalitarian human rights. So much has the ethic become a warranty of intellectual and moral respectability, not only among the cognoscenti but also among ordinary people! Those who perceive connections between the ethos of egalitarian-rights and excessive modes of social control are inclined to regard such excesses as an incidental hazard rather than an inescapable practical outworking of this pervasive juridical ethic.

For example, anyone teaching in an educational institution recognizes the weary acquiescence among colleagues in the relentless bureaucratic subversion of their proper objectives and activities. Lament and protest as they may,[36] they have been largely ineffectual in retarding the progressive undermining of the proper end of formal education—namely, the disciplined pursuit and communication of wisdom and knowledge—by the exclusive claims of scientific and "research" methods, combined with the administrative requirement of procedural "fairness," and a political agenda of equalizing academic attainment across the designated classes and groupings in society. As with practitioners in other vocational realms, the capitulation of educators to these pressures is depriving them of a shared, robust, coherent understanding of the specific goods and disciplines of their profession.

The Juridical Cultural Trajectory of Liberal Natural Rights

The task now is to provide a fuller account of the symbiotic interaction of the juridical ethos of modern liberal society with the political project of egalitarian rights and pursuit of technological control. Recall that in Locke's political theory the possession and pursuit by individuals of proprietary freedom, which grounds their natural right to private property and drives their technological mastery of the natural world, also grounds their natural right to judge and punish infractions of the natural law, injuries to themselves or to others. Even after individuals have surrendered to the civil community and its delegated government their unprofitable right of judging causes, their proprietary freedom within civil society still consists in their nonsubjection to other wills and to externally imposed obligations to which they have not consented; so Locke's citizen-proprietors retain a strong defensive interest in the routine judgment and punishment of rights violations but now pursue it through public judicial agencies.

Human Rights," *International Affairs* 81, no. 2 (2005): 436–9, building on her BBC Reith Lectures 2002: "A Question of Trust."

36. There has been no dearth of critical analysis of the negative impact of bureaucratizing on higher education from the 1970s onward: for example, Hans Daalder, "Trends and Dangers of Increased Bureaucracy in Higher Education: A View from Below," *International Journal of Institutional Management in Higher Education* 9, no. 1 (1985): 35–43; George Simpson, "Bureaucracy, Standardization, and the Liberal Arts: Evidence of Mass Production in Higher Education," *The Journal of Higher Education* 50, no. 4 (1979): 504–13.

Of course, a political thinker of the late seventeenth century could hardly have countenanced the juridical profile of late modern civil culture: its proliferation of freedom and entitlement rights, the increased appetite of citizens for rights surveillance and litigation, and the key role of the communications media in creating, sustaining, and satisfying the juridical temper of social relations. In liberal democratic societies over the last seventy years, the civil pursuit of maximal and equal emancipation of individuals from external and internal restraints on their proprietary freedom (i.e., on their rightful power of sovereign self-disposal) has produced an unprecedented proliferation of rights. Their promotion in political policy and codification in law has been called forth by sufficiently strong and widespread popular demand for public provision, and the popular demand has, in turn, been driven by scientific-technological advances in overcoming the defects and limitations of human life, combined with the influence of those inherited liberal ideas pervading the discourse of individual rights. Granted that many people have little reflective purchase on the core idea of the individual's proprietary freedom and its associated social, moral, and political ideas, judgments, and attitudes; nevertheless, they constantly absorb elements of this ideological complex from myriad social sources: notably, from formal education in the sciences and the humanities, and from all facets of the public communications media, print and electronic, information and entertainment, professional journalism and informal "chat."

Popular journalism across the communications media has been a key cultural educator in the ideas and ethos of liberal rights: especially, in the idea that citizens should retain a compelling concern with judging violations of their own and others' rights, quite apart from the authoritative public judgment of government. This civic concern or appetite is both stimulated and satisfied by the exorbitant professional investment of journalists in scrutinizing the conduct of public and private individuals, institutions, and enterprises, to expose their moral, social, and political misdemeanors and failures. Too often journalistic scrutiny today exceeds its moral remit of investigating and reporting unjust, incompetent, immoral, and injurious conduct seriously damaging to the common good, to approximate malignant gossip corrosive of public conversation. Intimately connected with this intrusive scrutiny has been the gratuitously inquisitorial character of much journalistic interviewing in the spoken media, supplanting the accurate relaying and educated analysis of newsworthy events. The belligerence of such interviewing suggests that public discussion should be aggressively conducted from positions of maximal distrust, because civil relations are riddled with insurmountable antagonisms. From its skeptical and relativist posture, popular journalism magnifies and celebrates the diverse and conflicting perspectives, judgments, and practices within society as the substance and guarantor of egalitarian freedom. Rather than undertaking, or even commending, the laborious search for rapprochement, it thrives on presenting the (supposedly) irresolvable combat of opposing positions, and similarly, on unmasking reasoned argument and debate as the power play of self-interested parties. Journalism maintains its hold on popular attention in the role of exacting referee of the pugilistic contests absorbing the realm of public intercourse.

The relentless exertions of popular journalism as public inquisitor and referee heavily reinforce the defensive, mistrustful, and judgmental ethos attaching to the ideology of proprietary rights and the pervasive threat of litigation accompanying it. In its dual roles, journalism can foster inflated and misguided popular expectations as to the services which the cadres of trained professionals staffing public and private organizations and enterprises should provide, contributing to the pressures that drive their administrators and employees to bureaucratic strategies of self-protection: to procedural rules of conduct and quantifiable measures of assessment having the universal "transparency" to stand up under inquisitorial examination, whether from journalistic, political, or judicial sources. Lamentably, the tyranny which the combination of popular and political expectations and surveillance may exert over professionals can incite the tyrannous conduct to which professionals are, themselves, prone in practicing their expertise, thereby inhibiting a mutual spirit of deference, modesty, and respect between practitioner and recipient in the provision of services, among other deleterious effects.[37]

Today, in liberal democratic societies, the limitations and restraints (temporal, spatial, moral, civil, and substantial) attaching to the older "representative" forms of popular judgment via the communications media have diminished, with the vast dispersal of popular judgment among countless individuals, broadcasting their approbation and condemnation, their adulation and contempt, directed at every conceivable object, on every conceivable occasion, from a multitude of social media platforms, often with a national or global audience. This largely formless, fluid, disordered, and uncontrolled social conduct of judgment, too often unreasoned and intemperate, if not violent and malevolent, threatens to undermine the indispensable constraints of civil intercourse and governmental practice, inviting a greater suppression of popular judgment by coercive legal, bureaucratic, technical, and ideological means, of which more severe and brutal versions have long been employed in despotic and totalitarian civil and political regimes.

Which Theological Alternative to Modern Liberal Natural Rights?

Christian academics, clergy, and, more generally, thoughtful and educated Christians who recognize the destructive dynamics of modern freedom, as I have presented them, will readily concur in understanding emancipation from bondage to be the conversion of human beings from absorption in their own capacities and productive labor, in projects of self-defense, self-vindication, and self-

---

37. Allen Verhey uncovers this dynamic in the medical context of hospital manager, therapist and patient in "Manager and Therapist as Tragic Heroes: Some Observations of a Theologian at a Psychiatric Hospital," *Studies in Christian Ethics* 21, no. 1 (2008): 7–25.

aggrandizement, in strivings to create and secure themselves through technical domination of human and nonhuman nature; and their conversion to the perfections of the triune God revealed in *his* work of creating, sustaining, justifying, and sanctifying. They will readily conceive emancipation to be the overcoming of the individual's proprietary self-possession by divine possession, self-love by the love of God, fleshly fear by heavenly fear, justification through works of law by justification through the cross and resurrection of Christ, humanly contrived certainty by the divinely bestowed certainty of faith, and self-aggrandizement by the Spirit's sanctifying grace. In short, they will profess emancipation to be God's own gracious work into which he has taken the church's communication of salvation in Jesus Christ.

As servants of this communication, Christians critical of the prevailing rights tradition must confront the issue of whether the concept of universal human rights can be extricated from the theoretical fabric into which it has been woven over four centuries, to be soundly and profitably employed within a biblical theological framework. Lamentably, serious theological and philosophical criticism of this fabric has been relatively sparse within most Christian denominations over the last seventy years, owing in part to the unrivaled moral and political prestige of the postwar documents issued by the United Nations, which brought universal human rights to national and international prominence as a public ideology: chiefly, the Universal Declaration of Human Rights of 1948 and the subsequent International Covenants of 1966 on Economic, Social and Cultural Rights and on Civil and Political Rights.

Although these documents did not employ the term "natural rights," they invoked the concept by indicating in their preambles an intrinsic relationship between "the inherent dignity and... the equal and inalienable rights of all members of the human family." At the same time, the documents rendered this relationship ambiguous by failing to give determinate conceptual content to the term "inherent human dignity" independent of the universal human possession of rights, despite the pronouncement in 1966 of the priority of "dignity" to "rights."[38] It is a historical irony that this failing, apparently necessitated by divergent understandings of human dignity across religious and cultural boundaries, probably facilitated the global spreading of the Western liberal tendency to identify the inherent dignity of human persons with their natural possession of specific rights.

Despite this failing, the following decade saw a spate of enthusiastic Christian theological endorsements of the Universal Declaration across the denominational spectrum, regularly explicating human dignity by drawing on the biblical doctrine of the *imago Dei*: the doctrine that mankind was originally created in the image of God, and that fallen humanity, corrupted by sin, has been, is being, and will be restored to God's image in Jesus Christ. It is significant that these theological

---

38. The Preamble to the International Covenant on Civil and Political Rights recognizes that the rights postulated by the Universal Declaration "derive from the inherent dignity of the human person."

explications, however differently nuanced, concurred in emphasizing relations of humankind and of individual persons to the triune God, initiated and sustained by God's own action. Equally striking was their apparent consensus about the unproblematic character of moving from a relational theological understanding of human dignity to the concept of inherent, "equal and unalienable" human rights. Out of ignorance or out of apologetic considerations, their authors assumed rights to express adequately the moral attributes of humanity undergirding political and legal justice and did not address critically the powerful liberal tradition of natural rights.[39] Fortunately, a steady stream of historical scholarship in rights theory and practice has progressively discredited the expression of such complacent assumptions by Christian moral and political thinkers.

Having said this, the Roman Catholic magisterial tradition of "social teaching" has distinguished itself in our postwar era of naive rights enthusiasm by its relative theological astuteness, owing largely to Pope Leo XIII's famous encyclical, *Rerum Novarum* (1891), which put its stamp on the subsequent magisterial integration of universal human rights into Catholic social and political thought.[40] While appealing principally to the thought of Thomas Aquinas, Leo's encyclical tapped into late medieval and early modern developments of the theory and practice of rights in scholastic theology and in civil and ecclesiastical corporation law. Forty years after *Rerum Novarum*, Pope Pius XI built more extensively on the civic corporative "rights" tradition. Post 1945 Catholic social teaching has aligned itself more closely, but not uncritically, with the majoritarian liberal democratic, pluralistic rights tradition, under the influence of such "modern" Thomists as Etienne Gilson and Jacques Maritain.

Selective mining of this legacy has enabled Roman Catholic social teaching to present more conservative accounts of natural rights, integrated into the longer canonist and scholastic theological tradition of law, predominantly around a Thomist/Aristotelian nexus.[41] Similarly, Protestant thinkers have uncovered in late- and post-Reformation Anglican or Reformed scholasticism and covenantalism (e.g., in the thought of Theodore Beza, Richard Hooker, and Johannes Althusius)

---

39. See Joan Lockwood O'Donovan, "Historical Prolegomena to a Theological Review of 'Human Rights,'" *Studies in Christian Ethics* 9, no. 2 (1996): 53 and n. 2.

40. Responding simultaneously to two aspects of the contemporary malaise, the industrial degradation of the laboring class in a laissez-faire environment and the seductive appeal for the downtrodden of atheistic socialism, Pope Leo's Catholic social vision and campaign of action placed in the foreground the right of the laborer (as well as the entrepreneur) to property, and the right of the family to fulfill its natural purpose of mutual love and provision.

41. For a comprehensive documentary collection of modern Catholic social teaching, David J. O'Brian and Thomas A. Shannon, eds., *Catholic Social Teaching: The Documentary Heritage*, 2nd edn. (Maryknoll: Orbis Books, 1992). For an interpretative presentation of the tradition, David Hollenbach, *Claims in Conflict: Retrieving and Renewing the Catholic Human Rights Tradition* (New York: Paulist Press International, 1999).

comparably Orthodox Christian frameworks for integrating natural rights,[42] or, like Nigel Biggar, have integrated conditional legal rights within a Christian moral right (law) matrix. Among the conceptual relationships in their sources which these contemporary interpretations of rights seek to conserve are: the subordination of rights to obligations, of subjective right to objective right, of natural right(s) and natural law to the totality of God's law revealed in the Scriptures, of individual freedom to communal bonds and authority, and of human nature to divine grace.

At the same time, the last fifty years of historical scholarship has given us greater appreciation of how heavily dependent the (preponderantly) Protestant framers of modern liberal rights theories were on premodern and protomodern juristic and scholastic developments. Better knowledge of the theoretical and practical trajectories of the earlier rights traditions has brought into clearer view the continuities with their modern sequel. These continuities substantially advance our discernment of resemblances between the modern political ethos and ethic and the late scholastic ethos and ethic. They provide fresh historical and theological grounds for questioning whether even the most admirable contemporary theological handling of subjective rights can wholly rescue the Christian humanist promise of the Western political tradition of rights from the *débâcle* of unbounded freedom, agonistic social relations, institutional legalism, and technological manipulation. They sharpen the suspicion that to move from objective human obligations to subjective human rights is to cross a deep theological fissure and end up on an unavoidably slippery theoretical and practical slope. The following chapter, therefore, has the two objectives of clarifying the theoretical continuities of the earlier rights traditions with their modern sequel and of indicating the theological alternatives to these earlier traditions furnished by English Reformation public theology.

---

42. For example, Alexander S. Rosenthal, *Crown Under Law: Richard Hooker, John Locke and the Ascent of Modern Constitutionalism* (Langham: Lexington Books, 2008); John Witte, Jr., *The Reformation of Rights: Religion and Human Rights in Early Modern Calvinism* (Cambridge: Cambridge University Press, 2008).

Chapter 4

CONTINUITIES OF THE PREMODERN AND MODERN NATURAL RIGHTS TRADITIONS

In order to display the theoretical continuities between natural rights prior to 1600 and after 1600 and to show what modern liberal formulations owe to the incremental developments of the earlier period, this chapter will treat these earlier developments in historical sequence.

Canonist Construction of Subjective Natural Right and Permissive Natural Right

Canon law glossators in the twelfth century introduced a novel use of the term "natural right" (*ius naturale*) to denote a rational moral power or capacity universally ascribable to individual subjects as moral actors. This novel subjective sense of *ius naturale* was in addition to, and not in replacement of the term's long-standing "objective" use to denote the objectively right order or relationship among individuals and things established by God's command or "law" (*ius, lex*) in creation. At the same time, canonists and theologians distinguished within the objective sense a "permissive" natural right, a divinely ordained ground or sphere of nonobligated moral choice, so enlarging the scope of human freedom.

The paradigmatic canonist case of permissive natural right was the power of the human community to "derogate" from the original order of God's good creation by introducing the institutions of property and political jurisdiction. This licit or permitted derogation from the natural order had the effect of challenging the sharp distinction made in the patristic and early medieval tradition between the law of nature (*ius naturale*) which ordered created human community, and the law of peoples (*ius gentium*) and of civil polities (*ius civile*) which ordered fallen human community.[1] To gauge the innovative character of the Decretist formulations, it

---

1. My study, among many, is indebted to Brian Tierney's argument in *The Idea of Natural Rights: Studies on Natural Rights, Natural Law and Church Law 1150–1625* and elsewhere for locating an early and decisive impetus for the Western development of natural rights theory in the work of twelfth-century canonists. Tierney draws on the canonist glosses,

is necessary to sketch the relevant theoretical parameters in Roman law and in patristic and early medieval theology.

Contemporary scholars broadly agree that the Roman legal tradition, from its classical period in the first two centuries to Justinian's sixth-century corpus, presents more than an occasional use, but not a systematic or paradigmatic use of the term *ius* as a right ascribed to individual subjects, such that they may be said to "have a right" (*ius habere*). The predominant uses of the term are objective, denoting an objectively right order or relationship among individuals and things, or human acts conforming to such an order, or the articulation of objective order in law (*lex*), whether natural, divine, or imperial.

Of import for the proprietary dimension of subjective right, classical jurists sometimes distinguished between having *dominium* ("lordship") and having a "right in" something. *Ius* they conceived as a *res incorporalis* ("immaterial thing") constituted by a legal relation between parties, while *dominium* was a proprietary power over objects to use and enjoy them without legal limitation.[2] However, the *dominium* of the Roman citizen/subject, although retaining its practical aspect of unrestricted disposal, was increasingly conceived as a *ius* in relation to the *dominium* of the emperor.[3] Moreover, Roman law produced many juxtapositions or convergences of right and property, as in the right to own, lease, possess, or use property, or "to be free from interference or invasion of one's property."[4] Roman law also recognized personal and public subjective rights and liberties attaching to specific social positions.[5] But the common thread running through all these types of subjective right is that they were inherent in and inseparable from the social, political, and legal order of the Roman Empire.

---

commentaries, and *summae* on Gratian of Bologna's compilation of ecclesiastical law commonly called the *Decretum* (c. 1140), and highlights the Decretists' debt to the study of Roman law texts in the *Corpus Iuris Civilis*, and to the Roman juristic concepts, principles, and rules contained in Gratian's canonical sources.

2. See *Inst.* 2.2: *Institutiones Justiniani*, ed. Paul Krueger, in *Corpus Iuris Civilis*, 3 vols, ed. Theodore Mommsen and Paul Krueger (Berlin: Berolini apud Weidmannos, 1872–95), 1:13. Ulpian at *Dig.* 7.6.5: *The Digest of Justinian*, ed. Theodore Mommsen with Paul Krueger, trans. Alan Watson, 4 vols (Philadelphia: University of Pennsylvania Press, 2011), I:241.

3. This process, traced by E. Levy in *West Roman Vulgar Law: The Law of Property* (1951), is summarized by Richard Tuck, *Natural Rights Theories: Their Origin and Development* (Cambridge: Cambridge University Press, 1979), 10–12.

4. John Witte, Jr., *God's Joust, God's Justice: Law and Religion in the Western Tradition* (Grand Rapids: Eerdmans, 2006), 34.

5. Ibid. For example, rights of patrons and guardians, of fathers over children, of public officials, the specific liberty of married women, of free persons, of slaves, surveyed in Charles Donahue, Jr., "*Ius* in Roman Law," in *Christianity and Human Rights: An Introduction*, ed. John Witte, Jr. and Frank S. Alexander (Cambridge: Cambridge University Press, 2010), 64–80.

The *iura* and *dominia* (rights and lordships) of Roman law were not categorically conceived as universal or established by nature or God, although any or all could occasionally be construed as embodying the universal, natural order of justice and right. Indeed, the speculative strand of Roman jurisprudence that most appealed to patristic theologians contrasted the *ius naturale* as the original practices of human community marked by the freedom and equality of individuals, and the *ius gentium* as the practices and institutions of existing societies: chiefly, waging wars (*bella*), taking and repatriating captives (*captivites*), enslavement and manumission of slaves (*servitudes*); separate property holdings (*dominia distincta*), transactions of purchase and sale (*emptiones, venditiones*); and political communities (*civitates*), magistrates, and written laws (*leges scribi*).[6] According to this strand of juristic speculation, all *iura* of the Roman legal order determining inequalities among persons would belong to *ius gentium* and *ius civile*, not to *ius naturale*.

In favoring this strand, the Church Fathers paid little heed to three Roman juristic alternatives: identifying the *ius naturale* with the instinctual inclinations to self-preservation, sexual intercourse, and propagation common to all animals;[7] identifying it with the *ius gentium* as taught by natural reason and instinct, and coeval with human society;[8] and assigning to the *ius naturale* the inception of property from the occupation or capture of what originally belonged to no one.[9] Rather, guided chiefly by the depictions of political subjection and worldly wealth in the Gospels and Epistles, reinforced by Roman Stoic ideas, patristic theologians assimilated the juristic disjunction between *ius naturale* and *ius gentium* to the biblical disjunction between the original ordering of creaturely relations and their subsequent ordering in the disrupted state of sin. They emphasized the equal moral vocation and freedom of created human beings subject to God's laws, their equality as objects of God's redeeming love in Christ, and the unnaturalness of the universal modes of human subjection in sinful society. The prevailing theological perspective, magisterially consolidated by Augustine of Hippo, justified all forms of coercive rule, public and private, as human disciplines of judgment and punishment necessitated by the corruptions of human nature: disciplines at once

---

6. For an extensively documented survey of the relevant writings of the third-century jurists, Tryphoninus, Florentinus, and Ulpian (e.g., at *Dig.* 12.6.64; 1.5.4; 1.1.1-4; 1.17.32), the early fourth-century jurist, Hermogenianus (at *Dig.* 1.1.5), and the sixth-century authors of Justinian's *Institutes* (e.g., *Inst.* 1.1.4; 1.2; 1.2.2; 1.2.11; 1.3.2), R. W. and A. J. Carlyle, *A History of Mediaeval Political Theory in the West*, 5th impression, 6 vols, Vol. 1: A. J. Carlyle, *The Second Century to the Ninth* (Edinburgh and London: William Blackwood, 1962), 33–79.

7. Ulpian's designation at *Dig.* 1.1.3: Watson, 1:1.

8. Gaius at *Dig.* 1.1.9: Watson, 1:1; Gaius at 41.1.1: Watson, 4:1

9. Paulus, quoting Labeo and Nerva Filius, *Dig.* 41.2.1: Watson, 4:16; Neratius, *Dig.* 41.1.14,1: Watson, 4:6.

expressive of God's wrathful judgment on sin and of his merciful will to preserve the goods of human society against sin's destructive forces.[10]

In addition, patristic theologians almost unanimously viewed inequalities of wealth as belonging to the postlapsarian condition, being the product of human vice, and the legal forms of property as serving a merely remedial purpose. Influenced principally by the New Testament's requirement of generous, self-sacrificial giving to the needy neighbor, and warnings against covetousness and greed, as well as by the pattern of common sharing of material goods in the apostolic church,[11] the Fathers and their successors regarded the institution of property as deviating from the "natural" community of possession and use of the earth and its fruits to fulfill common human needs.[12] Their paradigm of common use was the sharing of all creatures in God's indivisible bounty of air, sun, rain, sea, and the seasons—goods created as *koinia*, unable to be privately appropriated and possessed.[13] To this paradigm, the common use of divisible goods should approximate as closely as was practicable.

This original use, restored in Christ, was more perfectly approximated by the communal ownership and distribution of goods in the church's clerical and monastic estates but also in the donation of superfluous property by all the faithful to support the poor. For some theologians, support of the needy was a matter of divine justice in the distribution of the earth's abundance for the sustenance of all; conversely, the accumulation of wealth for private use amounted to robbing the needy of what was theirs by divine and natural right.[14] So Augustine opposed the human law of property that secured to owners a private, exclusive, and unrighteous use of things, to the divine law that awarded all things to the "righteous" who would use them righteously.[15]

Although aware of ambiguities in some of their legal sources, medieval theologians and canonists consistently followed the patristic mainstream in defining the *ius naturale* as the immutable divine right (law) that ordered rational humanity from its creation and was revealed to sinful humankind in the

---

10. Noteworthy in the case of slavery, however, was its progressive legal reforming under Christian emperors and the moral pressures for manumission.

11. Acts 2:44; 4:32-7.

12. For the adherence of early Paris-linked theologians to this position, Odd Langholm, *Economics in the Medieval Schools: Wealth, Exchange Value, Money and Usury according to the Paris Theological Tradition, 1200-1350* (Leiden: Brill, 1992).

13. This paradigm was widely transmitted through such influential passages as: Clement of Alexandria, *Paidagogus* 2.12; Basil of Caesarea, *Homilia in Destruam* 7; Ambrosiaster, *Comm. in 2 Cor.* 9.9.

14. Clement of Alexandria, *Quis dives* 31; Basil, *Homilia in Destruam* 7; Ambrose, *De Nabuthae* 3.11; *De officiis* 1.28; *Exp. de Psa cxviii* 8.22; Ambrosiaster, *Comm. in 2 Cor.* 9:9; Chrysostom, *De Lazaro* 2.4; Augustine, *In Psa cxlvii* 12; Gregory Magnus, *Regula pastoralis* 3.21.

15. Augustine, *Ep.* 153.26; *Tract in Ioh ev.* 6.25.

Decalogue and Christ's injunctions.[16] Nevertheless, the elaboration by Decretists of subjective *ius naturale* and permissive *ius naturale* indicated a departure from the patristic theological disjunction between the moral life of created and sinful human community.

As Tierney has documented, influential Decretists of the twelfth century defined *ius naturale* as a moral force or propulsion (*vis*) in the human soul, a power (*potentia*) of the moral actor, and a capacity (*habilitas*) for rational moral discernment, commonly designated as "free will" (*liberum arbitrium*).[17] The greatest Decretist, Huguccio (*c.* 1190), went so far as to render the subjective sense of *ius naturale* as its primary and proper sense, and the Golden Rule as derivative from it.[18] Tierney sets these conceptual novelties in the context of a flowering of interest in the individual, exemplified by the growing canonist concern with personal intention and will.[19] The shift to the ethical subject which he depicts may also be understood, however, as a shift away from the objective moral field in which the subject acts, from the objective justice of the concrete moral action, and from the transcending claim of divinely revealed precepts and examples delineating the moral field.

Rufinus in his *Summa Decretorum* (1157-9) advanced an influential division of the objective content of *ius naturale* into commandments, prohibitions, and demonstrations,[20] proposing that human customary and written law may make "additions" of an elaborating and concretizing kind to the commandments and prohibitions,[21] but may not derogate (i.e., subtract or detract) from them. Human law may, however, derogate from the demonstrations which nature "simply shows to be good" or "convenient," rather than obligatory. Locating among the demonstrations the natural right of equal human freedom and common human possession and use of the world's goods, Rufinus argued that the *ius gentium* and *ius civile* may derogate from these by instituting such practices as the subjugations

---

16. Civil law Glossators displayed more inconsistency than their canonist contemporaries in assigning principles and practices to *ius naturale* or *ius gentium* and were more inclined to include property within the *ius naturale* and to justify this by appeal to the Decalogue's prohibition of stealing.

17. Tierney cites Rufinus, Sicardus, Ricardus Anglicus and Huguccio, among others. *The Idea of Natural Rights*, 61-5. Hereafter *INR*.

18. Huguccio, *Summa decretorum*, MS. Admont 7, fol. 2rb (Introduction), cited in *INR*, 64.

19. See Harold J. Berman's discussion of the canon law of marriage and of contract in *Law and Revolution: The Formation of the Western Legal Tradition* (Cambridge, MA: Harvard University Press, 1983), 226-30, 245-50.

20. D. 1 (*On Gratian's Introduction to* D. 1 c. 1.) Translation from *Die Summa Decretorum des Magister Rufinus*, ed. H. Singer (Paderborn: Schöningh, 1902) in *From Irenaeus to Grotius: A Sourcebook in Christian Political Thought*, ed. and trans. Oliver O'Donovan and Joan Lockwood O'Donovan (Grand Rapids: Eerdmans, 1999), 300-1. Hereafter *IG*.

21. Ibid. For example, human law may elaborate the natural law of male-female sexual union into a ceremonial and legal code of marriage.

and enslavements of war, civil rule, and property. Although inseparable from the sinful propensities of fallen humanity, these practices are, for Rufinus, disciplines of restraint that serve and support the natural order, and so virtually constitute the social modes of natural right in existing human communities.

The demonstrations of Rufinus were ambiguous in a consequential way. Tierney interprets the category as a formulation of permissive natural right, positing a space of permitted human action, neither required nor proscribed, and so, of unfettered human choice. In doing so, he does not observe that Rufinus, in pursuing his argument, avoids this step toward a liberal freedom of indifference by affirming the moral necessity in sinful human society of the institutions established by customary and statutory laws, their indispensability to individual and collective obedience to the commandments and prohibitions of the natural law as "revealed in the Mosaic law" and "perfected by the Gospel." He thereby implies that "equal human freedom" and "common possession" are not divinely permitted social options for sinful human community.[22]

Later Bolognese glossators, however, constructed from the category of demonstrations a more expansive concept of permissive natural right, transparently on the path of liberal freedom. According to one English glossator:[23]

> In a second sense, natural law is used to mean licit and approved, neither prescribed nor prohibited by the Lord or by any statute, which is also called *fas* as, for example to reclaim or not to reclaim one's own, to eat or not to eat, to put away or not to put away one's unfaithful wife who wants to continue cohabiting . . . wherefore upon the Apostle's words "All things are licit for me" Ambrose comments "by the law of nature." (My translation)

As Tierney astutely notes, the glossator converts the apostle Paul's teaching on Christian freedom from Jewish ceremonial precepts into a general doctrine of permissive natural liberty.[24] Indeed, the passage indicates how complex theological tensions between divine and human law, between divine command and concession, may attract a liberal resolution involving the concept of permissive law.

Building on Rufinus, Huguccio offered a further route to harmonizing the *ius naturale* with the *ius gentium* and *civile*. He argued that the demonstration in the natural law of "common possession of all things" did not exclude, but rather permitted the alternative of "private property," and, moreover, he construed the demonstration as the permanent, unchanging rational judgment that in time of necessity, goods should be shared with the needy.[25] This route preserved the patristic

---

22. *IG*, 301.

23. S. Kuttner, *Repertorium der Kanonistik, 1140–1234* (Vatican City: Biblioteca apostolica vaticana, 1937), 202; cited in *INR*, 67.

24. *INR*, 68.

25. *Summa ad* D.1 c. 7, MS Admont 7, fol. 2va; cited in *INR*, 72 and also in Brian Tierney, *Liberty and Law: The Idea of Permissive Natural Law, 1100–1800* (Catholic University of America Press, 2014), 26–7.

understanding of common possession as an abiding moral feature of human society by inserting common possession into the broader moral-juridical structure of private property, at the cost of relaxing the patristic opposition of the created and the fallen moral orders. His harmonization would gain enduring prominence in the next century with Thomas Aquinas's interpretation of *communitas rerum* as the enduring moral requirement that owners manage their property for the benefit of others as well as for themselves, sharing their possessions in cases of necessity.[26] Significantly, Thomas conceived the human acquisition and ownership of things as merely a rational *addition* to natural right and not a *detraction* from it, as in Rufinus.[27]

Later canonists further closed the distance between natural right and human law by recasting the requirement of common possession into the moral right of an indigent in extreme need to take and use the superfluous property of the affluent without permission, or alternatively, to bring before an episcopal judge a legal claim for alms against a wealthy proprietor who unreasonably, intransigently refused them.[28] This speedy conversion of a natural subjective right into an available legal action evidences the juridical tendency of the concept of subjective right and the interests of positive law propelling its historical evolution.

Juridical Ecclesiology: Imperial Papalism and Ecclesiastical Corporatism

These cumulative initiatives in Decretist jurisprudence, tending to undermine inherited tensions between natural, human, and divine (revealed) right and law, were interconnected with two far-reaching ecclesiological developments over the medieval period: those of Roman imperial papalism and of ecclesiastical corporatism. Conceptually distinct but temporally interwoven, both developments extended the church's understanding of itself as a juridical and proprietary body. The foundations of Roman imperial papalism lay in the vast reforming project of Pope Gregory VII (Hildebrand, 1030–85) to emancipate the clerical estate from its corrupting secular ties to feudal tenure, marital responsibilities, concubinage, and simoniacal practices, under the Ottonian and Salian imperial dynasties, and, more comprehensively, to renew the integrity of Christian society through subjecting lay rule to clerical rule, and both to papal supremacy. The theological lynchpin of Hildebrand's reform was a juristic elaboration of the pope's primacy as successor to Peter's vicariate from Christ, which extended the church's power of "binding" and "loosing" beyond the realms of penance and purgatory to external government. The "power of the keys," which in earlier times had designated the general clerical authority of convicting sinners and declaring absolution, or at most, the apostolic authority of the whole episcopate, was increasingly reserved for the pope's sovereign rule over the Christian world. Over several centuries, canon lawyers

---

26. *Summa Theologiae* 2.2ae.66.2. Hereafter abbreviated *ST*.
27. *ST* 1.2ae.94.5 ad 3; 2.2ae.66.2 ad 1.
28. See *INR*, 73–4.

garnered from the *Corpus Iuris Civilis* of Justinian and its commentaries, and from the pseudo-Isidorean False Decretals, the images, allegories, principles, and concepts for explicating the papal *imperium* as universal in Christendom, legally unbounded, juridically unimpeachable, and inerrant.[29] The concept of "fulness of power" (*plenitudo potestatis*)[30] provided a catalyst for the systematic theoretical elaborations of the modes of the pope's exclusive lordship (*dominium*) from Christ in both proprietary and jurisdictional aspects. The early fourteenth-century apologists for Pope Boniface VIII in his notorious quarrels with King Philip IV of France (notably, Ptolemy of Lucca, Augustinus Triumphus, Giles of Rome, and James of Viterbo) construed all just or licit rule and ownership as deriving from the universal agency of Christ's earthly vicar, who exercised sovereign spiritual and temporal judgment over rulers and as well, universal and immediate lordship over temporal goods, to tithe and to tax proprietors.[31]

Papalist ecclesiology construed the universal society of the church as, at once, a mystical body (*corpus mysticum*) and a political body (*corpus politicum*): a spiritual unity after the pattern of its heavenly head and a political-legal hierarchy anchored in papal sovereignty. The role of its clerical government was to translate the church's divine-human essence through the agency of law into visible institutional structures: liturgical, doctrinal, disciplinary, administrative, and proprietary. But canon law also invested the visible church or its parts with a distinct form of unity, that of the corporation (*universitas*), with the range of proprietary and political rights established for corporations in Roman civil law.[32] Below papal

---

29. Roman law doctrines of imperial sovereignty—that what the emperor wills has the force of law (*Dig.* I.4.1; cf. *Inst.* I.2.6), that he is unbounded by laws (*legibus solutus, Dig.* I.3.31) and is the plenary legislator—were taken over for the pope and reinforced by a spate of papal legislation and new collections of canonical tradition. Pressed into service were the assertions in Pseudo-Isidore concerning the freedom of legal appeal to Rome, the pope's exclusive authority to judge bishops, and the immunity of the Roman see from judgment. A declaration of Rome's original possession of the norm of the apostolic faith became a touchstone of the doctrine of papal inerrancy. For a short summary, I. S. Robinson, "Church and Papacy," in *The Cambridge History of Medieval Political Thought c. 350–c. 1450*, ed. J. H. Burns (Cambridge: Cambridge University Press, 1988), 282–8.

30. The concept was a pseudo-Isidorean construction from a letter of Pope Leo I (460–1) in which Leo had told a papal legate that he was called to a share of ecclesiastical responsibilities (*in partem sollicitudinis*) but not to the "fullness of power" (*Ep.* 14.1). In the *False Decretals* Leo's phrases were applied generically to distinguish episcopal and papal authority (e.g., Ps.-Vigilius, *Ep.* 7, cited by Robinson in Burns, *History*, 282.

31. See, for example, *Giles of Rome on Ecclesiastical Power: The De ecclesiastica potestate of Aegidius Romanus*, trans. R. W. Dyson (Suffolk: Woodbridge, 1986). Parts 1, 2, 3 are excerpted in *IG*, 365–78.

32. For the legal structure of the medieval ecclesiastical corporation, Brian Tierney, *Foundations of the Conciliar Theory: The Contribution of the Medieval Canonists from Gratian to the Great Schism* (Cambridge: Cambridge University Press, 1955), 106–32.

and curial government, the medieval church presented a hierarchy of relatively self-governing, property-owning corporations formed at various administrative levels (congregational, parochial, diocesan, archdiocesan, etc.) and including a variety of establishments (e.g., monastic houses, confraternities, universities, and hospitals). Like its secular counterpart, an ecclesiastical corporation comprised a collective "fictive" subject vested with legal rights and obligations, as were its members. Typically, it had a head (*syndic, rector, tutor*) elected by the whole body (*universitas*), who might also be its representative at law (*proctor*) authorized to act for it. Certain prerogatives such as corporate rule-making belonged to the assembled members, with or without their head. Each corporation was the legal owner of property held for specific religious and charitable purposes and administered by its head.

Until the late thirteenth or early fourteenth century, the occasional Decretist attributions of corporative rights to the universal church were frequently absorbed by the Decretalists[33] into the spiritual and temporal plenitude of papal headship. Only the concerted assault on papal sovereignty mounted by royal and imperial publicists such as John of Paris, Marsilius of Padua, and William of Ockham, consistently presented the political and proprietary rights of the entire corporation of the faithful, clerical, and lay, as limiting the pope's plenary jurisdiction.

The canonist articulation of the ecclesial *corpus mysticum* in terms of the complex political-legal apparatus of an institutional hierarchy in which divine and positive human right mingled, politicized the church's spiritual communion, and spiritualized her political, proprietary order. This relatively seamless unification of political apparatus and spiritual communion, natural and divine right, held attraction for contemporary civil polities[34] and would contribute significantly to the development of constitutionalism in both secular urban republicanism and conciliar ecclesiology.

While structures of corporative rights could be legally and theoretically integrated into a monarchical polity, their political articulation inevitably introduced a degree of individualistic voluntarism, as jurisdiction was redistributed to the association of members as well as to its head. Moreover, the individual members of medieval corporations were frequently the origin, as well as the legal subjects, of rights and obligations, in that they regularly formed corporations for a variety of often overlapping economic, political, social, and devotional purposes by voluntarily swearing oaths, signing contracts, and subscribing to charters. The formation throughout Western Europe of largely independent urban polities out of existing corporate structures such as craft, mercantile, professional, and burgher

---

33. The Decretalists were canonist compilers and glossators of the papal Decretals.

34. For example, the regular presentation of the French kingdom as a *corpus mysticum* from the thirteenth century onward lent an exalted moral and religious aura to the national realm, which abetted Philip the Fair and his successors in their Gallicanizing of the church. For discussion of the civil *corpus mysticum*, E. H. Kantorowicz, *The King's Two Bodies: A Study in Medieval Political Theology* (Princeton: Princeton University Press, 1957), 207–72.

guilds produced relatively participatory, less hierarchical, and more culturally homogenous social and political bodies, with egalitarian and populist features.[35]

Formative Rights Theories: Marsilius and Ockham

The formulations of Marsilius of Padua and William of Ockham were significant for the historical course of subjective rights theory, owing to their unique employment of juristic and Aristotelian concepts to defend, on the one hand, the Franciscan order's theological discipline of poverty, and on the other, the political right of secular and ecclesiastical rulers and their subjects, against the assaults of papal imperialism. In relating subjective right to divine and human law and justice, these different thinkers revived the tensions in patristic moral, ecclesiological, and political thought which high papalist theology had collapsed, but not without theological damage to the earlier tradition.

Natural and Evangelical Nonproprietary Right

For the Franciscans, the most perfect discipleship bequeathed by their founder was participation in the earthly sufferings and destitution borne by Christ and enjoined on his disciples during their missionary journeys, when they were to seek and use only the barest necessities, to give away all superfluous goods, and to depend for their daily sustenance on the free alms of believers.[36] As the order grew numerically and its expanding ministries became more specialized, it came to define the discipline of poverty as requiring both a *minimal use* of material goods (*usus pauper*) and *renunciation of positive legal right* in these goods, so that the brothers' ministries were sustained by the property of others made available for their use.[37]

The ethic of legal poverty, as expounded by Bonaventure,[38] was indebted to Augustine's understanding of the intimate relationship between covetousness and pride in disordered human love. The soul's excessive love of other beings and things, its consuming passion to possess them, is always for the sake of aggrandizing its

---

35. Berman, *Law and Revolution*, 333-404; Anthony Black, *Guilds and Civil Society in European Political Thought from the Twelfth Century to the Present* (Ithaca: Cornell University Press, 1984), 49, 66.

36. Mk 6:7-13; Lk. 9:1-6. For a fuller account of the Franciscan theology of poverty see Joan Lockwood O'Donovan, "Christian Platonism and Non-proprietary Community," in Oliver O'Donovan and Joan Lockwood O'Donovan, *Bonds of Imperfection: Christian Politics Past and Present* (Grand Rapids: Eerdmans, 2003), 73-96.

37. Rome licensed the brotherhood's steady accumulation of material resources through a machinery for regular economic acquisition and alienation that did not involve the friars directly as legal agents.

38. *Apologia Pauperum*, *Opera Omnia* 8 (Florence: Quaracchi, 1898), 233-330.

own powers, which it seeks to possess privately, as belonging to itself rather than to their divine source and owner.[39] Bonaventure understood that proprietary right, by creating the possibility of defending a claim to earthly goods for oneself and against one's neighbor, exposed legal proprietors to a private, possessive attachment to their belongings. In voluntarily surrendering legal possession and use of goods, the brothers removed themselves from the temptation to covetousness and, above all, bore efficacious witness that "apostolic wayfarers" do not possess themselves and their powers, but are possessed by Christ, receiving from him immediately all the good that they are, have, and do, and receiving the truth, beauty, and goodness of the world as his gift. Bonaventure portrayed the "way" of apostolic dispossession as recovering the original use of the earth's bounty belonging to Adamic community.

The failure of Bonaventure's endeavor to avert growing antipathy between the Franciscan and papalist ecclesiologies and underlying Christologies climaxed in Pope John XXII's assault on the Franciscan discipline in a series of bulls during the 1320s repudiating the brothers' postulation of a natural and divine right of using earthly goods apart from positive legal right.[40] In a theological tour de force, John XXII interpreted Adam's lordship (*dominium*) over creation as an individual proprietorship, that is, exclusive administration and use of temporal goods. With the creation of Eve, this became common proprietorship; but after the Fall, individual proprietorship was reinstituted in a succession of divine property-grants, which, preceding the advent of the kings, demonstrated the continuing origin of property right in divine rather than human law.[41] Therefore, Christ's practice of "perfect poverty" was compatible with his having universal proprietary lordship (*dominium*) of temporal things, *as man and as God*, and even with his defending his property at law, as his apostles and disciples could likewise do.[42]

Marsilius and Ockham's refutations moved onto their adversary's theoretical ground by introducing the concept of subjective right, absent in earlier Franciscan defenses of the order's discipline. The formal concept of subjective right provided a moral-juridical counter to John XXII's controlling concept of ownership or full property right. Thus, Marsilius defined subjective right as "every controlled human act (*actum*), power (*potestas*) or acquired habit (*habitus*)" in conformity

---

39. Oliver O'Donovan discusses this relationship in *The Problem of Self-Love in St. Augustine* (New Haven: Yale University Press, 1980), 95–103.

40. *Ad conditorum* (1323), *Extravagantes D. Ioannis Papae XXII* in *Corpus Iuris Canonici* 2, ed. E. Friedberg (Leipzig, 1879): *Extrav.* 14.3, cols. 1225–9.

41. *Quia vir reprobus* (1329) quoted in Ockham, *Opus nonaginta dierum* (*Work of Ninety Days*), 26–8, 88–9, in *Guillelmi de Ockham Opera Politica*, 1–2, ed. H. S. Offler (Manchester: Manchester University Press, 1963); translation of 26–8, 88 in *William of Ockham: A Letter to the Friars Minor and Other Writings*, ed. Arthur Stephen McGrade and John Kilcullen, trans. John Kilcullen (Cambridge: Cambridge University Press, 1995).

42. *Quia vir reprobus*, 93–6, 115, 119. These arguments expanded on John XXII's declarations in his 1323 bull, *Cum inter nonnullos*.

with law;⁴³ and Ockham presented subjective right as the power (*potestas*) of an individual to perform a lawful act (or more frequently, as a "lawful" or "licit" power to act). While the two concurred that the subjective sense of *ius* was secondary and derivative from the sense of obligatory law,⁴⁴ they differed markedly in their interpretation of "law," Ockham favoring a rationalist and Marsilius a voluntarist conception. When referring to natural law or divine law (comprehending natural law), Ockham preferred to designate law as human "right reason" that is either "purely natural" or "taken from things revealed to us by God" in the Scriptures.⁴⁵ By contrast, Marsilius consistently presented law in its "proper" sense as the command of a human or divine lawgiver concerning what is just or unjust, beneficial or harmful, coercive over those who transgress it, and operating through punishment or reward.⁴⁶ In addition, he reiterated the voluntarist juristic concept of permissive law,⁴⁷ of which Ockham also availed himself.

Ockham's defense of Franciscan poverty followed the theoretical progression of John XXII's attack in *Quia vir reprobus*, moving from natural *dominium* to Christological, apostolic, and finally papal *dominium*. Against the pope's interpretation of Adam's lordship as exclusive ownership, Ockham interpreted it as the "common" power⁴⁸ of rationally ruling (*regendi*) and managing (*gubernandi*) the nonhuman creation, using the earth's resources for human sustenance and comfort, and in other "permissible" ways.⁴⁹ In line with the patristic vision, Adamic society, even before its fuller realization in the creation of Eve, was a community of sharing in the earth's abundance according to rational need, uninhibited by claims of mine and thine. Such sharing was not incompatible with regular or continuous management and use of things by individuals, alone or together, *without excluding claims*. Following his Franciscan predecessors, Ockham contrasted Adamic

---

43. *Defensor pacis*, Discourse Two 12.10: trans. Alan Gewirth (Toronto: Medieval Academy of America, 1980), 191. Hereafter *DP*.

44. The "power" may be in conformity with positive divine or human law (custom, pact or ordinance), or with natural right or "right reason." *Opus nonaginta dierum*, 2, 65. Hereafter *OND*: McGrade and Kilcullen, *A Letter to the Friars Minor*, 19–33, 48–59. Hereafter *LFM*.

45. See *OND*, 65: *LFM*, 51, 57–8; III *Dialogus* II.3.6: *LFM*, 286–90.

46. *DP* II.12.3-4: 188-9; cf. I.10.3–6: 35-6.

47. A command is "an affirmative statute obliging its transgressor to punishment"; a prohibition is "a negative statute obliging its transgressor to punishment"; a permission is "an ordinance of the legislator obliging no one to punishment." *DP* II.12.4: 189.

48. Here "common" (*commune*) means "to be communicated" (*communicandum*). *OND*, 27: Offler, *Ockham Opera Politica*, 2: 489.

49. *OND*, 26–8: *LFM*, 34–48; cf. *Breviloquium de principatu tyrannico* 3.7 in *Wilhelm von Ockham als politischer Denker und sein Breviloquiium de principatu tyrannico*, ed. Richard Scholtz and William Hiersemann (Stuttgart: Anton Hiersemann Verlag, 1952); *A Short Discourse on Tyrannical Government*, ed. A. S. McGrade, trans. J. Kilcullen (Cambridge: Cambridge University Press, 1992), 89. Hereafter *SD*.

lordship established by divine (i.e., natural) law with proprietary lordship established by legal judgment, describing the latter as "a principal human power of laying claim to and defending some temporal thing in a human court" or "of laying claim to some temporal thing and defending, holding, and controlling it."[50] He repeatedly asserted the centrality of the litigable claim to positive legal right.

For Ockham, as for Huguccio, the judicial order of fallen human community could not absolutely overrule the continuing order of divine (natural) justice and reason that would socially assert itself on occasion. Primarily this would occur when individuals in dire necessity used the goods of others without their permission; for the natural power of using goods to sustain one's life could not morally be renounced. But it would also occur outside of necessity, as when the owners of goods freely permitted their use by the Franciscans.[51]

On the important question bequeathed by Rufinus, whether the institution of property is commanded or merely permitted to fallen humanity by natural and divine law, Ockham's mature thought was complicated. In rebutting papal jurisdictional claims, he proposed that God had conferred on human beings by "special grant" the power to appropriate temporal goods for private use to restrain the avaricious appetite for these goods and ensure their proper management against neglect.[52] It is notable that Ockham read the Aristotelian argument for private management—that most people love common things less than their own things—as applicable only to postlapsarian humanity, whereas Aquinas applied it to prelapsarian humanity, conflating the created and fallen human conditions.[53] According to Ockham, human appropriation of goods preceded the introduction of "exclusive lordships" by communal custom, agreement, and ordinance (although some exclusive lordships were introduced by direct divine ordinance). God's special grant carried a command obliging persons to appropriate goods and to establish proprietary lordships where required by social "necessity," or "utility comparable with necessity."[54] But God's command did not oblige a community of individuals freely devoted to striving after perfection, who loved and cared for common things above their own. Thus, Ockham's account integrated prescriptive and permissive natural and divine law,[55] associating the latter with Christ's counsels of perfection followed by the Franciscans.

By contrast, Marsilius of Padua's defense virtually disregarded the concept of subjective natural right. He never discussed Adamic lordship and defined *ius naturale* in its objective senses as either a dictate of divine law (or of right

---

50. *OND*, 2: *LFM*, 28, 31.
51. *OND*, 65: *LFM*, 48–59.
52. *SD* 3.7: 89.
53. *ST* 2.2ae.66.2, 57.3. Aquinas cites the argument in support of the individual's possession of material things, deriving from humankind's God-given, natural competence regarding them.
54. *SD* 3.8: 91.
55. *SD* 3.7–8: 90–1.

reason conformed to divine law) or as a statute of positive human law widely observed among nations (*ius gentium*).[56] His dichotomy of human law and divine law displayed Averroist tendencies in sharply separating, while also aligning, human aspirations for happiness in this world and in the next world, embodied, respectively, in the civil and ecclesiastical domains. Marsilius invested civil life with a high degree of moral self-sufficiency and autonomous intelligibility and occasionally came close to inverting the traditional ordering of the secular to the spiritual realms.[57]

Marsilius defended the Franciscans' ex-proprietary use of temporal goods as conforming only to Christ's counsel of perfect poverty, not to a prior natural right of created humanity. Although Christ's counsel contradicts proprietary right, the Franciscan practice does not, both because the goods used by the Franciscans are obtained with the owner's consent and because the brother's renunciation of proprietary right accords with the civil legal principle that "a benefit is not bestowed on an unwilling person."[58] For Marsilius, then, the individual's freedom to use temporal goods without owning them, recognized both by human law and by divine permissive law,[59] mediates the moral opposition of Christ's counsel to legal proprietorship. This mediation, however, may implicitly be the mediation of natural right, given that Marsilius includes among the meanings of "ownership": "the human will or freedom in itself with its organic executive or motive power unimpeded," by which the individual is said to have "control of his acts . . . by nature."[60]

Evangelical and Civil Freedom and Lordship

The concept of the will as ownership (*dominium*), as the individual's unimpeded executive power of disposing of his or her judgments, capacities, and acts, was not a novel idea. Indeed, it was intrinsic to the mendicant vow of obedience by which the individual, for Christ's sake, relinquished his will, his self-ownership—which,

---

56. *DP* II.12.7–8: 190-1.

57. The Averroist strand of Marsilius' thought placed the maximum distance between acts designed for "living well" in this world and acts ordered to "living well" in the next (I.4.3; I.5.2). Whereas the former acts, governed by reason and art, may be regulated by positive human statutes and customs with worldly rewards and punishments (I.5.2-4; I.10.2-4; also II.8.3-5), the latter acts, governed by faith and the "evangelic law" of Christ, are regulated by rewards and punishments only in eternity (I.5.10; I.6.8,10; also II.8.5). Of major interest to Marsilius is the positive contribution of religious beliefs and practices to civic virtue and order, which appears to depend only on the former's ethical efficacy and not their truth or falsity (I.5.11,14).

58. *DP* II.13.3: 197. See *Dig.* 50.17.69.

59. Christ's counsel of perfection does not "oblige to punishment" those who do not follow it.

60. *DP* II.12.16: 193.

presumably, believers not bound by the wayfarers' vow retained in some measure.⁶¹ In defending the mendicant vow, both Thomas Aquinas and Bonaventure had set forth unequivocally the character of the individual's free will as ownership; moreover, they had made clear the dependence of the individual's *dominium* over external things on this interior *dominium*.⁶² The prominence of this concept of the will in moral and political theology was undoubtedly heightened by the late scholastic thematizing of human freedom as a natural and evangelical right, to which Ockham's thought gave considerable momentum.

In attacking papal jurisdictional claims, Ockham did not reiterate the prevailing conception of evangelical freedom as the freedom of individual believers chiefly to determine for themselves whether or not to follow Christ's "counsels of perfection": that is, of supererogatory works conducive, rather than necessary, to obtaining salvation.⁶³ Instead, he redefined the "liberty of the gospel law" as the divine restriction on church authorities, that they impose on Christ's followers "nothing, especially nothing heavy . . . supererogatory, or not required by natural law or explicit divine law," except in cases of "urgent necessity and clear utility" or of punishable fault.⁶⁴ His redefinition both expanded the scope of gospel freedom and converted it into a regular (but not absolute) immunity from oppressive ecclesiastical demands.

Of course, for Ockham, as for Marsilius, the believer's freedom was perfected in active obedience to Christ's law of salvation. Moreover, Ockham admitted the authority of the clerical hierarchy to promulgate Christ's law, and (contra Marsilius) to judge and punish violations of it with spiritual sanctions, while yet insisting that legislation of the individual's spiritual life was Christ's, not man's, prerogative.⁶⁵ However, his theologically sound assertion of Christ's authority neither required nor justified his redefinition of evangelical freedom as political immunity,⁶⁶ or

---

61. *Apologia Pauperum* 3.11-12. The Franciscan renunciation of property right exhibits the spiritual meaning of the mendicant vow to poverty, chastity, and obedience, in which the individual offers to Christ his will as well as his acts; or, in Anselm's analogy cited by Bonaventure, he offers both the ownership of the tree and its fruits. Elsewhere, Bonaventure defines human free will as having full *dominium* over its proper acts. *II Sent. Comm. Dist.* 25.1a.1.

62. *De perfectione spiritualis vitae*, in *Opera Omnia iussu Leonis XIII* (Rome, 1882-1971), 41:79; *ST* 1.2ae.1.2.

63. See Aquinas, *ST* 1.2ae.108.2 and Marsilius, *DP* II.12.4: 189.

64. *SD* 2.17: 54. The other literary *loci* for Ockham's defense of individual freedom against papal tyranny are *Octo Quaestiones* 1.6; III *Dialogus* 1.1.5-8; *De imperatorum et pontificum potestate* 2.1-9.

65. *SD* 2.3-5: 21-8.

66. Surprisingly, Nigel Biggar appears to defend Ockham's deployment of the Christian's spiritual freedom as a political immunity right, after he has rightly criticized Tierney for misrepresenting Ockham's understanding of "spiritual freedom" as "a core of spiritual autonomy inherent in the human person, granted by 'God and nature,' a freedom of choice

his extension of immunity to cover ecclesiastical infringements of civil as well as spiritual rights. In that the freedom of Christ's faithful protected them against violations of their rights as rational human beings, as secular proprietors and as rulers, papal rule, Ockham argued, could be neither the supreme source nor regular arbiter of secular proprietorship and jurisdiction.

Rather, the rights of temporal rulers, parallel to those of proprietors, descended from an original, direct divine grant to sinful humankind of a specific power to establish secular jurisdiction by common consent, subject to God's command to use it as necessity dictated.[67] According to Ockham, "the people" (i.e., the freely united body of rights-bearing individuals) transmitted to the ruler its collective powers (rights) of rule for the purpose of judging violations of the common utility. This transmission was the foundation of limited and just monarchical government, subject to divine and customary law and to constitutional provisions for electing, correcting, and deposing tyrannous rulers.[68] In the course of his political theorizing, Ockham came to incorporate under divine and natural law the institutions and principles traditionally designated as belonging to the *ius gentium*.[69]

Marsilius' demonstration of the limitation of ecclesiastical rule by divine law, like Ockham's, primarily consisted of an account, taken largely from the New Testament, of the powers which Christ possessed *as man* and bestowed on his apostles and their clerical successors: powers of performing and regulating the church's pedagogical, sacramental, and pastoral ministries. But his account admitted no this-worldly exercise of coercive disciplinary authority over the faithful, reserving it to Christ's divine-human judgment and punishment of sinners in "the future world."[70] Neither translating the spiritual freedom of believers into judicial immunity, nor admitting coercive jurisdiction into the apostolic priesthood, Marsilius surpassed Ockham in depoliticizing the community of faith and practice, and in assimilating ecclesiastical to civil jurisdiction. For him, the corporate will of the civil community and voluntary consent of its citizens alone established and protected the just order of the community's constituent parts,[71] by making binding laws and electing, correcting, and deposing the law executors. As part of the civil corporation, the institutional church was ordered by the civil government and subject to civil obligations, chief among which was that its

---

in responding to divine love and divine demands," rather than as 'the property only of the redeemed *Christian* person . . . granted by the Holy Spirit of God-in-Christ, and not by fallen nature." *What's Wrong with Rights?*, 45. https://academic-oup-com.ezproxy.is.ed.ac.uk/book/33698/chapter/288283666

67. *SD* 3.1–6: 71–87.
68. III *Dialogus* II. 3. 5–7: *LFM*, 281–98; *SD* 3.14: 99–100; 4.3–10: 111–25; 6.2: 158–63.
69. III *Dialogus* II. 3. 5–6: *LFM*, 281–93.
70. *DP* II.4, 113–26.
71. Marsilius' explication of civil jurisdiction in Discourse One sets the framework for demonstrating the limitation of priestly rule by divine law in Discourse Two.

teaching and practices inculcate the virtues necessary to the peace and sufficiency of communal life. Thus did the civil polity impose on the ecclesiastical sphere a commanding place for individual and corporate freedom and authority.

Evangelical and Naturalist Rights Theories: Wyclif and Gerson

Almost half a century later, John Wyclif theologically reoriented the theoretical and practical agenda of Ockham and Marsilius by assimilating natural to evangelical *dominium* as the universal foundation both of a nonproprietary, nonjuridical, clerical estate and of civil proprietorship and rule. His controlling thesis, borrowed from Richard Fitzralph,[72] was that the original, natural lordship of created humanity presupposed justifying grace. Adopting the Franciscan depiction of the post-resurrection Jerusalem church as the renewal of Adamic "dominion by grace," Wyclif proposed that God had historically reserved to the clerical estate the apostolic vocation of fully exemplifying the nonproprietary sharing of spiritual and material goods in Christ, in which all members and estates of the church variously participated.[73]

Wyclif's assimilation of natural to evangelical lordship set up an extreme dialectical relationship between evangelical and civil lordship (*dominium civilis*). On the one hand, he drew sharp moral contrasts between them unflattering to civil lordship;[74] on the other, he founded civil lordship on no other ground but God's grace in Christ that brought about righteous possession and use of earthly goods.[75] Unless civil ownership was an oblique expression of evangelical right, an imperfect conformity to Christ's law of love, lay proprietors would not be members of Christ's faithful household.[76] In addition, Wyclif recognized that even unjust proprietorship, lacking a foundation in evangelical lordship, had a remote basis in divine justice: it displayed the passive, extrinsic justice by which all creaturely being conforms to the will of its creator, and it served God's permission of evil for a time, to execute his purposes of punishing the unrighteous, testing the saints, and manifesting His mercy universally. To these divine purposes, legal property right and political jurisdiction were necessary as the means of restraining evildoing, including the evildoing of the clerical hierarchy who, in pursuing civil wealth and

---

72. Richard FitzRalph, *De pauperie salvatoris* written between 1351 and 1356.

73. *Tractatus De civili dominio*, ed. Johann Loserth for the Wyclif Society, 4 vols (London: Trübner, 1885–1904), 1.11, 3.6: I:73–80, 3:77–81. Following FitzRalph, Wyclif departed from the moderate Franciscan and papalist view of the primitive church as having a "double profession" of common property (the church's "purse") and of nonproprietary use of necessities (the apostolic missions), affirming instead her single profession of apostolic nonproprietorship.

74. Ibid., 1.18–19: I:126–33; also 1.11: I:76–7.

75. Ibid., 1.4: I:25–33.

76. Ibid., 1.6: I:39–42; 1.41: I:317–24.

jurisdiction, were flagrantly flouting Christ's command for the preaching estate and, as well, the venerable English law of ecclesiastical "dotation."[77]

Although Wyclif never foresaw that his assimilation of natural to evangelical lordship would imperil the jurisdiction and property of secular as well as clerical lords, the Paris theologian, Jean Gerson, saw this as certain. Convinced that "extrinsic" or "passive" divine justice and permission offered insufficient security to legitimate rule when exercised unjustly in the secular or ecclesiastical domains, Gerson provided a more robustly rationalist, voluntarist, and naturalist foundation for civil jurisdiction and property, building on Ockham, Aristotle, and Thomas.

Gerson's initial definition of *ius* as "an immediate faculty or power pertaining to anyone according to the dictate of right reason"[78] differed from Ockham's only in the addition of two words: "immediate faculty." "Immediate (*propinqua*)" indicated that the power could issue in act directly, lending the active character to *ius* missing in Wyclif; and *facultas* possibly carried the voluntarist connotation of power approved or permitted rather than prescribed.[79] His amplification introduced Thomist-Aristotelian formulations, in explicating "right reason" as "originally and essentially in God" and "participatively" in rational creatures[80] and identifying "superior" human reason with *synderesis*, the rational capacity of discerning the right and equitable.[81]

In addition, Gerson transposed Wyclif's Augustinian conception of "passive" or "extrinsic" creaturely justice into a naturalist Aristotelian key, attributing to all creatures, rationale and irrational, *iura* in the sense of inherent powers for specific actions on themselves and their environment in accordance with the dictate of divine reason.[82] His universal attribution of natural rights reappeared later in connection with his definition of *ius* as "an immediate faculty or power pertaining to anyone according to the dictate of primary justice." This followed his explication of "primary justice" as the creator's "perpetual and constant will to assign to everything what is proper to it," namely, its "being" and "worth." Gerson's revised definition united each creature's power, being and worth (goodness) with "the right or title to possess whatever . . . the absolute norm of primary justice

---

77. In prescribing "free alms" as the form of ecclesiastical "dotation," English law entitled the lay magistracy to compel the clergy to live "exproprietarily," without compulsory tithes and exactions, perpetual alms, the practice of simony and the machinery of ecclesiastical litigation. Ibid., 1.41, 3.16: I:325–8, 3:303–6.

78. *De vita spirituali animae*, Lectio 3 in *Oeuvres complètes*, ed. Palémon Glorieux (Paris: Desclée, 1965), 3:141.

79. Later, Gerson erroneously derived "*facultas*" from "*fas*," which could designate permissive natural right or law in juristic commentary. *INR*, 67.

80. *ST* 1.2ae.91.2.

81. *De vita*, Lectio 3: *Oeuvres complètes* 3:142; cf. *ST* 1.2ae. 94.1.

82. Ibid. cf. *De potestate ecclesiastica* 13: *Oeuvres complètes* 6:242; trans. *IG*, 527–8. See Annabel Brett's account of this transposition in *Liberty, Right and Nature: Individual Rights in Later Scholastic Thought* (Cambridge: Cambridge University Press, 1997), 79–85.

prescribes that it possess."⁸³ In presenting the ontological dimension of justice as the ordered totality or "system" of divinely appointed creaturely "rights or titles," Gerson programmatically accorded primacy to the subjective over the objective sense of *ius*—an exceptional theoretical position in Decretist commentary, not easily accommodated by Ockham, and wholly foreign to Aquinas.

However, this comprehensive attribution of natural rights remained somewhat extraneous to Gerson's primary thesis that the natural right exclusive to human beings presupposed human right reason and the natural lordship (*dominium naturale*) bestowed by God on Adam, including the subject's rights of freedom, of controlling his acts, and of taking inferior creatures for use and sustenance. This twofold lordship persisted in sinful humanity, independently of evangelical lordship founded in charity and forfeited by sin,⁸⁴ and underlay the civil lordship (*dominium civile*) of jurisdiction and property. Gerson's foremost concern in presenting primary justice as a system of universal creaturely rights was always to establish a strong natural foundation for human "rights, laws, jurisdictions and dominions (*dominia*)." Significantly, the literary context was his treatise on reform of church polity along conciliarist lines, in which his chief objective was to ensure that the plurality of clerical offices (especially episcopal offices) with their attached "rights" had a regular role in the corporate government of the universal church.⁸⁵ In the litigious and politically acrimonious ecclesiastical climate, Gerson presented the papal usurpation of the rights of lesser clerical office holders as "theft," thereby focusing attention on abstract, immaterial, and subjective faculties as objects of ownership, as property susceptible of being snatched away against the proprietor's will.⁸⁶ Just so, the conflictual church environment of conciliar theology throughout the fifteenth century gave prominence to the defensive purpose of individual and communal natural rights.

Thematizing Control and Freedom: Summenhart

A key development after Gerson was thematizing of the widespread assumption of rights theorists that *ius* in its subjective sense regularly had two (or three) aspects: being understood as an inherent power of a subject to act, as the subject's habitual relationship to an external object, and to his own act(s) in respect of that

---

83. *De potentate ecclesiastica* 13: *Oeuvres complètes*, 6:242.

84. *De Vita*, Lectio 3: *Oeuvres complètes* 3:145–7, 150–6.

85. Written during the Council of Constance (1414–18), *De potestate ecclesiastica* contributed to the emerging view of the universal church council, invested with the power of the "mystical" corporate whole, as an ongoing regulative, advisory, and disciplinary assembly, and not merely a latent potency to be exercised in rare emergencies. Expressing this view, the council's decree, Frequens (1417), called for papal convocation of "general councils" at regular, stipulated intervals.

86. *IG*, 527.

object. In his theological *opus* on contracts (1500), the eclectic thinker, Conrad Summenhart, explained that every right or subjective "power" (*potestas*) may be taken either "materially" as "a reality of the soul which elicits acts, in which sense ... [it] is an independent entity and not a relation," or "formally" as "a disposition [habitus] of the soul . . . towards its object and towards actions which it can produce with respect to the object."[87] He argued that, as an aspect of subjective right, the soul's habitual relationship to an external object and to its own actions in respect of it was appropriately termed *dominium* in a broad sense, and the right holder was appropriately termed *dominus* (owner). Dominion, then, consisted of the subject's control of the object by his act and control of his act in respect of the object, whether the object be a material thing or the action of others. For example, someone with a legal right to use a field owned by another (*ius utendi*) would have control over the field as an object of use, and control over the act of using it. Were the owner to prevent his use of the field, it would be theft of his right or dominion in both aspects. Even the wage laborer had "dominion" over the wage owed, as, in the event of his employer's withholding it, he could engage in acts, also under his control, of demanding the wage and suing for it in court.

Beyond the juristic context of theft and restitution, Summenhart's argument related to his thesis that an agent has as much right or dominion over a thing as he has freedom within legal limits to determine his action respecting it.[88] His thesis sharply focused theoretical interest on the degree of control characterizing dominion and the scope of licit or permitted freedom of action within the law's constraints. Summenhart's work thus made explicit the universal logic of proprietorship, control, and freedom that over four centuries had pervaded the conceptualizing of subjective natural right in moral, social, and legal contexts, and across the categories of right as *naturale, gentium,* and *civile*, as right *in* or *to* things, as right to act or to receive, and as freedom to act or freedom from compulsion.[89]

Toward Legal Assimilation and Overcoming of Natural Right

The focus on freedom and control as determinative for subjective right fuelled a broad theoretical movement toward assimilating natural right to human legal right. Natural rights took on a more individualistic, proprietary, juridical, and defensive character consonant with the proprietary and political arrangements of the *ius gentium* and the *ius civile*, reducing the discontinuity between pre-

---

87. *Septipertitum opus de contractibus pro foro conscientiae atque theologico* (Hagenau: Heinrici Gran, 1515), sig. Ev r; trans. Annabel Brett, in *Liberty, Right and Nature*, 38-9.

88. "Vnde tantum quisque habet iuris, vel dominii in aliquam rem: quantum actionis licet sibi exercere circa rem." *De Contractibus* 4, cited in *INR*, 248 n. 31.

89. While having a clear grasp of this logic, Richard Tuck in *Natural Rights Theories*, mistakenly attributes it only to a theory that gives prominence to "active" rather than "passive" rights, not recognizing its implicit universality throughout rights theory.

and postlapsarian community. Under the influence of juristic humanism, the discontinuity was restored, but within a radically libertarian reformulation of *ius naturale*. In the wake of Summenhart, the synthesizing work of Paris masters advanced this complex development.

The labors of Jacques Almain and Francisco de Vitoria, among others, were largely in response to papal infringements on established political and proprietary rights and spiritual freedoms: infringements grounded in the theory of papal supremacy, with supportive interpretations of "dominion by grace" and "evangelical right." While Almain continued Gerson's defense of the conciliar constitution of the church, Vitoria resisted the Spanish assault, claiming papal authorization, on the property, jurisdiction, and freedom of conquered populations in the Americas. For both theologians, theological resistance required the close and unassailable connections between natural and civil rights offered by Gersonian theoretical formulations, appropriated, it would seem, as timely elucidations of Thomist understandings of natural right and dominion.

Vitoria, founder of the "school of Salamanca" or "second scholastic," produced the most influential synthesis of Summenhartian and Thomist formulations. He ground all lordship over external things in the original, divinely bestowed lordship of the rational individual over his acts,[90] and, by giving a Summentarian gloss to Aquinas, identified human freedom with the individual's unobliged determination of acts permitted by law.[91] In addition, he gave a somewhat novel gloss to humankind's lordship by natural law over nonhuman creatures, proposing that, "every individual" as "lord of all created things . . . could use and abuse them . . . at will . . . as long as he did not harm other men or himself (my translation)."[92] Here and elsewhere, his depiction of humankind's created lordship converted it from the common, inclusive, and rationally restrained use of the nonhuman creation defended by Ockham into a semiprivate, unfettered, and arbitrary use of it by individual lords within the general precepts of natural law. Accordingly, individuals were permitted by natural law to establish properties incorporating

---

90. For example, *De Indis* 1.2–4 in *Francisco de Vitoria, Political Writings*, ed. and trans. Anthony Pagden and Jeremy Lawrance (Cambridge: Cambridge University Press, 1991), 241–8. Hereafter *VPW*. Also, *De justitia* 2.2ae.64.1.1-4: *On Homicide and Commentary on Summa theologiae 2a 2ae Q. 64*, trans. John P. Doyle (Milwaukee: Markquette University Press, 1997), 120–5.

91. For example, Commenting on *De justitia* 2.2ae.62.1; *INR*, 259.

92. "Non solum universitas et communitas . . . sed quilibet homo in statu naturae integrae, id est, stando in solo iure naturali, erat dominus omnium rerum creaturum et poterat uti et abuti omnibus illi . . . pro libero suo . . . dummodo non noceret alias hominibus vel sibi." *De justitia* 2.2ae.62.1; cited in *INR*. I am not convinced by Tierney's suggestion that the verb "abuti" probably has the meanings here of "to use up" or "to consume" (*INR*, 263 n. 36.), as these meanings are regularly expressed by the verb "*consumere*" and are not recognized meanings of "abuti" in later Latin dictionaries.

inferior creatures,[93] subject only to the natural law requirement affirmed by Aquinas of sharing belongings as human necessity demands.

Consistent with Vitoria's portrayal of Adamic lordship were the arguments of his political writings for confining lordship and rights to rational beings exclusively.[94] Two arguments stand out: irrational creatures cannot have legal rights (*iuria*) because they cannot be victims of an injustice (*iniuria*); and they cannot have rights over external things as they do not have rights over their own bodies, lacking *dominium* over their acts (following Aquinas[95]). Consequently, they may, without injustice, be deprived of external necessities and killed with impunity, even for sport. Human agents have no moral obligations to subhuman creatures, nor restraints in exercising dominion over them, but only obligations not to injure themselves or other needy human agents by using the creatures frivolously.[96] Even Vitoria's student, Domingo de Soto, who thematized the specific inclinations of irrational creatures under *lex naturale*, recognized no human obligations in managing and using them.[97]

The voluntarist, proprietary revision of natural dominion in the thought of Vitoria, his Paris contemporaries and Spanish successors, also gave reign to a more agonistic conception of created human relations and to greater concern with the natural right of individuals to defend against aggression their bodies, acts, and external possessions. This concern deviated from the longer theological tradition in which acts of self-defense belonged to the sinful human condition and ran counter to Christ's law of suffering love. In the early 1500s, theologians were reconfiguring the problematic relationship of killing in self-defense to biblical teaching, as Vitoria's lecture, *De homicidio*, exemplified. Here, Vitoria's approach to reconciling the two differed notably from Thomas's appeal to the principle of "double effect"[98] (which Vitoria also endorsed),[99] in that an issue for Vitoria was whether the inalienable right and duty of self-preservation *always required* the individual to defend his life to the point of killing another. He resolved the issue by adducing permissive natural and divine law: the individual, possessed of a limited lordship over his body under God's supreme lordship, was permitted to set aside his lordship when to accept death for another's sake would be the more perfect act

---

93. Ibid.
94. *De Indis* 1.4: *VPW*, 247–8. Exceptionally, in his commentary on *ST 2.2ae*. 57.3 he extended natural right to include the specific acts of irrational creatures.
95. *ST* 1.2ae.1.1–2, 6.2; 1.82.1 ad 3.
96. Commenting on *ST* 2.2ae.64.1. ad 2.
97. For evidence of this lacuna, Brett, *Liberty, Right and Nature*, 149–52.
98. Invoking this principle, Thomas argued that the act of killing is licit only if the intended effect is to save one's own life and not to kill the assailant, for the inclination to self-preservation belongs to natural law. *ST* 2.2ae. 64.7.
99. Commenting on 64.7: Doyle, *On Homicide and Commentary*, 193–5.

of Christian discipleship. In this instance, killing in self-defense was licit rather than mandatory.[100]

Vitoria's appeal to the individual's freedom in using his natural right was indicative of the voluntarist logic of rights prevalent in the economic and political domains. In the economic domain, increasingly detailed analysis of how, when, and to what extent the individual's natural property in his powers and actions could be transferred to another agent assisted their commodification as objects of economic exchange. In the political domain, issues concerning the retention and conveyance of the rights of individuals, civil communities, and rulers were occupying the theoretical foreground. Feeding both domains was the theoretical assimilation of natural right to human legal right via the rational individual's proprietary freedom.

However, a somewhat contrary depiction of natural right and its relation to legal right emerged out of the encounter of the Paris-Salamanca tradition with contemporary humanist jurisprudence, to advance the libertarian trajectory of liberal rights theory. The influential, Salamanca-trained jurist, Fernando Vázquez de Menchaca,[101] adapted and enlarged on the formulation of natural right (law) as "what nature has taught all animals (*quod natura omnia animalia docuit*),"[102] identifying natural right (law) with the instinctual inclinations (including to self-preservation) common to human and subhuman creatures. This Vitoria and Soto had also done, and Aquinas before them when distinguishing *ius naturale* and *ius gentium*.[103] But unlike Vitoria and Soto, Vázquez made no allowance for Thomas's controlling identification of natural right with the divinely given, rationally apprehended laws governing these inclinations in human beings;[104] nor for his assertion of the specifically human natural inclination to know truths about God and living in society.[105] Rather, Vázquez assigned all rational human inclinations to the *ius gentium*.

Vázquez thus portrayed the natural-right foundation of human society and jurisdiction in terms of the subrational inclinations of the human species, principally the inclination to self-preservation in its appetitive and defensive aspects, anticipating Hobbes. Investing the inclinations of all animate creatures with "natural freedom" conceived as the power of unrestrained and arbitrary action, he portrayed the *ius gentium*, from its inception in the primeval human community of common use and common freedom, as displaying the corrupting, as well as moderating, effect of human reason on natural inclinations. On his account, the growing inclination

---

100. *De Homicidio* 23–4: Doyle, *On Homicide and Commentary*, 95.

101. *Controversiarum illustrious usuque frequentium libri tres*, 1564. For an exposition of Vázquez' thought on natural and civil rights and liberty, Brett, *Liberty, Right and Nature*, 165–204.

102. Ulpian at *Dig.* 1.1.3; n. 7.

103. *ST* 2.2ae.57.3; *ST* 1.2ae.94.2; *Sententia libri ethicorum*, 5.12.

104. *ST* 1.2ae.94.2, 95.4.

105. *ST* 1a2ae.94.2, 95.4.

of human beings to self-aggrandizement and domination drove them over time to create jurisdiction and the positive laws of property, commerce, and contract—"the second *ius gentium*."[106] The civil rights of freedom and proprietary dominion protected the individual's natural faculties of freedom and dominion in a regulated and restricted social form and space, overcoming thereby the more damaging expressions and effects of their degeneracy. But unlike Hobbes, Vázquez came to depict these restrictive legal artifices as intrinsically unstable, because, imposing no natural moral obligation, they depended for their practical efficacy solely on individuals perceiving their utility for freely pursuing private advantage.[107]

Political Construction on the Natural Right of Self-Defense

Both the Paris Gersonians and their Salamanca beneficiaries made the natural right of self-defense a central plank in the foundation of political rule. Key to this was the theoretical stress placed by Gerson and his conciliarist followers on the moral continuity between the individual's natural right to "repel force with force," to the point of killing an assailant, and the political community's natural right to repel assailants from within and without by judgment and punishment, including capital punishment.[108] The Paris conciliarists attributed to both the natural civil polity and the supernatural ecclesiastical polity the natural right of defending their integrity against tyrannical rulers.

The conciliarist, Almain, harmonized the defensive natural right of individuals, communities, and governors with greater theoretical ease than did the Salamanca theologians, by consistently applying a voluntaristic, corporative model to natural political society. On this model, the natural corporation, formed by the consent of individuals to serve their common ends, was endowed with political rights to make corporate rules and to elect, regulate, correct, and punitively remove its governors. These communal rights were separable from, yet comprehended, the rights of

---

106. The progression from the instinctually driven individual to gathering in society, the rise of aggression, and the institution of jurisdiction and positive laws is charted in Book 1.

107. See Brett, *Liberty, Right and Nature*, 199–202.

108. Gerson formulated this continuity when arguing the right of the ecclesial body represented in a general council to resist an erring pope, *De auferibilitate sponsi* in Glorieux, *Oeuvres complètes* 3:294–313. Jacques Almain, *Libellus de auctoritate ecclesiae* (Paris, 1512) in *Conciliarism and Papalism*, trans. J. H. Burns and Thomas M. Izbicki (Cambridge: Cambridge University Press, 1997), 135–7. Their analogy diverges from, and does not, as Almain implies, simply complement Thomas's analogy (*ST* 2a2ae.64.2) between the lawfulness of cutting off an individual's putrid limb for the sake of his body's health and the community's putting to death of an evildoer for the sake of the common welfare, where the moral continuity resides not in the subjective right of self-defense but in the subordination of part to whole.

consenting members. The corporate body of consenting individuals was the original, constitutive, and ongoing source of governmental powers, never transferring or alienating its natural rights and powers to rulers, who, therefore, held delegated or ministerial powers to act representatively for the corporation assembled in council. Applying corporative principles to the church's supernatural, monarchical polity, Almain presented the General Council as holding directly from Christ the fullness of apostolic jurisdiction, and the pope as holding directly from Christ the ministerial exercise of this plenitude, permanently subject to, and bound by the Council.[109]

The immanent natural-rights logic of Almain's civil corporatism, appealing to divine right only as the remote source of natural rights, resembled the humanist republicanism of Marsilius rather than Ockham's constitutionalism. For Ockham, unlike Marsilius, had conceived the corporation as transferring jurisdiction to the ruler, who ruled under God's providence and law (and to an extent, under human customary and statute law), but not under corporate jurisdiction.[110] Correlatively, Ockham allowed rulers to be established by forms of political consent other than election[111] and preferred to justify their forcible removal by appeal to the natural necessity of preserving the common good under grave threat rather than to the community's natural right of self-defense.[112]

Vitoria's synthetic accounts of political rule, on the other hand, were closer to Ockham's in addressing the more complex tensions between individual, communal, and divine right and dominion. However, their impressive strengths were somewhat undermined by fluctuation and incoherence. Vitoria began his 1528 lectures on "civil power" by arguing along the Thomist lines that individuals were rationally obliged by natural and divine law to live within the civil association or "commonwealth" to meet the natural ends of fellowship, self-preservation, and defense. Then, switching to the discourse of corporative rights, he argued that, as the commonwealth was composed of rational, self-controlling individuals, each with the natural right of self-defense, it likewise had a natural "power and right" to order and defend the collective "body," even against its own members,[113] to provide for which it was obliged by practical necessity to entrust (delegate) its "powers and offices" to "rulers and magistrates."[114] Notwithstanding, he proceeded to assert that the sovereign power of kings was conferred immediately by God himself and not by the commonwealth, and to be exercised, as Ockham had proposed, only under God and not under the civil (or ecclesiastical) body.[115] Rather than adopting with

---

109. Burns and Izbicki, *Conciliarism and Papalism*, 153–65.

110. *SD* 4.5–8: 113–17.

111. Rulers could be established by a people's simple acclamation or by their acknowledgment of his title over time. *SD* 4.10–11: 122–7.

112. His preferred argument applied even to the removal of ecclesiastical rulers, including the pope. 3 *Dialogus* 1.2.20, 28: *LFM*, 171–7, 200–3.

113. *De potestate civili* 1.4: *VPW*, 11.

114. Ibid., 1.5: *VPW*, 12.

115. Ibid.: *VPW*, 16.

Ockham the Roman juristic idea that the civil community transferred its power of governing to the ruler, Vitoria contended that the commonwealth transfers to the monarch "authority" (*auctoritas*) but not "power" (*potestas*): it transfers the superior office of rule, but not the capability of ruling, which God alone confers.[116] Thus, the secular monarch exercises by immediate divine conferral the same power of ruling that belongs by natural and divine right to the commonwealth.

What Vitoria's account theoretically gained by qualifying the Roman transference theory of sovereignty was offset by ascribing to the civil community a natural right or power of acting which it could not naturally exercise, or transfer to another agent. Unconvinced, Soto adopted the Roman transference theory unqualified,[117] as Vitoria later did himself.[118] On another front, Vitoria and Soto's political thought suffered from inadequately resolving the theoretical conflict surrounding capital punishment between communal and individual dominion: between the commonwealth's divine and natural right to defend itself by executing harmful members and the individual's divine and natural right and duty of self-defense.[119] Vitoria's attempt at resolution was to argue for the obligation of the criminal condemned to death to escape his lawful punishment, if opportunity offered.[120] Soto, deploying Thomas's Aristotelian argument for capital punishment within the idiom of rights,[121] proposed that the malefactor betrayed his human rationality and lost his freedom (i.e., his proprietary *dominium* in himself), degenerating "into the lowliness and servitude of brute animals" who may licitly be killed *judicially* for the sake of the common good.[122] Thus, to the contemporary theorizing of voluntary transfers of individual and corporate natural rights, Soto added the involuntary forfeiture of an individual natural right.

Critical Summary and Reformation Alternative

This overview has attempted to display the cumulative theoretical contributions of premodern to modern developments of Western natural rights theory, and

---

116. In Relectio I, *De potestate ecclesiae* 1, Vitoria clarified this distinction, proposing that the term, "power" (*potestates*), may refer either to authorities that is, those in positions of superiority, or to capabilities, in this case, the capability of ruling. *VPW*, 50.

117. Soto, *De iustitia et iure libri decem* (Salamanca, 1556) I.6.4, cited in Brett, *Liberty, Right and Nature*, 157.

118. *Comm. ST* 1a2ae.105.1: *Commentaria al Tratado de la ley*, ed. Beltran de Heredia (Madrid, 1952), 81: *VPW*, 199.

119. Vitoria, *De potentate civili* 1.4: *VPW*, 11–12; Soto, *De iustitia et iure libri decem* 5. 1. 2 in corp; cited in Brett, *Liberty, Right and Nature*, 160 n. 112.

120. *De homicidio* 29: Urdanoz, *Obras de Francisco de Vitoria*, 1123. Cited in *INR*, 300.

121. *ST* 2.2ae.64.2, 3 ad 2.

122. *De iustitia et iure libri decem* 5, 1.2 ad 3; cited in Brett, *Liberty, Right and Nature*, 160.

coordinately, to show how premodern natural rights developments gave a new cohesion and direction to rationalist and voluntarist ideas previously associated with concepts and applications of objective natural right and law. The following critically summarizes these cumulative contributions and indicates the English Reformation theological alternatives to them.

First and most fundamental was the subjective concept of natural right as an original, universal power of the acting individual. The theorizing of natural rights coordinated two original powers: the agent's power of choosing among possibilities of acting, the right of freedom, and the agent's power of acting to preserve his or her life, the right of self-preservation. Theologians and jurists understood these powers to conform to objective natural right in its three senses: as the ordered relations among creatures and with their creator, as human actions conforming to these relations, and as the divine norms disclosed in Scripture and nature that reveal them. But with the emergence of subjective rights in moral theology and jurisprudence, the center of theoretical gravity shifted away from these objective senses of *ius naturale* and also modified them. The canonist category of permissive natural right, while not formulating an open-ended individual or communal freedom, nourished the conception of individual freedom of choice as a proprietary right of control over one's acts. With some impetus from Ockham, the handling of permissive natural right in the Paris tradition placed increasing emphasis on the *dominium* of human agents in their acts, their licit power as owners to dispose of their acts at will, culminating in the anticipation by Spanish thinkers of the modern moral paradigm of the individual's wide-ranging exercise of autonomous choice within a nonnegotiable framework of rational prescriptions and proscriptions.

In the perspective of English public theology, the idea of the moral agent making undetermined choices among divinely "permitted" or "licit" practical moral options is, overall, a misconception of the relation of human freedom and divine law that conflates divine law with human political law. Whereas in moral deliberation, judgment, and action, human law may define a space of permissive freedom in which individual and collective agents can make undetermined choices among multiple licit courses of action, God's law always demands that agents seek to discern and faithfully pursue the course of action most closely in accord with his revealed will. Faithful moral discernment seeks to determine the concrete obedience required in a particular moral situation. Prayerful deliberation, open to the Spirit's leading, illuminates the moral features of the situation, its relevant goods and evils, and the bearing upon it of divine commands and examples that do not clearly and decisively address it. Rather than thematizing human freedom as an interior right, power, or faculty of the human agent, English public theology focused attention on the divine-human relationship, making human moral agency immediately and directly dependent on God's prior action. The agent's moral deliberation, judgment, and action are good, profitable, and free, only as they originate in, and conform to God's communication of the universal and particular judgments of his creating, sustaining, redeeming, and sanctifying will.

Second, the formulation of permissive natural right in Rufinus provided a key theoretical foundation for subsequent justifications of property and coercive rule in the service of self-preservation which aimed at overcoming the moral tension between these institutions of human law and the natural law of created society portrayed by the Church Fathers as a common sharing of the earth's gifts among free and equal human beings. Whereas this moral tension had been preserved within the patristic understanding of property and coercive rule as providential disciplines of "unnatural" constraint and punishment for sinful humanity's disordered passions and actions, it was increasingly undermined by the tendency of scholastic jurists and theologians to endorse legal property right as the most beneficial social realization of the individual's natural rights.

Among the leading ecclesiastical and secular developments contributing to this tendency were three. The elaboration of the papal *plenitudo potestatis* over persons and property and its derivation from Christ's unlimited earthly lordship (*dominium*) fused divine and human judgment and right (*ius*) in the bestowal of political, proprietary, epistemological, and soteriological supremacy on the occupant of a single office. The alternative ecclesiastical model of hierarchical corporatism translated the spiritual unity of Christ's body into a hierarchy of relatively self-governing and property-holding corporations, envisaging the seamless unification of spiritual communion and political-economic apparatus, and even of political, epistemological, and soteriological authority. Civic political corporatism also inclined toward a monistic model of religio-moral-political integration, *corpus mysticum* and *politicum*, grounded in natural proprietary and juridical rights of sovereignty that could be invested in the ruler by transfer from the sociopolitical corporation, could remain with the corporation or be distributed by binding agreement between them.

While English Reformation public theology did not provide a succinct account of the natural right of created human society along patristic lines, it gave indirect support to the patristic conception by reinvigorating the soteriological vision of nonjuridical and nonpossessory ecclesial community, in opposition to papal imperialist and Puritan ecclesiologies. Patristic theologians had viewed created community through the lens of its eschatological renewal and restoration, anticipated by Christ's practice of noncoercive, spiritual rule and self-sacrificial poverty enjoined on his disciples, and by the common sharing of goods in the post-resurrection, apostolic fellowship of believers. For the English reformers, as for the Church Fathers, the decisive common good of the ecclesial community, beyond all human proprietary right and jurisdiction, was the Father's saving communication of himself in his Son by the power of the Holy Spirit—originally to his disciples, and through the apostolic witness of the early church, to succeeding generations of believers.

Central to Cranmerian public theology as to the continental Reformation was the doctrine that an adequate grasp of the moral good, right, and freedom of individuals and communities issues only from faithful reception of Jesus Christ, who manifests the unity of God's judgment and action in creation and redemption. Humanity created in the image of God cannot be understood apart from the renewed moral agency and action of humanity redeemed, dependent on sinful human beings' acceptance of their condemnation and reconciliation in Christ's death and resurrection. For this is God's vindication of his good creation in the historical contest with evil and his promise of its fulfillment in Christ's kingdom. An account of created humanity that disregards or sidelines its accomplished history and awaited future in Christ is necessarily vitiated and distorted.

Equally central to Cranmerian theology was the Reformation doctrine that God's imparting to human beings of his saving judgment is entirely his free action over which the church exercises no proprietary right or juridical control. In performing her apostolic ministry of communicating God's saving revelation, the church's practices are at the disposal of God's sovereign communication in and through the written testimony of his chosen witnesses collected in the Scriptures. They take neither a proprietary nor a judicial form, nor offer the type of certainty and security conveyed by such forms. Through the regular practices of prayer and praise, attending to the words of Scripture, confessing sins, and sacramental celebration, the Holy Spirit freely generates, nourishes, and purifies the faith, hope, and love of believers, renewing their freedom in the fellowship of Christ's resurrection life.

Corresponding to the church's mission, Tudor public theology presented the apostolic authority of the ordained ministry as essentially authority to preach and teach God's word, to intercede on behalf of the church, to celebrate the sacraments commanded by Christ, and to give pastoral counsel, exhortation, and consolation to Christ's flock. Belonging to the church's eschatological reality as the risen Christ's spiritual body, ministerial authority does not intrinsically extend to practices of coercive judgment belonging to the church's political reality as a community under law. In exercising ecclesiastical jurisdiction, the Tudor clerical hierarchy served and represented the lay monarch who held from Christ sovereign jurisdictional authority over the clerical and lay estates of his dominions. Although fraught with dangers, this handling of the duality of the church's spiritual and temporal rule preserved the patristic theological disjunction between the relationships and practices of created and fallen human society.

Third, scholastic elaboration of the functioning of the natural rights of freedom and self-preservation within the proprietary and juridical institutions of civil society progressively laid bare the controlling and defensive rationality of human lordship (*dominium*). According to later Paris masters and their Salamanca successors, individuals have proprietary right in and control over their own capacities and actions primarily and external things derivatively and a degree of moral and coercive control over the actions of others when protecting their own property against theft and injury. They have as well a limited proprietary right in their own life, unrestricted right in the life of inferior creatures, and discretion as to how they exercise their rights. This account had the negative implication of downgrading the moral status of the nonhuman creation, which derives entirely from its usefulness to human self-preservation and freedom. Unable to hold together coherently under the moral-juridical rubric of "rights" the wide-ranging *dominium* of rational creatures and the inclinations of irrational creatures for specific actions, Vitoria and Soto place irrational creatures outside the community of natural rights and corresponding obligations comprising the domain of natural and legal justice. Their juristic perspective occludes the goodness and beauty of lower creatures as God's handiwork and mirror of his perfections, and as objects of wonder, admiration, affection, and species-specific obligations on the part of human beings.

While Tudor public theology does not provide a systematic, biblically focused, alternative account of the relationship of humanity to the nonhuman creation, drawing on patristic, Franciscan, and Wycliffite resources, reformed homiletic and liturgical material offers a patchwork account reflecting the longer exegetical tradition that contains the following elements. All creatures, individually and in their ordered totality, mirror God's infinite goodness, wisdom, and majesty and have as their *telos* the praise of their creator, preserver, and restorer. Nonhuman creatures are ordered to humanity's spiritual praise, in that their sensible appearance and provisions for human welfare evoke in human beings reverent and thankful knowledge and love of God. The Father's bestowal on his human creatures of these spiritual and material benefits is mediated by his Word and Wisdom, incarnate in Jesus Christ, and by the Holy Spirit, who enables human beings to receive them. Sinful human beings are brought to a right regard for, and use of, lesser creatures through knowledge and love of Jesus Christ, in whose history is restored all that which is created, preserved, and governed by the Father's Word and Wisdom.

Fourth, increased attention to the controlling and defensive character of natural freedom and lordship exacerbated thorny issues in theorizing political rule by introducing avoidable clashes of natural rights. Two issues in point were: whether, in the matter of capital punishment, the community's natural right to defend the common welfare took moral priority over the natural right of individuals to defend themselves; and whether the civil community was obliged to transfer the exercise of its natural jurisdictional rights to an appointed magistrate. Albeit, Almain, handled these two issues with relative theoretical ease within his voluntarist, republican-leaning, corporative model of the civil polity: its participatory, representative, and regulatory mechanisms so integrated the natural self-protective rights of its members as to ensure the corporation's right to defend itself against their assaults with capital punishment; and it also ensured that the powers of elected rulers were delegated and accountable to the civil polity, not transferred from it. However, Vitoria's recognition of the more complex relations of divine to human right and *dominium* cast doubt on the adequacy of Almain's immanent corporatist framework for harmonizing natural rights and fulfilling natural justice.

Yet neither Vitoria nor Soto offered a morally plausible harmonization of the communal and the individual natural rights of self-defense in respect of capital punishment, or a coherent theological alternative to the problematic transference theory of sovereign political right/power. Vitoria's proposal of God's direct conferral of monarchial power underpinned its reality as coercive jurisdiction over civil society but left in limbo the commonwealth's natural right of jurisdiction. In a different way, the jurisprudential synthesis of Vázquez also exacerbated these tensions: identifying natural right with subrational, instinctual inclinations, and asserting the rational corruption of the individual's natural powers of liberty and self-preservation, it undermined the moral underpinning of customary and statute law by these natural powers and ensured that their legal protection would severely curtail their exercise. Thus, Vázquez' enterprise of overcoming the graver defects of natural liberty by legal right failed to produce the stable civil contract of subjection that Hobbes would later pursue scientifically.

The alternative account of political rule in Tudor public theology avoided the theoretical difficulties of politically integrating individual and communal natural right by eschewing altogether the conceptuality of subjective rights. Concentrating theoretical attention on the divine source of moral and political authority and the divinely given content and objectivity of right, it elaborated human freedom in terms of faithful obedience to divine law revealed in nature and history and sought to unify ruler and ruled within common bonds of obedience and obligation. It placed limitations on the ruler's *dominium* not by deriving it from, hedging it by, or assimilating it to, a prior individual or communal *dominium*, but by subordinating it to God's revelation of the creaturely goods and right relations which he ordained it to serve, the purpose and forms of its service, the principles and laws of its action, and the spiritual endowments to be entreated of God.

Admittedly, this alternative was not without theological flaws that detracted from its formidable strengths: it suffered from a tendency to inflate the divine constitution of political rule and to underplay some external sources of critical guidance and restraint. These weaknesses will be examined and assessed, along with its strengths, in Chapter 10, for rectification of its past missteps should strengthen the theological challenge presented by Tudor public theology to the Western development of subjective rights theory.

Chapter 5

THE PRIORITY OF SOTERIOLOGY

Our more detailed exploration of the resources of English Reformation public theology for framing a critical and constructive alternative to the natural rights moral and political tradition must have its starting point in soteriology: in the account of God's reconciling and renewing judgment of humankind and the world in the death, resurrection, and ascension of Jesus Christ. For this reforming tradition approaches the individual and common life of created and fallen human beings only from within the revelation to faith of their reconciliation and renewal in Jesus Christ. For the English, as for the continental reformers, this soteriological starting point is inseparably wedded to an epistemological account of Scriptural authority.

The soteriological perspective of Reformation anthropology has many implications for formulating and resolving the anthropological issues posed by natural rights theory in its premodern and modern phases. While posed in a distinctive way by natural rights theory, these issues are perennial to theological anthropology and to its elaboration in ethical and political thought. They may all profitably be seen to relate to the broad theological task of explicating the biblical doctrine of "the image of God" (*imago Dei*): the doctrine that mankind was originally created in the image of God, and that fallen humanity, corrupted by sin, has been, is being, and will be restored to God's image in Jesus Christ. This doctrine has always been the biblical *locus classicus* for expounding the uniqueness of human being within the created order: that is, the singular worth, ontological and moral status of human creatures, generically and individually, distinguishing them from inferior creatures.

A Soteriological Approach to the Imago Dei

From its historical inception, conceptualizing natural rights within a Christian theological framework has necessarily engaged with this doctrine, explicitly or implicitly. Scholastic jurists and theologians directly invoked the doctrine in setting forth the created human rights/powers of rational freedom and dominion over the nonhuman creation. Contemporary Christian theologians have consistently employed the *imago Dei* doctrine to explicate its secular humanist sequel, the concept of "human dignity," which has occupied a similarly pivotal position in the discourse of universal human rights. As we observed earlier, in employing the *imago Dei* doctrine, theologians have commonly emphasized the relations of human beings to the triune God, initiated and sustained by God's own action.

A compelling theological issue, then, concerns the intrinsic association of the *imago Dei* (or its modern successor, "human dignity") with rights or moral powers inherent in individual and communal subjects. Undoubtedly, the issue is most starkly presented by the late modern liberal identification of the inherent dignity of human beings with their autonomous freedom, understood as sovereign ownership (possession and use) of their capacities and actions, their natural right of self-disposal through choice. Nevertheless, the issue is also presented by the scholastic identification of the human image of God with the natural rights of freedom and dominion. In fact, the issue is broader than whether the *imago Dei* or human dignity may be conceptualized in terms of rights. It is whether either can be conceptualized in terms of any immanent or self-standing human structure, quality or capacity, such as freedom, dominion, self-consciousness, linguistic communication, or social relatedness. In short, the issue is whether a trinitarian relational account of the *imago* precludes or may accommodate a naturalist or essentialist account that deflects attention away from God's initiative and action to human initiative and action.

Although Tudor public theology does not address this issue thematically, its position is clear: that the human image of God can only be conceptualized in terms of the dynamic relations of human creatures in every dimension of their individual and communal being to God's manifold and unceasing action as Father, Son, and Holy Spirit. The pivotal relation in this divine-human dynamic is that of sinful human beings to God's saving action in the history of Jesus Christ, and only from within this relation can human beings know themselves as created and sustained by God. Conceptualizing the *imago Dei* in detachment from this knowledge is exposed to the deceptions and distortions of sinful human reasoning. Thus, the *imago Dei*, which sinful human beings need to lay hold on, is the renewed image of Jesus Christ in his full humanity, revealed in the totality of his reconciling and renewing action. For Jesus Christ is both the means and the end (*telos*) of created humankind's reconciliation with God.

In the context of quarrels with Catholic contemporaries over the way in which sinful human beings participate in the renewed *imago Dei*, English reforming bishops were reluctant to give theological content to the created image, fearful of conceding a false soteriological role to natural human capabilities. Consequently, only late and insufficient attention was explicitly paid to the topic of created humanity in the official homilies and doctrinal Articles. However, in various implicit ways, all the reforming instruments of the Tudor church—the vernacular Bible prefaces, doctrinal homilies, Articles, and Prayer Book services—upheld the dialectical relationship within the biblical canon between the beginning and the end of the history of creation: that is, the end as *telos*, inaugurated by the Father's eternal Word taking on human flesh, comprehends and determines the beginning; the beginning as original order is presupposed by its final completion and historical dynamic. Thus, the created human "image"[1] is determined by the Father's eternal Word spoken in Jesus Christ, but not yet determined by the Father's Incarnate Word as wholly renewed humanity, proleptically present in the community of Christ's faithful people.[2] Further consideration of the ways in which this dialectic is upheld in the reforming theology and practices of the Tudor church, and its ethical and political implications, will be given in later chapters; but our prior task in this and the next chapter is to present the Tudor homiletic and doctrinal treatment of God's uniting of humanity through faith and repentance with his singular historical work of salvation in the life, passion, death, resurrection, and ascension of Jesus Christ. Both the strengths and weaknesses of the Tudor treatment reflect the characteristic synthesis of Lutheran and Reformed sources in the English rendering of the Pauline tradition of understanding "justification."

Without wishing to understate the weaknesses, we shall begin by summarizing those features of official Tudor soteriology which, in our judgment, comprise its strengths. 1. The work of salvation is presented as fully accomplished and entirely God's own, not dependent on human volition and action to give it effect. 2. The primary biblical paradigm for conceptualizing God's accomplished work in Jesus Christ is the judicial paradigm of the Father's reconciling judgment as sovereign ruler. This paradigm comprehends and validates the constitutive concepts of sinful humanity's moral and political life—justice and mercy, condemnation and vindication, giving and keeping (or violating) law, right-doing and wrongdoing, merit and guilt, punishment and satisfaction, restraint and protection, and so on—while at the same time displaying their limitations and contradictions. 3. Tudor soteriology enriches and deepens the juridical paradigm by interweaving it with other biblical concepts and images of God's saving action in Christ, previewing and inviting fuller theological development and integration of these different soteriological strands. 4. The account of God's justification of sinners keeps attention fixed on their union through faith with Christ's accomplished work of righteousness and does not allow its deflection to an ecclesial process such as the penitential discipline, intending to build upon Christ's work. 5. The merit of every human act (including that of faith) is excluded from the causal framework of justification, whether the merit be conceived as inherent in the act or as externally bestowed by God. 6. The account focuses on the Holy Spirit as the agent by which the spiritual "benefits" of Christ's work of righteousness are communicated to sinners and does not recognize the operation in the human soul of divinely bestowed spiritual gifts apart from the personal communicating presence of Christ's Spirit of Holiness. 7. Human good works are affirmed as the indispensable completion of God's justifying action. 8. In proximity to Melanchthon and Bucer, the account emphasizes the enduring authority of God's revealed law for a "true

---

1. Gen. 1:26-7, 5:1-2.
2. Col. 1:15-20, 2 Cor. 4:4, Heb. 1–2, Phil. 2:7; Rom. 8:29; 1 Cor. 15:49.

and lively faith" in Christ that "worketh by charity," conceiving charity as willing and joyful obedience to God's law perfectly interpreted by Christ's example and commandments.

God's Accomplished Work of Salvation

The primary concern of Edwardian soteriology as presented in its core homiletic documents—Cranmer's three sermons in the 1549 collection on salvation, faith, and good works—is to articulate the total and exclusive dependence of sinners on the Father's accomplished work of justification in his Incarnate Son. Adopting an early pattern of evangelical soteriology, Cranmer declined to expatiate widely on the trinitarian dynamic of God's saving work but concentrated on what he considered to be the crucial features of St. Paul's theology of atonement.[3] Fortunately, the soteriological homilies in the Elizabethan collection, treating the birth, passion, and resurrection of Jesus Christ and the descent of the Holy Spirit, are more expansive and rounded, supplying some important additional trinitarian and Christological material. The following will examine Cranmer's programmatic homiletical account of God's justifying work, supported by the 1553 Articles, before passing to the Elizabethan homiletic and doctrinal contributions.

As befits preaching of the gospel, Cranmer begins his homily "Of the Salvation of Mankind . . ." by presenting God's continuing work of justification as his ongoing response to the universal need of sinful human beings.[4]

> Because all men be sinners and offenders against God, and breakers of his law and commandments, therefore can no man by his own acts, works, and deeds, seem they never so good, be justified and made righteous before God; but every man of necessity is constrained to seek for another righteousness or justification, to be received at Gods own hands, that is to say, the remission, pardon, and forgiveness of his sins and trespasses in such things as he hath offended. And this justification or righteousness, which we so receive by God's mercy and Christ's merits, embraced by faith, is taken, accepted, and allowed of God for our perfect and full justification.

---

3. A notable example is Melanchthon's dogmatic insistence, in opening the 1521 edition of his *Loci Communes Theologici*, that theology restrict its focus to the needs of the sinner and the benefits of Christ's work. *Loci Communes Theologici* (1521), trans. Lowell J. Satre, in *Melancthon and Bucer*, ed. Wilhelm Pauck (Philadelphia: The Westminster Press, 1969), 20–2.

4. *MWL*, 128; *GH*, 24. All quotations from Cranmer's three homilies are from the 1547 Grafton edition, repr. *MWL*, 128–49, and are followed by the corresponding page references in *GH*.

These dense introductory sentences, encapsulating the contemporary evangelical understanding of the universal plight of sinners devoid of justifying righteousness and of God's merciful bestowal of the "justification or righteousness" of forgiveness of sins, dependent on "Christ's merits,"[5] yield Cranmer's controlling theological principle: that in his work of justifying righteousness, God's wisdom "tempered his justice and mercy together." In dealing with offending humanity, universally enslaved by transgressing his law, God in his "great wisdom" would "neither by his justice condemn us unto the everlasting captivity of the devil and his prison of hell, remediless for ever, without mercy; nor by his mercy deliver us clearly, without justice or payment of a just ransom." Rather, God himself provided the "just ransom" of our deliverance from captivity (Rom. 3:23-24) in the sacrificial "offering" on the cross of Jesus Christ.[6] Christ was sent "to fulfil the law for us," and by shedding his blood, to make "satisfaction or . . . amends to his Father for our sins, to assuage his wrath and indignation conceived against us."[7]

Cranmer's account of Christ's atoning work condenses the blend of judicial, cultic, and political/economic concepts, metaphors, and images drawn from the Scriptures and developed in the church from the early Fathers onward: concepts of God's condemning judgment and punishment, of paying the penalty and making satisfaction for violations of his law, of expiatory and propitiatory sacrifices and offerings to God to deal with sin, and of ransom or redemption from the captivity of slavery by payment of a price. With his evangelical contemporaries, Cranmer principally drew these concepts, metaphors, and images from Paul's epistles to the Romans and Corinthians and focused attention on his conceptualizing of atonement in its intimate connection with justification.[8] The controlling problematic of divine salvation for Cranmer, as for his distinguished predecessor, Anselm of Canterbury,[9] concerns the unity of God's justice and mercy. Reduced to its bare bones, it is that God in his justice requires that sinful humanity do what it cannot do—make satisfaction for sin, pay the price of redemption from the captivity of sin; God in his mercy, by uniting himself with humanity, makes the satisfaction, pays the just price required of humanity, and, in so doing, overcomes the law's condemnation of humanity by perfectly fulfilling the law. Cranmer pursues this problematic through the progression of Paul's argument in Romans and elsewhere.

---

5. Rom. 1–5.
6. *MWL*, 129; *GH*, 25.
7. *MWL*, 129; *GH*, 24.
8. It is worth noting that the concepts of atonement and justification in Paul's soteriology continue to be a hornet's nest of controversies among exegetical scholars.
9. Anselm of Canterbury schematized Christ's atoning work as satisfaction in his influential treatise *Cur Deus Homo?* (1098) and in *De Conceptu Virginali* (1100), following the lead given by Augustine's mature soteriological thought.

Cranmer begins where Paul begins, with the captivity of sinful human beings to "ungodliness and wickedness" and their standing under God's condemnation understood to be the cause of their enslavement (Rom.1:18-32). With Paul, he declares the universality of human bondage both to sin (3:9-18) and to condemnation by God's law (3:19-20), a declaration that will be reiterated in the account of "original or birth sin" given in the Edwardian Articles (Art. VIII). Lamentably, however, Cranmer ignores a key detail of Paul's argument which should not be ignored, even in homiletic pedagogy: that to sin is originally and fundamentally to suppress the truth. Sin began, Paul proposes, with human beings suppressing the truth of God's "invisible nature," specifically, of his "eternal power and Godhead" (KJV) plainly revealed to them in his creatures, by not honoring him as God or giving thanks to him, but, instead, worshipping and serving creaturely idols fashioned by their darkened imaginations and feigned wisdom (Rom. 1:18-25). Consequently, sin continued with human beings suppressing the truth of their own nature and moral relationships (1:26-31).

Since God's eternal power and deity is revealed in the wondrous plenitude and arrangement of created beings and goods, and in his sovereign, steadfast, wise, and bountiful government, Paul's depiction of sin's genesis recalls Adam and Eve's mistrustful refusal of their Creator's unconditional authority to command them for their entire good and their attempted usurpation of his supreme wisdom and ruling power. Although humanity's generic disobedience is echoed in Cranmer's reference to the "breaking of the law" by which "the world [was] wrapped in sin,"[10] he does not explicitly relate God's law to his truth—an omission not remedied in Article VIII's description of the universal corruption of Adamic nature in terms of nonsubjection of the "lust of the flesh" to "the law of God." Thus, he effectively overlooks Paul's crucial depiction of sin as human beings' suppression in action of who God is and who they are, their denial of the relational identities of Creator and creatures whose being is from, in, and to God.

Unless this connection of law-breaking and suppression of God's revealed truth is explicitly made, the justice of God's judgment that sinners *are worthy of death* (Rom. 1:32, KJV), central Cranmer's soteriology, lacks intelligibility. For Paul, God's judgment on sinners is just, in that it pronounces the measure of their defection or straying from the life-giving and goodness-bestowing truth that determines right action. Thus, death is both the intrinsic outworking of their defection and God's pronouncement on it. Both dimensions are included in Paul's depiction of death as the *wages of sin* and the desert (merit, reward) of sinners. The priority of sin over death in Paul's depiction is the priority of spiritual over physical being and of spiritual over physical corruption or deprivation of being. As human life hangs on obedient knowledge of God and of his creation, so human death is the "sting" in the tail of disobedient knowledge. This priority is also central to Paul's conception of the twofold captivity of sinful humanity: to sin first, which is simultaneously captivity to "a base mind and to improper conduct" (Rom. 1:28, RSV), and then

---

10. *MWL*, 128; *GH*, 25.

to death, to physical disintegration portending interminable separation from God. Cranmer encompasses the twofold enslavement of humanity in his reference to the "perpetual captivity of the devil, and his prison of hell."[11] But this power of the devil wielded through sin, and over death, also lacks intelligibility unless Satan is the original Deceiver, the relentless seducer of humanity to fabrications and deceptions (Gen. 3:1-7); for temptation always draws those tempted away from the order of being, truth, and goodness.

Although not rectifying his omission of Paul's understanding of human sinning and law-breaking in terms of suppressing the truth of creation, Cranmer's presentation of Christ's saving work on the Cross as sacrificial atonement, as redemption and ransom, and as fulfillment of the law, has other soteriological strengths. To begin with, his depiction of the Father's "wrath and indignation" against sin and sinners (6) is wholly consonant with the pervasive Old Testament depictions of God's anger (*aph*) and fury (*chemah*) against the sins of Israel, of Israelites, and of the nations, and with Paul's depiction of God's wrath (*orgē*) in Romans chapters 1–5 and 9, which stands out as somewhat rare in the New Testament. The overriding intention of Cranmer is to portray in dramatically personal terms "God's fixed and determined response"[12] to all that transgresses his holy will for his creatures. God's "fixed and determined response" to the transgression and the transgressor is, simultaneously, his condemnation and his punishment, which must fall either on the offender or on a representative: a person or thing who can occupy the offender's place in the court of God's judgment.

Although Paul, unlike the author of Hebrews, makes little explicit use of images and ideas drawn from Israel's sacrificial cult, an important concession occurs in Rom. 3:24-25, where he says of sinners universally that "they are justified by [God's] grace as a gift, through the redemption which is in Christ Jesus whom God put forward as a propitiation (*hilastērion*) by his blood, to be received by faith (ESV)." Cranmer's presentation of Christ's death on the Cross as a sacrificial atonement for the sins of all, in the Articles XIV and XXX as in his homily, blends the sacrificial and juridical conceptuality of atonement, in the spirit of this passage. Its logic is that, in his sacrificial death, Jesus Christ representatively bore God's final condemnation and punishment of all sin and all sinners and thereby averted his everlasting wrath from falling on those who have deserved it. It was as the sinless human being whom God himself elected and provided to stand in solidarity with sinful humanity that Jesus Christ propitiated God's wrath, or, in other words, satisfied his justice (Art. XIV), by freely suffering in his flesh the universal penalty for sin: physical death presaging spiritual death (2 Cor. 5:21; Rom. 3:25).

---

11. *MWL*, 129; *GH*, 129.

12. David Peterson, "Atonement in the Old Testament," in *Where Wrath and Mercy Meet: Proclaiming the Atonement Today*, ed. David Peterson (Milton Keynes: Paternoster, 2001), 9.

Paul's logic of Christ's representative atonement, adopted by Cranmer, accorded with Israel's cultic provisions of atonement in recognizing that representative bearing of another's sin, in the senses of carrying the other's guilt and suffering the other's ordained and deserved punishment, required an identification of offender and representative victim, which neither could bring about of themselves, but only the offended party, by setting the terms of the representation. Israel's God, as both offended party and judge, dictated these terms in his covenant law and, moreover, enabled his people to fulfill them. Of the offender he required, and to the offender he would give, heartfelt acknowledgment and repentance of the evil committed. Of the animal victim he required that it be pure, whole, and unblemished—his acceptance of which established it as such.[13]

In setting out the purpose and effect of Christ's self-sacrifice on the Cross, Cranmer also fuses purgative and propitiatory conceptions. Giving himself over to death, Christ bore the guilt of human sin as well as its punishment: the guilt of sin comprehending the spiritual and physical "blemish" or "wound" left by sin, its "stain" or "uncleanness" (impurity), and the sinner's responsibility or deserving (desert). Christ's shedding of his blood has washed sinners so thoroughly, says Cranmer, that "there remaineth not any spot of sin that shall be imputed, to their damnation."[14] Here, as in Israel's cult, the logical gap has been overcome between the appointed victim's *representation of the offender* in which the offender participates and the victim's *substitution for the offender*. Through God's own action, the sprinkled blood of the slain offering cleanses the sinner of his defilement, and, by bearing the sinner's dessert, the victim averts God's wrath from him. Significantly, Cranmer presents Christ's self-sacrifice as simultaneously removing the cause of human beings' enmity to God and the cause of God's enmity to human beings, so bringing about their reconciliation. In carrying the sin and guilt of all to the Cross, God's Son truly put them to death, definitively ridding sinners, we may say, of their deprivation and untruth, while at the same time vindicating the Father's judgment on them.

Beyond the Israelite cultic logic of atonement, Cranmer's sermon on salvation affirms with Paul and other New Testament writers that it was the eternally beloved Son of the Father who encompassed all humanity in a sacrificial satisfaction worthy of his Father's acceptance. Regrettably, he does not elaborate this affirmation along the Christological lines of Col. 1:15-20, reflecting on Paul's insight (assuming his authorship) that in "the image of the invisible God, the first-born of all creation" (1:15), "all the fulness of God was pleased to dwell, and through him to reconcile to himself all things . . . making peace by the blood of his Cross (1.19-20)." Later

---

13. For the provisions of ritual atonement in the Old Testament, apart from Peterson (above), see: Richard E. Averbeck, "'Offerings and Sacrifices' and '*kpr*,'" in *New International Dictionary of Old Testament Theology and Exegesis*, ed. W. A. VanGemeren, 5 vols (Carlisle: Paternoster, 1997), 4:996–1022; W. S. Wurzburger, "Atonement: Jewish Concepts," in *Encyclopedia of Religion*, 2nd edn. (Detroit, London: Macmillan Reference, 2005), I, 593–4.

14. *MWL*, 128; *GH*, 24.

homilies, as we shall see, make some progress toward recognizing the importance of this insight.

In addition, Cranmer combines the forensic/cultic depiction of Christ's work on the Cross with the emancipatory depictions of redemption, ransom, and deliverance. In making a full and perfect "sacrifice and satisfaction" for the sins of all humankind, Christ's death was the redemption (Rom. 3:24 *apolytrōsis*) of sinners: it was the *price* of their liberation (1 Cor. 6:20, 7:23), the *ransom* that delivered sinful humanity from Satan's captivity by breaking the power of sin over death.[15] This intimate relationship between sacrifice and liberation is especially present in Paul's reference to Christ as "our paschal lamb" (1 Cor. 5:7), recalling the Passover sacrifice of Exodus 12, which inaugurated God's deliverance of Israel from its Egyptian captivity and ratification of his covenant rule over his chosen people. While Cranmer's homily, in speaking of God's "payment of a just ransom," goes well beyond Paul, nevertheless, it nowhere suggests that the ransom was "just" because it respected the devil's proprietary "right" over humankind (a patristic theory discredited by Anselm among others).[16] Rather, for Cranmer, the Son's payment to the Father was just because it freely covered sinful humanity's just desert of captivity to the devil.

Finally, Cranmer presents Christ's fulfilling of the law as a separate strand of his saving work distinguishable from the other two. Christ's fulfilling of the law was his perfect knowledge and love of his Father's will terminating in obedient action throughout his earthly life and climaxing in his blamelessly suffering the death of the body to which the law's condemnation consigned sinful humanity. His fulfilling the law overturned the law's condemnation, emancipated humanity from "the law of sin and death" (Rom. 8:2), and opened to human beings the possibility of life lived in the liberty of Christ's righteousness. Cranmer concludes his exposition of God's justifying work with Paul's key passage in Rom. 8:3-4: "That which was impossible by the Law, inasmuch as it was weak by the flesh, God sending his own Son in the similitude of sinful flesh, by sin[17] damned sin in the flesh, that the righteousness of the Law might be fulfilled in us, which walk not after the flesh, but after the Spirit."[18]

Cranmer passes on to expound the sinner's justification by faith in Christ without commenting on this vital transitional passage connecting God's accomplished

---

15. *MWL*, 129; *GH*, 25. Article 30 also combines these metaphors.

16. Origen elaborated and gave historical currency to a theory which took with legal literalness the idea that humankind in sinning had sold itself into servitude to the devil, becoming his property, which Christ had to buy back at a just price. Among later theologians critical of the devil's proprietary rights, Anselm of Canterbury concedes that sinful humankind is justly abused by the devil, with God's just permission, but denies any intrinsic justice to the devil's act, and any notion of just possession, humankind, and the devil remaining the rightful possession of God alone. *Cur Deus Homo*, 1.7.

17. "by sin": Cranmer follows Tyndale (1534) and The Great Bible (1540).

18. *MWL*, 129; *GH*, 26.

work of righteousness in Jesus Christ to his ongoing work of righteousness in those who by faith are in Christ. For the connecting reality is the Spirit of Jesus Christ, crucified and resurrected, who, even in their mortal lives, draws the faithful into the Son's exalted life of obedience to the Father's truth, giving them a foretaste of their final imaging of Christ's glorious rule. It is a measure of Cranmer's Lutheran truncation of God's accomplished work of justification in this homily that he does not mention the resurrection of Jesus, and so stops short of Paul's unequivocal declaration that Jesus "was delivered [to death] for our offences and was raised again for our justification (Rom. 4.25 KJV)." Of course, the homily on salvation is not Cranmer's last word on the resurrection and ascension of Christ or on the justification of sinners. Throughout his two following homilies on faith and good works he assumes Christ's living presence before the Father and the imparting of the Holy Spirit to the faithful. In addition, Article IV presents as fulsome an affirmation of the bodily resurrection and ascension of Jesus as one could wish.[19] Cranmer does not, however, provide homiletical treatment of the relationship between Christ's bodily resurrection and his salvation of sinners.

Overall, it must be conceded that Cranmer's account of God's completed work of salvation in Jesus Christ does not draw broadly enough on Paul's soteriological themes, nor those of other New Testament writers. Moreover, despite his invocation of Old Testament soteriological themes taken over in New Testament writings, he makes little explicit reference to God's unfolding of his saving promises, fulfilled in Jesus Christ, in the prophetic traditions that contribute to the Pauline interpretation of salvation in Israel's history.

Resurrection and Creation, Justification, and Revelation

Turning to the Elizabethan soteriological homilies, they consist of five sermons: one on the nativity of Christ, two on his death and passion, one on his resurrection, and one on the "coming down" and gifts of the Holy Spirit. Of the first four, two are, unambiguously, edited versions of Edwardian sermons, and another could originally be of the same vintage, whereas the fifth is more probably Elizabethan in origin, perhaps from John Jewel. While the immediate rationale of their inclusion was to provide doctrinally and pastorally rich sermons for the most important liturgical occasions of the church calendars—Christmas, Good Friday, Easter, and Whitsunday—they were, assuredly, also selected, edited, or composed with an eye to the soteriological lacunae in the Edwardian homilies. While endorsing

---

19. "Christ did truly rise again from death, and took again his body with flesh, bones, and all things pertaining to the perfection of man's nature, wherewith he ascended into Heaven, and there sitteth, until he return to judge men at the last day." Also, Article 29 on "the Lord's Supper" follows the "Black Rubric" of the Communion service in situating Christ's human body exclusively in heaven.

the emphases of Cranmer's account of God's accomplished work of justification in Jesus Christ, they addressed the need for a fuller and more balanced presentation.

Taken together, these homilies made notable soteriological contributions. They set forth the resurrection and ascension of Jesus Christ as the decisive completion of his triumph on the Cross and related this more complete understanding of Christ's triumph to the doctrine of the Incarnation and Christ's "two natures" as true God and true man. They gave fuller expression to the trinitarian relations and action in which Christ's saving work is embedded and upon which it depends and, as well, to the unity of God's action in his creation and justification of humankind. They paid closer attention to the history of Israel as foreshadowing God's promise in Christ and clarified the relationship between the revelatory and the atoning dimensions of God's action in Jesus Christ. Together, the sermons enhanced the internal coherence and the Scriptural fidelity of the official homiletic presentation of Christ's saving work and brought it into line with the doctrinal/theological scope of the church's formal liturgy and of its official formulary of faith.

Naturally, the resurrection and ascension of Jesus are treated most extensively in the Easter homily, edited from Richard Taverner's *Postils on the Epistles and Gospels* (1540). Taking 1 Cor. 15:14-22 as its starting point, the homily attributes to the apostle Paul certainty that the resurrection of Jesus Christ is "the ground and foundation," "the very lock and key" of Christian faith and practice; for in Christ's resurrection lies the justification of sinners and their establishment in the hope of eternal life and righteousness.[20] Christ's resurrection is presented as the completing movement of a single divine action, the first movement of which was Christ's death on the Cross. The two movements (or phases) are distinguishable, but also inseparable, so that depicting Christ's accomplishment on the Cross cannot stop short of the third day. With Cranmer and the apostle Paul, the homily depicts Christ's death as taking away human sin and God's "malediction" on it, "a ransom of them both"—as overcoming the devil, destroying death, and the "damnation" of hell.[21] However, the homily's author and editor understand that these depictions of the accomplishment of Christ's death—removing, delivering, ransoming, and destroying—are backward looking: they chart the initial and not the terminal phase of God's saving action, the exodus from Egypt rather than the sight of, and entry into, the promised land. The homily holds together the backward and the forward glances: Christ's death has broken through and overcome all the obstacles thrown up by human sin to the fulfillment of God's gracious purposes for his human creatures, to place humanity on the brink of its fulfillment.

It is in Christ's resurrection that God pronounces the acquittal of sinful humanity, welcomes humanity into his presence, and establishes the rule of the Spirit of righteousness within humanity:[22]

---

20. "Of the Resurrection of our Saviour Jesus Christ," *GH*, 429-32.
21. *GH*, 431.
22. *GH*, 433.

It had not been enough to be delivered by his death from sin, except by his resurrection we had been endowed with righteousness. And it should not avail us to be delivered from death, except he had risen again, to open for us the gates of heaven, to enter into life everlasting . . . [1 Pet. 1:3-5]. . . . He died to destroy the rule of the devil in us; and he arose again to send down His Holy Spirit to rule in our hearts, to endow us with perfect righteousness.

The clear message of the homily is that God, in raising Jesus Christ from the dead, has unfolded the final end toward which Christ's deliverance of humanity by his death is ordered. He has unfolded the restoration and perfection of human life in righteousness for which Christ on the Cross overcame the power of death, purchased forgiveness of sins, and cleansed all humanity from the stain and guilt of sin. The "lively hope" into which sinners have been "begotten . . . by the resurrection of Jesus Christ" (1 Pet. 1:3) is of their own resurrection, to reign with the Father and the Son in "everlasting bliss," as souls endowed with imperishable righteousness and holiness through the indwelling Spirit, and "bodies . . . glorified in immortality and joined to [Christ's] glorious body."[23] The homily pays balanced attention to the historical and the eschatological dimensions of Christ's resurrected life and action. Initially, it strongly emphasizes the publicity of Christ's resurrection appearances, his "bodily presence" to his disciples over forty days, providing visible and tangible proof of his victory in the grave over sin, death, and the devil. Then its focus shifts to the indwelling of the ascended Christ and his Spirit of Holiness within the human heart by faith, translating the faithful "in hope" to the everlasting life of heavenly glory in fellowship with Christ, and replenishing them "with all righteousness" as "a seal and pledge of [their] everlasting inheritance" of spiritual and corporeal bliss.[24]

A weakness, perhaps, of the eschatological vision is the relative absence of a larger cosmic and social horizon, leaving uncertainty as to whether Jesus Christ glorified is the archetype of the spiritual and corporeal renewal of elect individuals or of the whole creation order. This weakness, also detectable in the Edwardian and Elizabethan Article IV on Christ's resurrection and the Edwardian Article XXXIX on "the resurrection of the dead," may be regarded as an aspect of the neglect of the doctrine of creation coloring the Edwardian homilies, and both sets of doctrinal articles (apart from the bare reference to God as "the maker and preserver of all things both visible and invisible").[25]

Among the three happy exceptions to this neglect in the Elizabethan homilies is the homily on Christ's "Nativity and Birth," featuring more prominently the relation of salvation to the original creation order. It sets the stage for an exposition

---

23. *GH*, 434.
24. *GH*, 433–4.
25. On the occlusion of creation by redemption in the Articles, O'Donovan, *On the Thirty-Nine Articles: Conversations with Tudor Christianity*, 2nd edn. (London: SCM Press, 2011), 63–74. Hereafter, *TA*.

of the Incarnation and the "two natures" of Jesus Christ by elaborating on the creation and fall of Adam and the succession of God's covenant promises to fallen humanity. It stresses the perfection of Adam in terms that call to mind Calvin's fulsome descriptions of created humanity in his 1559 *Institutes*: "endued with all kind of heavenly gifts," "sound ... in all parts, both inwardly and outwardly," "made altogether like unto God in righteousness, in holiness, in wisdom, in truth." Adam also enjoyed a perfection of worldly existence, living in "tranquillity and pleasure," with a comfortable "abundance" of all the goods "that he might justly require or desire to have," and the divinely granted lordship to "rule" the nonhuman creation and "use [it] at his pleasure."[26] Despite his spiritual perfections, however, Adam in the "time of prosperity and wealth" was still susceptible of forgetting himself and God, so as to break the single divine commandment "most unmindfully, or rather most wilfully," "giving ear" to the devil's "crafty suggestion."[27] The homily's presentation of humankind's primal sin is that of a self-assertive suppression of the relation of creature and creator in its ontological and moral dimensions, goaded by the devil's misrepresentations. The outcome of Adam's forgetful disobedience was his becoming "accursed" rather than "blessed," "abhorred" rather than "loved," "vile and wretched" rather than "beautiful and precious" in the sight of his Maker and Ruler, the "image of the devil" rather than of God.[28]

The homily's presentation of Adam's created perfection and fall into sin has several features deserving of attention. First, its reference to the perfections of created human nature as "heavenly gifts" may indicate that they not only have their source in God but are continually imparted by him, being productions of his presence to and in the human soul, and not productions of human powers or faculties. Its author may be implying the activity of God's eternal Word and Spirit from the beginning, illuminating the knowing human mind, directing the desiring human will, and bringing its spiritual acts to fruition.[29] Second, the homily's invocation of the universal tendency of flourishing humanity to forget itself and God suggests an inherent frailty in the finite human understanding and will. Inhering in human modes of knowing and enjoying, administering and using fellow creatures are two contrasting, but closely related temptations. One is for self-conscious human beings to harbor an inflated estimation of their status and powers within the physical and moral universe, and to strive to secure them against their creator and ruler. The other is for human beings to immerse themselves in finite activities and their objects, to the point of reifying them,

---

26. *GH*, 400, cf. *Institutes* I.15.3-8.
27. *GH*, 400-1.
28. The second homily on Christ's passion produces this same antithetical pair *verbatim* in describing the consequences of Adam's act of disobedience. *GH*, 419.
29. If so, he would concur with Calvin's 1553 commentary on Jn 1:4: "The life was the light of men" (cf. *Institutes* 2.2.12), and his speculation in *Institutes* 2.12.17 about Christ's continuing headship of created humanity by the power of his Spirit, had humanity not fallen into sin.

losing sight of their transcending orientation to the Creator as his handiwork. Third, the homily describes the consequences of Adam's disobedience largely in terms of transformed relationships with both God and the devil. Humanity's subjection to the antihuman rule of the devil in which it takes on the devil's image or likeness places it under God's truthful and just abhorrence and enmity. From both relationships spring the incapacities of corrupted human being.

Thus, recovery of the divine image is, before all else, recovery of God's loving, cherishing, and delighting recognition of his human creatures. The Messiah, promised even to Adam and his progeny, is the Father's beloved Son, who by his perfect sacrifice and satisfaction rescued sinners from their just condemnation to Satan's rule of sin and death, and restored them to God's favor.[30] That the crucified and resurrected Messiah was "perfect man" and "perfect God" was indispensable to his justification of sinners: indispensable to his representation of sinners before God which won their acceptance and vindication and indispensable to their incorporation by his Holy Spirit into his resurrection life, which produced faith and the spiritual fruits of faith among his disciples.

Into these familiar arguments for Christ's "two natures" the homily weaves aspects of Christ's revelatory mission. It presents his earthly ministry as the unfolding revelation of his humanity and his divinity: on the one hand, of the frailty and vulnerability of the human condition subject to suffering and death in its physical, social, legal, and moral forms; and on the other, the divine powers of forgiving sins, casting out devils, healing "with his only word," knowing "the thoughts of men's hearts," having natural forces at his command, rising from the dead, and ascending into heaven.[31] The Incarnate Son is, simultaneously, the revealing Word of the Father to his human creatures and the revealing Word of his human creatures to the Father. Jesus Christ came among sinners "to bear witness unto the truth, to teach and preach the words of his Father, to give light unto the world." As "very God" he revealed to sinful human beings what their captive understanding had suppressed: their heavenly Father's sovereign authority, eternal wisdom, cleansing righteousness, and boundless, condescending love.[32] As "very man" he manifested true human being, the human *imago Dei*, the adopted son in whom the Father delights; by his obedient self-giving to the Father, and through the Father, to his human kin, Christ made known his Father's eternal will for all humanity.[33]

The homily's considerable theological achievement is to expound God's revelation of his eternal Image in the creation and in the justification of humanity as one unified revelation, so that created humanity has no other *telos than* justified humanity and cannot be conceived apart from its relationship to the Father

---

30. *GH*, 406–7.
31. *GH*, 405–6.
32. Citing Jn 18:37; Lk. 4:17-21, 43; Mt. 11:27; Jn 8:12. *GH*, 408.
33. *GH*, 408–9.

through his Word manifest in Jesus Christ.[34] The homily succeeds in reattaching the controlling anthropological tropes of Edwardian Pauline soteriology—those of "the old Adam" and "the new Adam," fallen and redeemed humanity, condemned and justified humanity, to the structural element of creation present in Paul's theological architecture. It portrays the revelation in Jesus Christ of the human image of God—created, corrupted, and perfectly renewed—as an indivisible revelation, so that no one moment may be treated in abstracting isolation from the others. Cranmer's homilies fail on this account, owing to his preoccupation with the implications of Adam's fall for God's work of justification in Jesus Christ, and with the danger posed by Pelagian and legalistic constructions of justification.

Addressing the need for a fuller account of the person and work of the Holy Spirit (recognized by the Edwardian and Elizabethan bishops) is the first part of a two-part sermon for Whitsunday on the Spirit's "coming down" and "manifold gifts," frequently ascribed to John Jewel. Naturally enough, the homily initially focuses on the Holy Spirit's gathering of the community of the faithful through the preaching, hearing, and confessing of God's Word in Jesus Christ, beginning with the apostolic witness to all nations at Pentecost; but it is concerned more broadly with the divine person and work of the Spirit as proceeding from the Father and the Son. It presents the Spirit as universally active in the communication of the Father's saving Word to humankind: preeminently in the Son's Incarnation, from his conception in Mary's womb; most dramatically, with the Father, at Christ's baptism; throughout his miraculous earthly ministry and that of his disciples; but also by Israel's patriarchs and prophets looking forward to the fulfillment of God's promises; and by Christ's followers and disciples during his earthly ministry.[35] However, one theater of the Spirit's revelation of Christ is notably absent from the homily: the theater of apostolic prophecy or apocalyptic visions of the last things. The Tudor episcopal reformers did not encourage their flocks to dwell on the detailed speculative imagery in the New Testament, especially in the book of Revelation, concerning Christ's return in judgment, the general resurrection of the dead, and the consummation of all things in his Kingdom, nor did they wish to draw attention to the divine inspiration of such visionary communications.

In passing seamlessly from the Spirit's revelation of Jesus Christ, resurrected and ascended, to the Spirit's sanctifying action, the homily displays the interpenetration of the two activities of "quicken[ing] the minds of men" to receive the truth, wisdom, and command of Christ and of "stirring up good and godly motions in

---

34. To assert this unity of divine revelation and of humanity's *telos* does not entail the further assertion that the eternal Son of the Father would have become incarnate, had humankind not sinned. One can still concur with the second sermon for Good Friday that, if humanity had not "presumed to transgress the will of God in . . . Adam, then Christ, 'being in the form of God,' needed not 'to have taken upon him the shape of a servant'; . . . being 'the true bread' of the soul, he needed not to hunger; being the healthful 'water of life,' he needed not to thirst; being 'life' itself, he needed not to have suffered death." *GH*, 422.

35. *GH*, 455–6.

their hearts . . . agreeable to the will and commandment of God."[36] As the Spirit's sanctifying work belongs to the following and later chapters, our task now is to draw together the resources of the Tudor presentation of God's completed work of justification for framing a theological alternative to the anthropology of liberal natural rights.

Toward a Dynamic, Relational, and Christological Imago Dei

The dynamic, relational, Christological anthropology offered by English Reformation public theology presents a radically critical and constructive alternative to the rationalist, voluntarist, and essentialist anthropology of the Western natural rights tradition which locates the dignity of human creatures—their unique ontological and moral status—in their proprietary freedom and control as self-reflecting subjects. Foregoing all naturalist or essentialist accounts of created humanity that conceptualize the *imago Dei* in terms of immanent, self-standing human structures, qualities, or capacities, the reformers' alternative account focuses on the united action of Father, Son, and Holy Spirit to restore and renew the *imago Dei* in the history of Jesus Christ. This soteriological lens fixes attention on divine rather than human initiative and action: God's completed work of salvation in Jesus Christ determining the history of created humanity and the nonhuman creation beyond the causal nexus of sinful human reasoning, volition, and action. Only God's renewal of his image in the humanity of Jesus Christ brings fully to light created humanity's dependent adherence to the Father's Word in the Spirit's power, enabling effective and authoritative human action within and over the creation.

The Incarnate Son's revelation of renewed humanity in his obedient knowledge and self-expending love of the Father and his fellow creatures lays bare the modern liberal misconstruction of the unique moral fabric of human life in terms of immanent human powers of autonomous and creative will, reason, and action, ordered to the principal ends of individual self-protection and self-development. It exposes this misconstruction's disregard of the essential openness of human beings to the commanding claim and power of God's righteous and loving will for their common life; its blindness to the intrinsic unity in created human moral community of rational freedom, love, and law: of freely giving oneself to God and to one's fellow creatures and of being bound by an irresistible, transcendent, and immanent imperative.

The prevailing ideal of human agency in egalitarian-rights society, that of autonomous self-disposal in action, leaves no room for the ecstatic moral agency of human obedience presented by Christ's self-giving on the Cross, in which God disposes of the agent's action, and freedom resides in the alignment of the human with the divine will brought about by the Spirit. It is this alignment, even unity,

---

36. *GH*, 456. Citing 1 Cor. 3:16, 6:19; Rom. 8:9; 1 Jn 2:27; 1 Pet. 4:14.

of wills that enables human beings to embrace the loss of "self-control" inherent in suffering, chosen or unchosen—a loss wholly repugnant to the proprietary conception of the subject's freedom. This unity enables individuals to embrace suffering on behalf of others as an imperative of divine love within the disordered relationships of fallen community, and as participation in Christ's redemption of human agency by his sacrificial suffering and death.

Furthermore, the liberal misconstruction of human moral community in terms of natural subjective rights makes coercive jurisdiction and law indispensable to moral community per se: for the entire development of natural rights theory into late modernity shows subjective rights to be inseparable from jurisdiction: to be either inherently proprietary and justiciable or superfluous to ethical and political thought. Late and second scholastic theologians were driven to adopt more proprietary, defensive, and juridical formulations of natural rights by both theoretical and practical pressures to resolve the inherited contradiction between humanity's natural right of nonproprietary, nonjuridical use of the world's resources, conceived relationally in theistic and Christocentric terms, and humanity's natural right of liberty, conceived in immanent, rationalist, proprietary terms, of which legal property right was the social embodiment.

In the perspective of English Reformation anthropology, to make jurisdiction indispensable to moral community is to suppress the moral ambiguities of human jurisdiction and the ineradicable tension between love and justice in the conflictual society that requires jurisdiction. Fundamentally, it is to suppress the different modalities of divine rule in human society as created, fallen, and restored. Against this suppression, Jesus Christ's sacrificial satisfaction to God the Father in the court of divine justice for humankind's defiant violation of his law testifies definitively that God's condemning and acquitting judgment is coterminous with human sinfulness, as is the discordance between justice and mercy, law and love, which the Son's atonement overcomes. Apart from humanity's bondage to sin, God's rule and law are not judicial: his judgments do not convict, condemn, punish, or vindicate his human creatures, as do human public judgments established by him.

For the English reformers, following the Western patristic tradition, the persisting necessity of political and legal judgment in human society testifies that Christ's overcoming of humanity's bondage to sin and of the law's condemnation is not fully revealed in our human historical existence. The uniting of sinful human beings with Christ's righteousness, with his perfectly ordered love, is an ongoing work of the Holy Spirit in this passing age of the Old Adam, wherein human sinning and the law's condemnation are still operative but deprived of any future in Christ's coming kingdom. The absence of human jurisdiction from the Western theological vision of created and perfected human community under God's rule of commanding love calls into question the attribution to human beings of the natural right of proprietary freedom and its satellite rights, and with them, the theoretical erection of political jurisdiction on the natural rights foundation.

For the English reformers, human political jurisdiction is not a rational human contrivance for collectively managing, protecting, and enlarging individual and corporate rights of self-preservation, liberty, and their institutional embodiments.

Rather its source is God's providential ordination of a communal condemnation of human wrongdoing and vindication of well-doing, expressing his just condemnation of sinful works and his merciful will to protect the fragile common goods of human life from sin's ravages. Its practical limitations and inherent tensions derive from its divinely ordained, not humanly contrived, purposes. Moreover, human jurisdiction also stands under God's condemning judgment on account of the inescapable infection of its practices with sinful proclivities, paramount of which are to usurp God's rule and to tyrannously dominate fellow human and nonhuman creatures. Both proclivities were operative in the judicial condemnation to a torturous and humiliating death of Jesus Christ, the human incarnation of God's rule of love. Christ's revelation on the cross of the unity of justice and love in God's saving rule discloses in their depth and breadth the limitations and moral ambiguities of human jurisdiction.

The chasm separating the benefits to sinful humanity of God's saving rule from those of communal jurisdiction is conveyed by the plethora of biblical conceptual motifs employed by the Tudor homilists to depict Christ's completed work of justifying righteousness. Drawing on Old and New Testament patterns, the Tudor homilies interweave the central juridical soteriological paradigm with motifs of spiritual purification of human life from sin's stain, emancipation and rescue of the whole creation from the tyranny of destructive and disintegrative forces, the breaking of demonic power over sin and death, and participation of faithful humanity in God's promise of an eternal communion with himself and with one another that fulfills his sovereign law of love. This larger soteriological fabric contains and interprets the juridical logic of Christ's satisfaction, enmeshing it within the multiple strands of God's trinitarian revelation of himself in action toward and in the world. These encompass God's overflowing generosity in creating finite goods, his continuous sustaining of creaturely goods amid the chaotic disruption of human sin, his overcoming of sin and the law's condemnation, and inaugurating an eschatological community beyond communal practices of judgment and punishment: a communion of openness and joy, humility, forbearance, and forgiveness, conforming in time to the image beyond time of Jesus Christ.

In bringing into focus the structures, conditions, and ends of human life through the lens of God's accomplished work in Jesus Christ, the Tudor homilies break through the barriers thrown up by immanent forms of anthropological analysis to the emancipation of human beings from their present forms of bondage. For the immanent forms of sinful humanity's diminished self-understanding cannot begin to plumb the depths of, or to surmount, the negativities of human existence in the *saeculum*: the intolerable burden of human beings' self-determining freedom, of their failure and guilt as moral actors, of their isolation and alienation from one another, of their drive for manipulative control of their human and nonhuman environment, and of conflicting individual and collective aspirations and undertakings.

The imperative of redirecting the theoretical quest of human emancipation away from immanent human powers is further explored in the exposition to follow of the Tudor treatment of God's ongoing work of justifying humanity, his bringing sinful human beings to a lively faith in Jesus Christ and repentance of their sins. Chapter 6 engages more closely with the wholly negative moment in the dynamic divine-human relationship: the moment of "loss," "destruction," "effacement," or "darkening" of the human *imago Dei*. In English Reformation soteriology, this moment too is portrayed within the Father's judgment of wayward humanity in the suffering and death of his Son which brings to light, at once, the full scope of the Father's rejection of human corruption and disablement by sin, and his recognition and acceptance of the renewed human image in Jesus Christ. Thus, the unity of faith and repentance is key to sinful human beings' recovery of conformity and communion with the Father's eternal Word, the everlasting *imago Dei*.

Chapter 6

GOD'S ONGOING WORK OF JUSTIFICATION

BRINGING SINNERS TO FAITH

We turn now to the English reformers' public account of God's ongoing work of justification: the completion in individual and social life of his accomplished justification of all humanity in Jesus Christ.[1] Facilitating our expository task is the relatively homogenous character of the documentary material. Compared with Cranmer's relatively sketchy and truncated account of God's completed work in Jesus Christ, his homilies on salvation, faith, and good works provide a quite comprehensive account of God's ongoing work of justification, fully elaborating the liturgical motifs of the Edwardian prayer books. Consequently, the Elizabethan homilists were content to reiterate his reforming orthodoxy with occasional modest expansions. Likewise, the Articles simply summarize Cranmer's teaching, only offering additional theological clarification around predestination.

Aspects of "A True and Lively Faith"

Cranmer's account of God's ongoing work of justification is somewhat distinctive in presenting it as *one work* in two parts: the first part being God's uniting of sinners with Christ's work of righteousness and the second, the outworking of this union in bringing forth works acceptable to God. Thus, he deviates from much reforming soteriology by incorporating sanctification into justification via his concept of faith, rather than treating sanctification separately as a further divine work. In approaching the relevant New Testament, and especially Pauline, texts, Cranmer draws on selected patristic and contemporary writings (of Augustine especially, and Luther, Melanchthon, Bucer, and Calvin) but, for apologetic reasons, makes explicit appeals largely to the Church Fathers, Latin and Greek.

---

1. For a detailed historical analysis of the intricate cross-currents in theological formulations of justification preceding and including the sixteenth-century controversies, Alister E. McGrath, *Iustitia Dei: A History of the Christian Doctrine of Justification* (Cambridge: Cambridge University Press, 1986).

First and foremost, Cranmer presents God's justification of sinners as uniting them with his merciful work of righteousness in Jesus Christ. Sinners are united as recipients or beneficiaries of the Father's mercy and of Christ's justice. Their justification is God's communication to them of the benefits of Christ's accomplished work of making satisfaction to the Father for human sin or paying sin's debt, of washing away sin's stain, of overcoming the law's condemnation and fulfilling its righteousness, of abolishing the demonic tyranny of death. Sinners' reception of Christ's benefits takes the form of a "true and lively faith," definitively described by Cranmer as "a sure trust and confidence of the mercy of God through our Lord Jesus Christ, and a steadfast hope of all good things to be received at God's hand."[2]

Cranmer's three homilies show faith to be "true" and "lively" in the following aspects. First, the object of faith is entirely what the Father has done, is doing, and will do for sinners in his Son, Jesus Christ, and not at all what sinners themselves can do toward their justification, with or without God's special aid and/or gift. At the same time, faith's focus on God's action in Christ reveals the sinner's existential condition. Second, faith necessarily brings forth "good works": that is, interior and exterior actions pleasing to God and to the neighbor. Although works of love are no part of the causal nexus of justification, they are intrinsic to repentant and hopeful faith as its "fruit." The form taken by works of love is obedience to Christ's commandments, which are for faith the authoritative disclosure of God's perfect law for human action. Third, faith certifies itself: it demonstrates its truth by means of its practical fruits, giving reflexive assurance of their justification to faithful actors. A closer look at these defining aspects will show the importance for the soteriological structure of Cranmer's ethics of his expansive understanding of faith, encompassing hope as its forward-looking dimension and love as its active fruition.

The Single Object of Faith

True faith has for its entire object the Father's past, present, and future action for sinners in his Son, Jesus Christ. Its object is the divinely revealed and certified truth that the Father "will forgive and forget our offences for his Son's sake"; that he looks favourably on us and cares for us "as the father . . . over the child whom he doth love," protecting and defending us, and patiently correcting us; that his Son will be "our perpetual Advocate and Priest, in whose only merits, oblation, and suffering . . . our offences be continually washed and purged," until the Father finally makes us "inheritors with him of his everlasting kingdom."[3] True faith looks only to God's free and gracious, yet fixed and unswerving, acceptance of unworthy

---

2. *MWL*, 135; *GH*, 37.
3. *MWL*, 135–6; *GH*, 37–8.

sinners for the sake of Jesus Christ and on account of his righteousness, alone.[4] In considering the cause of God's favor toward us, faith fixes its gaze firmly on Christ's perfect justice and the working of God's mercy through it.[5]

In the view of Cranmer and like-minded reformers, the soteriological traditions of the Roman church had corrupted faith by deflecting its gaze away from God's justifying work in Christ and onto his justifying work in sinners. These traditions construed justification as God's work of making sinners just, of rendering them worthy of divine acceptance and forgiveness of sin, by assisting them to meritorious acts and infusing in them meritorious spiritual states that would in some respect cause God's pardon. Thrusting Christ's saving work on the Cross into the background, their analysis concentrated on the complicated causal process of human effort and divine grace by which sinners appropriated the merit of Christ's sacrificial satisfaction on the Cross.

In these traditions, the process of justification was intimately linked with the discipline of sacramental penance: the threefold work of contrition, confession, and satisfaction by which sinners obtained forgiveness of their post-baptismal sins, including divine remission of both the guilt (*culpa*) and the punishment (*poena*), eternal and temporal, which their mortal and venial sins had merited.[6] The discipline was erected on two core soteriological axioms: the baptized person in committing a mortal sin[7] lost the gift of sanctifying grace imparted to the soul in the sacrament of baptism, and with it the promise of eternal life; and restoration of the gift of sanctifying grace and its corresponding promise would come only through *poenitentia*, the "voluntary self-punishment for sin required by God's justice,"[8] which was simultaneously a spiritual virtue (penitence) and an ecclesiastical sacrament (penance). The soteriological fulcrum of penance was the conversion of the penitent's sorrow for past sins (her "attrition") into true "contrition" by the gift of sanctifying grace (*gratia gratum faciens*). There were two prevailing conceptions of this conversion of attrition to contrition, which may be labeled, broadly speaking, Thomist and Scotist.

On the Thomist view, the divine infusion of sanctifying grace into the penitent's soul transformed her imperfect sorrow, dominated by servile fear of divine

---

4. *MWL*, 132; *GH*, 32.

5. Ibid.

6. For historical accounts of the discipline of sacramental penance, B. Poschmann, *Busse und Letzte Ölung, Handbuch der Dogmengeschichte*, vol. iv, pt. 3 (Freiburg: Herder, 1951): *Penance and the Anointing of the Sick*, trans. and rev. F. Courtney (London: Burns and Oats 1964); Thomas Tentler, *Sin and Confession on the Eve of the Reformation* (Princeton: Princeton University Press, 1977); Oscar D. Watkins, *A History of Penance*, 2 vols (New York: Burt and Franklin, 1961).

7. Mortal sins were traditionally defined as violations of the Decalogue.

8. Ashley Null, *Thomas Cranmer's Doctrine of Repentance: Renewing the Power to Love* (Oxford: Oxford University Press, 2000), 34; citing *Manipulus curatorum*, Pars. 2, tract. 1, cap. 1, fol. 65r.

punishment, into sorrow springing from perfect faith and love of God, expelling all fear. The imparted habit of sanctifying grace effected a double movement of the penitent's free will, toward God (the *motus* of faith and love) and against sin (the *motus* of contrition), simultaneously inaugurating the healing of the sinner's disordered nature and rendering her acceptable to God.[9] While the penitent's preparatory disposition of inadequate sorrow—itself a work of "prevenient" grace (*gratia gratis data*)—was requisite for God's gift of sanctifying grace, it did not merit the gift. By contrast, the action of sanctifying grace did merit justification *de condigno*, that is, according to God's gracious ordination of this reward for this work.[10]

The causal relations between the infusion of sanctifying grace, the act of contrition, and the remission of sin were painfully complicated in Thomist thought because Aquinas conceived each of the three moments as exercising reciprocal causality on the other two. This causal reciprocity permitted integration of the three moments with the parts of sacramental penance—contrition, confession, and absolution—by combining the Aristotelian distinction of material, formal, and efficient causality with the traditional theological distinction of visible sacramental sign and its invisible object. In sacramental penance, the infusion of sanctifying grace was the formal and efficient cause of the penitent's interior act of contrition signified by the external acts of confession and satisfaction, which was the material cause of the infusion of sanctifying grace and so, of the forgiveness of sins[11]; while the priest's absolution, in conjunction with the penitent's exterior acts of confession and satisfaction, was the instrumental cause (*causa instrumentalis*) of the infusion of sanctifying grace, and so, of the forgiveness of sins.[12] Thus, this penitential account of the "process of justification" sought to render forgiveness of sin "a conjoint result" of both the supernatural virtue of contrition and "a benefit of Christ's passion . . . communicated through absolution . . . *ex opere operato*."[13] The theory's major weakness was the obvious disjunction between temporal and causal relations. Skeptics questioned the plausibility of the sacramental absolution

---

9. Aquinas, *ST* 1.2ae.113.6, 111.2; also McGrath, *Iustitia Dei*, 106–7; Poschmann, *Penance*, 165, 169–70.

10. *ST* 1.2ae.114.1; also McGrath, *Iustitia Dei*, 113–14. As McGrath points out, merit *de condigno* is defined by some proportional relationship between the intrinsic moral worth of an act and God's estimation of it (*iustitia secundum proportionem quandam*), but God's assignment of particular worth to an act rests, nevertheless, on his prior gracious ordination.

11. IV *Sent*. d. 17 q. 1 a. 4 sol. 1 and 2, cited in Poschmann, *Penance*, 170.

12. IV *Sent*. d. 22 q. 2 a. 1 sol. 2, and ad.1, cited in Poschmann, *Penance*, 170–1.

13. Null, *Cranmer's Doctrine of Repentance*, 44. When sacramental grace is communicated wholly by the inherent power of the sacrament to which the recipient raises no spiritual barrier, it is bestowed *ex opere operato* ("by the work worked"); whereas, when the reception of sacramental grace depends on the antecedent meritorious disposition of contrition in the recipient, grace is bestowed *ex opere operantis* ("by the work of the worker"). Also, Poschmann, *Penance*, 171–2; Tentler, *Sin and Confession*, 263–81.

acting antecedently on the penitent's contrition through her intention to undergo the sacrament of penance, and the plausibility of the penitent's contrition meriting forgiveness of sins by virtue of the subsequent absolution. [14]

Some skeptics found the Scotist account more attractive; for, instead of attempting to hold together in one tortuous causal network the efficacy for forgiveness of both contrition and absolution, Scotus separated them into alternative sequences. In one sequence, attrition of a sufficient degree merits sanctifying or informing grace *de congruo* (i.e., by virtue of God's gracious covenantal investing of the act with disproportionate worth), which converts attrition to contrition directly, bringing forgiveness of sin. Although forgiveness is bestowed extra-sacramentally, penance is not rendered superfluous, as the penitent's contrition entails the intention to undergo penance. In the other sequence, a lesser degree of attrition in the penitent is converted to contrition and awarded forgiveness exclusively by the power of priestly absolution *ex opere operato*, on condition of there being no obstacle of mortal sin in the path of sacramental grace. Whether the means of justification is merit *de congruo* or sacramental absolution alone, remission of sin is "by the extrinsic denomination of the *acceptatio divina*":[15] that is, by God's free, covenantal determination of these means of acceptance and, fundamentally, by his free predestining of the individual sinner to salvation.

It is important to be aware of the subtleties and complexities of the Thomist and Scotist theologies of justification, with their cross-fertilizing variations and adaptations, in order to focus precisely the objections of Cranmer and his English evangelical colleagues to these Augustinian traditions which circulated widely in contemporary penitential manuals for priests and in vernacular Christian handbooks and sermons—the Scotist tradition apparently dominant in England and in Cambridge circles.[16] The Cranmerian homilies make clear that the *fundamental* quarrel of evangelical reformers with these traditions was not that they denied the need of sinners for particular or "special" operations of God's grace to acquire meritorious virtues and perform meritorious acts, as, for the most part, they insisted on these operations. Nor was the *fundamental* quarrel that these traditions viewed the merit awarded by God to human dispositions and acts (whether or not divinely assisted or "infused") as corresponding to, or even demanded by, their intrinsic worth. Rather, the *fundamental evangelical objection* was that these penitential approaches to justification deflected the attention of faith away from its only proper object: the Father's unfathomable mercy and Christ's

---

14. Poschmann, *Penance*, 171–2.

15. McGrath, *Iustitia Dei*, 97; also Poschmann, *Penance*, 187; Null, *Cranmer's Doctrine of Grace*, 46–7; Tentler, *Sin an Confession*, 263–81.

16. In providing an overview of the penitential theological backdrop to Cranmer's evolving views on faith and repentance, Ashley Null draws on Latin penitential manuals, popular handbooks and sermon collections widely circulating in the English church, including the erudite *Treatise concerning . . . the Seven Penitential Psalms* of John Fisher, Cambridge luminary and Cranmer's teacher. Null, *Cranmer's Doctrine of Grace*, 30–4.

perfect justice. To dwell on such intermediate causes of the justification of sinners, even though they be conceived as originating in Christ's accomplished work of righteousness, was to deflect faith away from Christ's righteousness, withholding the fullness of glory owing to him. The intention of St. Paul's insistence that "faith without works justifieth us"[17] was to keep faith focused exclusively on Christ's merits or deserving and to repudiate deflection and defection to human merit or deserving, however dependent the latter on divine liberality and condescension. For Cranmer, the apprehensive, receptive moment of faith is first and foremost: "when it seeth and considereth what God hath done for us."[18]

At the same time, Cranmer and his reforming colleagues were convinced that, in focusing entirely on Christ's merit and deserving, faith simultaneously plumbed the depths of the sinner's undeserving. The unwavering light of Christ's merit revealed the sinner's imperfection to be "so great," so pervasive, that nothing within him is "apt to merit and deserve any part of [his] justification."[19] In this sense alone is the single focus of faith a double focus: to focus on the actions, and correlatively, the perfections, of the divine Father and Son brings into focus the counteractions and the imperfections of the human creature as an inverted image.[20] God's self-abasement, freely undertaken to rescue, restore, and reunite with himself his lost and wayward human creatures, reveals not only the breadth and depth of his love and wisdom, his unchanging and ever-dependable justice, and his unconquerable and conquering life and power but also the depth and breadth of human self-aggrandizing pride and malevolence, the superficiality and deception of human love and knowledge, and the impotence and futility of human striving to possess God and the highest spiritual realities. Repentance, then, is an indispensable dimension of faith's receptive moment. Our knowing embrace of God's mercy and promises in Jesus Christ is necessarily that recognition of our own guilt and deprivation only available at the foot of Christ's Cross: it is our existential turning away in horror and sorrow at the defilement and corruption of our humanity that renders us unworthy beyond measure of the Father's love for us and forgiveness of us in his Son. In this double motion of the soul, the sinner wholly relinquishes "the office of justification" to God, confessing it to be "not a thing which we render unto him, but which we receive of him."[21]

True knowledge of our unique selves in our contingent, concrete, historical determinations is knowledge of our universal humanity standing under the judgment and the promise of Christ's cross. In promising us a renewed integrity and more glorious destiny in his resurrected and glorified body, Christ's triumph on the Cross confronts us with our self-inflicted wretchedness in having lost the image of God's Word in which we were created. Cranmer understands this twofold

---

17. Eph. 2:8-9; Phil. 3:9; Gal. 2:21; 3:21.
18. *MWL*, 136; *GH*, 30.
19. *MWL*, 133; *GH*, 33.
20. *MWL*, 129-31; *GH*, 27-31.
21. *MWL*, 131; *GH*, 31.

knowledge as the noetic ground of the reordering of our desire and will, of our existential orientation, which reception of Christ's gift entails.

The Liveliness of Faith

As an interior human act, faith, along with repentance, hope, charity, and fear of God, contributes nothing to our righteousness before God. Cranmer is as determined as his continental mentors to strip the preposition "by" in the phrase "justification by faith alone" of any causal connotation. He contends that St. Paul, along with the Church Fathers,[22] merely indicated by this phrase that faith does what "none other of our virtues or works properly doeth," namely, "directly send us to Christ for remission of our sins."[23] Thus, the work of faith is the divinely given mode, and not a meritorious cause, of the sinner's justification. Our embrace by faith of God's promises in Christ is, indeed, our embrace of Christ's righteousness, but as the extrinsic cause of our acceptance by the Father. It is truly our reception of Christ's merit, our uniting with Christ's merit. But as truly, it is the Father's "imputation" to us of Christ's merit: that is, his situating us within and under Christ's merit as he looks upon us in judgment. As the Father judges us within and under Christ's justice, he acquits us of our guilt and deserved punishment.

Our act of receiving God's work of righteousness in Jesus Christ is, simultaneously, surrender to, and possession by God's saving purposes for us. For Cranmer, the surrender of repentant faith is "true" and "lively" because informed by love and hope. Never mere intellectual assent to God's revealed word nor mere "persuasion" of God's revealed truth, faith is the sinner's total, wholehearted responding to God's merciful and gracious countenance with humble gratitude, loving devotion, and confident expectation. Apprehending and receiving the revelation in Christ of God's saving perfections, faith prostrates the sinner before God in worshipful reverence and unreserved dependence, while raising him up in ardent love and yearning for Christ's goodness above all created goodness; likewise, faith subjects the sinner's will to God's sovereign command in holy fear and ready obedience, while it directs his expectation with full assurance to God's promised future.

Cranmer's amplification of the liveliness of faith over his three homilies is a continuous assault on the scholastic distinction between two genres of faith (paralleling the two genres of repentance): namely, "the faith of assent" (*fides assensus*) or "unformed faith" (*fides informis*) and "faith formed by love" (*fides caritate formata*). Cranmer's previous public assaults on this distinction had proved unavailing, as it had featured prominently in Henry VIII's conservative theological

---

22. Cranmer features quotes from Hilary, Basil of Caesarea, and Ambrose, but also cites passages in the writings of Chrysostom, Cyprian, Augustine, Prosper, Oecumenius, Photius, and Anselm. *MWL*, 130-1; *GH*, 28-9.

23. *MWL*, 132; *GH*, 32-3.

manual of 1543 (*The King's Book*). The manual distinguished between faith "in itself" as the persuasion "wrought by God in man's heart" wherein he intellectually assents to the whole body of God's revealed truth in Scripture and the church's tradition, and faith annexed with hope and charity, where persuasion is joined with "a sure confidence and hope to attain whatsoever God hath promised for Christ's sake, and an hearty love to God, and obedience to his commandments."[24] While, according to the manual, only the perfected "faith formed by love" is "effectual" in meriting justification for the sinner, the imperfect "unformed" faith, remaining even in believers guilty of mortal sins, provides a cognitive foundation for recovering effectual faith through the sacramental discipline of penance.[25]

Henry's demise freed Cranmer to expatiate on the evangelical conviction of *one faith only*. In deference to the letters of James (2:14-26) and Paul (2 Tim. 3:2-9; Tit. 1:16), Cranmer's homilies admit that Scripture discriminates another faith "which bringeth forth (without repentance) either evil works or no good works," but this is shown to be "a dead, devilish, counterfeit, and feigned faith" that leaves its possessors, whether devils or humans, wholly "in their damnable estate."[26] Accordingly, in his homiletic depictions of faith's intrinsic liveliness or fruitfulness, as in many passages in the 1552 prayer book, Cranmer enlarges on faith's relationship with works and disciplines of love directed toward God and the neighbor through which the Holy Spirit freely acts.

For Cranmer and his evangelical associates, pressing home faith's intrinsic fruitfulness from the pulpit was central to the theological conversion and reeducation of Catholic clergy and laity whose natural antagonism to apparent soteriological novelty was intensified by conservative Catholic representations of the moral indifference and antinomianism of a soteriology that had substituted the imputed justice of repentant sinners for their actual justice, their becoming just. Vindication of evangelical soteriology in the face of such representations involved continual, forceful assertion of the double-pronged necessity of good works to faith and of faith to good works. As summarized in the Elizabethan Articles XII and XIII, respectively, faith issues necessarily in works "pleasing and acceptable to God in Christ," and only works springing from faith are pleasing to God.[27]

Chief among the regular disciplines of faith is that of humbly and penitently confessing "our manifold sins and wickedness . . . before the face of Almighty God our heavenly Father . . . to the end that we may obtain forgiveness of the same by his infinite goodness and mercy."[28] At "all times," but especially "when we assemble and meet together,"[29] "the Scripture moveth us" to acknowledge, and

---

24. *The King's Book*, 9–10.
25. Ibid., 11–12.
26. *MWL*, 133, 135–6; *GH*, 33–4, 36–8.
27. *TA*, 140–1.
28. The exhortation to corporate confession, Morning Prayer, 1552, *BCP*, 50.
29. Ibid.

not to "dissemble nor cloak," before God, the evil fruits of our corrupted nature which betray our adherence to Christ's promises and impede the healing action of his Spirit within us. Accordingly, in the reformed service of Morning Prayer from 1552 onward, the assembled worshippers confess:[30]

> Almighty and most merciful Father, we have erred and strayed from thy ways, like lost sheep. We have followed too much the desires and devices of our own hearts. We have offended against thy holy laws. We have left undone those things which we ought to have done, and we have done those things which we ought not to have done, and there is no health in us.

The vast scope and inscrutability of our sins is discerningly conveyed by Cranmer's fellow homilist and Catholic controversialist, John Harpsfield, in commending King David's frequent confession:[31]

> how well weigheth this holy man his sins, when he confesseth that they be so many in number and so hid and hard to understand, that it is in manner impossible to know, utter, or number them! Wherefore, he having a true, earnest, and deep contemplation and consideration of his sins, and yet not coming to the bottom of them, he maketh supplication to God to forgive him his privy, secret, hid sins, to the knowledge of which he cannot attain.

Liberation by faith from the law's condemnation is not in this present life permanent emancipation from the grievous burden of sin, for this burden borne faithfully is the essence of contrition, as the 1552 corporate confession before communion makes clear, in portraying the "remembrance" of our "misdoings" as "grievous" and their "burden" as "intolerable."[32] If anything, firm trust in the Father's abundant mercy extended to us for his Son's sake, increases our remorse for sins continually committed, as these are the measure of our ingratitude for God's immeasurable love and condescension. Our sins are an outrageous affront to the moral rationality of faith, which harbors a deep desire to imitate divine generosity and a deep fear of offending it. This rationality is captured in Cranmer's sermons by his repeated affirmation that, "if we be not desperate persons, and our hearts harder than stones," considering the "great and merciful benefits" promised to us in Jesus Christ will "move us to render ourselves unto God wholly . . . to serve him in all good deeds, obeying his commandments . . . evermore dreading willingly to offend such a merciful God and loving Redeemer in word, thought, or

---

30. Ibid.
31. "Of the Misery of Mankind," *GH*, 19. In exhorting the faithful to penitential self-reflection and confession, this Catholic publicist does not mention or even allude to the discipline of sacramental penance, his reticence perhaps displaying the impressive reformist scope of contemporary Catholic sympathies or his remarkable diplomatic restraint.
32. *BCP*, 50.

deed."³³ Completing this observation, the Edwardian Article X on grace declares that the Holy Spirit "doth take away the stony heart and giveth a heart of flesh."³⁴

It is the faithful intention to render ourselves wholly to God in loving service that keeps the discipline of repentance from degenerating into the outworking of despair and sustains its enhancement of our moral agency and action. In the deepest sorrow over sin, faith does not lose sight of the eschatological signs of spiritual renewal in which all members of Christ's body participate. Thus, confession of sin properly terminates in a petition for the manifestation of God's restorative action in our lives. Illustrating the pattern of the corporate confessions and following prayers of absolution in the 1552/9 prayer books, the confession at Morning Prayer concludes by beseeching God:³⁵

> Restore thou them that be penitent, according to thy promises declared unto mankind, in Christ Jesu our Lord. And grant, O most merciful Father, for his sake, that we may hereafter live a godly, righteous, and sober life, to the glory of thy holy name.

While repentant faith has no illusions about the spiritual frailty of sinful humanity and the resourcefulness of tempting spirits, it has confidence in the Father's imparting of the Holy Spirit to those whom he has justified, so that, even now, the "old man" is being overtaken by the "new." Faith does not embolden us to boast before God or our neighbor that our sinful nature is regenerate, but it emboldens us to act, in the firm hope that our action may prove "acceptable," "pleasing," to our Heavenly Father, through Jesus Christ.

For Cranmer's homily on faith, as for the Letter to the Hebrews, the boldness of faith to act is the practical bond uniting God's chosen people in every generation: a central thread of continuity in salvation history, from the Israelite patriarchs to the church of the present day. Here Cranmer focuses in the *active faith* of Israelites God's work of universal salvation (somewhat compensating for his homiletic neglect of other foci in Israel's history). He waxes eloquent about the astonishing works performed by the church's Israelite "fathers, martyrs, and other holy men" out of a faith that was not only trust in the sovereign "maker and governor of all men," or "a special confidence" in Israel's divine "comforter . . . maintainer, and defender," but a fully fledged seeking "for all benefits of God the Father through

---

33. Ezek. 36:26-27 "I will take out of your flesh the heart of stone . . . and I will put my spirit within you." *MWL*, 134; *GH*, 35. In the same vein, the author of the sermon on "falling from God" says that God's "face of mercy" shown in Jesus Christ to the truly faithful "doth so lighten their hearts that they . . . be transformed to his image, be made partakers of the heavenly light and of his Holy Spirit, and be fashioned to him in all goodness requisite to the children of God." *GH*, 84.

34. *TA*, 139.

35. *BCP*, 51.

the merits of his Son."³⁶ The import of Cranmer's argument is that of Hebrews 11: Christ's coming to earth has made available to us through his Spirit a "greater faith and surer trust" than was available to those who awaited his coming; so that "we should no less, but rather more, give ourselves wholly unto Christ both in profession and living."³⁷

For Cranmer, a greater faith entails a more certain hope and a more perfect charity. As to hope, he declares, we who have heard Christs promises in the Gospels "know that when God shall appear, we shall be like unto him, for we shall see him even as he is. And whosoever hath this hope in him doth purify himself, like as God is pure (quoting 1 Jn 3: 2-3)."³⁸ According to his passage, our hope of finally conforming to Christ's purity in our inner being is already an incipient purification of our inner being: of our desiring, knowing, and willing. The hope intrinsic to faith is the mode in which the perfecting of our being, which is everlasting life, is active in our present struggle with "the old Adam." Hope is the proleptic participation of the faithful in God's final purification of their love. In hope the faithful set their minds "to serve God, for God's own sake, and for his sake also to love all neighbours, whether they be friends or adversaries, doing good to every man, as opportunity serveth."³⁹

The Obedience of Faith

Here and throughout his homilies, Cranmer makes clear that to set our minds to serve God in our present life takes the form of attending to and keeping his commandments (1 Jn 2:3-5, 1 Jn 5:3-4).⁴⁰ The faith of repentant sinners brings forth "motions" and "works" pleasing to God by setting them to walk in the way of God's law, the way of obedience to his commandments. For God's commandments proclaimed in the Scriptures disclose "the pathway" of faith working through love: they disclose the implications for human action of all God's revealed judgments and actions in creation and in salvation. Most importantly, Christ's commandments, interpreted within the whole of his ministry, are the hermeneutical key to the totality of divine commandments. They are for Cranmer the authoritative disclosure of God's law to created and fallen humanity, the sure revelation of perfect human conformity, inward and outward, to his revealed will. They do not supersede, but fulfill and interpret, God's previous revelations to Israel of the order of created beings and ends, the shared goods and structures of human community, the right relations of human beings to God, to one another, and to the nonhuman creation. All previous revelations have their historical telos in the revelation of God's suffering and triumphant self-giving in his incarnate Son, true

36. *MWL*, 137–8; *GH*, 41.
37. *MWL*, 138; *GH*, 41–2.
38. *MWL*, 138; *GH*, 43.
39. *MWL*, 139; *GH*, 45.
40. *MWL*, 138; *GH*, 42–3.

God and true man, for the salvation of his creation, and so must be interpreted as anticipations of this final revelation of moral community. Christ's commandments are a practical commentary on this final revelation.

The supreme authority and hermeneutical centrality of Christ's commandments is concisely conveyed by Cranmer's summary of God's law concluding his "Homily of Good Works Annexed Unto Faith." Mindful of Christ's exhortations to perfection in the Sermons on the Mount and on the Plain, Cranmer's summary shows Christ's law of love to be the perfecting fulfillment of the Mosaic Decalogue.[41] God's will, Cranmer tells us, is that we should surrender ourselves wholly to him, trust in his promises, "love him in prosperity and adversity, and dread to offend him." For his sake, we should "love all men, friends and foes," be solicitous for their welfare and only do them good, because they are created in his image and redeemed by Christ, as we are. We should not only obey our "superiors and governors . . . for conscience sake," but seek "to serve them faithfully and diligently"; likewise, we should honor our fathers and mothers with unstinting attention to their needs and wishes, beyond fulfilling their demands. We should never oppress, kill, beat, slander nor hate any man; but love, help, succor, and speak well of all, even those who slander and hurt us. We should not steal or covet our neighbor's goods, but content ourselves with what we justly receive, and bestow our goods charitably, as the need of others requires. We should "commit no manner of adultery, fornication, nor other unchastness, in will nor in deed."

Far from being novel, Christocentric exegesis of the Decalogue comprised the ethical core of the longer theological tradition from the patristic period and was congenial alike to Lutheran and Reformed theologians. It had deep roots in the Augustinian tradition, and most germanely, in its late-medieval flowering exemplified by the writings of such English theologians as Robert Grosseteste and John Wyclif which were influential in some English and continental and reforming circles. This tradition understood the Decalogue to be God's law given with the creation but promulgated to his chosen nation of Israel under the universal condition of human sinfulness. Its purpose was to render this elect part of sinful humanity a "foreshadowing symbol" of the future heirs of Christ's fulfillment of the law, bringing human liberation from sin and from the law's restraint and condemnation.[42]

Features of the older tradition reappear in the ethics of early English Lutherans such as Robert Barnes, John Frith, and, most notably, William Tyndale, whose doctrinal manifestoes and biblical expositions were widely circulated, and lent a particular nuance to the Reformation dialectic of law and gospel. While recognizing the generic meaning of "the Law" as "the ministration of death," of God's wrathful condemnation of sin that drives the sinner to repentance and faith in Christ's promises of pardon and favor, the English Lutherans laid heavy stress on the indispensable role of Christ's commandments within the gospel's "ministration of life," on their centrality to the inward and outward, individual and communal

---

41. *MWL*, 149; *GH*, 64.
42. Augustine, *Contra Faustum* 19.18, 25–6; *De civitate Dei* 15.2.

obedience wrought by the Spirit of the risen Christ.[43] Cranmer's ethics are of this complexion, stressing the positive, directing, and enabling operation of Christ's law in the hearts of the faithful. For Cranmer as for Tyndale, to love Christ is to love God's law and to desire to fulfill it.[44]

In this respect, Cranmer and Tyndale's handling of the law moved away from the Lutheran-Calvinist schema of the law's residual "uses" in the era of grace toward a greater incorporation of the law into the work of grace. Even so, it did not abandon the association of God's commandments with the continuance of weakness and sin in the repentant believer, assumed by Melanchthon's and Calvin's explications of the law's use to instruct the faithful in God's will.[45] Indeed, Cranmer's urgent pastoral concern in these homilies is that repentant sinners persevere in "observing" Christ's commandments and not stray from the path of faith working through love into the seductive byways devised by Rome of meritorious devotion, penitential satisfaction, and ecclesiastical obedience. The controversies of Jesus with the "Pharisees, Sadducees, and Scribes" over Israel's legal inheritance provide the template for Cranmer's prophetic lines of attack on papal traditions of public worship, personal and collective piety, discipline and jurisdiction judged to be idolatrous, superstitious, hypocritical, and usurping of secular authority.[46]

In assigning moral priority to God's promulgated laws, Cranmer's intention was not to deny or diminish Scripture's revelation of aspects of faithful human action in various epistemological and literary modes: in the narrative of God's actions (coterminous with his speech) in the creation of the world, the history of creation and its consummation, providing the encompassing framework for historical narratives of human conduct of various moral complexions and for other genres of human moral reflection: for example, parabolic, allegorical, and proverbial. Nevertheless, Cranmer, the theological homilist, resembles the earlier Luther and Melanchthon in eschewing ontological speculations, based on "natural" order, as the groundwork of ethical reflection.

The Certainty of Faith

After showing from Scripture that hopeful, repentant, and loving faith necessarily brings forth hopeful, repentant, and loving acts, Cranmer's homily on faith proceeds

---

43. See 309–10 n. 471,

44. For example, William Tyndale, *A Pathway into the Holy Scripture* (1525–32) in *Doctrinal Treatises and Introductions to Different Portions of the Holy Scriptures by William Tyndale*, ed. Henry Walker (Parker Society, Cambridge: Cambridge University Press, 1848), 5–28.

45. Philip Melanchthon, *Loci Communes Theologici* (1535), ed. Heinrich Ernst Bindseil, in *Corpus Reformatorum* (1854), 21:405–6. Hereafter *CR*. John John Calvin, *Institutio Christianae Religionis* (1559), ed. Wilhelm Baum, Edward Cunitz and Edward Reuss, *CR*, 30 (1864): 261–2.

46. *MWL*, 144–8; *GH*, 53–63.

to show that faith necessarily "certifies" its truth by its works. It exhorts believers to "certify" or ascertain the truth and liveliness of their faith by examining their past interior and exterior acts as to their conformity to God's commandments. For Cranmer, this discipline of self-reflection is indispensable to faith, primarily in affording to believers assurance of God's saving presence and work in their lives, and also in arming them against the self-deception of falsely claiming to observe God's commandments, having been seduced by the "fantasies" of corrupt religious "imaginations."[47] Cranmer's concluding exhortation lays out these two benefits:[48]

> Therefore, as you profess the name of Christ, good Christian people, let no such phantasy and imagination of faith . . . beguile you; but be sure of your faith, try it by your living, look upon the fruits that cometh of it, mark the increase of love and charity by it towards God and your neighbour, and so shall you perceive it to be a true lively faith. If you feel and perceive such a faith in you, rejoice in it, and be diligent to maintain it, and keep it still in you; let it be daily increasing, and more and more be well working, and so shall you be sure that you shall please God by this faith, and at the length, . . . so shall you . . . come to him and receive "the end and final reward of your faith."

Lest Cranmer's rousing exhortation be suspected of encouraging in believers an un-nuanced consciousness of regeneration and perfectionist strivings, attention must be paid to the opening admonition, "let no such phantasy," which plainly conveys that faith's maturation involves deepening awareness of sin's beguiling power as well as joyful confidence in sin's continual overcoming. Cranmer's presentation of certifying faith broadly follows the dialectical logic of 1 John in its succession of quotations, beginning with the inner compulsion of the faithful to confess their sins penitently before God (1 Jn 1:8-10). Central to this logic is the interpenetration in faith of the knowledge and love of Christ's commandments, received as the practical expression of the Father's saving truth and the power of the Holy Spirit. Given that knowledge and love of Christ's commandments belong to faith as such, it follows for Cranmer as for 1 John, that the faithful judgments of the "conscience" on past acts will be approving as well as reproving. Whereas the reproving judgments of the faithful increase their awareness of the stubborn residue of sinfulness in their inward dispositions, the continuing vitiation of their desires and intentions, and their innumerable capitulations to temptations in their acts and omissions, the approving judgments increase their joyful, thankful consciousness of the Spirit's work of obedience within them.

Rather than dispelling the spiritual ambiguities of the believer's situation as *simul iustus, simul peccator*, Cranmer's concept of faith proving itself sets these within the eschatological, Christological frame of 1 John. Cranmer's focus is the eschatological reality of the believer's abiding in Christ by lively faith which is her

---

47. *MWL*, 140, 144–8.
48. *MWL*, 140–1; *GH*, 47.

proleptic participation in Christ's knowledge and love of the Father (1 Jn 2:5-6, 27-29; 4:7-18). As Christ's knowledge and love of the Father is everlasting life, the final fulfillment of faith is proleptically present in faith (5:10-20). For Cranmer, the election of believers in Christ is their abiding in him: it is the eschatological inception of their eternal future with Christ, of which they cannot be deprived.[49] While still tormented by evil inclinations and all too often succumbing to them, the truly faithful are, nevertheless, actively ruled by the Holy Spirit who, once imparted, never utterly departs from them but continually orders their desiring, knowing, and willing throughout life's earthly pilgrimage, generating interior acts of contrition and intention "to lead a new life," and exterior acts of obedient service to God and to the neighbor.[50] The perseverance and maturation of believers in faith and assurance is not a project of spiritual striving controlled by their own wills, but a free, unmerited and continual communication from the Father and the Son through the Holy Spirit, experienced and acknowledged as such.

Assurance, Election, and Predestination

Cranmer's homiletical treatment of the perseverance and assurance of faith largely anticipates the scope and length of the Edwardian Article on "predestination and election" (XVII), modestly amended by the Elizabethans.[51] The bulk of Article XVII traces the sure progression of God's predestined, by the Spirit's varied working, to the attainment of "everlasting felicity," and extols the vital role of assurance of election in strengthening the faith and love of believers but also warns against the devil's use of predestination to drive "curious and carnal persons, lacking the Spirit of Christ," into despair or into reckless immorality. Besides distilling Cranmer's homiletic treatment of election, the article provides additional theological clarification in its opening and closing. The Elizabethan article's opening definition of predestination runs as follows:[52]

> Predestination to life is the everlasting purpose of God, whereby (before the foundations of the world were laid) he hath constantly decreed by his counsel secret to us, to deliver from curse and damnation those whom he hath chosen in Christ out of mankind, and to bring them by Christ to everlasting salvation, as vessels made to honour.

---

49. *MWL*, 138–9; *GH*, 42–3.

50. Cranmer's conviction about the perseverance of true faith is not shared by all contributors to the Edwardian homilies. The author of the homily on "falling from God" repeatedly and emphatically avers that a lively faith, truly received, and the indwelling Spirit, may be lost in the believer/s carnal life. *GH*, 81–90.

51. *TA*, 143–4.

52. *TA*, 143.

Consonant with the soteriological, Christological, and pastoral slant of everything that follows, the definition refers only to predestination to life, making no concession to the theory of "double predestination" favored in Reformed Augustinian circles. Moreover, the Elizabethan editors heighten the definition's Christological focus by amending the Edwardian Article's phrase "whom he hath chosen out of mankind" to "whom he hath chosen in Christ out of mankind." Undoubtedly, their design was to block any Reformed tendency to treat predestination as a speculation about the sovereign will of the Creator God to dispose of his human creatures with arbitrary, proprietary freedom, as would later appear in the Puritan Lambeth Articles (1595) and the Westminster Confession of Faith (1647).[53] As importantly, they discerned the original article's intention of paraphrasing rather than interpreting the New Testament language.[54]

From the start, the wording of the definition invokes the great Pauline blessing of Eph. 1:3-14: the blessing of the Father's eternal will to unite all things in his Son (1:9-10) that comprehends his having chosen a heritage of adopted sons for Jesus Christ before the foundation of the world (1:5-6). Predestination to life is God's everlasting purpose because it transpires within the everlasting love between the Father and the Son. To be "chosen in Christ," says Oliver O'Donovan, means that "the elect" participate in Christ's "position as the object of the Father's favour from eternity."[55] The election of human beings in Christ, like their creation, is the revelation in time of the eternal outpouring of the Father's Spirit of love on the Son, rather than the revelation of a primordial principle of abstract sovereignty.

Unlike the Lambeth Articles and Westminster Confession, the Cranmerian article does not assert the predestining of particular individuals, nor confine to these the intended benefits of Christ's passion.[56] While affirming God's unchanging determination "to deliver from curse and damnation" and "bring . . . to everlasting salvation" those "whom he hath chosen in Christ," the article discourages us from construing the predestined in terms of set numbers or members by counseling us to "receive God's promises in such wise, as they be generally set forth . . . in Holy Scripture"[57]—that is, ventures O'Donovan, as addressed to "the class of human-beings who will hear and obey God's word."[58] Finally, while presenting the elect as chosen "out of mankind," the article does not deny, or otherwise diminish, their representative solidarity with, and service to the whole of humanity and all

---

53. See Gibson's comparison of this definition with the relevant Lambeth Articles in C. S. Edgar Gibson, *The Thirty-Nine Articles of the Church of England*, 5th edn. (London: Routledge, 1906), 474–7 and Oliver O'Donovan's comparison of the whole Article 17 with the corresponding chapter 3 of the Westminster Confession, in *TA*, 82–7.

54. Gibson documents this intention from the source passages in Romans 8 and 9 and Ephesians 1, *The Thirty-Nine Articles*, 463–4.

55. *TA*, 83.

56. Gibson, *The Thirty-Nine Articles*, 474–7; O'Donovan, *TA*, 85–7.

57. *TA*, 144.

58. *TA*, 86.

its members, after the pattern of Christ, their renewing and perfecting head and archetype.

Faith and Moral Action: Toward an Ethic of Dispossession and Repossession

In its four aspects, the Cranmerian theology of "true and lively faith" sets forth an existential renewal of human agency and action that stands over against the proprietary profile of human existence in liberal natural rights theory. To show this, it is salutary to summarize this existential renewal as a dynamic of the three interpenetrating moments of possession, dispossession, and repossession. In the course of being united by faith with God's accomplished and promised work of justification in Jesus Christ, sinners are taken out of themselves and dispossessed of themselves as they are possessed by the Father's Word through the Spirit's power. Being possessed by Christ, they possess Christ and his Spirit of Holiness, and, simultaneously, they possess anew, in the knowledge and love of Christ, themselves, their neighbors, and the whole of God's creation.

The first moment of renewed human agency and action is the passive receptivity of faith: receptivity to being possessed in the sense of captivated or enthralled by the Truth and the Good, from above and beyond finite humanity. This possession of human beings is God's gracious word of saving judgment on sinful humanity, in which the Father's infinite mercy toward sinners is united with the Son's sacrificial fulfillment of justice for them. The passive receptivity of faith to divine possession is the pervasive awareness by sinners of their deprivation of truth and goodness, their existential unworthiness, impotence to judge and to act well, undeserving of another's affirmation and love. But in being possessed by God's saving judgment in Christ, faith is actively receptive, laying hold on Christ's obedient self-giving as the extrinsic truth, good, and justice (right, merit) of the Father's acceptance of us.

The active reception of faith is our willing surrender (our assenting or consenting) to Christ's possessing us, and simultaneously, to Christ dispossessing us of our past sinful and sinning selves. The motion of contrition belonging to faith is our recognizing the intolerable burden of owning past sins from which Christ's perfect satisfaction on the Cross has delivered us; the motion of hope is our acceptance of being stripped, dispossessed, of the nest of proprietary or possessive relations comprising our sinful self-identities: relations to ourselves, to others, to our nonhuman environment, but primordially and preeminently to the absolute Other, to God. At the core of these proprietary relations is our sinful human striving to secure against all threat and challenge our powers to invest ourselves with meaning and worth, to maximize our spiritual and material resources and dispose of them in acts of use and enjoyment, with as little qualification, determination, and limitation as possible from beyond ourselves. Although this striving is limited by the ineradicable givenness of ourselves to our conscious intentions and reflections in the threefold temporal constitution of human consciousness (of past, present, and future), we conceal the givenness of ourselves under the pretense that we continuously create or produce ourselves out of the controlling dispositions of our conscious willing. Thus, our striving to secure our proprietary powers over ourselves is also a striving to secure the illusion that we have determined and can determine ourselves apart from and over against God's unceasing action toward us.

Sinful human striving in every generation is, therefore, first and foremost against the transcendent life-infusing power, form-imparting archetype, and worth-bestowing good that is the triune God, revealed in Jesus Christ. Against the Giver of Life, sinful human beings in every generation have set the creative and destructive possibilities of their imagination and their practical and technical reasoning; against the Giver of Form and Law, they have set their own authority to legislate, command, and manage; against the Giver of Goodness, they have set their own authority to estimate, claim, and bestow worth. Nevertheless, modern human beings have taken sinful human strivings into uncharted theoretical and practical territories, pursuing their creative and destructive possibilities in an unprecedentedly fluid and plastic universe, assimilating law-giving to an unprecedented project of autonomous self-regulation, and goodness to an unprecedented bestowal of "value" by the unfettered passions of equal individual and collective agents. Always and everywhere, the striving of human beings to secure their proprietary powers runs counter to neighborly love and conserving oversight of the nonhuman creation. But modern society appears dominated on an unprecedented scale by relationships of acquisitiveness and competitiveness, calculation and manipulation, suspicion and deviousness, methodical doubt and skeptical violence, and control and exploitation of human and nonhuman nature. By virtue of being excessively proprietary, these relations are excessively juridical: pervaded by legal rules and instruments, by establishment and adjudication of rival and reciprocal rights, enforcement of demands and claims, and judgment and punishment of noncompliance and infringement.

Such relationships not only express but generate and exacerbate the anxiety, guilt, despair, and self-loathing besetting human beings incapable of facing ultimate questions concerning their identity and worth, the meaningfulness of their lives, and their standing in and beyond their world. For, as proprietary subjects, we are crippled in our moral agency by the fear that our resources comprise an insufficient basis for our standing before others and before the absolute Other. What we need and crave, consciously and unconsciously, is faith that dispossesses us of all false pretension to ground ourselves, to dispose of ourselves, to claim or appropriate for ourselves, to know and value ourselves, even to unmask and devalue ourselves: faith that relinquishes our semblance of proprietary right to the true possessor and shepherd of our souls and bodies, the Father's Beloved, whom we encounter as already possessing and ruling us through his Holy Spirit. By faith we encounter Christ as the Father's Word of address to us, who already knows us, values us, and judges us, already claims us and disposes us. Only in being conformed to his loving knowledge and judgment of us, to his commanding claim on us and will for us, do we truly and freely, in knowledge and love, possess ourselves, determine ourselves, and dispose of ourselves.

Moreover, by faith we are also conformed to Christ's loving knowledge and judgment of our neighbors, to his claim on them, and will for them. Our lively faith, informed by love and hope, situates us alongside our neighbors as known and judged, claimed and disposed by Christ, overcoming our temptation to regard their good as undermining or diminishing our good, and to construct on that base of existential enmity an exploitative, competitive, hostile, manipulative, and judgmental relationship to them. Faith reveals to us that we and our neighbors participate in a single divine-human community of created, fallen, and eschatological good, a single divine-human economy of creating, preserving, and renewing love, in which there is only one divine-human measure, estimator, valuer, and judge: the eternally active Word of God.

Our calling, as the English reformers laid out, is to know, to love, and to act within this divine-human economy: within it we may venture to communicate the Father's Word to our neighbor, to present Christ to our neighbor, without being guilty of usurpation. Within it we may encounter God's law as liberating guidance along the pathway of our practical lives together, illuminating the complex moral landscape of our concrete deliberations and giving form to mature judgments. Within it our desires and imaginings may correspond to the good and the evil divinely revealed to us, and so find completion in efficacious and beneficial human action.

Finally, the divine-human community recognized by faith extends to created realities beyond the human: to animate and inanimate creatures which also belong to Christ in their distinctive ways, and whose being, meaning, worth, and action are also established by the Father's creative and redemptive Word through his Spirit. We humans act rightly toward these creatures in accordance with our divinely ordained lordship or dominion over creation, as we know and esteem them within the divine-human economy. This means that our use and enjoyment of them conforms to their positing, determination, and destining by the Father's Word and Spirit, prior to human purposes for them. It means use and enjoyment of them bounded by God's revelation to human rationality of the totality of generic and teleological relations structuring the nonhuman creation: including the design of creatures for specific actions (functions, motions) constituting their specific good, the multiple contributions of each species to the welfare of other species, the intricate fabric of interdependence across multiple species comprising "the balance of nature," and, finally, the ordering of all creatures to their transcendent source and end.

These generic and teleological relationships constituting nature as a totality or unified whole are widely recognized within the organic and ecological sciences today, but with significant division over their ethical implications for human action. A theological consideration of the moral obligations inhering in human use and enjoyment of nonhuman creatures must keep in view their individual and specific modes of praising God in their being, acting, and manifold forms of service within his creation. But it must also concede the tragic fallenness of the whole creation on account of human sin, its subjection to systemic disruption, distortion, and disharmony among creatures, and the implications of this for human valuing of and acting on inferior creatures. Faithful human dominion soberly accepts the inevitability of struggle, conflict, and frustration in the human pursuit of "subduing" the natural environment, but within the discernable, relations of created nature and the promise of final reconciliation. Thus, far from removing believers to some Archimedean point of knowing, valuing and acting outside of the totality of creation, the ecstatic, Christocentric determination of faith anchors them firmly to God's promise of renewal for this totality.

Chapter 7

SCRIPTURAL COMMUNICATION OF GOD'S WORD OF SALVATION

In English as in continental reforming theology, the soteriological and epistemological themes of *sola gratia/sola fide* and *sola Scriptura* were densely interwoven. Reforming theologians understood the written testimony of Scripture to be the unique historical connection between the Spirit's revelation of God's Word in Christ to his original disciples and his revelation of God's Word to subsequent generations of believers. They understood the historical coming to birth of Scripture—the gestation over centuries of the Hebrew Scriptures, the writing of the apostolic testimonies to Christ's person and work, and their assembling and arrangement in a literary canon together with Israel's recorded testimony to God's Word—to comprise a single, unrepeatable temporal work of the Holy Spirit within the community of God's faithful people.

The Sufficiency and Authority of Scripture

Across the range of official Tudor theological documents—the prayer book liturgies, the vernacular Bible prefaces, the homilies, and the sets of Articles—Holy Scripture is exalted as the wholly sufficient and supremely authoritative *medium* of God's communication to sinful human beings of his saving Word spoken in Jesus Christ. As "sufficient to salvation" (Article V, 1553) or "for salvation" (Article VI, 1571), "the Holy Scriptures" are constitutive for the knowledge of God's Word intrinsic to "true and lively faith." The priority of God's saving word in Christ over the Scriptural medium of human knowledge—the priority of the soteriological over the epistemological—is succinctly conveyed in the Edwardian and Elizabethan Articles by their placing the statement of Scripture's sufficiency after three articles on Christ's person and work (II, III, IV).

In imparting his saving word to sinners through the Scriptural text, God imparts knowledge of Christ as the Truth, the Way, and the Life. The knowledge imparted by God is objective: its object, the history of God's speaking and acting in the person of Jesus Christ, is independent of the knowing subject. At the same time, the knowledge is subjective, involving a dialogical encounter of the knowing subject with Jesus Christ in which the subject is addressed and transformed. In and through human practices of reading, speaking, and hearing spoken the words of Scripture, God continually addresses his word of salvation to human beings, giving them effectual knowledge of Jesus Christ in which their thinking, willing, and acting are conformed to him. The "sufficiency of Scripture for salvation" does not, then, denote a quality internal to the textual corpus. It does not simply denote the literary rationality or coherent meaning of its order of words, as the term might do if applied to a literary work of fiction or poetry conceived as comprising a totality of interrelated meanings. Rather the term denotes the relation of the text in its entirety and in its constituent parts to a reality transcending it: to the totality of God's speaking and acting in his creation and salvation of humankind and the world. The relation of the biblical testimony to that which is testified by it is not, however, one of mere external correspondence, but one of participation and invocation as well as representation: in communicating the reality of God's speaking and acting, the biblical text participates in and invokes that transcending reality, without, however, encompassing it, or being identical with it.

Thus, Tudor reformed bishops held out the book of the Bible in its physical objectivity as the single proper focus for faith, over against the indiscriminate proliferation of objective foci for faith in the church's tradition. The official Bible prefaces and sermons encourage the acquisition and reading of the Scriptures (at least, the New Testament) by individuals and within households, and, further, they encourage the active, disciplined engagement of the individual's faith with the meaning of biblical texts. Their authors sometimes conceptualize the saving sufficiency of Holy Scripture within spatial metaphors, referring to the biblical text as the "fountain" and "well" from which "may be drawn out" all "truth" and "doctrine" necessary for salvation, the terrain where earnest seekers after knowledge of "God or themselves" should "search,"[1] where they may "gather witnesses of that salvation which is in Jesus Christ."[2]

The terrain for seeking and finding God's salvation in Christ extends over the "canonical books of the Old and the New Testament of whose authority was never any doubt in the church."[3] This appeal to the unchallenged testimony of the church in all ages excludes from the Old Testament canon the Apocryphal books, because doubts about their authority had arisen on account of their presence in the Greek Septuagint, but not in the Masoretic textual tradition of the Hebrew Scriptures. Knowing that the apostolic, early church, and patristic writers made confident use of the Greek Septuagint, the English reformers were here adopting an uncharacteristic position, informed by the judgment of contemporary humanist scholarship that the Masoretic Hebrew textual tradition was older and more authentic.[4]

---

1. *GH*, 7.
2. Preface to *The Bishops' Bible* (Richard Jugge, 1568).
3. Art. VI, 1571: *TA*, 136–7.
4. In fact, the Masoretic Hebrew textual tradition was produced between the seventh and tenth centuries CE, and its relation to pre-Christian Hebrew textual traditions is complicated.

The Textual Structure of Scriptural Sufficiency

Apart from their concern to circumscribe the textual domain of Scriptural sufficiency, Tudor theologians were concerned to organize reading of this domain in conformity with the structure of Scriptural sufficiency inhering in the relations of the textual witness to the theological-historical realities witnessed by it. An important window on the Tudor understanding of this structure are Cranmer's tables for the recitation of psalms and readings ("lessons") from the Old and New Testaments at the daily services of Morning and Evening Prayer and the celebration of Holy Communion. As we have seen,[5] Cranmer's lectionary for Morning and Evening Prayer provided for the sequential reading through of the psalms every month, the bulk of the Old Testament once a year (with minor additions from the Apocrapha),[6] and the New Testament three times a year (excepting the Apocalypse, reserved for occasional feasts), both Testaments being read in parallel cycles, at the rate of one chapter per lesson. To reduce interruptions to his scheme of sequential reading, Cranmer severely pruned back the church's calendar of festal commemorations, requiring special or "proper" lessons, to those of New Testament saints and All Saints. While the Elizabethan prayer book altered the Cranmerian scheme by providing Proper First Lessons for Sundays,[7] the selection of chapters continued to follow the canonical sequence, except on principal feasts of the church.

By contrast, Cranmer's handling of the readings of Epistle and Gospel at Holy Communion was less revisionary, largely taking them over from the Western church's venerable tradition preserved in the Sarum rite. These readings define the seasons of the church's liturgical calendar in observance primarily of the key theological moments of God's work of salvation in Jesus Christ: expectation of Christ's coming (Advent), the Incarnation (Christmas), the manifestation of Christ's rule (Epiphany), penitential anticipation of Christ's passion and death (Lent), celebration of Christ's resurrection (Easter), ascension (Ascension), and the Holy Spirit's descent on Christ's disciples empowering them for mission (Whitsunday). The final season celebrates the Trinity, observing various ecclesial and moral dimensions of God's trinitarian work (Trinity).

To begin, Cranmer's scheme for sequential reading of the Scriptures almost in their entirety indicates that an aspect of Scriptural sufficiency is the narrative intelligibility of the text's witness to God's action in the world's creation, history, and fulfillment. This intelligibility is, above all, Scripture's witness to the consistency of

---

5. pp. 51, 52 n. 52.

6. Included in the lectionary were a handful of readings from the books of Judith, Tobit, Baruch, Wisdom, and Ecclesiasticus, considered edifying, "for example of life and instruction of manners." *TA*, 137.

7. In addition, the Book of Genesis is now begun at Septuagesima (the ninth Sunday before Easter), as in the Breviary, and not on January 1, as in Cranmer's lectionary, following the civil calendar.

God's revelation of himself, his human creatures, and his intentions for them, in the sequence of his dealings with them constituting the history of creation.

The sequential reading of texts from the Old and New Testaments in parallel cycles, starting at Genesis 1 and Matthew 1, highlights both the separateness and the unity of the two Testaments' witness to God's speaking and acting: the Old Testament being the testimony of the Israelite people to their unique historical inception, mission, and destiny in God's work of salvation; the New Testament being the testimony of the apostles and evangelists to Christ's unique historical person, action, and destiny in God's saving work. The parallel cycles of readings indicate that the theological sufficiency of each Testament entails its hermeneutical interdependence with the other. At the same time, the three cycles of New Testament readings annually, against one of the Old, accords with the superior hermeneutical position occupied by the apostolic testimony to Jesus Christ in the gospels, the epistles, and Acts.

Conforming to the church's long tradition of biblical interpretation, Tudor theologians award the apostolic testimony to Christ unrivaled weight in interpreting the testimony offered by the vast array of Israel's Scriptural writings, understanding that the history of Jesus Christ finally and irrevocably interprets the past history of salvation. For the New Testament shows Jesus Christ to be the transcending perfection or fulfillment of Israel's recorded traditions of salvation history, and Israel's traditions to be anticipations of this fulfillment, whether or not they are explicitly prophetic.[8] While Old Testament prophecies of God's future action have a special role in confirming the truth of the apostolic testimony to Christ, they convey knowledge of a lower order, not having arrived at the clarity and fullness of apostolic knowledge.

To Tudor reformers, the apostolic testimony in all its theological richness, complexity, and diversity discloses the modes in which the nonapostolic writings of the Hebrew canon point to Christ. It discloses the soteriological analogies belonging to Israelite history, which anticipate the Father's saving word and work in his Son: analogies of God's judgment and vindication of his chosen people, of human waywardness and divine patience, of communal and individual suffering and divine rescue, of faith in God's promises and repentance of evil, of devotion and obedience to God's revealed law, and of sacrificial atonement for sin and cleansing from it. All these analogies are drawn in the Edwardian and Elizabethan official sermon collections.

Within the New Testament the evangelists' narrative depictions of Christ's person, life, and ministry are supremely authoritative on two accounts: on account of their originating in the apostles' direct, extensive experience of Christ in the flesh (including his resurrected flesh) and on account of their carrying the apostles' commission from Christ himself to proclaim to the world his message

---

8. The author of "An Information for Them Which Take Offence at Certain Places of the Holy Scripture" interprets the whole of Israel's recorded testimony to the history of salvation as the foreshadowing and anticipation of fulfillment in Christ. *GH*, 368-81.

and the message about him. The apostolic recollections of Christ's teachings, exchanges, miracles, and other actions, of his suffering, death, and resurrection appearances, comprise a uniquely privileged body of knowledge in respect of both their empirical and their interpretative veracity. In a unique sense, their testimony is the original human hearing and speaking of God's saving word in Jesus Christ, upon which all previous and subsequent hearing and speaking of God's Word have depended. Consequently, Tudor theologians approach the evangelists' accounts with the greatest reverence and attentiveness, confident that perceived differences, even divergences, among them in theological perspective and emphasis and in narrative detail are susceptible of harmonization.

Tudor theologians bring this same confidence to the larger task of integrating the distinct strands of apostolic interpretation of God's work of salvation in Christ. Programmatic for the biblical hermeneutical task in its entirety are the words of Christ himself, vigorously commended in the opening lines of the Preface to the Bishops' Bible: "Search ye the Scriptures, for in them ye think to have eternal life, and those they be which bear witness of me."[9] By translating the ambiguous second person plural verb, "search" (ἐραυνᾶτε in Greek, *Scrutamini* in Latin) as an imperative rather than indicative verb—"Search ye the Scriptures . . ." rather than "You search the Scriptures."[10]—the Tudor Bible translators rendered Christ's challenge to the Jews as a universal hermeneutical directive and a general exhortation to Scripture reading issued to all potential readers of the Jewish Scriptures, and prophetically understood, of the New Testament Scriptures as well.

This key exhortation and claim of Christ demonstrated to Tudor exegetes not only the supreme epistemological and hermeneutical authority of the New Testament corpus of writings but also the abiding authority for faith of the Jewish Scriptures. Taken together with the declarations in 2 Tim. 3:15-17 and 2 Pet. 1:20-1 of God's inspiration of the scriptural testimony to Christ, Jesus's words affirm the indispensability of the Jewish Scriptures for saving knowledge of himself and, by implication, deny the supplanting or superseding of their prophetic witness by the apostolic testimony. The Edwardian and Elizabethan Articles highlight this point by placing immediately after the pronouncement of Scripture's sufficiency in Article V (VI) the unequivocal statement of Article VI (VII): "both in the Old and New Testament everlasting life is offered to mankind by Christ,"[11] and the homilies follow suit.[12]

---

9. Jn 5.39, Bishops' Bible.

10. Tyndale's translation of Jn 5:39 in his 1534 New Testament was repeated virtually unchanged in subsequent official Bibles: Search the Scriptures, for in them ye think ye have eternal life: and they are they that testify of me. Modern translators, on the grounds of contextual coherence, prefer "You search the Scriptures because you think that in them you have eternal life; and it is they that bear witness to me" (RSV).

11. *TA*, 138.

12. For example, "An Information . . .," *GH*, 368–9.

For Tudor theologians, the scope of the apostolic testimony to the history of Jesus Christ is central to Scripture's sufficiency. The combined cycles of liturgical Scripture readings at Morning and Evening Prayer and Holy Communion situate the climactic moments of God's saving action in Jesus Christ within the larger soteriological fulcrum of his earthly history. They show that the faithful are united with their Saviour not only in his passion, death, resurrection, and ascension but throughout his earthly life as the Father's Incarnate Word of judgment and promise. Moreover, the whole body of apostolic recollection, repeatedly heard and read, itself testifies that the unity of the faithful with God's incarnate Word of judgment and promise entails their unity with the presence of the Word in Israel's history, from God's calling of Israel's patriarchal forbearers to Israel's hopes of national restoration. To become one with Christ is to become one with Israel's hope for a wholly efficacious priestly sacrifice and intercession, an irreversible Messianic deliverance from the alien tyranny thwarting the corporate pursuit of holiness, and a prophetic repromulgation of the Mosaic law that would elicit complete obedience. Finally, it is to become one with the representative universality of Israel's history and hope of salvation, in which the whole community of humankind and other created beings is judged and renewed for eternity.[13]

The Divine and the Human Historical Genesis of the Text

While the production of the Scriptures by the Spirit's inspiration elevates them as a vehicle of God's word above all other bodies of writing, it does not render them other than a body of human writings, exhibiting the features of other human writings. Thus, Tudor exegetes regard analysis of the biblical text as a human literary enterprise extending over many centuries to be intrinsic and not foreign to a theological grasp of its sufficiency for salvation. As students of the humanist biblical scholarship afoot in Northern Europe and widely involved in the task of Bible translation, Tudor exegetes aim at expounding the *intended* meaning of textual units of Scripture, bringing to bear historical, linguistic, and formal literary considerations.

Formative for their orientation to the biblical writings are the general textual, hermeneutical, and theological reflections on Scripture offered by their continental contemporaries (Erasmus, Luther, Melanchthon, Zwingli, Bullinger, Bucer, Calvin, etc.) and by the Church Fathers, headed by St. Augustine. Paramount in this orientation is the hermeneutical primacy of the "literal sense" of the Scriptural text and its identification as the text's historical meaning and the meaning intended by its author.[14] For Tudor exegetes and their continental mentors, the literal sense

---

13. Isaiah 24–27; 53, 65; Ezekiel 37. On this prophetic hope, N. T. Wright, *Resurrection of the Son of God* (London: SPCK, 2003), 115–28.

14. G. R. Evans, *The Language and Logic of the Bible: The Road to Reformation* (Cambridge: Cambridge University Press, 1985) gives a concise account of the background

of textual units is not the "naked" rehearsing of temporal events, of the mundane acts of God, or of human beings with mundane desires, emotions, and intentions, which medieval exegesis could dismissively ignore as the most inconsequential of textual meanings. The literal sense is no longer to be construed through the medieval "architectural metaphor"[15] as the crude foundation of a rising structure of "spiritual" senses largely disconnected with it: the allegorical, pertaining to the church's faith and doctrine; the tropological, pertaining to moral conduct; and the anagogical, pertaining to the heavenly objects of hope.[16] Rather, for evangelical exegesis, the text's literal or historical sense circumscribes the field of God's temporal act(s) of self-revelation to his human creatures and their temporal act(s) in response, to which the text's "spiritual" or theological sense(s) are intended by the author to refer. Thus, Tudor exegetes understand the literal sense of any biblical text to include one or more "spiritual" (theological) senses, referring to any aspect of God's trinitarian being and action temporally disclosed to his creatures or to any aspect of the being and acting of creatures, (generically or concretely) in their original, fallen, redeemed, and restored conditions and relationships, past, present, and future. This plenitude of theological meaning, belonging preeminently to the whole text of Scripture, but also, in various degrees, to its internal units of various magnitudes and complexity, is central to Scripture's epistemological sufficiency and authority.

Tudor exegetes are aware that the literary and theological scope of biblical textual units is often ascertainable only by diligent study and reflection, with the aid of scholarly tools. The search for what Tyndale calls "the order and process of the text"[17] may be of indefinite length, depending on the obscurity or ambiguity of textual meaning(s) and relationships to the material preceding and following it. However, as Augustine and other patristic exegetes understood, the inspiration of Scripture guarantees that illumination and clarification of such obscurities

---

of these identifications in scholastic developments in biblical textual criticism and interpretation, including the significant analytical contribution of John Wyclif.

15. Evans, *The Language and Logic of the Bible*, 42.

16. Walter J. Ong's historical analysis of the role of alphabetizing language in the cultural tendency to "spatialize" linguistic meaning casts light on the logic of the fourfold exegetical schema. "The arrangement in space" presented by the letters of an alphabetic script provides "maximal symbols of order and control, probably because the concepts of order and control are kinaesthetically and visually grounded." "The fixity of space" and "the possibility of segmentation" suggested by the term "literal" foster the impression that "literal meanings, meanings according to the letter," being "so clear and distinct," are "fixed and neatly segmental too." *The Presence of the Word: Some Prolegomena for Cultural and Religious History* (New Haven: Yale University Press, 1967), 45–6.

17. *The Obedience of a Christian Man*, in *Doctrinal Treatises and Introductions to Different Portions of the Holy Scriptures by William Tyndale*, ed. Henry Walker (Parker Society, Cambridge: Cambridge University Press, 1848), 305; "Preface to the Five Books of Moses," 393.

and ambiguities are to be found in surrounding, parallel, and larger textual units, with plainer and/or more developed theological content[18] and that textual units of narrow theological scope derive further intelligibility from their broader, fuller theological contexts. Tyndale's biblical prefaces and expositions are replete with demonstrations of how decisive these implications of biblical inspiration are for a proper discrimination of textual units and their literal, theological meaning, whether they comprised historical narratives and chronicles; codes of moral, judicial, and ceremonial law; corporate and individual prayers and songs of worship; or sustained theological reflection.[19] In addition, the widespread employment by Tudor biblical scholars of the "common-place" method of assembling biblical passages in comprehensive collections around particular topics exhibits their confidence in both the narrower textual and exegetical benefits and the broader hermeneutical and theological benefits, afforded by intertextual reading.

Of course, the English reformers' exegetical approach appears to exaggerate the continuities and harmonies of the literature when viewed from the perspective of modern historical-critical approaches to the biblical writings that emphasize their multiplicity of internal divisions, the diversity of their oral and written sources, their editorial processes, and their varied contexts and purposes. Later centuries of scholarship have produced more rigorous analysis of the discontinuities of traditions, outlooks, styles, intentions, purposes, and functions presented by the literature, and likewise, by the changing historical contexts of institutions and practices. Putting aside sixteenth-century scholarly limitations, the reformers' theological bias toward unity of biblical textual meaning is expressed in the prohibition in the Edwardian and Elizabethan Article XXI (XX) against the church "so expound[ing] one place of scripture that it be repugnant to another."[20] While this bias may have somewhat inhibited the scholarly exploration of tensions within the biblical corpus, it is defensible on the broad hermeneutical plane and also as a critical reaction to the excessive textual fragmentation entailed in the traditional scholastic exercises of "spiritual" biblical interpretation and biblical proof-texting.

---

18. Says the homily, "A Fruitful Exhortation to the Reading and Knowledge of Holy Scripture": "Although many things in the Scripture be spoken in obscure mysteries, yet there is nothing spoken under dark mysteries in one place but the self-same thing in other places is spoken more familiarly and plainly to the capacity both of learned and unlearned." *GH*, 14. Cf. Nihil enim de illis obscuritatibus eruiter quod non planissime dictum alibi reperiatur. Augustine, *De doctrina Christiana*, 2.8: ed. R. P. H. Green (Oxford: Clarendon Press, 1995), 62.

19. Exemplary is Tyndale's exegesis (against the medieval schema) of "The letter killeth, but the spirit giveth life" (2 Cor. 3:6), which demonstrates at length that the literal or theological meaning of the words "letter" and "spirit" is given by the logic of the larger constellation of verses preceding and following 3:6. *The Obedience of a Christian Man*, *Treatises and Introductions*, 308–9.

20. *TA*, 145–6.

Moreover, Tudor reforming theologians were not slow to embrace current scholarship, being thoroughly conversant with, and hugely impressed by, the epistemological gains of humanist textual criticism, chiefly in uncovering the verbal errors of the Latin Bibles (principally the Vulgate), but also in exposing the historical spuriousness of such key legal documents of the Roman tradition as the *Constitutum Constantini* (*Donation of Constantine*) and the *Pseudo-Isidorean* (*False*) *Decretals*. In addition, the widespread involvement of Tudor episcopal theologians with the work of Bible translation, either undertaking it themselves or appraising its fruits in the succession of continental and English translations, gave them an appreciation not only of the virtue of scholarly suspicion but also of the cumulative character of historical and textual scholarship.

Nowhere is there expressed a more unalloyed conviction of the progressive character of biblical textual and exegetical scholarship than in the prefaces of Tudor vernacular Bibles. Miles Coverdale set the trend in the Prologue of his 1535 English Bible translation by expatiating on the mutual aid and advancement afforded by a multiplicity of independent biblical scholars, working "with diligence and faithfulness" to translate and interpret the Scriptures.[21] He expresses complete confidence that their "sundry judgements of the text," submitted "in meekness to the spirit of truth in the congregation of God," increase knowledge and understanding for all; for some judgments are thereby shown to be more accurate and discerning than others. Moreover, he proposes, dissatisfaction with another's textual rendering, if arising out of humble devotion to the common task, does not breed contempt in the more able, but rather offers an occasion for their further exertion. With similar enthusiasm, Archbishop Matthew Parker in his Preface to the 1568/72 Bishops' Bible extolled the benefits of successive, diverse biblical translations.[22] After duly conceding the inevitability of error in the labor of deciphering "books so profound in senses, so passing our natural understanding," and the providential role of textual "obscurities" and "ambiguities" in taming the arrogance of readers, keeping them from "contempt" for the Scriptures, Parker assures his readers that the Spirit, in delivering these books, intended the complete unfolding over time of their true meaning, and has continually bestowed "abundant gifts and graces" on his church for accomplishing this work.

Among the scholarly "gifts" or resources for furthering a historical understanding of the biblical text, Tudor translators and exegetes appreciated the contribution of extra-biblical literary and linguistic research. Although the primary purpose of this humanist research was limited to establishing the range of meanings or uses of single words and verbal constructs in the broad linguistic contexts of the biblical material, it constituted an important recognition of contextual terrains to be investigated and utilized in the learned enterprises of biblical translation and exegesis.

---

21. *The Holy Scriptures of the Olde and Newe Testamente with the Apocripha* (London, 1847).

22. *The Holie Bible: Conteynyng the Olde Testament and the Newe* (London, 1568), iii.

Beyond this limited humanist focus, Tudor exegetes were driven by contemporary polemics to pay scholarly attention to historical difference, historical otherness, particularly in respect of Israelite manners, practices, and institutions transmitted by Old Testament texts. They were compelled to approach a host of Old Testament passages with historical-cultural sensitivity, to counter their moral and cultural disparagement by Catholic traditionalists bent on arguing that widespread, indiscriminate "hearing and reading of God's word" bred "heresy, carnal liberty, and the overthrow of all good order" in commonwealths.[23] So the official Elizabethan homiletic riposte to these Catholic assaults addressed several categories of biblical "offences"—against polite manners, against natural law, and against divine law—defending a selection of offending passages against their detractors with a mixture of historical-cultural and theological argumentation.[24]

Most commendable in this homily is the author's epistemological and methodological insight into, on the one hand, the unity of theological and historical judgment in the scholarly pursuit of textual meaning, and, on the other, the necessary theological accommodation of historical tensions arising at the level of social and cultural practice and of literary and theological expression. For the Tudors, as for ourselves, it is the *theological* undertaking to accommodate historical and textual tensions within the dynamic unity of faith presented by the canon of biblical writings that demonstrates "the sufficiency of the Holy Scriptures for salvation." Without this ongoing labor of clarifying the unity for faith of the biblical testimony to God's revelation in Jesus Christ, the testimony would appear to require completion by some external oral or written tradition. By illuminating the coherence of the written witness to Christ, theological investigation displays the biblical text in its historical objectivity to be the complete—and so, uniquely authoritative—historical revelation of Christ by the Holy Spirit.

This uniquely authoritative revelation constitutes both the absolute horizon of meaning and the structural focus of meaning within which the faithful pursue saving knowledge, and are bound together, communally united, in their pursuit. Tudor Bible prefaces and homilies consistently portray interpretation of the Scriptural witness to Christ as a *common* spiritual labor of believers. Of

---

23. *GH*, 368.

24. For example, the homily, "An Information . . ." in the Elizabethan collection defends Israel's seemingly rude legal custom of a widow pulling off her nearest kinsman's sandal and spitting in his face before the magistrate upon his refusal to marry her (Deut. 25:5-10), by stressing the purely ceremonial-symbolic and legal meaning of the gesture as a vindication of the woman and reproach to her kinsman for his grave violation of divine law. Similarly, the homily mitigates the offense of patriarchal concubinage as it appears in the Genesis narratives of Sarah and Hagar (16:1-6), Rachael and Bilhah, and Leah and Zilpah (30:1-13) by carefully delineating the legal and social relations of wives and maid-concubines within the patriarchal household, emphasizing the lawful and ordered character of the sexual practices involved, before theologically explicating the institution as God's moral concession to "the fathers" for the sake of fulfilling his promise to them. *GH*, 372, 374.

course, reforming theologians are greatly concerned with the spiritual openness of individual believers to the word of Christ spoken in the Scriptures: with their having an ardent and sincere desire to "find Christ as their saviour . . .,"[25] as the one who *reveals* and *fulfills* all the needs of faith. They are, however, also concerned that faithful seekers of Christ apply themselves with diligence, reverence, and humility to study and ponder Scriptural texts, availing themselves of every communal aid to understanding afforded by learned interpretation and application of texts in preaching, teaching, and counseling.[26] When their own understanding falters and perplexities assail them, faithful readers wait patiently and prayerfully on the Spirit's illumination[27] and consult those of greater wisdom, learning, and authority to advise.[28] Even in their solitary engagement with the Scriptural text, the faithful benefit from the communal fruits of past and present engagement, drawing on textual, exegetical, and hermeneutical resources available within the historical community of reading, including authoritative doctrinal standards or rules which help to guide their intellectual journey to maturity of understanding. Mindful of their own limitations and their neighbor's welfare, they neither rashly speculate nor pontificate or dispute in public, about Scriptural obscurities and ambiguities. The strongest admonishments for mishandling Scripture are directed at the disputatious and the scornful, the "idle babblers and talkers of the scripture" who "have respect only to . . . how they may bind and loose subtle questions,"[29] and to the "scorners, jesters, and deriders" of its testimony, who seek Christ only "as Herod did under the pretence of worshipping him, to destroy him."[30] These cut themselves off from the ongoing communal reception and transmission of the Scriptural tradition.

Redemption of Historical Community: Scripture as Divine and Human Tradition

The Tudor church's public account of the sufficiency and authority of Scripture for salvation presents this body of literature as the supremely authoritative tradition, at once human and divine, of every community of believers in Christ. Scripture is

---

25. Preface, *Bishops' Bible* (1568).
26. Cranmer's 1540 preface set the tone by repeating with approval John Chrysostom's exhortation to his flock to prepare for, and to reflect on, his weekly sermons on biblical passages during their private or domestic study of the Scriptures. *MWL*, 119.
27. "Only search with a humble spirit, ask in continual prayer, seek with purity of life, knock with perpetual perseverance, and cry to that good Spirit of Christ, the Comforter . . . Christ himself will open the sense of the Scriptures, not to the proud or to the wise of the world, but to the lowly and contrite in heart." Preface, *Bishops' Bible*.
28. *MWL*, 122–3; "A Fruitful Exhortation . . .," *GH*, 12–14.
29. *MWL*, 122.
30. "An Information . . .," *GH*, 380; Preface, *Bishops' Bible*.

communal tradition, having originated and developed, been canonically ordered and received, translated and interpreted, within the historically determinate communities of Israel and the apostolic church of believers in Christ. As divine, the Scriptural tradition unifies the distinct historical moments of God's communication of his saving Word to sinful humanity. It unifies God's past and present communicative acts: the Spirit's revelation of Jesus Christ to his disciples and followers of the apostolic generation, terminating in the collected writings of the New Testament and the worshipping community gathered around them, and the Spirit's ongoing revelation of Jesus Christ to sinners, individually and corporately, through the assembled apostolic writings. The ongoing corporate reading, recitation, and interpretation of the Scriptures are the instruments by which the Spirit of the risen and exalted Lord forms and manifests his bond of communion with his people and among his people, uniting every generation of the church in their faithful practices of listening and proclaiming, from the patriarchs onward.

Tudor public theology and practice affirm the supreme epistemological authority within the Scriptural tradition of the apostolic testimonies to Jesus Christ while safeguarding the historical integrity and authority of Israel's foreshadowing witness to God's saving word. The divine givenness of the Scriptures' coherent witness to God's word is everywhere assumed, but as the ground and possibility of fruitful scholarly investigation into the complex literary and theological continuities and discontinuities of the textual tradition. Fulsome recognition is accorded to the interdependence in the hermeneutical task of the individual and the community with its recognized authorities, national and international, as the faithful severally and collectively "search for Christ" in the Scriptures, and scholarly biblical labors enhance and discipline individual and communal reading of the Scriptures.

As communal tradition, the Scriptures have formal resemblance to every other communal inheritance from the past of metaphysical and poetic imagination, historical recounting, moral wisdom, and disciplines of thought and of practice, which, having been absorbed, learned, refined, enlarged, and revised over time, give direction, substance, and energy to communal vision, knowledge, and action in the present. And as with other community-creating and sustaining traditions, the Scriptural tradition comprises the integrative framework or matrix within which less-encompassing traditions (literary, artistic, scholarly, social, political, technical, and material) emerge and flourish. Consequently, the English reformers do not simply pit the Scriptures against human tradition as such: rather, they pit the uniquely authoritative and sufficient witness of the Scriptural tradition to the history of God's salvation in Christ against "merely human traditions" which detract from, or undermine, its witness. They revere the Scriptural tradition of witness as a unique divine and human historical work through which the Holy Spirit imparts to the faithful the "image" and "presence" of God's Incarnate Word of Truth, Good, and Life. Moreover, in witnessing to God's promised fulfillment of his historical work of salvation in the future revelation of Christ's kingdom beyond history, the Scriptural tradition is uniquely eschatological, uniting members of Christ's community with their eternal destiny in Him.

Tudor public theology displays the immanent-historical and transcendent-eschatological functioning of the Scriptural tradition: its spiritual unification of successive historical communities, undergirding in each the freedom of faithful imagining, thinking, judging, and acting. The community formed by the history of God's communication of his Word in the formation and the reception of the Scriptural writings is the community of communities: that is, the unity of faith and practice of socially and culturally distinct historical communities. The historical concreteness of the Scriptural writings mediates the historical concreteness of all hearing and proclaiming of God's Word. At the same time, the saving revelation imparted by the Scriptural tradition is the universal matrix and measure of the truth, goodness, beauty, and freedom imparted by every other human tradition.

As matrix and measure, the Scriptures disclose to their faithful hearers and readers the positive and negative dynamics of "merely human traditions." The Scriptures disclose the ambiguities of human traditions' guiding and shaping of communal authorities and communal practices, to nurture or to inhibit the free achievement of common and individual goods. The English church reformers were acutely aware of the ambiguities infecting the history of interpreting and applying the canonical Scriptures within the communities of Christian believers, and so, of the necessity for informed and searching criticism of what is authoritatively handed down, in the light of the universally authoritative textual foundation. They understood that the Scriptural text demands continual communal transmission to which deferential respect should be freely granted, but not to the extent of excluding critical appeals to the textual foundation against its contemporary transmission.

The implication for communal tradition per se, in the fallen condition of human historical existence, is that both an authoritative transmission and a transcending ground for critical appropriation are necessary to the temporal achievement of truth, goodness, and beauty. Whatever its ground, the aim of critical appropriation is to correct, adapt, and revitalize what has been authoritatively transmitted, not wholly to repudiate or overthrow it. The historical particularity of communal tradition must remain, to some degree, an object of loyalty and admiration, a carrier of universality, rather than an offense to rationality, sentiment, imagination, and skill.

Thus, as the supremely authoritative tradition of the universal community of believers in Christ, Scripture shows tradition to be an intrinsic aspect of human historical existence: the form taken by the dependence of human knowing, thinking, feeling, and acting upon a communal past. In late modern society, such dependence on the communal past has suffered a double assault from a false universalism in which an ideology of universal human freedom is wedded to a universal scientific-technological rationality. Set loose from its earlier theological matrix, the theoretical tradition of liberal natural rights has become an ideology of maximizing egalitarian freedom, of emancipating the individual and collective exercise of choice from as many external and internal constraints as possible. The chief instrument of this emancipation of the will is scientific-technological rationality, occupied with manipulating and controlling the world of natural and historical givens to accord with the will's dictates. Both the sovereign will and technological rationality are disengaged from the past and exclusively future-oriented, engaged in a revolutionary project of deconstructing and reconstructing the elements of human and nonhuman life. Thus, the late modern terminus of the tradition of liberal natural rights currently threatens the dissolution of all traditions outside of its project of emancipation and conquest.

All communal historical inheritance; all traditions of thought and practice; and all professional, vocational, creative, and productive spheres of contemporary societies informed by past learning and skill have, to a troubling degree, fallen victim to the liberal-technological dynamo defining modernity, as earlier chapters have argued. That aspects of this dilemma are increasingly attracting popular protest, critical analysis, and practical resistance should offer encouragement rather than hope to inheritors of the Scriptural tradition who can perceive the fragmentary, partial, and superficial character of contemporary responses and their susceptibility to deception and defeat. For the inheritance of Scripture is *the* historical medium through which God—the ultimate source, form, and end of all created being, truth, goodness, and beauty—unambiguously reveals himself to human beings, so that, in receiving God's revelation of himself through this tradition, they can more truly appreciate the necessity and benefits of communal tradition and more effectively address its deficiencies. Through engagement with the Scriptural tradition members of late modernity can come to a truly profitable and efficacious understanding of why liberal-technological repudiation of this form of dependence on a common past will create an antihuman future of spiritual deprivation, darkness, and division.

Through the working of the Holy Spirit, the biblical tradition opens human beings to realize truth, goodness, and beauty in their common present by revealing their common participation in God's completed creation, historical redemption, and promised perfecting beyond history of the whole of human and nonhuman life. This revelation is the one sure ground on which to resist the liberal-technological eclipse of traditions because it imparts to the faithful the capacity to purify "merely human traditions" of harmful dross and enhance their impartation of truth, of good, and of beauty. Such purification extends to the Western tradition of human freedom and the technological control of elements of the human and nonhuman world in the service of freedom. In these pivotal theoretical and practical spheres, purification involves grasping created human freedom in its historical and eschatological relation to the uncreated Ultimate Good and to the totality of penultimate created goods, and as well, grasping the purposes, moral parameters, and limitations of human technologies.

Chapter 8

THE CHURCH'S COMMON WORSHIP INFORMING THE PRACTICE OF FAITH

The Tudor account of the sufficiency and authority of Scripture entails an account of faith as *common reception* of God's saving word spoken in Jesus Christ through the Scriptures. The preceding chapter explored this common reception of God's word in the structured reading aloud of Scripture in the church's regular worship, the work of faithful Scriptural translation and interpretation, and the faithful development and transmission of the Scriptural tradition. The present chapter will explore more fully the practices of worship as corporate modes of obedient attending to and responding to God's word, and the paradigmatic role occupied by these practices in the Tudor vision of the church as a community of faithful action.

The Visible Church as Worshipping Community

Central to Tudor ecclesiology is the conviction that God continually speaks his word of salvation through the testimony of his chosen voices to his gathered people and amid his gathered people. In Tudor worship, reading aloud and recitation of Scriptural passages dramatically renders the written words of Scripture transparent to God's continuing acts of speaking to and with his faithful, the written words becoming an interval in the stream of divine-human communication, of reciprocal speaking and hearing in which the initiative remains with God. In God's temporal self-revelation to his people, as in the self-disclosure of human beings to one another, the spoken word places persons, in their spiritual interiority, in the presence of one another and of the Other.[1] The dynamic of addressing and being addressed creates, sustains, and orders personal relationships, and gives rise to the social "we," the community of "I"s. Thus, while faith's possession of Christ by active "hearing" of God's address is the most personal and interior of spiritual motions, being *my* acceptance of the Father's merciful judgment of *me* in Christ and *my* reception of all the benefits of Christ's accomplished work of salvation extended to

---

1. The medium of human speaking, says Ong aptly, "binds interiors to one another as interiors." *Presence of the Word*, 125.

me, nevertheless faith is not private possession; for the gift received—the Father's saving Word, the agency of reception—the Spirit of Christ, and its form in life—active knowledge and love—are common.

Tudor public ecclesiology passes easily between the spiritual fellowship of the faithful in Christ and the structured social reality of the worshipping church, conceived to be the visible medium of the spiritual fellowship. It portrays the fellowship of faith as continually generated, nourished, strengthened, and purified through the practices of corporate worship, in which God's saving word is spoken and received by the gathered company, and the Spirit of the resurrected and ascended Christ is at work in a preeminent way, incorporating believers into Christ's resurrection life. While not denying that the universal church on earth has a visible reality in all professing Christians, Tudor public theology consistently presents the church as Christians concretely assembled in this time and place but also universally assembled in every place on earth. (The faithful departed are excluded, out of reforming concern to discourage Scripturally unfounded speculation and practices respecting their "state" before the parousia.[2]) Tudor liturgical language invoking the church is almost entirely the simple language of "we" and "us," combining concreteness with universality. Only occasionally do the boundaries of the national church come into view, in the regular prayers for the monarch and governing authorities, the welfare of society, and specific clerical orders. The faithful assembled in worship, along with the building devoted to worship, are similarly given prominence throughout the eight homiletic treatments of the church in the Elizabethan collection.[3] Although the continuity of ecclesiological priorities and positions exhibited by these homilies may be owing to the single authorship of John Jewel,[4] they are, more importantly, in broad agreement with the ecclesiological priorities and positions of the prayer books and the Articles.

On the constituent practices of corporate worship, the prayer books and the homilies wholly concur. In the invitation to penitential confession opening Morning and Evening Prayer, these are: "to knowledge our sins before God . . .,

---

2. Notably, the prayer for "the whole state of Christ's church" in the 1549 Communion service becomes the prayer for "the whole state of Christ's church militant here in earth" in the 1552 service (p. 52 n. 78) and no longer incorporates thanksgiving for the lives of the saints and petitions for the faithful departed. *FSPB*, 221-2, 382. (A reformed thanksgiving for and commendation of the faithful departed was restored in 1662.)

3. These are: "the Right Use of the Church or Temple of God and of the Reverence due unto the same," "Against Peril of Idolatry and Superfluous Decking of Churches," "Repairing and Keeping Clean and Comely Adorning of Churches," "Concerning Prayer," "The Place and Time of Prayer," "Common Prayer and Sacraments . . . ministered in a Tongue . . . understanded of the Hearers," "Worthy Receiving and Reverent Esteeming of the Sacrament of the Body and Blood of Christ," and "The Coming Down of the Holy Ghost and the Manifold Gifts of the same."

4. Jewel wrote the celebrated defense of English church reform, *An Apology of the Church of England* (1562), against the hostile declarations of the Council of Trent.

to render thanks for the great benefits that we have received at his hands, to set forth his most worthy praise, to hear his most holy Word, and to ask those things which be requisite and necessary, as well for the body as the soul."[5] To these, the homiletic summaries of the practices of worship add "truly to celebrate his holy Sacraments"[6] (which are no part of Morning and Evening Prayer). The closest approximation in the Articles to this concurrence is the definition of the church in Article XX (XIX) as "a congregation of faithful men, in which the pure word of God is preached, and the Sacraments be duly ministered, according to Christ's ordinance."[7] The narrow compass of this definition of the church relates to its specific ecumenical function as a public statement of the *notae ecclesiae*, that is, of those visible "marks," widely agreed on by continental reformers, for recognizing particular worshipping communities as belonging to Christ's church. The definition was not intended to encompass, nor does it strictly encompass, all the practices integral to worship in Tudor ecclesiological thought and practice. Rather, the practices of preaching and ministration of the sacraments are two forms among others within worship of attending to and responding to God's saving word spoken through the Scriptures.

Liturgical Forms of Attending to God Speaking

In regular Tudor worship, the pivotal form of congregational attending to God's speaking through the words of Scripture was listening to appointed passages of text read aloud from the Old and New Testaments, but this was accompanied by two secondary and dependent forms: listening to preaching of the Scriptural word and recitation of shorter or longer units of biblical text in praise, meditation, and prayer, sung or said by minister, congregation, and/or choir.

Scripture Reading and Preaching

The centrality of Scripture reading to God's saving conversation with his people was reflected not only in the hermeneutical seriousness with which the liturgical readings from Scripture were organized but also in the primacy assigned to Scripture reading over preaching. In reformed English worship, as previously, services without preaching preponderated, preaching being normally confined to the Sunday service of Holy Communion, and even then, absent from many churches. Chiefly owing to the dearth of theologically literate clergy in Edward VI's church and, later, to Elizabeth's will to restrain theologically literate clergy from spreading dissenting and controversial views, reading from the official

---

5. *BCP*, 50.

6. "Of the Right Use of the Church or Temple of God . . .," *GH,* 154; also, 159, 166–7, 275, 343.

7. *TA,* 145.

homilies was regularly the prescribed substitute for preaching on the appointed (or other) biblical texts.

Consequently, Elizabethan apologists for of the 1559 Book of Common Prayer, of which the most masterful was Richard Hooker, were compelled to defend the extensive liturgical reading of the Scriptures against the increasingly vociferous claim of Presbyterian dissenters that the word of Scripture preached is alone the lively "word of God" capable of breeding faith, whereas the "mere" reading aloud or hearing of the Scripture is capable only of preparing for faith or nourishing faith.[8] With his evangelical predecessors, Hooker affirmed the writing of the Scriptures to be the original, uniquely authoritative and efficacious human *preaching* of God's saving truth to all generations succeeding the prophets and apostles, so that reading aloud of the prophetic and apostolic writings to later generations continues *their preaching* and carries *their* authority and efficacy. By contrast, subsequent preachers' exposition, interpretation, and application of God's word given in the Scriptures are not in themselves God's word;[9] nor are they new works of the Holy Spirit enhancing or adding to his original work. The Presbyterians' grave error was to invest preaching with the additional efficacy of inspired communication, residing in qualities of the preacher and his performance, above the text's own communicative power. Rather, post-apostolic preaching derives its efficacy from the Scriptural text's divinely inspired communication of meaning and is nothing other than an undertaking to draw out this meaning in a disciplined and coherent manner. Its efficacy lies in exhibiting what has already been given in the biblical text and what has been given remains the substance of its expository, exegetical, and hermeneutical undertaking.

Implicit, if less developed in Tudor public theology, are the ways in which the settled schedule of Scripture readings contributes to the primacy of liturgical reading over preaching. Most importantly, by ensuring that reading and hearing

---

8. Richard Hooker, *Of the Laws of Ecclesiastical Polity* 5.22.4 in *The Folger Library Edition of the Works of Richard Hooker*, general ed. W. Speed Hill, 6 vols (Cambridge: Belknap Press of Harvard University Press, 1977–93) 2:89–90. Hereafter *WRH*. The Presbyterian, Thomas Cartwright had asserted: "Although reading do help to nourish the faith which cometh by preaching, yet this is given to the preaching κατ' ἐξοχήvi, i.e. by excellency, and for that it is the excellentest and most ordinary means to work by in the hearts of the hearers." *A Reply to an Answer made by M. Doctor Whitgift against the Admonition to the Parliament*, in *The Works of John Whitgift*, 3 vols, ed. J. Ayre, Parker Society (Cambridge: Cambridge University Press, 1851–3), I:159 [126], 2:376–7, 395.

9. Says Hooker: "we are to know that the word of God is his heavenly truth touching matters of eternal life revealed and uttered unto men; unto Prophets and Apostles by immediate divine inspiration, from them to us by their books and writings. We therefore have no *word of God* but the Scripture. Apostolic sermons were unto such as heard them his word, even as properly as to us their writings are. Howbeit not so our own sermons, the expositions which our discourse of wit doth gather and minister out of the word of God." *Laws*, 5.21.2: *WRH* 2:84.

of the Scriptural word is common throughout the church, the lectionary is instrumental to the Holy Spirit's shaping of a common reception of God's word among his people. It embodies the common authority and efficacy of the church in proclaiming God's word spoken in the Scriptures. By outwardly uniting all congregations in their attending to the Scriptures, it shows all congregations to be united in the promised unveiling of Christ's saving truth to the faithful by the Holy Spirit. It shows every reader and every preacher to carry representatively the authority and efficacy promised to all believers attending to God's word, to communicate, through the power of the Spirit, his truth spoken in the Scriptures.

Preachers bear this representative authority in seeking to expound the meaning of Scriptural passages for a particular congregation in its particular circumstances, to bring to their communication of Scriptural meaning the immediacy of God's address to *this people today*, along with the prophetic warning: "harden not your hearts."[10] Their illumination of the scriptural testimony must focus its immediate, pressing challenge to the hearers. At the same time, the Scriptural passage(s) addressed should neither be constantly dictated by current circumstances, nor by the preacher's particular proclivities. By providing preachers with texts not of their own choosing, the lectionary invites fresh attention and application, and presents a communicative task more open, demanding, and disciplined than preaching only on favored passages, themes, and positions. Thus, preaching on assigned readings most advances the far-reaching project of the Tudor church's lectionary to make the whole of the scriptural testimony to Christ available as an object of clerical and lay study.

Finally, enabling the gathered faithful to hear the text(s) read prior to preaching implies that their expectation to hear God's word efficaciously preached is hopeful, but not slavish. It implies that the faithful are not exempted from a thoughtful, inquiring response to preaching; for all who have heard the Scriptures read must measure the preacher's words by what they have already heard and digested. They must be prepared for the Holy Spirit to answer their corporate petition for faithful, stimulating and nourishing preaching in the way they least desire: with lazy, dull-witted, careless preaching, or worse, with wayward and seductive preaching, challenging them to "test the spirits."

Despite the defensiveness of the Tudor church hierarchy's response to the perceived lack of competent and trustworthy preachers, Tudor bishops understood the vital benefits of sound preaching for individual and corporate faith and regretted the frequent resort to the official homilies, which provided topical expositions of the Scriptures rather than close textual exegesis. However, they also perceived the virtues of the homilists' "common-place" method of developing the theological components of their topics by copious use of quotations and paraphrases from both Testaments. In many cases, the homilists, drawing on wide-ranging, diverse portions of the biblical text, succeeded in expounding their material as a coherent tradition of witness.

---

10. *Venite exultemus domino* (Ps. 95).

The Lord's Prayer and Other Scriptural Recitations

Apart from reading and preaching, liturgical recitation of passages of Scripture during common prayer took a variety of liturgical forms, exemplifying the many facets of divine-human intercourse. At the same time, the liturgical prominence of the Lord's Prayer displays the unity of all these forms and facets; for the prayer taught by the gracious and lively Word of God himself shows all hearing and responding of human beings to God's Word to be hearing and responding to their "sovereign good" as well as their "supreme truth."[11] The Word of the Father spoken and heard is truth illuminating the human understanding as it is goodness ordering human desire and action. All prayer acknowledges "Our Father in heaven" to be the giver of every good gift and the crowning of every happiness, whether prayer takes the form of penitential confession, praise, thanksgiving, or petition. In Tudor public prayer, the Lord's Prayer is *the prayer* which frames the prayers of the faithful, opening the regular services of worship and concluding a significant liturgical sequence within them.[12] It frames congregational prayer not only as the perfect model of human prayer, showing its proper progression of thought and affection; but, more importantly, as the prayer which Jesus Christ, our risen and exalted advocate with the Father, has instructed us to pray. When we pray as Christ has instructed us, his Spirit unites our prayer with our advocate's heavenly intercession for us, rendering our own unworthy and infirm efforts acceptable to God.[13] Therefore, the Lord's Prayer frames the prayers of repentant sinners as their possibility and their perfecting.

Among the shorter recitations from Scripture are the terse lines addressed to the congregation before key corporate and individual acts, to heighten their spiritual focus: for example,, words of penitential exhortation and assurance before congregational confession of sin, of encouragement to generous giving before the collection of alms, and of confidence in our salvation by Jesus Christ before the prayers of Eucharistic celebration. These are a counterpoint to the recitation of longer, denser Scriptural "songs and hymns" less precisely related to the sequence of worship—chiefly, the psalms and the majority of canticles comprising a substantial portion of the services of daily prayer—which make several valuable contributions to Tudor worship.[14] Primarily, they embody the historical continuity of the worship of God's elect people. From early times, the church recognized the psalms as gems of Israel's tradition of worship: the choicest expression in prayer of

---

11. *Laws* 5.23: *WRH* 2:110.

12. In Holy Communion, the Lord's Prayer opens the service and, from 1552, directly follows congregational reception of the sacrament. In Morning and Evening Prayer, the Lord's Prayer directly follows absolution, and again, the congregational recital of the Apostles' Creed.

13. Hooker argues similarly against the Puritan contention that the Lord's Prayer is a model to be followed rather than words to be recited. *Laws* 5.35.3: *WRH* 2:143–7.

14. The psalms and canticles overlap, in that several psalms (67, 95, 98, 100) are used as canticles recited daily.

her spiritual and political inheritance, a kaleidoscopic image of Israel's faith in its entire emotional range, and a poetic condensation of her oral and literary witness to the human condition and to God's creative and redemptive action.[15] For the Tudor church, as for her predecessors, daily recitation of the psalms transmitted to the present generation of Christ's disciples the living tradition of Israel's faith transformed by the event of God's Incarnate Word.

Pivotal to the church's inheritance of Israel's living tradition are the three canticles of the New Testament, *Magnificat* (Song of Mary), *Benedictus* (Song of Zechariah), and *Nunc Dimittis* (Song of Simeon) from Luke's Gospel,[16] for these record the very moments at which Israel's expectation becomes gospel proclamation. The *Magnificat* uniquely articulates the proclamatory rationale of the church's action centered in corporate worship: namely, to glorify God by imparting, in the power of the *Holy* Spirit, the Father's Incarnate Word of salvation. The *Benedictus* and *Nunc Dimittis* poetically memorialize the first, prophetic welcoming into the world of Israel's savior by Israel's sons who long for his coming. Other canticles from the Psalms,[17] the Apocrypha,[18] and the patristic church[19] render praise and thanksgiving to God for his entire work of bringing forth and sustaining the ordered creation, and rescuing Israel, humankind, and the whole creation from eternal exile from God's living presence.

Singing the Scriptures

Recitation of the psalms and canticles provides a major congregational voice in corporate worship, conveying solidarity and reciprocity. The assembled faithful speak with one voice, in unity with all the faithful who have spoken or sung the texts through the ages, but they also speak to one another as fellow members of Christ's body. In both aspects they are obeying the injunction of Eph. 5:18-19, to "be filled with the Spirit, speaking unto yourselves in psalms and hymns and spiritual songs, singing and making melody to the Lord in your hearts."[20] However, the style of recitation may accentuate one or the other aspect. Congregational singing of the metrical psalms in unison or simple harmony, so popular in

---

15. Hooker's celebration of the psalms could hardly be outdone by the ancients for poetic mastery: "Heroical magnanimity, exquisite justice, grave moderation, exact wisdom, repentance unfeigned, unwearied patience, the mysteries of God, the sufferings of Christ, the terrors of wrath, the comforts of grace, the works of Providence over this world, and the promised joys of that world which is to come, all good necessarily to be either known or done or had, this one celestial fountain yieldeth." *Laws* 5.37.2: *WRH* 2:150.

16. Lk. 1:46-55, 68-79; 2:29-32.

17. *Venite exultemus domino* (Ps. 95), *Jubilate Deo* (Ps. 100), *Cantate domino* (Ps. 98), *Deus misereatur* (Ps. 67).

18. *Benedicite omnia opera Domini Domino* (Song of the Three Young Men, vv. 35-68).

19. *Te Deum Laudamus, Gloria in Excelsis Deo* (Holy Communion).

20. *The Great Bible*, repeating Tyndale; cf. Col. 3:16.

Elizabethan worship, accentuated the single massed voice in corporate declaration of Scripture whereas the alternative Tudor style of antiphonal psalmody—that is, the alternating recitation of the poetic stanzas by two corporate voices, accentuated the dialogical dimension of rehearsing Scripture, the reciprocal sharing of it with one another. The antiphonal style was the more ancient and continuous tradition of the church, retained in Tudor worship where the canticles and the psalms were recited in Coverdale translation, either said or sung to adapted Gregorian chant.[21] Historically, the Reformed style of metrical psalmody was a shaping force in Anglican parish worship without trained choirs until the mid-nineteenth century, which saw the adoption by Anglo-Catholic congregations of simple forms of Gregorian plainsong, and also the composition and large-scale dissemination of "Anglican chants" for the Coverdale Psalms, with broad and durable congregational success.[22] In cathedrals and churches with choral foundations, antiphonal psalmody always held sway, enriched by the collection of harmonized Anglican chants, which is still growing.

Two musical developments elevated the Tudor tradition of singing the vernacular Scriptures to a further level of musical complexity: the composition of part settings for the canticles and the composition of English anthems. Both had their inception in the Edwardian church, but their flowering (like antiphonal psalmody) in the later Elizabethan, Jacobean, and Caroline churches, with such distinguished composers attached to the Chapel Royal as Thomas Tallis, John Sheppard, William Mundy, Richard Farrant, William Byrd, Thomas Tomkins, and John Bull.[23] Canticle settings for Morning and Evening Prayer were often composed in pairs (*Venite* and *Benedictus*, *Magnificat* and *Nunc Dimittis*) and in conjunction with the *Preces* and *Responses* of the two services. English anthems were typically musical arrangements of one or more Scriptural verses for part voices and instrumental accompaniment, often with soloist(s). The greater freedom allowed to composers by the reformed liturgies, as compared with their Latin predecessors, to select and combine Scriptural texts[24] increased their attentiveness to the meaning of the words and the expressive challenge they posed.[25]

Indeed, the whole orientation of the vernacular liturgies toward the intelligibility and spiritual power of the words of Scripture and of common prayer played a significant role in fostering the more expressive and dramatic musical handling of words that emerged in the second half of the sixteenth century, involving the

---

21. The alternating voices belonged to the presiding minister and the congregation or to the two sides of a divided congregation or choir.

22. Gant, *O Sing Unto The Lord*, 294–300.

23. See p. 40, n. 88 and n. 89.

24. The Latin rites had many fixed liturgical texts for which composers were expected to provide musical arrangements.

25. Le Huray, *Music and the Reformation in England*, 141–8.

contrasting use of solo and choral voices and a new feeling for tonality.[26] For the liturgical rationale of music was no longer to communicate to worshippers the transcendent, incomprehensible mystery and beauty of sacramental realities, or to furnish an elevating background for the sentiments of their private devotions. Composers were now required to enhance the meaning of the words which they set, for singers and listeners alike, calling forth emotional responses that deepened spiritual comprehension of the realities represented by them.

While the episcopal restraint of liturgical music in the reformed English church produced some unjustified casualties, its general aim was not to suppress the self-transcending and ecstatic experiences of faithful worshippers but to intellectually purify and clarify them, integrating them into the full comprehension of faith. The challenge to the musician, lucidly conveyed by Richard Hooker,[27] was to wed the sensual delight afforded by his art to spiritual insight, representing (and thereby arousing) the affections intrinsic to faith's apprehending and loving the truth conveyed by the words. The musician's responsibility and his danger were commensurate with the benefit he might bestow; for, as the reformers intuitively, if imprecisely, discerned, music's capacity to unfold temporal experience as an ordered totality of passions transcending the discontinuity and fragmentation in experience—that is, its evocation of eternity in time—might either assist or undermine the Spirit's revelation of God's redemption of human time in Jesus Christ. It might either communicate or obscure the tensions between the time of sinful humanity, the time of Jesus Christ incarnate, crucified, and resurrected, and the eternal future of Christ's kingdom. Sensing this ambiguity of music, the English reformers, for the most part, required that it be brought under the discipline of the word of Scripture.

Attending and Responding to God Speaking in Corporate Worship

Regular Tudor worship displays the intimate relation between attending to God speaking through the Scriptural voices and through congregational prayer, for attending to God's speaking is the attitude of prayer: of trusting supplication, ardent expectation, and reverent receptivity. It is fitting that the concentration of the worshippers' affection in their prayerful intercourse with God should frame the concentration of their intelligence in receiving the Scriptural witness to God's saving truth, which comprises the centerpiece of the church's worship, directing and disciplining, empowering and ennobling the faltering speech and understanding of repentant sinners.

The psalms and canticles of daily worship epitomize for worshippers the inseparability of offering praise and thanksgiving to God. Offering praise or

---

26. See Le Huray's analysis of music in the period from 1570 to 1640, *Music and the Reformation in England*, 227–73; also, Gant, *O Sing Unto The Lord*, 105–80; Davies, *Worship and Theology in England*, 1:398–404.

27. *Laws* 5.38.1: *WRH* 2:151–2.

"magnifying God's name" is the "peculiar service" rendered "to his Majesty by his people,"[28] and God's majesty encompasses the transcendent perfections of his rule, calling forth reverent and fearful adoration from his worshippers. Yet God's majesty also comprehends the blessings to his creation issuing from these perfections—his stable and provident ordering of human life and community, loving protection, and succor of all creatures, merciful extending of forgiveness and renewing grace to helpless sinners, constant guidance and strengthening of the faithful in heavenly and earthly virtues, and all within his promise of life everlasting—calling forth joyful thanksgiving for the "innumerable and unspeakable benefits bestowed upon us."[29]

The congregational petitions laid before God in prayer also declare the breadth of his perfections and blessings, particularly the petitions in the frequently recited Litany,[30] which range over the whole spectrum of spiritual and physical necessities belonging to individual and communal life. God's faithful people "call upon him" in their need, but God desires our prayers, as the homilist says: "not because he either will not or cannot give without our asking"; for he knows better than we do our desires and our necessities, and his mercies outstrip our imagination. Rather, God would have us "pour out the secrets of our hearts before him and crave help at his hands" that "we might acknowledge him to be the Giver of all good things and behave ourselves thankfully towards him."[31] The rationale of petitionary prayer is eloquently summarized in the following collect:[32]

> Almighty and everlasting God, which art always more ready to hear than we to pray, and art wont to give more than either we desire or deserve: Pour down upon us the abundance of thy mercy, forgiving us those things whereof our conscience is afraid, and giving unto us that, that our prayer dare not presume to ask; through Jesus Christ our Lord.

The unity of all the forms of attending and responding to God's Word in corporate worship—reading, reciting, and preaching from Scripture, praising, thanking, supplicating God and confessing before him in prayer, and celebrating the sacraments—lies in their communicating God's full communication of himself through the Scriptures and uniting worshippers with the salvation wrought for the whole creation in the history of Jesus Christ. Of these practices, ministration of the sacraments of Baptism and the Lord's Supper are, by divine ordination, uniquely

---

28. "Of the Right Use of the Church or Temple of God . . .," *GH*, 154.

29. Ibid.

30. The Litany was to be used weekly on Sunday, Wednesday, and Friday, and in special liturgies, including those of "ordering" (ordaining deacons and priests, and consecrating bishops.)

31. "An Homily Concerning Prayer," *GH*, 320.

32. *BCP*, 193. Cranmer's expansive translation of the Sarum collect for the twelfth Sunday after Trinity.

efficacious in uniting worshippers with the climax of Christ's history, his saving death and resurrection, and, so, with the promise of "free forgiveness of our sin," "holiness," and "joining in Christ."[33]

Corporate Worship as Archetypical Obedience to Christ's Rule

Corporate worship may be regarded as paradigmatically encompassing all the church's essential works of trinitarian and Christological love—of discipleship, fellowship, and ministry—falling outside of it. For works of generous, forgiving, merciful, self-sacrificial, and joyful service to the neighbor express a faith and hope continually formed and nourished through the practices of worship; and the extra-liturgical works themselves manifest the constitutive aspects of liturgical practices. Individually and collectively, the practices of worship, being informed by faithful reflection on the testimony of Scripture and on ecclesial tradition, communicate to the worshippers the structure of faithful human action per se, whatever its specific purpose and form of service.

Tudor public theology, therefore, sets forth the practices of corporate worship as the primary and determinative instance of faithful human action *coram Deo et hominibus*, the foremost visible and audible response of the faithful to God's saving word in Jesus Christ. Through speech and through ritual signs, corporate worship communicates the constitutive aspects of faithful human action, with generative meaning and power for action outside the sphere of corporate worship. Moreover, in showing faithful action to be the embodiment of God's saving rule over, in, and through his people on earth, corporate worship constitutes the spiritual and institutional nexus of God's earthly rule, the most transparent anticipation of its eschatological fulfillment.[34]

We shall briefly indicate the aspects of faithful human action conveyed by Tudor worship (reflecting on earlier discussions) before examining their articulation in the service of Holy Communion. The first aspect is the grounding of faithful action in the free consent of sinful human beings to God's revealed judgments: chiefly and determinatively, their consent to the Father's judgment of condemnation and reconciliation directed toward themselves in the death and resurrection of his Son. To hear and consent to God's judgment of themselves in Jesus Christ opens to sinners the possibility of hearing and consenting coherently to God's judgments

---

33. "Of Common Prayer and Sacraments," *GH*, 355.

34. My interpretation of Tudor ecclesiology as investing the church's core practice of worship with paradigmatic or archetypal meaning and power for faithful action is indebted to Bernd Wannenwetsch's exploration of the church's common worship as the "grammar of Christian life" and the "first instance" of her corporate obedience to God's rule, in *Gottesdienst als Lebensform—Ethik für Christenbürger* (Stuttgart: Verlag W. Kohlhammer, 1997); trans. M. Kohl, *Political Worship: Ethics for Christian Citizens* (Oxford: Oxford University Press, 2004).

revealed in all his works. Corporate worship, then, continually points to Christ's accomplished work of righteousness as the primary object of faith and shows faith originating within the divine subjectivity of his Spirit who incorporates believers into Christ's resurrection victory over all antihuman and nihilistic forces of evil.

The second aspect of faithful human action conveyed by common worship is the communal character of its agency. The agent of faithful action is never the self-conscious subject in detached isolation from others, the self-positing ego standing over against others. It is always the "I" that is also "we": the faithful person in fellowship with others. The liturgies of corporate worship convey the expectation that perfected human agency in the Kingdom of God will be wholly common, communicative, and consensual: that it will be the mutual participation of persons in the Spirit's judgments, mutual sharing in the knowledge, love, and freedom of Christ. In manifesting by word and deed the promise of reconciled freedom, the Tudor liturgies do not affirm that institutional practices of worship are, in and of themselves, the perfected action of reconciled community. Rather, they affirm that faithful human agency is divinely imparted where the Word of God is purely preached and the sacraments administered according to Christ's commandments. The English liturgies display the subject of every obedient act of worship as the whole company of Christ's faithful people to which every worshipping individual and congregation is joined in a real communion of minds and wills. This communion is the bond of faith, hope, and love in the Holy Spirit which every faithful act both presupposes and strengthens. Although identifying the church universal with "the church militant" on earth, the prayer books of 1552 and 1559 abundantly attest the extension of the worshipping subject across time as well as space, primarily by the historical ecumenicity of their content.[35]

The third aspect of faithful human action is its conformity to the outer rule of the canonical Scriptures as the authoritative revelation of God's word of salvation in Jesus Christ, which comprehends all God's judgments and actions toward his creatures. Tudor worship reveals that within God's justifying, redeeming, liberating word spoken through the Scriptures is a commanding and directing word, which establishes the path of faithful human action. God speaks his commanding word through the Scriptures in a multiplicity of literary ways: in cosmological, legendary, and historical narratives; in parables, prayers, prophecy, proverbs, and other sayings; in human exhortation and counsel; and divine blessing and cursing as well as direct divine commands. In these manifold modes, God shows what is pleasing and what is abhorrent to him, what is consonant and dissonant with the stable orders of creaturely life, and the temporal consequences and final ends of human obedience and disobedience. He calls individuals and communities

---

35. Cranmer was ecumenical both in contemporary liturgical borrowings and in frequently retaining more of the tradition than even Lutheran colleagues: for example, his preserving more of the traditional canticles, versicles, and responses in Morning and Evening Prayer, and over seventy of the church's ancient and medieval collects in translated and adapted forms.

to faithful action in the here and now, illuminating the moral terrain of their acting, guiding their deliberation, and eliciting desire for appropriate goods. All these ethical modalities have a presence in Tudor worship: primarily in the canonical sequence of readings in daily prayer, and in preaching and homilies that abundantly invoke them across the range of their moral guidance, exhortation, and remonstration. Nevertheless, the reformed English liturgies, like the homilies, give priority to God's explicit commandments as disclosing the moral implications of all his recorded judgments and actions, and, above all, to Christ's commandments as the hermeneutical key to the totality of divine commandments, and so to the Bible as the external rule of Christian action.

The fourth aspect of faithful action is its conformity to the inner rule of the Holy Spirit. The regular English services convey in their structure and prayers the correspondence between the outer and the inner determinations of renewed human moral agency and action. They convey the proleptic participation of faithful human agents, by the activity of the divine Spirit, in the freedom and lordship of the risen and ascended Savior. This is freedom not only from the law's condemnation of past sins but from the oppressiveness of the law's present demands, encountered as external and alien constraints on the agent's willing and acting. The promised rule of the Holy Spirit—also referred to as God's "heavenly" and "special" grace—is communication to the faithful of Christ's lordship over the law, his perfect obedience to His Father's will, in which true human knowledge is wedded to proportionate and appropriate desires and affections, bringing about effectual action. As the ordinary and seasonal collects express,[36] the Holy Spirit will make Christ's lordship present to the faithful by particular operations throughout their unique individual and communal moral histories.

The Sacraments as Faithful Action

The 1559 liturgies of the Lord's Supper and Public Baptism coherently articulate these four aspects of faithful action, so to present the church as the community of Christ's saving rule. Thus, to confine our discussion to the communion service is for expediency. While mindful of the bitter disputes that have dominated the interpretation and assessment of these sacramental liturgies since the mid-nineteenth century, particularly regarding the relationship of their contents to Cranmer's shifting sacramental reflections, our principal concern is with the theological coherence of the communion service, both internally and with the Homilies and Articles, which affords us a degree of interpretative freedom from Cranmer's own expositions. Although plainly expressing decisive features of Cranmer's sacramental theology, the 1559 liturgies, like their 1552 predecessors, do not clearly or unambiguously express all its controversial elements.

---

36. See p. 52.

Let us begin by noting the features common to baptism and communion as "sacraments," according to the definition given in the Edwardian and Elizabethan Articles XXVI (XXV):[37]

> Sacraments ordained of Christ be not only badges or tokens of Christian men's profession; but rather they be certain, sure witnesses and effectual signs of grace and God's good will toward us, by which he doth work invisibly in us, and doth not only quicken, but also strengthen and confirm our faith in him.

The sacraments of baptism and communion not only have the outward visibility of "badges or tokens" of a common Christian "profession," but are ordained by Christ to be "sure witnesses and effectual signs" of God's grace and favor toward us. Christ's command that his disciples perform these signs enfolds his promise that they effectually convey what they materially image and verbally signify, as instruments of God's ongoing, invisible work "in us" to "quicken," "strengthen and confirm our faith in him." Graciously given to Christ's elect people, the sacramental signs are his appointed carriers of their common faith. Their communal reality and *telos* is eloquently highlighted in the Edwardian Article's opening quote from Augustine: "Our Lord Jesus Christ hath knit together a company of new people with Sacraments, most few in number, most easy to be kept, most excellent in signification."[38] Although, lamentably, dropping this quote, the Elizabethan revisers indirectly affirm the centrality of corporate action to the spiritual efficacy of the sacraments by retaining the injunction that they "were not ordained by Christ to be gazed upon or to be carried about, but that we should duly use them."[39] Thus, Articles XXVI (XXV) clearly indicate the constitutive aspects of faithful action displayed by both sacraments: grounding in faith's consent to God's saving judgment, common agency, the outward rule of Scripture, and the inward rule of the Spirit of grace.

Holy Communion

The Christological Ground of Faithful Action. Despite its liturgical parallels with the service of Public Baptism,[40] the service of Holy Communion is distinctive in its sustained liturgical focus on Christ's accomplished work of righteousness on the Cross as the basis of the Father's reconciling judgment of sinners, which is the object of faith and basis of faithful human action. Despite the centrality of this

---

37. TA, 147–8.

38. TA, 147. Augustine, *Epis.* 54.1: "sacramentis numero paucissimis, observatione facillimis, significatione praestantissimis."

39. TA, 147–8.

40. Gordon P. Jeanes has extensively charted and theologically discussed such parallels in the services of 1549 and 1552 in *Signs of God's Promise: Thomas Cranmer's Sacramental Theology and the Book of Common Prayer* (London: T&T Clark, 2008), 187–240.

basis to the baptismal service, its liturgical focus is somewhat more divided, with greater emphasis placed on the action of the regenerating Spirit in the advent, growth, and fruition of faith. The undivided focus of the Communion liturgy is Christ's passion and death as the pivotal representative act of God's Incarnate Son that accomplishes the reconciliation to the Father of humankind and the world. Its doctrinal focal point is the rhetorically lavish proclamation in the Eucharistic prayer of Institution that Jesus Christ on the Cross "made there (by his one oblation of himself once offered) a full, perfect, and sufficient sacrifice, oblation, and satisfaction, for the sins of the whole world."[41]

The whole sequence of pre- and post-communion prayers—that is, the penitential prayers and exhortations, and the prayers of congregational oblation and thanksgiving—draws attention to Christ's *unrepeatable* suffering and death as the sole merit on which the Father's forgiveness and deliverance of sinners depends, and to repentant faith in the merit of Christ's passion as the sole form in which sinners lay hold of the Father's pardon and deliverance. Communicants must attend the "heavenly feast" in "the marriage garment required of God"[42]: bewailing and confessing before him their "manifold sins and wickedness" committed against his "divine majesty,"[43] fully trusting in, and giving hearty thanks, for the Father's abundant mercy and Christ's "exceeding great love" for sinners exhibited on the Cross.[44] They must eagerly seek reconciliation with enemies and forgiveness for their offenses against others, while forgiving offenses against themselves, and earnestly intend to lead amended lives, "following the commandments of God."[45] Conversely, would-be communicants who manifestly spurn the "marriage garment" should be pastorally warned not to presume to approach the Lord's "holy table" in their faithless, obdurately sinful state.[46]

Significantly, it is after the penitent faithful have been united with Christ's sacrifice by their spiritual partaking of his flesh and blood, that they offer up to their heavenly Father a twofold oblation: of "praise and thanksgiving" and of themselves, their "souls and bodies" as "a reasonable, holy, and lively sacrifice."[47] The faithful have come to divine worship and the Lord's Table conscious of their empty-handedness: apart from their contrite faith and gratitude, they have only their unworthiness and need of cleansing to bring before God in a prayer of trusting supplication:

> We are not worthy so much as to gather the crumbs under thy table, but thou art the same Lord whose property is always to have mercy. Grant us therefore

---

41. *BCP*, 263.
42. Optional exhortation to worthy reception, *BCP*, 257.
43. "General Confession," *BCP*, 259.
44. Exhortation to worthy reception, *BCP*, 258.
45. *BCP*, Invitation to receive the sacrament, *BCP*, 259.
46. *BCP*, 258.
47. *BCP*, 264.

(gracious Lord) so to eat the flesh of thy dear Son Jesus Christ, and to drink his blood, that our sinful bodies may be made clean by his body, and our souls washed through his most precious blood.[48]

Mindful of their supplication, they may, after reception, express confidence in the spiritual washing received in their sacramental union with Christ crucified, by offering up to the Lord, together with "praise and thanksgiving," their entire spiritual and corporeal selves as an acceptable sacrifice.[49]

The spiritual eating and drinking of Christ's body and blood by his faithful people is their prayerful recollection of his atoning sacrifice, in which their Savior, in the unity of his humanity and his godhead, gives himself afresh to them in personal union. It is not Christ's "natural," "corporeal," or "substantial" presence in the material elements of bread and the wine which "nourishes" and "increases" faith in his members, but rather Christ's giving of himself to be spiritually "eaten, chewed, and digested" in their expectant and obedient giving and receiving of these elements.[50] It is within the sequence of prayer immediately preceding reception, wherein the faithful recollect Christ's sacrificial death, his institution at the Last Supper of a "perpetual" memorial, and his words and actions of blessing and distributing the bread and wine,[51] that these material elements become for the faithful "lively" or "effectual" "signs and tokens" of their participation in Christ's sacrificial victory on the Cross. Although the bread and wine, owing to their natural use in providing vital bodily sustenance to human beings, have an inherent symbolic power to signify vital spiritual nourishment and refreshment, their precise sacramental signification and instrumentality as a vehicle of Christ's self-giving to the faithful derives from their use within the corporate remembrance in words and action of Christ's saving sacrifice, conforming to the apostolic testimony to his example and command.[52] As the absence of the *Epiclesis* from the 1552 Prayer

---

48. Prayer of Humble Access, *BCP*, 263.
49. Prayer of Oblation and Thanksgiving, *BCP*, 264.
50. *An Answer unto a Crafty and Sophistical Cavillation Devised by Stephen Gardiner Against the True and Godly Doctrine of the Most Holy Sacrament of the Body and Blood of Our Saviour Jesus Christ* (1551) 1.8; also, 1.20-4, 32-43, in *Writings and Disputations of Thomas Cranmer Relative to the Sacrament of the Lord's Supper*, ed. John Edmund Cox (Cambridge: Cambridge University Press, 1844), 15, 25-9, 35-47. Hereafter *WD*. The "*Cavillation*" refers to Gardiner's *Explication and Assertion of the Catholic Faith Touching the most Blessed Sacrament of the Alter* (1551), a confutation of Cranmer's *Defence of the True and Catholic Doctrine of the Body and Blood of Our Saviour Christ* (1550), itself a riposte to Catholic assaults on the 1549 Communion service.
51. Prayer of Institution (or Consecration of the Elements), *BCP*, 263.
52. Cranmer often repeats that "the nature of the sacraments require[s] that the sensible elements should remain in their proper nature, to signify an higher mystery and secret working of God inwardly, as the sensible elements be ministered outwardly." *An Answer* 1.33-4: *WD*, 37.

witnesses, to call down the Holy Spirit's sanctifying action on the elements per se is misplaced, when their communicative power is already given by the Spirit in the congregational recollection of Christ's saving sacrifice and commanded memorial. In this faithful and obedient recollection by Christ's adopted sons and daughters, the nonhuman world is sanctified, drawn into Christ's promise of eternal life.

Through this symbolic "showing forth" of Christ's broken body and spilt blood, faithful recollection feeds on the crucified Savior and, by the Spirit of the resurrected and exalted Savior, receives the spiritual benefits of his passion. Chief among these is the assurance, drawn from this "seal" or "pledge" of Christ's steadfast, redeeming love, that "he doth so join and incorporate himself to us, that he is our head, and we his members, and flesh of his flesh, and bone of his bones, having him dwelling in us, and we in him."[53] Like Baptism, administration of the Lord's Supper is a unique communication of Christ's word of life, for it presents Christ to all the senses and not only the auditory.[54] But through this sensual possession of Christ, the faithful ascend beyond the sensible to feed spiritually on their crucified and glorified Savior, enthroned in heaven on the Father's right hand, in the unity of his godhead and corporeal manhood.[55]

This ascent of faithful communicants to Christ is definitive of the spiritual dynamic of their possession of him throughout their earthly life. Thus, the collect appointed for Ascension Day is the prayer for all days: "Grant, we beseech thee, Almighty God, that like as we do believe thy only-begotten Son our Lord to have ascended into the heavens; so we may also in heart and mind thither ascend, and with him continually dwell."[56] In ascending to dwell with and in the Son by the power of his Spirit, the faithful are not deserting or devaluing the Father's material gifts of bread and wine. On the contrary, by the promised illumination of their knowing and purification of their desiring and willing, they are enabled to grasp the multilayered meaning and goodness of the physical elements in their natural being and uses, as well as the eschatological meaning and goodness in their sacramental use. And just as ascent to Christ is the universal motion of faith, so the promised illumination and purification extends to faithful knowledge, appreciation, and use of the whole nonhuman creation in its materiality and corporeality and not only the sacramental elements.

Individual and Common Agency. Throughout the communion service, the liturgical action in which the worshippers participate is at once intensely inward and private, and at the same time, palpably common and communicative. The sustained presence of the corporate "we" in supplication, praise, thanksgiving, confession, and oblation constantly reminds the worshippers that they are united with their Savior in his suffering unto death and heirs of his risen and glorified

---

53. *Defence* (1550) 1.16, incorporated into *An Answer* 1.40: *WD*, 43.

54. *Defence*, 1.12, *An Answer* 1.38: *WD*, 41; also, *An Answer* 3.156, quoting Chrysostom: *WD*, 153.

55. *Defence*, 3.185–6; *An Answer* 3.190–1: *WD*, 183; also, *An Answer* 4.246: *WD*, 235.

56. *BCP*, 166.

life, not as separate, isolated individuals, but as fellow sharers in Christ's history. Not that the liturgy neglects the individual vocation of faith: it is "I" (not "we") who declares my faith when I recite the "Apostles' Creed" in Morning and Evening Prayer, renewing the pledge of faith taken for me at my Baptism, and later by me in preparing for Confirmation.[57] However, even here, or especially here, in each individual's affirmation of this assumed creedal consensus of the early church,[58] the unity of the individual and the communal vocation of faith is powerfully demonstrated.

It is precisely because the nourishing gifts of Christ's presence in the sacramental action come not only "from above" but also from among Christ's members that reception of them by the faithful is presented as assurance from the Father that "we be very members incorporate in thy mystical body, which is the blessed company of all faithful people, and be also heirs through hope of thy everlasting kingdom."[59] The earthly perseverance of Christ's faithful toward the heavenly consummation of his reign is their perseverance in a communion, a "holy fellowship" that is "catholic" as well as "apostolic," as the Nicene creed declares.[60] The practical, moral dimension of Christ's "holy fellowship" is exhibited by the prayer's concluding petition to the Father "to assist us with thy grace, that we may . . . do all such good works as thou hast prepared for us to walk in." Common partaking of the faithful in the sacrament is the effectual sign of their harmony and concord in action as well as their unity in belief, understanding, and sentiment. Their memorial participation in Christ's act of reconciling self-sacrifice on the Cross is echoed and imaged in manifold acts of self-sacrificing and reconciling service within and beyond Christ's visible body.

The Rule of Scripture. The climax of the pivotal "Prayer of Institution" is the rehearsal of Christ's gracious invitation and command to his disciples at the "Last Supper":[61]

> in the same night that he was betrayed, [Christ] took bread, and when he had given thanks, he break it, and gave it to his disciples, saying, Take, eat, this is my body which is given for you. Do this in remembrance of me. Likewise after supper he took the cup, and when he had given thanks, he gave it to them, saying, Drink ye all of this, for this is my blood of the new testament, which is shed for you and for many, for remission of sins: do this as oft as ye shall drink it in remembrance of me.

---

57. Loosely following Roman tradition, the more concise (so-called) "Apostles' Creed" was used in the service of Baptism and the Confirmation Catechism, while the doctrinally enlarged Nicene Creed was used in the service of Holy Communion.

58. See p. 225 n. 5 on the historical provenance and authority of the three creeds of Tudor worship.

59. The second (alternative) post-communion prayer of thanksgiving, *BCP*, 265.

60. *BCP*, 251.

61. *BCP*, 263.

The liturgical interlacing of the Matthean phrases, "Take, eat" and "Drink ye all of this" (Great Bible) into Paul's account in 1 Cor. 11:23-25 highlights the convergence of invitation and command in Christ's words. The juxtaposition of "Take, eat . . ." and "Do this . . .," "Drink ye . . .," and "Do this . . ." conveys to the communicants that in the sacramental action of receiving the bread and the wine, Christ gives himself to their "remembrance" as the saving and commanding word of life. The efficaciousness for faith of their reception of the sacrament depends on their embracing the unity of invitation and command, promise and law, in Christ's self-giving. Thus, prior to communicating, they humbly beseech the Father: "grant that we, receiving these thy creatures of bread and wine, according to thy Son our Saviour Jesus Christ's holy institution, in remembrance of his death and passion, may be partakers of his most blessed Body and Blood."[62] The crucified and glorified Savior gives himself freely to sinners, but he is only received by their wholehearted devotion to his revealed will. Moreover, as Christ's saving invitation and command, his saving promise and rule, are revealed by the written apostolic testimony of the gospels and epistles, obedient reception of the Incarnate Word involves subjection to his authoritative communication in the Scriptures.

While focusing on Christ's commanding word of self-sacrificial love, anticipating his passion, the Communion liturgy also draws attention to God's commanding word of creative goodness, bringing forth and sustaining the cosmic totality of finite beings in their ordered relationships. For the sacramental centrality of table fellowship around breaking and eating bread, blessing and consuming wine, conveys the intrinsic relationship of the human community's dependence on God's nonhuman creation to God's saving work in Christ. In referring to the bread and wine as "these thy creatures," the Prayer of Institution intimates that it is God's providential care for his creation, beyond human work or resourcefulness, that provides for the natural necessities, as for the spiritual necessities, of human community; and that the grain and the grapes have a creaturely relation to their maker prior to their productive use by human beings. At the same time, the sacramental use of God's "creatures" of bread and wine looks forward to the fulfillment of all creatures in the eternal Sabbath Rest, in which the human lords of creation participate in the perfection of God's work by desisting from their own labor, to lead creation's hymn of praise and thanksgiving.

Notwithstanding the presence of creaturely relations, the Communion service, like Baptism, gives liturgical priority to the Father and the Son's explicit commandments, as the external rule of Christian practice.[63] By opening the service with a rehearsal of the Decalogue immediately after the Lord's Prayer, the liturgy gathers the company of the faithful in the public proclamation of its common rule. After the minister pronounces each commandment, the faithful "ask God's mercy for their transgression of the same," and beseech him to "incline our hearts to

---

62. Ibid.
63. See the discussion of the relation of Christ's commandments to the Mosaic Decalogue, 280–2.

keep this law."⁶⁴ "Keeping" of God's law is open to those who obediently embrace Christ's invitation and command to be united with his obedient sacrifice on the Cross through the recollection of faith, partaking in the memorial of his passion. For this command of Christ, in which the liturgical sequence climaxes, opens to sinners the soteriological reality of all God's commands as an expression of his merciful love, and the eschatological reality of obedience as abiding in Christ, and through Christ, in one another.

The Rule of the Spirit. The obedient recollection of faith, which unites us with Christ's obedient suffering unto death and his resurrection and ascension into glory, is the gift of the Holy Spirit. In "the communion of the body and blood of the Lord," the Elizabethan homilist tells us, "the operation of the Holy Ghost [is] the very bond of our conjunction with Christ," wrought through faith.⁶⁵ Although the pre- and post-reception prayers focus on Christ's indwelling and not on the Spirit's mediating presence, the earlier (ante-communion) prayers affirm the Spirit's preparation as essential for receiving Christ, cleansing "the thoughts of our hearts . . . that we may perfectly love thee, and worthily magnify thy holy name."⁶⁶ As the Holy Spirit is active with Christ himself in Baptism, regenerating the faithful sinner into Christ, so both Son and Spirit are active in the "spiritual feeding" (i.e., feeding in the Spirit) of the faithful on Christ in the Lord's Supper.⁶⁷ Indeed, both Spirit and Son are continually active, Cranmer tells us, "so long as we dwell in [Christ]."⁶⁸ How could it be otherwise?—for the Holy Spirit "doth quicken the minds of men, stirring up good and godly motions in their hearts which are agreeable to the will and commandment of God."⁶⁹

In the communion service, the appointed collects for ordinary and festal time portray various dimensions of the Spirit's active rule in faithful human agency and action, through which Christ's members participate proleptically in his freedom and lordship over the law. Although the collects regularly invoke the action of "God" (implicitly, the Father, to whom prayers are generally addressed) or of God's "grace" rather than of the "Holy Spirit," they consistently portray God's action on or within the "hearts" of the faithful as the Holy Spirit's action. Not surprisingly, the collect for Whitsunday is exemplary:⁷⁰

---

64. *BCP*, 248-9.
65. "Of the Worthy Receiving and Reverent Esteeming of the Sacrament," *GH*, 442.
66. *BCP*, 248.
67. "And as Almighty God by his most mighty word and his holy Spirit and infinite power brought forth all creatures in the beginning, and ever sithens hath preserved them; even so by the same word and power he worketh in us, from time to time, this marvellous spiritual generation and wonderful spiritual nourishment and feeding, . . . comprehended and received of us by faith. *Defence* 3.15, *An Answer* 3.207: *WD*, 198; also, 3.70: *WD*, 70-1.
68. *Answer* 3.71: *WD*, 71.
69. "Concerning the Coming Down of the Holy Ghost . . .," *GH*, 456.
70. Translation of Sarum Missal xxxii: *The Collect in Anglican Liturgy: Texts and Sources 1549-1989* (Alcuin Club Collection, no. 72), comp. and ed. Martin R. Dudley (Collegeville:

> God which as upon this day has taught the hearts of thy faithful people by the sending to them the light of thy Holy Spirit: Grant us by the same Spirit to have a right judgement in all things, and evermore to rejoice in his holy comfort; through the merits of Christ Jesu our Saviour, who liveth and reigneth with thee in the unity of the same Spirit, one God, world without end.

The collects eloquently convey the manifoldness of the Spirit's motions in making Christ's lordship present to the faithful, moment by moment, by particular operations: illumining their judgments, strengthening their resolution, affording assurance, generating good and appropriate desires and affections, and suppressing wayward ones—bringing about effectual action in the unique succession of moral situations comprising their individual and communal histories.[71] Two arresting examples are the following collect for Easter Day[72] and Cranmer's own composition for the Fourth Sunday after Easter.[73]

> Almighty God, which through thy only begotten Son Jesus Christ hast overcome death and opened unto us the gate of everlasting life: We humbly beseech thee, that, as by thy special grace preventing us, thou dost put into our minds good desires, so by thy continual help, we may bring the same to good effect; through Jesus Christ, who liveth and reigneth with thee and the Holy Ghost, ever one God, world without end.

> Almighty God, which dost make the minds of all faithful men to be of one will: Grant unto thy people, that they may love the thing which thou commandest, and desire that which thou dost promise; that among the sundry and manifold changes of the world, our hearts may surely there be fixed, where true joys are to be found; through Christ our Lord.

With the phrase "as by thy special grace preventing us," the Easter collect affirms God's acting on the imagination of the individual to bring to consciousness particular desires to perform particular good works, and, further, his acting to bring about the actual performance of these works. The second collect, as many

---

The Liturgical Press, 1994), 77; *BCP*, 168-9.

71. Examples include the Collect for the Ninth Sunday after Trinity: "Grant to us Lord we beseech thee, the Spirit to think and do always such things as be rightful, that we which cannot be without thee, may by thee be able to live according to thy will . . ." Translation of Sarum Missal xlii: Dudley, *The Collect*, 81; *BCP*, 188. Also, the Collects for the First Sunday in Lent and the Nineteenth Sunday after Trinity, *BCP*, 109, 204.

72. Expansive translation of a Latin prayer that came into the Sarum Processionale from the Gregorian Sacramentary: Dudley, *The Collect*, 73; also Frederick Armitage, *A History of the Collects* (London: Weare & Co., 1919), 67; *BCP*, 152-3.

73. Dudley, *The Collect*, 75-6; Armitage, *A History*, 90; *BCP*, 163. The revised 1662 collect begins: "O Almighty God, who alone canst order the unruly wills and affections of sinful men . . ."

others, affirms implicitly that, in the promised renewal of the moral subject, there is no disjunction between knowledge and will, reason and desire, and the will and the affections; neither is there conflict between the moral judgments of individuals or between individual and communal judgments, for the Spirit's imparting of Christ's love is the unifying thread of the individual as of the common moral life, "the very bond of peace and all virtues," in the words of another of Cranmer's own collects (echoing Eph. 4:3).[74]

Corporate Worship and the Renewal of Faithful Action, Then and Now

Through the Scriptural tradition of testimony to the history of his creating and saving Word, the Father continually creates and sustains communal traditions of attending to and responding to his speaking. By the power of the Spirit, overcoming the infirmities of sinful human knowledge and affection, these communal traditions of practice faithfully communicate God's living Word. English Reformation public theology presents the visible community of the faithful as the structured social reality constituted primarily by practices of corporate worship, recognizing these practices to be paradigmatic or archetypal exemplars of faithful human action, uniquely and powerfully conveying its aspects as a communication of God's own self-communicating action within and among his human creatures. Together with the regular worship of Morning and Evening Prayer, the liturgies of Holy Communion and Baptism comprise the core practical tradition of the reformed English church, continuous with practices of past generations reaching back to the apostolic period and to Israel's historical existence.

The uniqueness of Scripture as divine and human tradition is reflected in the uniqueness of the practices of worship as archetypal exemplars of faithful human action. The practices of worship are human practices, definable in nontheological discourse as communally established, regularly repeated, coherent, and complex sequences of cooperative acts, ordered to the realization of goods and ends to which they are intrinsically related.[75] At the same time, the goods and ends to which these cooperative acts are ordered are extrinsic as well as intrinsic, being the Father's impartation of his Word and the Spirit of Holiness. Consequently, the practices are not adequately comprehended by a nonsoteriological discourse of human "practice." In exemplifying faithful human action, in communicating its constitutive divine and human aspects, the practices of worship are central to God's renewal of human agency and action and overcoming of its idolatrous tendencies.

---

74. The collect for Quinquegesima: "O Lord, which dost teach us that all our doings without charity are nothing worth: Send thy Holy Ghost and pour in our hearts that most excellent gift of charity, the very bond of peace and all virtues, without the which whosoever liveth is counted dead before thee . . ." Dudley, *The Collect*, 65; *BCP*, 106.

75. We are adopting Alasdair MacIntyre's definition of a communal practice in *After Virtue: A Study in Moral Theory* (London: Duckworth, 1981), 175.

First, these practices communicate faith, not as a single temporal act, determinative for all future action, but rather a constant or continuous interior act accompanying other interior and exterior acts: an act of trust and hope that, united with our crucified, resurrected, and exalted Savior, we can achieve some good, some conformity to Christ's obedient love, in our earthly desires, intentions, and outward action; and, finally, that we as agents will be fulfilled and perfected in eternal communion with Christ. The practices also communicate faith as repentant, as disowning our past disobedient action performed out of, and for ourselves, apart from Christ. And they show that our remorseful recollection and contrite confession of our sins before God is not an exercise of intricate analytical inspection of past acts to render them morally transparent, for any attempt to approximate such moral comprehension and transparency is delusive[76] because we are only granted clarity about the pervasiveness of sin in our moral histories and our need for continual purification of our moral agency, as the church's daily confession declares.[77]

Faith's repentance must extend to the failures of the church's practices of worship to communicate God's saving Word and the obedient response of faith. As these practices are susceptible to human frailty and sin, despite the grounding of their authority in Christ's promises, they cannot be philosophically conceived as progressively enhancing our "human powers to achieve excellence" in their performance, or as "systematically" extending our "human conceptions of the ends and goods involved."[78] The centrality of penitential confession in worship testifies that its practices do not comprise *a project* of cultivating "virtues" or "habits" (i.e., spiritual powers to act), and perfecting or continually extending performance through repetitive, reflective action (practice). Rather, the practices of worship are forms of waiting upon God's communicative freedom. As such, they uphold the confidence of the faithful in God's promise to render them avenues of his restoring and sanctifying self-communication, but in his good time, the time of the Holy Spirit's acting, determined by no human project of moral formation through communal tradition.

Second, the practices of worship communicate the commonality of faithful action, its common subject, comprising all who by faith possess Christ, and in possessing him, possess themselves and their neighbors in his knowledge and love imparted by the Holy Spirit. By his Spirit, they know and love themselves and their neighbors as forgiven sinners, buried, raised, and exalted with Christ and, despite their unworthiness, called to participate in his renewed humanity. Although

---

76. On the morally delusive character of interpreting one's past actions, Kazuo Ishiguro's novel, *The Unconsoled* (London: Faber and Faber, 1995) is as discerning as it is entertaining.

77. "Almighty and most merciful Father, we have erred and strayed from thy ways, like lost sheep. We have followed too much the devices and desires of our own hearts. We have offended against thy holy laws. We have left undone those things which we ought to have done, and we have done those things which we ought not to have done, and *there is no health in us*. But thou, O Lord, have mercy upon us miserable offenders."

78. MacIntyre, *After Virtue*, 175.

imperfect in this passing age, their earthly communion, rooted in worship, supports the neighbor's good in myriad ways, without fostering indiscriminate intimacy or uniformity and homogeneity of desire, thought, and judgment, corrosive of individuality and independence of spirit. Rather, in their commonality, faithful persons gratefully accept their own unique makeup and that of others, allowing the distinctiveness of each to flourish, without breeding mistrust and enmity, and disagreements to be resolved and contained, without destructive division.

Third, the practices of worship, in communicating faithful action as waiting upon God's present address by attending to, reflecting upon, and responding in prose and song to Scripture's testimony, declare God's Word as justifying and liberating, commanding and directing, and faithful action as answering Christ's present invitation and obedient to his present command. Although one with his word spoken in the Scriptures, Christ's present word of invitation and command—the concrete opportunity that he lays before us and the concrete command that he lays on us—is neither given by nor within the church's tradition of practice. That is primarily because, as the Tudor collects attest, God's gifts and commands outstrip our habitual desires and imagining, encompassing the newness of the actual situation in which he is placing (has placed) us, individually and corporately. Consequently, the church's traditions of practice may only anticipate God's present invitation and command and situate the faithful to hear it.

Fourth, the practices of worship communicate faithful action as issuing from the Holy Spirit's illumination for agents of the present meaning of God's law, guiding their discernment and deliberation concerning the moral complexities of their particular circumstances. In these practices, the Spirit discloses to agents the unity of God's unchanging purpose in the person and action of Christ, articulated in the plurality of his commands. The worship of Christ's disciples in the Spirit displays the unity of God's law, summarized in Christ's twofold love command: "You shall love the Lord your God with all your heart, and with all your soul, and with all your strength, and with all your mind; and your neighbour as yourself."[79] The common participation and shared communication of the faithful in practices of worship according with God's law display the seamless, twofold service of faithful action to God and to the neighbor; for these practices are simultaneously communal modes of recognizing, celebrating, and proclaiming God's glorious acts, and modes of upholding and strengthening the neighbor in faith and good works. Common worship admits no tension, rivalry, or discontinuity between the two ends of service, but manifests their unity in every faithful human act.

The Struggle of Spiritual Worship against Idolatry, Then and Now

As the primary practical obedience of the faithful to God's rule, common worship is in this time of waiting the sensible human image of God most acceptable to

---

79. Lk. 10:27; Mt. 22:37, 39, combining the commands from Deut. 6:5 and Lev. 19:18.

him. It is the outward form taken by faith's continuous inward act of pure "spiritual worship" of him. Common worship is the imaging of God's perfections that Christ himself has commanded, carrying the authorization of the apostolic witness to him. Its practices involve waiting on, attending to, interpreting, and communicating the Father's Word spoken in Jesus Christ through the Scriptures, of death and resurrection, promised fulfillment, present invitation, and command. The rationale of all these practices is to place the faithful at the disposal of God's self-revealing address, to render them receptive to his communicating presence.

Idolatrous corruptions of Christian practices have, by contrast, the rationale of placing God's sovereign word of salvation at human disposal, of managing his self-revealing address through the Scriptures, of converting future promise into present fulfillment, the certainty of faith into the surety of achieved work, and the transcending newness of divine invitation and command into the immanent expectation of merely human tradition. Tudor evangelical reformers, as we have seen, judged the traditional practices of contemporary Catholic worship to be corrupted by this idolatrous rationale, from their handling of the Scriptures in liturgical reading and preaching to their ceremonial handling of the sacraments of the mass, baptism, and penance. In the reforming view, Catholic devotion focused reverence and confidence in practices, procedures, persons, and material things apart from God's saving and commanding word of Jesus Christ. The resulting accumulation of ritual actions and material symbols and images lacking evident apostolic authorization impaired faithful receptivity to God's self-communication and impeded faithful communication of his word of address. The immediate sensible fulfillment they provided subverted the "not yet" of eschatological expectation and the ascent of faith to spiritual communion with Christ.

The chief biblical *locus* of the English reformers' rigorous iconoclasm was the second prohibition of the Deuteronomic Decalogue, understood as a separate divine commandment. Its double prohibition of the production and the worship of "any graven image" or "likeness" of either God or his creatures was understood to assert a necessary relation within an environment of worship between producing images and worshipping them. The Elizabethan homily "Against Peril of Idolatry" identified this necessary relationship via Rom. 1:23 as the proclivity of sinful human beings to exchange "the glory of the immortal God for images of mortal creatures produced by their own art."[80] Infatuation with the imaginative power, sensible beauty, and "cunning" workmanship of their representations, as well as with spiritual control over what is represented, comprises the link between the production and the worship of images and, as such, casts doubt on the conventional opposition of "Christian images" to "pagan idols." The sermon's probable author, John Jewel, drawing extensively on Heinrich Bullinger's iconoclastic reading of classical and Christian history,[81] denies that any humanly produced visual image can truthfully communicate God's perfections as sovereign, active spirit. While

---

80. *GH*, 177.
81. *De Origine Erroris in Divorum et Simulacrorum Cultu* (1539).

regarding the carved or cast or molten image (Deut. 27:15),[82] as the epitome of the dumb, dead, and immobile idol, the author will not allow that painting, even with a narrative subject and intention, can truthfully communicate the person and actions of the Father, his Incarnate Word or the Holy Spirit. For, unlike the spoken and written word, representation of God by means of "a gross, bodily, and visible similitude" is a reductive falsification of his reality which entraps the affections, reasoning, and judgment of beholders in the sensible world, instead of lifting their hearts to God.[83] To the captivated beholder, the sensible representation possesses aspects of the represented and manifests a luminosity eliciting worship.[84]

In the somewhat different case of sculpted and ornamented images of the saints and painted depictions of their legendary virtues and supernatural feats, the unmediated sensible representation, often lavishly worldly, simultaneously augments and assimilates to itself, in the minds of beholders, the saints' blessed and active, post-purgatorial existence and powers, thereby giving the beholders special access to the various protective, assisting, and intercessory activities imputed to the saints' pre-resurrection afterlives.[85] Drawing attention to the parallel activities assigned to gods in the Roman pantheon, to whose idols supplications and worship were also addressed, the homily concludes that falsifying images elicit carnal responses from the spiritually immature, rather than appropriate admiration of, and desire for the saints' spiritual gifts.[86]

Lamentably, the Cranmerian theology of spiritual worship succumbed to an iconoclasm that, drawing on biased and erroneous historiography and lacking theological-exegetical balance and subtlety, propelled an indiscriminate demolition of the realm's Christian artistic and architectural heritage. Its theoretical failings and practical excesses have rendered Tudor iconoclasm as repellent to later generations of Anglicans and historians of all stripes, as it was to non-iconoclastic reforming contemporaries. To aesthetically sensitive and educated people, Tudor iconoclasts

---

82. *GH*, 171.

83. *GH*, 215.

84. The homily follows Bullinger in repudiating Gregory the Great's defense of Christian pictorial art in churches in his Epistle to Serenus: "For it is one thing," argues Gregory, "to worship the picture, and another thing by the picture of the story to learn what is to be worshipped. For that which Scripture is to them that read, the same doth picture perform unto idiots (or the unlearned) beholding." *In Registro sive epistol. Libro*, Parte 10, Epistola 4, cited in Bullinger, *De Origine Erroris*, cap. 24, fol. 117b. Reproduced in English translation, *GH*, 195. Following Bullinger, the homily dismisses Gregory's distinction as pagan, and discredited by Augustine, Lactantius, and Clement. *GH*, 230–1.

85. The speculative eschatological backdrop to images of the saints is emphasized in Article XXIII (XXII) against purgatory: "The Romish doctrine concerning purgatory, pardons, worshipping and adoration as well of images, as of relics, is a fond thing, vainly invented, and grounded upon no warranty of Scripture, but rather repugnant to the word of God." *TA*, 146.

86. *GH*, 230–5, 266.

appear ignorant of the capacity of the work of art, in whatever material medium, to communicate action, narrative, and a reality beyond the sensible totality which it comprises. They appear unappreciative of the internal dynamics of the artistic image (of planes, curves, lines, colors, bodily postures, and facial expressions), which give a transcending openness to its formal completeness and enable the work to convey spiritual truth about its human subject or to impart affective knowledge of God's relations to his creatures.

These considerable defects conceded, Tudor iconoclasts may, however, have grasped some aspects of the logic and progress of idolatry in the long proliferating production and devotional use of images within the pre-Reformation worshipping environment. More importantly, with the mainstream of continental reformers, they upheld the dialectical superiority of the spoken and written word in communicating the being and acting of God and sought to bring the production and reception of images by the faithful under the discipline of the biblical testimony and a theologically sound liturgical and homiletic pedagogy. Thus, in appreciating the benefits for us today of the English reformers' public theology and practice of corporate worship, we should not too readily dismiss from consideration its iconoclastic component.

Overall, this public theology and practice, in communicating the constitutive aspects of faithful individual and communal action, furnishes us with an ecclesial tradition of emancipation, capable of illuminating and transforming the complex dynamic of idolatrous bondage infecting liberal-technological society. To those laboring to understand and to resist the interlocking forms of tyrannous control over our practical lives together, this ecclesial tradition demonstrates the centrality of the church's worship to the Spirit's forming and sustaining individual and communal moral freedom throughout centuries of assault from diverse social and political faces of sin's tyranny. Most fundamentally, it shows the centrality of the church's common worship to the emancipation of our action from the idolatrous spiritual and practical project of proprietary self-possession, in which we strive for the sovereign disposal of ourselves that belongs to God alone. Common worship simultaneously illuminates the depth and scope of this project as the existential core of sin's captivity and communicates the ground, the subject, the structure, and the power of our emancipation. It communicates God's possession of us sinners in the earthly ministry, death, resurrection, and exaltation of Jesus Christ, and our promised possession of God in Christ, and of ourselves and one another in Him; it communicates the common rule by which we belong to Christ's temporal and eternal kingdom, and the power of his Spirit by which we grow into his likeness.

As the practice of receiving the Father's judgment and vindication of us in the cross and resurrection of his Son, common worship delivers us from our idolatrous strivings for self-justification, for securing our own worth and dignity apart from God and neighbor. As the practice of receiving ourselves and all beings as creatures of divine love and participants in an abiding and knowable order of being and goodness, common worship delivers us from our idolatrous strivings to create and sustain ourselves autonomously, and in pursuit of our unfettered purposes, to reduce our own and others' bodies and the nonhuman world to the mere stuff of technical manipulation and control. As the practice of receiving God's promise of restoring and perfecting his human and nonhuman creation by his everlasting presence, common worship delivers us from our idolatrous strivings to design and generate our future out of our corrupted imaginings and powers, our aspirations progressively to perfect individual and communal life by means of homogenizing and leveling processes and mechanisms.

Finally, the iconoclastic component of the Tudor theology and practice of common worship may goad theologians today to consider the contribution made by the unrestrained proliferation of visual images to the spiritual and practical malaise of liberal-technological society, at the core of which is the loss of faith in Christ and of faith's practical disciplines. The lens of Tudor iconoclasm may help us discern the oppressive and exploitative ways in which production and dissemination of visual images function across our social media: to magnify autonomous freedom of choice and the plasticity of the human makeup; to homogenize popular aspirations and desires along consumerist, materialist lines; to reinforce scientific reductions of humanity to a bundle of evolutionary instincts and techniques for self-preservation; to glorify the pugilistic rituals of society; to foster human strivings for perfection focused on the body and its powers; to infiltrate human relationships with simplistic, stereotypical projections, suppressing the complexity of moral reflection and deliberation; and to nourish inflated and misguided expectations of the common benefits and fulfillment achievable by political, economic, and social management.

While the current source and dissemination of such images may be extraneous to the church's contemporary practice, her practice has not proved entirely inured to their spiritual and social distortions. In our late modern age of social media saturation, Christian thinkers would do well to recollect that, to remain faithful, the church's traditions of practice—above all, those of worship—have always stood in need of a critique of visual images.

Chapter 9

AUTHORITY IN THE CHURCH

In conveying the aspects of faithful human action, the practices of Tudor common worship convey the spiritual fellowship of the faithful as a fellowship of equality. They set forth as a present hope a communion of persons whose equality resides in their liberty and their liberty in their common love of and conformity to God's will for them. As the worshippers' united act of consent to God's saving judgment in Jesus Christ, common worship expresses their equal standing as recipients of Christ's promises. Fellow participants, even now, in the external rule of God's revealed word and the internal rule of Christ's Spirit of freedom and love, the faithful are empowered and impelled to proclaim God's judgments to one another. In preaching, teaching, interceding, exhorting, consoling, and counseling, in exercising moral judgment on their neighbor's behalf and for themselves, the faithful stand alongside one another as equal beneficiaries of God's merciful and saving judgments. They stand neither above nor below their fellows, neither commanding them nor commanded by them.

It is imperative for us to add that the faithful also stand alongside those who have not yet heard or received God's saving judgment in Christ, whom they are commissioned, as servants of the Spirit's work, to gather into the community of lively faith. For the equal standing of those who have received Christ's promises rests on the equal standing of those who are called to receive Christ's promises: namely, every sinner. Tudor common worship scarcely conveys the missionary task given in the universal calling of sinful humanity, largely owing to the prevailing persuasion within Christendom that the work of mission was virtually complete, displaying the church's insufficient cognizance of the new horizons opened up by the early colonial ventures. Of enduring significance, however, is that the Christological and eschatological equality of the faithful, constantly expressed in Tudor worship, implicitly excludes abstract and naturalistic formulations of the equal moral worth of human beings.

Upon this Christological and eschatological equality, the Tudor liturgies superimpose an order of communal authority among the faithful and of corresponding vocational division between minister and congregation. The minister leads the congregation in praise and prayer, intercedes on behalf of the congregation, invites congregational confession, and declares to the penitent faithful "the absolution and remission of their sins," reads from and preaches on the Scriptures, gives exhortations and warnings to the congregation, and administers the sacraments of baptism and holy communion. Corresponding to their statement of the *notae* of the "visible church," the Edwardian and Elizabethan Articles XXIV (XXIII) define the communal office and authority of "the minister" as that of "public preaching" and "ministering the Sacraments in the congregation."[1] As the practices of the "visible church" communicate God's saving word in Jesus Christ spoken in the Scriptures, so the church's primary public ministry is a ministry of the Word: exegetical, theological, catechetical, and pastoral. Summarized by the prayer for the "church militant," that "all bishops, pastors and curates . . . may both by their life and doctrine set forth thy true and lively Word," this ministry is to be an instrument of the Holy Spirit in bringing sinful human beings to repentant faith in Christ, and in broadening and deepening their faithful understanding and obedience.

Hence, this ministry has need of endowments of an intellectual and a moral kind, both freely bestowed by the Spirit and acquired through vocational preparation and persevering application. Respecting their acquisition, the community has the dual responsibility of fostering them through pedagogy and validating them through testing. The authority belonging to the occupant of a ministerial office derives, consequently, from his communal appointment and validation as well as from his demonstration of the relevant endowments. Article XXIV (XXIII) recognizes this by asserting the legal necessity of the community's "calling" and "sending" to public ministry:

> It is not lawful for any man to take upon him the office of public preaching, or ministering the Sacraments in the congregation, before he be lawfully called and sent to execute the same. And those we ought to judge lawfully called and sent, which be chosen and called to this work by men who have public authority given unto them in the congregation, to call and send ministers into the Lord's vineyard.[2]

The article assumes that, in the English church, public authority to examine and select candidates for official ministry lies with the episcopal hierarchy and is coordinate with the legal authority of lay and clerical patrons to nominate candidates to livings and benefices. Thus, the article exhibits the interpenetration of "spiritual" and "political" authority pertaining to the church's public ministry of the Word.

Spiritual and Political Authority in the Articles

Beyond the sphere of "calling" and "sending" ministers, other articles disclose the full ecclesiastical breadth of the interpenetration of spiritual and political authority.

---

1. *TA*, 147. The immediate source of this article appears to be Article 10 of the Thirteen Articles (1538), recalling Article XIV of the Augsburg Confession. Martin Davie, *Our Inheritance of Faith: A Commentary on the Thirty-Nine Articles* (Malton: Gilead Books, 2013), 448.

2. *TA*, 147.

Directly addressing the matter of church authority, the Elizabethan Article XX asserts the church's "authority in controversies of faith," that is, her authority to give binding decisions on controversies over the articulation of the common faith, on the assumption that some controversies cannot be left entirely to the hazards of fraternal discussion and negotiation. Thus, the article invests the church with both the epistemological authority to judge the truth of conflicting articulations of the common faith and the political authority to require public assent to its judgments; and it grounds the twofold authority in the church's apostolic mission as "a witness and a keeper of holy writ." The ground of the church's authority is, simultaneously, its limitation, given that Article XXI (XX) prohibits the church from ordaining what is "contrary to God's word written" and from decreeing "anything against the same," nor "besides the same . . . [enforcing] anything to be believed for necessity of salvation."[3] These prohibitions imply that the unity of the scriptural testimony to God's word should be reflected in a unified witness of the organized community of faith, disciplined by Scripture.

The same ground of the church's authority to give binding doctrinal definition is reiterated in the stipulation of Article VII (VIII) that the Nicene, Athanasius, and (so-called) Apostles' Creed "ought thoroughly to be received: for they may be proved by most certain warrants of holy scripture."[4] Clearly, the authority of the three creeds rests primarily on their being demonstrably faithful theological distillations of God's word revealed in Scripture, and only secondarily on their prescription by the Tudor church government. At the same time, the article's intention is not to undermine the time-honored historical argument for the prescription of these creeds: that they embody an original theological consensus in the apostolic and patristic churches.[5] Articles I–IV have already prescribed adherence to this theological consensus in their statements of trinitarian and Christological orthodoxy (Articles I–IV). Nevertheless, the potency of this historical argument is dependent on the creeds' discernible conformity with the written prophetic and apostolic witness. Reinforcing this point is Article XXII (XXI)'s trenchant pronouncement on the fallibility of all church councils: "forasmuch as they be an assembly of men, whereof all be not governed with

3. *TA*, 146.
4. *TA*, 138.
5. The historical argument was weakened, but not demolished, by scholarship from the mid-seventeenth century onward. In the view of modern scholarship, the "Nicene Creed" is an expanded version of the creed issued by the Council of Nicaea (325), carrying the authority of the Council of Constantinople (381) accepted by all Latin and most Greek churches. The Western (Latin) text of the "Apostles' Creed" was a fifth-century, probably Gaulish, elaboration of a fourth-century, widely used, Roman baptismal creed. The Latin text of the "Athanasian Creed" was a late fifth- or early sixth-century Gaulish composition using Western trinitarian terminology and contributing little to the argument from primitive ecumenical consensus. For a basic survey, J. N. D. Kelly, *Early Christian Creeds*, 3rd edn. (London: Longman, 1972).

the spirit and word of God, they may err, and sometimes have erred, not only in worldly matters, but also in things pertaining unto God."[6]

The opening sentence of the Elizabethan Article XX asserts not only the church's "authority in controversies" but, as well, her "power to decree Rites or Ceremonies." Although the two powers are inevitably connected, the deferred elaboration of the latter power to Article XXXIV on "Traditions of the Church" indicates a somewhat different logic from the former. For, as Article XXXIV (XXXIII) makes clear, decreeing "rites or ceremonies" involves establishing, perpetuating, and revising communal traditions that are less directly and exclusively controlled by God's word spoken in the Scriptures, in that they engage a spectrum of theological, moral, and cultural judgments which cannot be shown to be required or precluded by the scriptural testimony. These traditions, predominantly of worship, are subject to a looser Scriptural discipline accommodating greater diversity of understanding and practice. Thus, the Article begins: "it is not necessary that traditions and ceremonies be in all places one, or utterly like. For at all times they have been diverse, and may be changed, according to the diversity of countries, and men's manners, so that nothing be ordained against God's word."[7]

The Elizabethan Article further specifies: "Every particular or national Church hath authority to ordain, change, and abolish ceremonies or rites of the Church ordained only by man's authority, so that all things be done to edifying."[8] This further specification has two noteworthy elements (to which this chapter will return). One is its use of the term "edifying" to summarize that looser consonance of church practices with the purpose of building up the church's faith, ruled by the Scriptures. The prominence of the principle of edifying (building up) in Paul's letters[9] ensured a major role in continental and English reforming discussions about practices. The other element is its designation of those practices falling within the authority of "particular or national" churches to determine, as "ordained only" by human authority, so emphasizing the independent functioning of communal judgment under the guidance of Scripture and the Holy Spirit. The positivist political tenor of designating practices authorized by the national church as "ordained only" by human authority is reflected in the Article's pronouncement:

> Whosoever through his private judgement, willingly and purposely doth openly break the traditions and ceremonies of the Church, which be not repugnant to the word of God, and be ordained and approved by common authority, ought to be rebuked openly . . . as he that offendeth against the Common order of

---

6. *TA*, 146. The article continues: "Wherefore things ordained by them, as necessary to Salvation, have neither strength, nor authority, unless it may be declared, that they be taken out of holy scripture."

7. *TA*, 152. The forerunner of this article is Article 5 of the *Thirteen Articles*.

8. *TA*, 153.

9. For example, 1 Cor. 14, Eph. 4.

the Church, and hurteth the authority of the Magistrate, and woundeth the consciences of the weak brethren.

Departures from common practice are, foremost, offenses against the national church's legally established order and the authority of "the Magistrate"; and as such, they chiefly wound the consciences of "weak brethren."

As Article XXXVI (XXXVII) makes clear, the offended magistrate is the sovereign civil magistrate, "unto whom the chief government of all estates of this realm, whether they be Ecclesiastical or Civil, in all causes doth appertain." (XXXVII).[10] In abandoning the Edwardian Article's designation of the monarch as "Supreme head in earth, next under Christ, of the Church of England and Ireland," the Elizabethan Article more strictly circumscribes royal governance as political and elaborates its lay character:

> we give not to our princes the ministering either of God's word, or of the Sacraments.... But that only prerogative which we see to have been given always to all godly Princes in holy Scriptures by God himself, ... that they should rule all estates and degrees committed to their charge by God ... and restrain with the civil sword the stubborn and evil-doers.[11]

Typical of Tudor public theology (as Chapter 10 will expound), Article XXXVII stands in both the Eusebian Hellenistic imperial kingship tradition and the Carolingian Germanic tradition of regarding the unitary rule of Israelite kings over their kingdoms as the divinely revealed template for Christian monarchical rule. Also characteristic is its Pauline highlighting of the retributive and coercive character of civil rule. The magisterial establishment in public law of secular and ecclesiastical practices and duties is seen as a defense of their communal authority against neglect, repudiation, or violation by dissenters.

Taken together, all the foregoing articles provide a cursory and formulaic summary of the Tudor theology of authority in church and commonwealth that both distinguishes the evangelical/sacramental authority of the minister from the jurisdictional authority of the magistrate and indicates the theoretical and practical scope of their interpenetration. This summary encapsulates the Tudor vision of the common life of sinful and redeemed humanity ordered by two universal authorities and practices: the authority of evangelical proclamation *directly constituted by* God's saving word of judgment given in Jesus Christ, and the authority of giving binding communal judgment *constituted under* God's condemning and reconciling word of judgment. In the Tudor vision, these two authorities and practices determine human moral agency and action in its dual reality, as restored through Christ's conquest of sin and death on the Cross and

---

10. *TA*, 154–5.
11. *TA*, 155.

awaiting fulfillment, and as struggling under the wages of sin and subject to the law's condemnation.

For the most part, Tudor public theology, reflecting the mainstream of English reforming thought,[12] upheld an institutional, as well as theoretical, separation of these authorities and practices: the church's ministries and practices of proclamation do not include public judgment; neither do the ruler's practices of public judgment include the church's proclamation. Whereas the church as Christ's body is ruled directly by her divine Head through the Holy Spirit, who binds together believers in a spiritual community of repentance, faith in Christ's promises, and obedience to his commandments; the church as a political society is ruled by the magistrate's coercive judgments about right and wrong, coercive because carrying temporal rewards and punishments. It is not that the church as Christ's body is a community without judgment but rather that believers are denied, individually and collectively, any judge but God in Christ who is both judge and judged. Thus, the church's essential response to Christ's judgment is her evangelical mission of proclaiming the gospel in acts of worship and self-sacrificing love. For the duration of this age, however, in which the Old Adam is being overtaken by the New, the different, even antithetical, authorities and practices of proclamation and jurisdiction remain dialectically interdependent. In that the church's proclamation is supported by a legal framework established and enforced by human government, the church is institutionally part of the body politic, yet not of its juridical essence. Conversely, in that the work of human government, defining the body politic, is itself defined and empowered by the church's proclamation, human judgment is a service within the church, but not of its evangelical essence.

The distinguishing of public judgment from the church's evangelical authority and practice, inspired not only by contemporary strands of *zwei Regimente* theology (Lutheran and Reformed) but by the late-medieval conception of a "spiritual church" radically articulated by Marsilius and Wyclif, is for much of the Tudor period a key distinguishing feature of the Anglican "establishment" perspective on external church discipline, over against Roman, (English) Presbyterian, Separatist, and Anabaptist perspectives. On the prevailing Anglican view, expressed in the Articles, so far as the external church needs public judgment, it is to be rendered by or under the supreme lay governor. When, therefore, English bishops issue binding public judgments in whatever ecclesiastical sphere—doctrinal, liturgical, administrative, or (more narrowly) disciplinary—they directly act as the monarch's ministers, whereas when they preach and celebrate the sacraments, they directly act as Christ's ministers.

The fullest public account of ministerial authority is given by the Tudor liturgies of "ordering" priests and deacons and consecrating bishops, since treatment of the

---

12. In this reforming mainstream, I would include such Henrician and Elizabethan theologians and lawyers as William Tyndale, Christopher St. German, Thomas Cranmer, Thomas Cromwell, Richard Sampson, Edward Fox, Thomas Starkey, William Marshall, John Rogers, Hugh Latimer, Nicholas Ridley, John Ponet, John Jewel, and John Whitgift.

church's official ministries is conspicuously absent from the two sets of homilies, possibly owing to the reticence of their authors to pronounce on sensitive issues of clerical and episcopal office, ministry, and authority. These issues concerning the inheritance of the apostolic commission by succeeding occupants of ministerial offices—in what offices and by what mode of transmission—rest on two fundamental issues: namely, whether Christ conferred permanent jurisdictional authority on the apostolic ministry and whether the exercise of jurisdiction contributes intrinsically to the apostolic proclamation of the saving gospel. Positions on these issues have a crucial bearing on understanding the relationship of civil and ecclesiastical jurisdiction to the church's apostolic mission. Given that the official documentary sources for the position(s) taken by Tudor public theology on these ministerial issues address them in a general, sometimes imprecise and oblique manner without developed theological argument, we must pursue a more comprehensive and precise grasp of these positions through comparison with the alternative positions of Catholic adversaries and Reformed ("Puritan") critics.

Tudor Ministerial Orders against Catholic Traditions

The evangelical soteriology of Edwardian and Elizabethan public theology contained an implicit rejection of the canonist and papalist traditions of unifying sacramental and juridical powers in the episcopal hierarchy by means of the church's "power of the keys" to "bind and loose," that is, to retain and remit sins.[13] In its mature scholastic formulation, the episcopal exercise of the "power of the keys" encompassed jurisdiction in two spheres or fora: in the "interior forum" of conscience and in the "exterior forum" of church polity.[14] While the former jurisdiction was exercised over voluntary penitents in the sacramental discipline of penance, the latter was exercised over penitent and impenitent violators of church order and law, frequently through ecclesiastical courts.[15]

Two medieval developments somewhat obscured, without ever eclipsing, the unified episcopal power of judgment in both fora inherited from the patristic church's discipline of public penance.[16] One was the advent of private penance

---

13. Mt. 16.19, 18.18; Jn 20:23; Watkins, *A History of Penance*, 1:3–26.

14. This terminological pair is well established by the end of the thirteenth century, demonstrated by its systematic use in, for example, John of Paris, *De potestate regia et papali* (1301), 12–13.

15. For the developing historical interrelationship between of the internal and external fora of jurisdiction in the Roman canon law, James A. Brundage, *Medieval Canon Law* (London and New York: Longman, 1995).

16. In the patristic discipline, the bishop was involved in excommunicating offenders for grave sins, liturgically "enrolling" penitents, hearing confessions, assigning and supervising penitential satisfaction, and on the completion of satisfaction, reconciling penitents with the church in a public liturgy of ecclesiastical forgiveness. In this liturgy,

administered by parish priests, which removed publicity from the sacrament; the other was the theological inflation of papal jurisdiction, which exaggerated the division between the sacramental powers bestowed by Christ on all the apostles equally and the unbounded jurisdictional power bestowed on Peter uniquely, in which the other apostles had only a derivative, determinate share.[17] Nevertheless, countervailing trends toward the unifying of interior and exterior jurisdictional powers proved victorious. Possibly, the most historically consequential of these was the extension of Petrine *jurisdiction* to cover direct remission of purgatorial punishment for sins committed (and consequently, remission of penances imposed), through distribution among the faithful, living, and dead, of "the church's treasury *(thesaurus)*" of supererogatory merit. This novel scholastic theology of "indulgences" emerging in the thirteenth century[18] invested the pope, as Christ's earthly vicar, with universal jurisdictional power of disposal over the church's spiritual property, so as to utilize "the commutation value" of spiritual merits belonging to the heavenly company of Christ crucified and the holy martyrs.[19] Thus, voluntary subjection to papal jurisdiction increasingly offered believers various secure routes to membership in the eternal communion of saints, as well as defining their post-baptismal membership in the visible church.

Reinforced by the theology of indulgences and the expanding commerce in them, the church's interpretation of the sacrament of penance as an exercise of clerical jurisdiction held sway up to the Reformation and the Council of Trent. The council's fourteenth session, countering reforming "heresies," decreed that the priest's absolution of the confessed penitent is "not a bare ministry only, whether of announcing the Gospel or of declaring that sins are forgiven, but is after the manner of a judicial act, whereby sentence [of remission] is pronounced by the

---

God's sanctifying grace and pardon were not conferred on the penitent by an episcopal pronouncement of absolution, but sought for the penitent by intercessory prayers and the invocation of the Holy Spirit in the laying on of hands by bishop and clergy. The patristic bishop was theologically conceived to be the embodiment and instrument of the church's sacramental and jurisdictional unity, knitting together the faithful spiritually by offering the eucharistic sacrifice, and knitting together the spiritual and the corporate community by conducting the church's discipline of penance. Although all presbyters (priests) came to be foci of the church's sacramental unity, having received the power of eucharistic celebration (the "power of order") directly from Christ at their ordination, they were not, similarly, foci of the church's juridical unity; for they received the power of spiritual jurisdiction from the bishop, whereas he received the power directly from Christ through the sacrament of episcopal consecration. Poschmann, *Penance*, 44–109.

17. Augustinus Triumphus, *Summa de potestate ecclesiastica* (1326), 68. 3 ad 2; Alvarus Pelagius, *De Statu et planctu Ecclesiae* (1340), chs. 54, 68.

18. For the evolution of the theology of indulgences from the eleventh to the sixteenth centuries, Poschmann, *Penance*, 219–32.

19. The bishop's power to grant indulgences was derivative, dependent on papal authorization.

priest as a judge."²⁰ Consequently, "the absolution which a priest pronounces upon one over whom he has not either an ordinary or a delegated jurisdiction ought to be of no weight whatever."²¹

Also indicative of the trajectory of late-medieval Roman ecclesiology toward close integration of the jurisdictional and the sacramental was the transferred application of the term *corpus mysticum* from the consecrated eucharistic host²² (replaced by the term, *corpus verum*) to the church's governing hierarchy. Besides reflecting current eucharistic concerns, this terminological shift reflected the ongoing cross-fertilization of canonist and civilian legal thought and of Roman ecclesiology and secular political theology considered in Chapter 4.²³ Out of this cross-fertilization emerged a common employment of *corpus mysticum* to denote simply *res publica*: that is, the complex organization of jurisdictional rights constituting the political corporation and personified in the supreme ruler— whether Roman emperor, pope, or national monarch.²⁴ In high papalist theory, the ruler's personification of the ecclesiastical *corpus mysticum* entailed a merging of epistemological and political authority. Drawing on the revival in contemporary jurisprudence of Hellenistic portrayals of the imperial ruler as the "living law" (νόμος ἔμψυχος, *lex animata*), the earthly fountain of law who has all laws, natural and civil, within his breast (*scrinio pectoris*),²⁵ papalists interpreted these formulaic epithets of Roman law²⁶ in an absolutist manner, to extol papal imperial judgments as the self-sufficient and infallible mediation of God's will. As *lex animata*, the church's earthly shepherd pronounced Christ's judgments, made Christ's law incarnate, and on this basis was *dominus absolutus* over lesser rulers and property,

---

20. "Quamvis autem absolutio sacerdotis alieni beneficii sit dispensatio, tamen non est solum nudum ministerium vel annuntiandi evangelium, vel declarandi remissa esse peccata; sed ad instar actus judicialis, quo ab ipso, velut a judice, sententia pronuntiatur." Fourteenth Session (November 25, 1551), De Sanctissimis Poenitentiae et Extremae Unctionis Sacramentis, VI, The Canons and Dogmatic Decrees of the Council of Trent, trans. J. Waterworth, in *Creeds of Christendom*, 3 vols, ed. Philip Schaff (repr. Grand Rapids: Baker Book House, 1977), 2:152.

21. "nullius momenti absolutionem eam esse debere, quam sacerdos in eum profert, in quem ordinarium aut subdelegatam non habet jurisdictionem." De Sanctissimis Poenitentiae et Extremae Unctionis Sacramentis, VII, *Creeds of Christendom*, 2:153.

22. cf. 1 Cor. 10:17.

23. pp. 186–9.

24. For discussion of this cross-fertilization, Kantorowicz, *The King's Two Bodies*, 193–272; Michael Wilks, *The Problem of Sovereignty in the Later Middle Ages: The Papal Monarchy with Augustus Triumphus and the Publicists* (Cambridge: Cambridge University Press, 1963), 151–83.

25. Literally translated, "within the writing case of his breast."

26. *Novellae* 105.2.4 and *Glossa Ordinaria* on *Dig.* 10.3, v *usum imperatorem*, or on *Cod.* 25.2, v *In iuris*.

endowed with *plenitudo potestatis*, that is, with unbounded and unimpeachable public power to command, administer, judge, legislate, and act.²⁷

Challenges to papalist theory and practice elicited more modest formulations of papal plenitude. In the sphere of secular jurisdiction, plenitude entailed merely a "casual jurisdiction" of the pope over secular rulers, licensing papal interference with their government only when peril to the church's welfare rendered it necessary. Originally deployed by late-medieval publicists of imperial and royal causes before being adopted by both conciliarists and their moderate papalist opponents, the general logic of "casual jurisdiction" comprehended arguments more or less restrictive of the grounds and scope of papal interference in other jurisdictions.²⁸ In the sphere of ecclesiastical jurisdiction, by contrast, conciliarist and moderate papalist theologians were in much less accord over the doctrine of plenitude.

Conciliarists located the plenitude of governing authority, along with inerrancy in judgments of faith, in the whole earthly body of Christ assembled in council, and assigned to all governing offices, including the papal office, determinate, and bounded jurisdiction.²⁹ Their argument combined Christological ecclesiological concepts and naturalist political concepts: concepts of the church's Christological unity and power, and the equality and collegiality of bishops in apostolic authority, and concepts of the inalienable natural rights of political corporations to elect,

---

27. This wedding of absolute epistemological authority and absolute governmental power in the papal office is given fullest development throughout the *Summa de potestate ecclesiastica* of Augustinus Triumphus and the *De ecclesiasticus potestate* of Giles of Rome (Aegidius Romanus) c. 1301.

28. Sixteenth-century Thomist critics of conciliarism, such as Francisco de Vitoria, Tommaso de Vio (Cajetan), Francisco Suárez, and Robert Bellarmine, admitted broader grounds and parameters for the pope's "indirect" temporal authority than did the Sorbonnist conciliarists: Pierre D'Ailly, Jean Gerson, Jacques Almain, and John Mair. The Thomists interpreted the pope's plenitude as superior jurisdiction over secular rulers, to reform by direct and coercive intervention secular laws and policies judged gravely damaging to spiritual goods, when the church's purely spiritual appeals had failed to correct. (Vitoria, *De potestate ecclesiae*, Relectio I.5.6-9; Suárez, *Defensio fidei Catholicae et apostolicae*. . . 3.5.21-3; Bellarmine, *De summo pontifice* 5.6.) By contrast, the Sorbonnist conciliarists, following Ockham, denied any *iuro divino* grounds for direct papal intervention with secular jurisdiction, insisting that all papal acts of censure and correction of secular rulers must not exceed the cognizance and the penalties of spiritual jurisdiction (i.e., admonishment, suspension, and excommunication). However, such acts might be intended to incite and might actually incite, independent civil censure of rulers, for example, papal excommunication of a secular rule leading to his/her deposition by lesser civil magistrates.

29. For conciliarists, the New Testament *locus* for the church's plenitude of authority to "bind and loose" is Mt. 18:17-18. This passage supplies the hermeneutic for Christ's promise of the keys to Peter in Mt. 16:19: namely, that here Peter personifies the whole church in its spiritual and juridical unity. The implication drawn is that the Roman church and its bishop do not have primacy over the universal church assembled in council.

correct, and punish rulers, to be represented in assembly, and to formulate and consent to laws.[30] By contrast, the moderate papalists, rejecting conciliarist analogies between natural civil corporations and the supernatural corporation of Christ's body, defended Christ's immediate bestowal on Peter of plenary jurisdiction, making him the church's single earthly head and carrier of her inerrancy in definitive judgments of faith.[31] Though the apostles, some papalists conceded, held their equal jurisdiction immediately from Christ, they also held their jurisdiction *under* Peter,[32] or even *from* Peter, as a sharing in, or devolution of his plenary jurisdiction.[33] Likewise, the bishops hold their jurisdiction *under* the pope, or even *from* the pope.

From the soteriological and ecclesiological perspective of the evangelical architects of Tudor church establishment, the divisions between conciliarist and papalist theologians were less significant than their convergence in conceiving the church's ministry as a wedding of sacramental and jurisdictional powers in a plurality of offices. Tudor divines rejected the soteriological centrality of priestly jurisdiction in both the internal and the external *fora*, regarding it as a legal positivizing of the apostolic "power of the keys." As we have seen in Chapter 6, English evangelical soteriology opposed Roman traditions of explicating the penitential *processus iustificationis* of baptized sinners on the ground of their deflecting faith from attending entirely and exclusively to the Father's saving action in his Son. In rejecting the various causal networks constructed by scholastic theologians to relate penitents' work of contrition, confession, and satisfaction to ecclesiastical absolution and the divine remission of both the guilt and the punishment (eternal and temporal) merited by sins, English reforming divines rejected the confessor's juridical actions of assessing the gravity of penitents' sins and imposing appropriate satisfaction, of judging the quality of their sorrow from their confession, in order to give or withhold the sacramental pronouncement of absolution. The evangelical doctrine of *sola gratia/sola fide* left no room for the causal role either of the penitent's merit or the confessor's judgment in God's

---

30. Primary sources for conciliarist thought include: Jean Gerson, *De ecclesiastica potestate* in *Oeuvres completes*, ed. Palémon Glorieux, 6:210-50 (Paris: Desclée, 1965); Nicholai de Cusa, *De concordantia catholica*, Opera Omnia 14, ed. Gerhard Kallen (Hamburg, 1959–68); Jacques Almain, *Libellus de auctoritate ecclesiae* (Paris, 1512), ed. and trans. J. H. Burns and Thomas M. Izbicki in *Conciliarism and Papalism* (Cambridge: Cambridge University Press, 1997), 134–200; Giovanni Domenico Mansi, ed., *Sacrorum conciliorum nova et amplissima collectio*, 31 vols (Venice, Florence, 1759–98), vol. 27.

31. The papalists read Jn 21:17 as Christ committing the care of the whole church to Peter and regarded this passage as confirming Christ's bestowal of plenary ecclesiastical jurisdiction on this one disciple in Mt. 16:18-19.

32. Vitoria's position (*De potestate ecclesiae*, Relectio II, 4.1–5.4) against Torquemada's denial that the apostles held jurisdiction immediately from Christ (*Summa de ecclesia* 2.54).

33. Cajetan's position, *Auctoritas papae et concilii sive ecclesiae comparata* 3.

work of justifying sinners, thereby undermining the whole hierarchical edifice of priestly penitential jurisdiction.

At the same time, English reforming theologians perceived the connection of juridical penance with the ecclesiological aberrations of absolutizing the visible church's epistemological authority in the papal or conciliar *magisterium*, absolutizing clerical sacramental efficacy in the sacrificial mass, and absolutizing obedience to the pope as essential to membership in Christ's spiritual body. Collectively, these developments within the Roman tradition comprised for the English evangelical reformers a cumulative project to usurp, control, or possess God's rule of salvation in Jesus Christ. Set free from its Henrician restraints, Edwardian and Elizabethan public theology recast the church's apostolic ministry in a nondominative, nonpossessive, proclamatory "key."

Evangelical Ministries in the Liturgies of Ordering

The Cranmerian liturgies for conferring Holy Orders, which underwent no significant verbal revision in successive Tudor prayer books, recognize differences in dignity, responsibility, and spiritual equipment among the historic orders of deacon, priest, and bishop within a common evangelical (proclamatory) conception of the three ministries.[34] The historic orders are neither so sharply distinguished as in the Roman and Orthodox traditions nor reduced to a single order as in most continental reforming churches. Although the diaconate is presented as preparatory and auxiliary to the priesthood,[35] all three ministries are shown to be "apostolic" in two leading respects: the intention of each is to imitate the apostolic communication of God's saving truth within the context of its particular tasks; this intention is pursued under, or in subjection to, the apostolic testimony.[36] The apostolic mimesis of each distinctive form of ministry is the primary meaning of its "apostolicity": of secondary importance is the *precise* historical grounding of each ministry's distinctive authority, tasks, and equipment in the ordination and "sending" by Christ and/or the apostles.

This is not to deny that the New Testament evidence for Christ's sending of the apostles and disciples, and the apostles' sending of deacons, presbyters, and overseers of presbyters, remains decisive for understanding of the tasks and forms of authority necessary to the church's ministry. What remains of secondary importance is whether the several orders originated in Christ's explicit command

---

34. The Cranmerian liturgical form recognizes only these three orders, suppressing the additional orders (e.g., of subdeacon, acolyte, exorcist, reader, and doorkeeper) implicitly envisaged by the wording of the enabling Act of Parliament. See *HAL*, 92–3.

35. The closing collect and final rubrics of the service convey the hope and expectation that the candidate's faithful and competent service in "this inferior office" will lead to his being "called unto the higher ministries in thy Church." *FSBP*, 448.

36. For this Tudor conception of the apostolicity of the church's ministries, *TA*, 114–16.

and induction, or in inspired apostolic (or even immediately post-apostolic) command and induction, and which specific tasks are allocated to which order. Thus, Cranmer's preface to the 1550 Ordinal, reproduced in every edition, offers only a general grounding of the offices of deacon, priest, and bishop in the apostolic church and subsequent tradition: "It is evident unto all men, diligently reading holy Scripture, and ancient authors, that from the Apostles' time there hath been these orders of Ministers in Christ's Church: Bishops, Priests, and Deacons."[37]

Confident of the consonance of the three ministries with the New Testament evidence, Cranmer's liturgies of ordering and consecrating seek to articulate their common and distinctive features in overlapping sequences of liturgical acts. The particularities of each ministry are focused within shared theological and practical parameters. Common to all three services are: integration into the church's regular celebration of Communion "upon a Sunday or Holy day,"[38] incorporation of the Litany, ministering of the Oath of the King's Supremacy, presentation and questioning of the candidate(s), readings from the Epistles and Gospels, exhortation concerning the duties of the ministry, prayers for the candidate's (s') undertaking, laying on of hands and commissioning, and delivery of the "instruments" of office.

Integration of the services of ordering into the church's calendar of congregational worship emphasizes the public and congregational character of the ordained ministries:[39] their being chiefly within and for the whole congregation of the faithful, assembled and acting in public, whether locally or supra-locally. This publicity parallels the Tudor church's replacing a ministry of private confessions, private baptisms, and private masses with a ministry of common public practice. Fittingly, the whole congregation participates in the liturgical inauguration of public ministry, joining in prayer for the candidate and, spiritually, in the laying on of hands, witnessing and hearing the candidate's presentation, examination, and commissioning, instructed by the apostolic wisdom and exhortations in the readings. The petitions of the Litany reinforce the collective scope of the ministry at multiple levels, for they encompass the spiritual and material welfare of the whole of society and all its members, the ruling monarch, and the occupants of both ecclesiastical and civil offices. In addition, the candidate's oath to recognize and defend against papal usurpation the unitary and supreme "authority, power, and jurisdiction" of the monarch over his realm and dominions, and the church within them, establishes (with lamentable polemics) the territorial, jurisdictional basis, and boundaries of the candidate's authorized ministry. By invoking the whole kingdom in the authorization of parochial and diocesan ministries, the oath

---

37. *FSBP*, 292.
38. Ibid.
39. The design of the three liturgies of ordering and consecration allows for the possibility of two or even three orders being conferred at the same service of Communion: the deacons being "ordered" after the Epistle, the priests after the Gospel, and the bishop consecrated after the Creed. *HAL*, 93.

unites the ascending levels of ministerial care, organization, and administration, and places every ministry in the service of this complex totality.

All three liturgies give precedence to the appointed Epistle and Gospel readings over the other liturgical elements, acknowledging the comprehensive authorizing role for Christian ministry of God's commanding and enabling Word spoken through the Scriptures. Where alternative New Testament readings are offered, the more evangelical, missionary passage is set as the first, and presumably preferred, option; subsequent liturgical elements build up the proclamatory account of each ministry. Accordingly, the liturgy for ordering deacons offers the alternative Epistle readings of 1 Tim. 3:8-16 and Acts 6:2-7. Although both passages lay out the spiritual and moral requirements of the diaconal ministry, the first orients the ministry within "the congregation of the living God" to the "liberty of faith" in Jesus Christ, while the second highlights the ministry's practical character, in contrast to the apostolic "administration of the word."[40] Furthermore, while the auxiliary ministry of the diaconate involves the various duties of assisting at the celebration of Communion and conducting baptisms, reading aloud the Scriptures and Homilies in divine service, instructing youth in the Catechism, and organizing the distribution of alms, the duty of communicating God's truth revealed in the Scriptures is uppermost in the examination of the candidates, in the special prayer for their ministry and in their commissioning and presentation with the instrument of their office. The liturgy's interpretation of the deacon's traditional role of liturgical Gospel reading as a modest theological ministry is clear both from the requirement that every candidate proves himself "sufficiently instructed in Holy Scripture"[41] and from the bishop's delivery of the New Testament to each newly authorized deacon, with the words: "Take thou authority to read the Gospel in the Church of God, and to preach the same, if thou be thereunto ordinarily commanded."[42]

The priesthood, for which the diaconate is a preparation and testing ground, is the primary evangelical, pedagogical, and pastoral ministry, consisting of preaching and teaching God's word, celebrating the dominical sacraments, gathering in, nurturing, succoring, and disciplining Christ's flock so as to bring it to oneness and maturity of faith. Of the alternative Epistle readings for the ordering of priests, Acts 20:17-35, 1 Tim. 3, the first is a template for the lifelong vocation of apostolic proclamation, being Paul's farewell peroration to the elders of the church at Ephesus. Of the three alternative Gospel readings, Mt. 28:18-20, Jn 10:1-16, Jn 20:19-23, the first is the risen Christ's commissioning of his disciples to teach and baptize "all nations," the second, the rule of the Good Shepherd in his sheepfold, and the third, the risen Christ's imparting to his disciples, with their commission, the Holy Ghost and the power of retaining and remitting sins. The lengthy episcopal exhortation to the candidates recapitulates the themes of all three Gospel readings (excepting

---

40. 1 Tim. 3:15-16 and Acts 6:2, Great Bible.
41. Preface to the Ordinal (1552), *FSBP*, 438.
42. *FSBP*, 444–7.

the power to retain and remit sins) within the controlling framework of the first. The candidates are called to be "the messengers, the watchmen, the Pastors, and the stewards of the Lord, to teach, to premonish, to feed, and provide for the Lord's family."[43] They are exhorted to constant and earnest prayer for the "heavenly assistance" of the Holy Spirit and to daily application of themselves to the Holy Scriptures, studiously "reading and weighing" them, and "framing [their] manners" to them, so that they may accomplish the difficult and perilous labor of bringing all Christ's sheep committed to their charge to "agreement in faith and knowledge of God," to "ripeness and perfectness of age in Christ."[44] The same evangelical, pedagogical, and pastoral orientation dominates the examination of the candidates and visually climaxes with the delivery to each of the Bible (without the traditional chalice and paten), accompanied by the words: "Take thou authority to preach the word of God, and to minister the Holy Sacraments in this congregation where thou shalt be so appointed."[45]

Notably, the laying on of hands by the officiating bishop and attending priests retains the traditional accompaniment of Christ's words from Jn 20:22-23: "Receive the Holy Ghost: whose sins thou doest forgive, they are forgiven; and whose sins thou doest retain, they are retained," completing them with: "and be a faithful dispenser of the word of God and of his holy Sacraments."[46] That the final imperative supplies the hermeneutic for the clerical authority of "loosing" and "binding" is indicated by the delivery of the Bible immediately following and a concluding collect situating the penitential declaration of absolution within the whole apostolic ministry of witness to salvation in Christ.

Of the readings for the liturgy of episcopal consecration, the Epistle, 1 Tim. 3:1-7, highlights the overlapping character and tasks required of the "presbyter" (πρεσβύτερος) and the "bishop" (ἐπίσκοπος) in apostolic churches, while the Gospel, Jn 21:15-18—a *locus classicus* of Petrine rule—highlights the distinctive governing authority of bishops. The liturgy gives other mixed signals on the relationship of the two offices: the liturgical "sending" of bishops is not a further "ordination," but rather a "consecration"; nevertheless, the liturgy of consecration (echoing those of ordination) designates bishops as a separate "order of ministers" in Christ's church. There is no explicit appeal to the traditional Scriptural bases for discriminating the ministerial orders: namely, Christ's sending of the Twelve and the Seventy with different commissions[47] and the apostle Paul's investing of Timothy and Titus with authority to appoint and discipline presbyters.[48] However, the close alignment of the episcopal and apostolic ministries is affirmed in the invitation to congregational prayer, which recalls Christ's night of prayer before choosing and

---

43. *FSBP*, 454.
44. *FSBP*, 453-4.
45. *FSBP*, 457.
46. Ibid.
47. Lk. 9:1-3, 10:1-12.
48. Tit. 1:5.

sending forth his apostles, and the fasting and prayer of the disciples at Antioch before sending forth Paul and Barnabas.[49]

A single, notable difference distinguishes the examinations of candidates for the priesthood and episcopate. This relates to the bishop's obligation to "correct and punish" such persons within his diocese "as be unquiet, disobedient, and criminous," according to the authority that he has "by God's word" and that "shall be committed" to him "by the ordinance of this realm."[50] For Scripture witnesses that jurisdiction (public judgment) over human community is secular: it belongs to the *saeculum*, to the external battle of fallen humanity against the worldly forces of lawless disorder and, as such, is exercised by the secular ruler elected and established by God for that purpose. Thus, the faithful secular ruler rightly devolves the exercise of public judgment over the church to ministers with the (nonjurisdictional) apostolic authority of spiritual oversight and care.[51]

A key element of the bishop's distinctive apostolic authority is conveyed by the traditional words of commissioning with the imposition of hands, drawing on 2 Tim. 1:6-7: "Take the Holy Ghost, and remember that thou stir up the grace of God, which is in thee, by the imposition of hands."[52] The import of the formula is sacramental, intending communication of the presence and power of the Holy Spirit by the laying on of hands, a communication vouchsafed to the apostles by Christ. As with the "true" dominical sacraments of Baptism and the Lord's Supper, the inward spiritual impartation in conjunction with the outward act is God's response to the supplications of his people. Those performing the sacramental action (whether the archbishop and attending bishops laying hands on the episcopal candidate, or the bishop and attending priests laying hands on the clerical or diaconal candidates) are empowered by the Spirit to act representatively, as did the apostles, for the whole community of the faithful in their charge. Their communal sacramental authority is, therefore, directly apostolic and Christological and not mediated by the secular sovereign.

Overall, the liturgy of consecration conveys episcopal authority and ministry as centrally and preeminently "spiritual" (i.e., evangelical, sacramental, and pastoral) rather than "secular" (political, juridical). A symbolic indication of the decentralizing of episcopal jurisdiction is the omission in 1552 of delivery to the newly consecrated bishop of the pastoral staff, the traditional symbol of the bishop's juridical rule, the delivery of ring and miter having been dropped in 1549. These omissions leave the Bible alone as the visible instrument of the episcopal office, delivered with the imperative: "Give heed unto reading,

---

49. *FSPB*, 460.

50. *FSBP*, 461–2.

51. According to Cranmer in 1540, the apostolic churches, in the absence of a divinely ordained Christian ruler, were constrained to settle matters of external order and discipline by consent among themselves, and, at times, by appealing to the apostles' superior, divinely bestowed, pastoral and disciplinary oversight. *MWL*, 116–17.

52. *FSPB*, 462.

exhortation, and doctrine. Think upon these things contained in this book . . . and be diligent in doing them: for by doing this thou shalt save thyself and them that hear thee."[53] Finally, the concluding supplications present all the episcopal acts of shepherding Christ's church, maintaining and promoting her apostolic obedience to God's word in faith and practice, as forms and extensions of the ministry of proclamation.[54]

Together, the church's liturgies of ordination and consecration show her corporate apostolic ministries to be essentially those of communicating the spiritual reign over the faithful of God's word of salvation in Jesus Christ. Her ministries intrinsically involve practices of communicating faith, through which Christ's faithful people participate in his resurrection life and promised future. They do not intrinsically involve practices of jurisdiction in either the internal or external forum. As the spiritual body of the risen Christ, the church is ordered exclusively by the saving word of Christ's triumph on the Cross, spoken and heard, enacted and seen, by the action of the Holy Spirit within her members. Her proclamatory practices and ministries spring from and replenish the spiritual unanimity of the faithful: their being of "the same mind," united in desire, knowledge, will, and action.[55] Having corporate worship at their core, these ministries both express and strengthen the common judgments of Christ's members about what is right, fitting, edifying, and timely to do, and so are pivotal to their witness in faithful action to Christ's coming kingdom.

Yet the Tudor liturgies do not lose sight of the continuing need of Christ's faithful people for jurisdictional authority. There are, arguably, two further liturgical instances of the interpenetration of evangelical and jurisdictional authority in the pastoral ministries of the clergy. The first occurs in the rubrics prefacing the Communion service, requiring the "curate" firmly to admonish against partaking of Communion such parishioners who have scandalized the congregation by their "open and notorious" evil-living, wronged their neighbor(s) "by word or deed," or persisted in a known relation of "malice" and "hatred" with another (others), until such time as they have demonstrated to all offended repentance and amendment of life.[56] While the curate's act carries strong communal and spiritual authority and serves both pastoral and judicial ends—warning offenders against divine condemnation and exhorting them to faithful repentance and its practical fruits, and protecting the spiritual welfare of the corporate ecclesial

---

53. *FSPB*, 463.

54. "Most merciful father, we beseech thee to send down upon this thy servant thy heavenly blessing, and so endue him with thy holy spirit, that he preaching thy word, may not only be earnest to reprove, beseech, and rebuke with all patience and doctrine, but also may be . . . an wholesome example in word, in conversation, in love, in faith, in chastity, and purity." *FSBP*, 463.

55. According to the apostle, Paul, to "be united in the same mind" (1 Cor. 1:10) is "have the mind of Christ" through reception of "the Spirit which is from God" (1Cor. 2:12, 16).

56. *BCP*, 247.

body against corrosion—its semiprivate character and admonitory form render it something less than a juridical act of suspension. The second instance occurs in the opening address of the Lenten liturgy of "Commination" [or threatening of divine punishment]. The liturgy is said to substitute for the primitive church's Lenten discipline of putting "notorious sinners . . . to open penance . . . that their souls might be saved . . . and . . . others admonished by their example," until the desired restoration of the earlier discipline.[57] Whereas, however, the patristic practice unambiguously blended the pastoral and the juridical, the Tudor liturgy's general recitation of biblical threats and exhortations, combined with penitential prayer, is wholly pastoral. Yet both instances recognize the possible, if not inevitable, juridical dimension of certain pastoral tasks of the church's apostolic ministries. These are forms of communicating God's saving Word, vehicles for nurturing faith and repentance, but in a paternal and disciplinary mode, so that they may border on, or overlap with, properly judicial action. However, the primarily spiritual aims and effects of these disciplinary tasks of preaching and the manner in which they are conducted distance them from the logic of social condemnation and vindication, of coercive restraint and correction of evildoing, characteristic of public judgment.

For the most part, then, Edwardian and Elizabethan public theology and practice communicated a tension between the pastoral ministry of the Word and the ecclesiastical public judgment that protected it. Exemplifying this tension is John Jewel's somewhat differently nuanced handling of pastoral discipline in his 1561 *Apology of the Church of England*. Jewel presented the church's "power of the keys" as the preaching of God's word of forgiveness to the contrite penitent and of eternal censure to the stubbornly impenitent, while coupling this proclamatory pastoral action with the minister's readmission to the church's fellowship of notorious and criminal offenders after evidence of their amendment, and his exclusion from it of unbelieving and contumacious offenders (following 2 Tim. 3:13). The single rationale of these disparate forms of ministerial action is the apostolic commission to "publish abroad" God's efficacious word of salvation; so that "the keys" with which the ministers "shut or open the kingdom of heaven" are "knowledge of the Scriptures" and "interpretation of the law."[58] For Jewel, then, the ministers declare judgment in the primary pastoral sense of "expounding" the "Gospel and the Law," rather than in the strict juridical sense of determining the gravity of offenses perpetrated, distributing proportionate punishment, and assessing satisfaction paid; but Jewel's evangelical penitential paradigm has assimilated apostolic juridical elements.

---

57. *BCP*, 316.

58. *Apologia Ecclesiae Anglicanae* (London, 1562) Part II.6-7: *An Apology or Answer in Defence of the Church of England*, trans. Lady Anne Becon (London, 1564) II.6-7, in *The Works of John Jewel*, ed. John Ayre, 4 vols (Parker Society; Cambridge: Cambridge University Press, 1845–50), 3:11–12 (Latin), 3:60–1 (English).

The Reformed Discipline against Tudor Ministerial Orders

Unfortunately, the Tudor tension between the church's proclamatory and juridical action tended to obscure the *intrinsically public dimension* of her proclamation. From the Henrician period onward, the public theology and practice of the Tudor church tended to absorb the claim to public authority of the church's proclamation into the sphere of political jurisdiction. Protracted quarrels over Elizabeth's church settlement exposed to new light both the theoretical strength of the Tudor reforming inheritance in protecting the primacy of evangelical proclamation and its theoretical weakness in assimilating the public authority of evangelical practices and ministries to the authority of jurisdiction. These controversies were the more bitter because they were domestic: the foremost dissenting voices, those of the Presbyterian divines, were in many respects reputable churchmen within the Elizabethan establishment fold. The exaggerated posturing on both sides was generated, in part, by the extent of their doctrinal and theological consensus. Nevertheless, beneath the hyperbolic polemics lay theological differences that would prove a lasting "thorn in the flesh" for the historical progeny of the Elizabethan settlement.

Imposition of the modestly revised 1552 prayer book and ordinal in 1559 elicited a more or less equal measure of discontent among Catholic traditionalists and reform-minded English divines, a number of whom had experience of Reformed city churches on the continent during the Marian persecution.[59] The 1560s witnessed a revival in clerical circles of the earlier protest against royal prescription of traditional vestments, offensive for their "idolatrous" associations.[60] This challenge to the queen's authority to impose decisions on *adiaphora* or "things indifferent," that is, traditions neither proscribed by God's word nor commanded as necessary to human salvation, departed from the position adopted by the majority of magisterial reformers: Luther, Melanchthon, Bucer, Vermigli, Bullinger, and Calvin had all defended the magistrate's authority in "indifferent" matters of church order.[61]

---

59. The English exiles from the Marian persecution had formed congregations in the Reformed cities of Emden, Frankfurt, Strasbourg, Zürich, Basel, Geneva, and Aarau.

60. In Edward's reign, dissent from the albe and cope prescribed for the celebration of communion in the 1549 prayer book was inspired by the reservations of both resident foreign divines (Bucer, Vermigli, Ochino, and Laski) and their continental mentors (Bullinger and Calvin) about the continuing use of these vestments in the English church. The original protagonists in the 1560s vestiarian dispute had all been exiles in Calvin's Geneva.

61. Bernard J. Verkamp, *The Indifferent Mean: Adiaphorism in the English Reformation to 1554* (Athens: Ohio University Press, 1977), 66–78, 87–8; Kirby, *The Zurich Connection and Tudor Political Theology*, 204–33; MacCulloch, *Thomas Cranmer*, 471–85; Clyde L. Manschreck, *The Role of Melanchthon in the Adiaphora Controversy* (New York: Penguin Random House, 1967), 166–71.

By the 1570s, influential dissenters had escalated the challenge into a full-scale assault on the worship, ministerial orders, and discipline of Elizabeth's church establishment, condemned as a wholesale contravention of God's explicitly revealed laws. Under the sway of Genevan ecclesiology imbibed under Theodore Beza's leadership, the Cambridge-bred theologians, Thomas Cartwright and Walter Travers, nurtured over two decades a wide-ranging clerical and lay movement for the establishment of Calvinist order and discipline in the English church, with arguments that struck a relatively novel soteriological, epistemological, and ecclesiological chord in the English setting.[62] Their theological consolidation of the Reformed project combined a thematizing of corporate "sanctification" with a legalistic hermeneutic of biblical authority and a juridical ecclesiological reorientation. To this theological project and its exponents the episcopal defenders of Elizabeth's church establishment frequently applied the derogatory epithet "Puritan."[63] Although scholars today employ the term "Puritan" to cover a fairly broad spectrum of sympathy in the Elizabethan church with aspects of this reforming orientation, we shall employ the term primarily for the Presbyterian cutting edge.

In certain respects the Puritan thematizing of "sanctification" had firm roots in the Edwardian evangelical tradition of public theology, despite the term's conspicuous absence from it. We have seen the central place occupied in Cranmer's homilies by the liveliness of faith in producing good works and by certification of faith by its fruits. However, Cranmer's treatment of "lively" faith exhibited a Lutheran emphasis on the priority of "passive" over "active" righteousness, underpinned by the individual believer's consciousness of being "*simul justus et peccator.*" With the Puritan shift of attention to communal and institutional dimensions of sanctification, this dialectical consciousness gave way to a more perfectionist orientation. Exacerbating this tendency was the strongly revisionist character of militant Puritan ecclesiology, aiming at "root and branch" renovation of English church polity. Although replacement of prayer book worship by Genevan-style worship featured prominently in the Puritan platform, its central planks included adoption of presbyterian (Reformed, Genevan) ministerial order and government, both of which came to be subsumed under the umbrella concept of "discipline."

Cartwright's sensational lectures of 1570 on the Book of Acts[64] furnished the apostolic standard of presbyterian church polity by which the Anglican *status*

---

62. The arguments were more familiar in Scotland, owing to the reforming leadership of the Genevan-trained John Knox.

63. Ironically, the term had originally surfaced in the previous decade in Catholic polemic against the anti-Roman reforming pretension of restoring the church to its primitive purity of doctrine, worship, and ministry by stripping away centuries of polluting papal accretions. Leonard J. Trinterud, *Elizabethan Puritanism* (New York: Oxford University Press, 1971), 6–9.

64. Cartwright had recently been installed as Lady Margaret Professor at Cambridge University when he delivered the lectures on Acts that would cost him his professorship and cause his removal to Geneva.

quo was to be judged and corrected. Informed by their brash proposals, the Puritan manifesto of 1572, An Admonition to the Parliament,[65] contended that restoration of the first two marks of a true church — "preaching of the word purely, ministering of the sacraments sincerely" —depended on restoration of the third mark — "ecclesiastical discipline"[66]—encompassing restoration of offices and procedures approved by the apostles for appointing godly and learned ministers to congregations, and for admonishing, punishing, correcting, and reforming "disordered" ministers and congregational members. The Admonition's argument exhibited the close interweaving of perfectionist and juridical ecclesiology and legalistic biblical interpretation that would dominate Puritan confrontation with the establishment for the remainder of Elizabeth's reign.[67]

Unsubtle polemics aside, the establishment strategy of portraying Puritan arguments as Romanist or Anabaptist had an element of truth, for all three positions sought assurance of salvation in communal offices and practices and in detailed models or rules of absolute authority. Drawing these from Scripture rather than from church tradition or ongoing communal inspiration, Cartwright and Travers expounded the presbyterian polity as God's universal, necessary, and perfect law for his holy commonwealth: the perpetual eschatological image of his heavenly kingdom.[68] They presented its constitution of offices and practices, in their liturgical, organizational, and disciplinary detail, as promulgated by Christ, instituted by his apostles, and authoritatively set forth in God's written word.[69]

---

65. The *Admonition* was published in the wake of the queen's obstruction of parliamentary consideration of proposals for prayer book revision and episcopal disciplining of mild clerical nonconformity (1571–2). G. R. Elton, *The Parliament of England 1559–1581* (Cambridge: Cambridge University Press, 1986), 205–11. Also, discussion in W. H. Frere and C. E. Douglas, eds., *Puritan Manifestoes: A Study of the Origin of the Puritan Revolt* (London: SPCK and New York: E. S. Gorham, 1907) and Patrick Collinson, *The Elizabethan Puritan Movement* (London: Routledge, 1967).

66. Frere and Douglas, *Puritan Manifestoes*, 9.

67. The Admonition elicited a protracted public controversy between Thomas Cartwright and John Whitgift, then Regious Professor of Divinity at Cambridge and responsible for Cartright's loss of his professorship. Whitgift's *Answer to the Admonition*, appearing in late 1572 or early 1573, quickly elicited Cartwright's *Reply to the* Answer, which Whitgift parried with his *Defence of the Answer* in 1574, eliciting from Cartwright in the same year a *Second Reply* in two parts. For analyses of this controversy, John S. Coolidge, *The Pauline Renaissance in England: Puritanism and the Bible* (Oxford: Clarendon Press, 1970), 1–54; Peter Lake, *Anglicans and Puritans? Presbyterian and English Conformist Thought from Whitgift to Hooker* (London: Routledge, 1988), 1–70.

68. See especially Travers, *A Full and Plain Declaration of Ecclesiastical Discipline Out of the Word of God* (Heidelberg: Michael Schirat/London, 1574), 9–11.

69. Comprising the church's permanent constitution were: (1) the offices of elder, doctor, pastor, and deacon, with their respective functions of disciplinary enforcement (elder), doctrinal and catechetical teaching (doctor), preaching, exhortation, and

Their presentation rested on two premises concerning the scope of divinely revealed law: that in the Scriptures, God has provided "general" and "special" laws to regulate all beliefs and actions; and that special law is the more perfect for leaving as little as possible "undetermined and without the compass of the law,"[70] subject to the discretion of fallible sinners. Taking the Mosaic legislation of the Pentateuch to be the paradigm of divine law, Cartwright and Travers found in the New Testament writings a body of commands of equivalent specificity and particularity to regulate the offices and practices of Christ's godly commonwealth.[71] Drawing rules from single and repeated acts of Christ, the apostles, and evangelists, along with their exhortations, commands, and admonitions (reinforced by passages from the Old Testament and early patristic writings), Cartwright and Travers produced a detailed vindication of presbyterian worship, ministries, and church government and corresponding indictment of Elizabeth's establishment counterparts. In claiming epistemological certainty for the presbyterian constitution, both theologians were undaunted by glaring weaknesses in the available Scriptural evidence. Not only did their historical construction depend on contestable interpretations of the recorded practice and dictates of the apostles and their successors, but they were compelled to hypothesize that the church's most primitive offices of "apostle," "evangelist," and "prophet," along with such spiritual equipment as conveying the Holy Spirit by the laying on of hands, were ordained by God only for the nascent church, and not as her "ordinary" and "perpetual" earthly endowment.[72]

Crucial to the dynamic presbyterian edifice of corporate sanctification were the practices of private and public discipline: those of fraternal examination, instruction, and admonishing of one another by the faithful, combined with official scrutiny, censure, punishment, and correction. To fulfill its wide-ranging remit, public discipline would take a variety of forms: local or regional "conferences" of ministers ("prophesyings") providing occasions for constructive scrutinizing of the preaching of colleagues; congregational visitations of pastors and elders to manage (among other tasks) the exclusion from communion of insufficiently

---

sacramental administration (pastor), and charitable distribution (deacon), beside which Cartwright admitted bishops or "superintendents," intending a regional office with certain administrative duties; (2) the governing structure of parochial "consistory" or "council" comprised of local church officials above deacon, and provincial, national and general synods or "conferences" (with representation from the consistories), forming a hierarchy of appeal in cases of appointment, deposition, suspension, and excommunication; and (3) the "lawful calling" of all church officials, consisting of appointment by God, that is, the vocational assurance of the candidate's conscience, and by church authorities, that is, the candidate's election and ordination by the consistory.

70. *The Second Reply of Thomas Cartwright against Master Doctor Whitgift's Second Answer, Touching the Church Discipline* (Heidelberg: Michael Schirat/London, 1575), 94.

71. The proximity to Zwingli's ecclesiological legalism is striking. See Bernard J. Verkamp, "The Zwinglians and Adiaphorism," *Church History* 42, no. 4 (1973): 486–504.

72. Cartwright, *Second Reply*, 327; Travers, *Declaration of Ecclesiastical Discipline*, 132–6.

reformed "papists" and their offspring from receiving baptism; consistory and synodical proceedings to remove "ignorant ministers" from office; suppress "papistical" ceremonies, and sever the obstinately heretical or immoral from the godly community. Of these disciplinary forms, "prophesyings" succeeded most in getting a temporary foothold within the Elizabethan church, winning considerable appreciation of their pedagogical benefits from episcopal overseers, participating clergy, and self-selected lay audiences.[73]

The harsher, punitive side of the Puritans' reforming project came to expression in their demand for the civil adoption of certain Mosaic judicial laws, the literal commands of which they considered permanently binding in the absence of scriptural testimony to God's explicit revocation of them. Foremost among these were the laws commanding the death penalty for persistent transgressors against "the first table" of the Decalogue, that is, against "true religion and . . . the service of God," the dishonoring of God name and glory being the fountain of all human criminality and lawlessness, of all violations of "the second table." While adopting Calvin's view of the moral consequences of violating the first table,[74] Cartwright and Travers starkly contradicted his denial of the permanently binding force of the Mosaic judicials, insisting instead that their "equity" or general moral intent was inseparable from their concrete commands.[75] This further step in assimilating the laws of Christian polity to the divinely appointed, uniquely sanctifying laws of the Israelite nation imbued judicial acts with definite saving significance.

In attempting to repulse the Puritan attacks on multiple fronts against the public theology and practice of Elizabeth's church, the shifting arguments of establishment defenders at times succumbed to, and exacerbated, inadequacies in the church's reforming inheritance, as consideration of two key planks in the episcopal campaign for "conformity" demonstrates. The foremost plank of this campaign was to uphold the distinction of the magisterial reforming mainstream between *the invisible church* governed immediately by Jesus Christ through his word and composed of his faithful and elect members, and *the visible church* governed under Jesus Christ by the sovereign Christian magistrate. While this alignment of the invisible church with Christ's government through his word is unproblematic when intending to affirm that only Christ's faithful are ruled spiritually by him, it is

---

73. A measure of the success of "prophesyings" was Archbishop Edmond Grindal's refusal to implement the queen's policy of suppressing them, prompting Elizabeth to sequester him in his palace at Lambeth. Patrick Collinson, *Archbishop Grindal 1519-1583: The Struggle for a Reformed Church* (London: Jonathan Cape, 1979), chs. 12-15, and *The Elizabethan Puritan Movement*, 178-89.

74. Cartwright, *Second Reply*, 117-18; Jean Calvin, *Institutes* (1559) 2.8.11.

75. Standing firmly in the scholastic legal tradition and its patristic foundations, Calvin held that commonwealths could be rightly governed by the common law of nations rather than the law of Moses, because only the equity or charity at which human legal enactments aimed was permanently binding, not the enactments themselves, including those appointed by God for the Jewish polity. See *Institutes* (1559) 4.20.14-16.

problematic when intending to deny any other visibility to the church than its civil establishment. For Christ visibly reigns in and over his people through the faithful human communication of his rule in the corporate practices of worship. Worldly in their commonality and publicity, these practices of communication are outward signs and instruments of Christ's inward rule through his Spirit's illuminating, cleansing, and unifying action in the hearts of worshippers. Through the Spirit's action, the practices are efficacious in unifying the faithful, independent of other "worldly" sources of unity.

In the polemical context of unrelenting pressure to vindicate the monarch's government of church order and ministry, its defenders undermined this defining unity of corporate action and common faith by stressing the invisibility of Christ's government of the church to the detriment of its vital visibility. Confronting Puritan insistence that, in the first place, the juridical imposition of uniform practices *from above* violated the evangelical and disciplinary freedom of local ministry, and in the second, their imposition *by the civil magistrate* violated the evangelical and disciplinary authority of ministerial offices per se, the Anglican conformists were constantly pushed to uphold the monarch's sovereign jurisdictional authority over the visible church at the expense of the evangelical and pastoral authority of her ministries. What was most needed for a faithful witness to the visibility of Christ's government was a balance of jurisdictional to evangelical authority more favorable to the latter, combined with a concerted search for theological and practical accord across divisions in the church.

The second plank of the conformist campaign of resistance to the Puritan project was employment of the distinction between "things necessary" and "things indifferent" (*adiaphora*) to salvation. Contraversially employed by Melanchthon and his colleagues in 1546 to justify acceptance by the Lutheran churches of Saxony of traditional Catholic practices imposed by the Emperor Charles V,[76] the concept was also used to justify variability among the liturgies, ministries, and disciplines of the reforming churches. Referring to God's revealed law in Scripture, the distinction paralleled the canonist-scholastic distinction between the "commands" (prescriptions and proscriptions) and the "permissions" of the natural and divine law, and was similarly vulnerable to voluntarist and positivist legal glosses (as detected earlier in Article XXXIV).[77] But, contrary to the scholastics' theoretical use of permissive natural and divine law to enlarge the practical and political freedom of individuals, the English reformers and their continental colleagues (Lutheran and Reformed) principally used the concept of *adiaphora* to undergird the political freedom and authority of independent churches over their members. Most continental reformers concurred that "indifferent" or "permitted" practices should have a permissive warrant in Scripture (which might merely be silence or absence of a prohibition) and would conform to the general Scriptural (especially Pauline) principles that all be done "in order and comeliness," preserving outward

---

76. Tierney, *Liberty and Law*, 160–2.
77. p. 334.

peace (1 Cor. 14:33, 40), with charity toward the neighbor (Mk 12:31, Rom. 13:9) and for the church's "edification" (1 Cor. 14:26).[78]

Deeply reluctant to accept the concept of ecclesiastical "*adiaphora*," the English Puritans subverted it by requiring that such practices conform to their confident applications of the general Scriptural principles. Against this subversion, conformists were sometimes more inclined to defend the authority of government to make dispositions for the church's worship, ministry, and discipline that were "not repugnant" to God's clearly revealed law than to argue for the conformity to God's revealed law of actual governmental dispositions made for the church by demonstrating their *coherent theological rationality*. This failure marred the polemical works of John Whitgift, who, as Archbishop of Canterbury (1583–1604), directed the establishment response to Puritan nonconformity over two decades. His long-winded literary combat with Cartwright over the elements of Elizabethan prayer book worship and ministry, displaying shifting delineations of the scope and guiding principles of *adiaphora* (by both sides), did not produce a wholly coherent account of the different ways in which the established church's worship and ministerial orders "edified" the faithful by conforming to the reign of the risen Christ over and within his people witnessed in the Scriptures.[79] It did not, therefore, provide an adequate theological matrix for the prayerful deliberation by church authorities over corporate responses to Christ's present commands adequate to their concrete claims (whether the responses be required, or only fitting and circumstantially possible, and as such, susceptible of variation and rational contestation across churches), within which the limited, variable, and somewhat arbitrary dispositions of human government would find a legitimate place.

This absence from Whitgift's argumentation threatened to undermine the validity of his single most stable proposal concerning *adiaphora*: namely, that all corporate practices edify by virtue of their incorporation into the laws that "keep godly peace and unity" in the visible church.[80] This pivotal proposal reiterated the logic of the Elizabethan article XXXIII on "traditions of the church," which closely associated the edification of ecclesiastical "ceremonies and rites" with their ordaining by "common authority," and gave moral priority to the political offense of disrupting the church's "common order." The proposal's virtue was its balancing of two sources of edification in politically prescribed practices: namely, the communication of God's rule through the magistrate's divinely ordained authority, and the prevention of factious dissent and quarrels over doctrine and practice

---

78. Bernard J. Verkamp, "The Limits upon Adiaphoristic Freedom: Martin Luther and Philip Melanchthon," *Theological Studies* 36, no. 1 (1975): 52–76.

79. *Defence of the Answer to the Admonition, Against the Reply of Thomas Cartwright: Tractates I-VI, VII-X*, in *The Works of John Whitgift*, ed. John Ayre, 3 vols (Parker Society; Cambridge: Cambridge University Press, 1851–3), vols 1 and 2. Hereafter *WJW*.

80. *WJW*, 2:5–6, 57–61.

that impede the faithful hearing of God's word.[81] Whitgift's balance somewhat redressed a Tudor tendency (discussed in Chapter 10) to portray obedience to public authority as *the decisive outward expression* of obedience to God's rule.

In addition, Whitgift made conceptual moves to subordinate juridical action to the church's proclamatory ministries and practices of nurturing faith and its practical fruits. Significantly, he conceived the obedience of the faithful to the church's existing laws as nonjuridical, in the sense of not standing in judgment. By obeying a public ordinance of which they are critical, the faithful virtuously refrain from raising their own judgment above the common judgment; whereas, in openly controverting and disobeying ordinances not evidently contradictory to Scripture, they enter unnecessarily into contentious judgment with their fellow believers. The "spirit of complaint" that shows no forbearance toward "imperfectly reformed" communal practices is uncharitable toward all neighbors: toward Catholic sympathizers, by alienating them further from evangelical truth; toward tender reformed consciences, by inflating the offense presented by such practices; and toward both those who command and who obey the practices, by impugning the integrity of their faith.[82]

On the disciplinary front, Whitgift credibly laid out the Anglican alternative to the Puritans' overly inquisitorial and juridical culture of communal sanctification. He stressed that a community of faith and repentance has no place for its members' probing and exposing the hidden sins of one another, rather than confining their probing and exposing to their own sins.[83] Consequently, the clergy are to exercise discipline primarily through warning, admonition, and exhortation directed to the whole congregation from the pulpit. Hearing this prophetic word, each of the faithful judges herself, just as each confesses her sins in the corporate confession, and each receives the declaration of God's absolution given to all. To inconspicuous sins, including those of unreformed Catholic lay and clerical traditionalists, the clergy administer a general pedagogical correction, unless private counsel is solicited.

Whitgift confines public judgment and punishment of individual sins in the established church to conspicuous offenses: open violations of divine and human laws that cause scandal and incite public complaint. For such lay and clerical misdemeanors as spreading heresies, blaspheming, fornication, harming another in person, reputation or property, nonattendance at Sunday worship, and nonconformity to prescribed liturgical forms, the church has a range of penalties at her disposal, from suspension of the sacraments to fines, incarceration, and excommunication.[84] Whitgift locates all the ecclesiastical penalties for conspicuous,

---

81. *WJW*, 1:5–6; 2:5–8, 57–62.
82. *WJW*, 1:319–26, 377.
83. *WJW*, 1:44; 3:79–80, 102, 230.
84. Instructive, if not fully authoritative, legal delineation of these penalties is found in the material assembled under the titles *de poenis ecclesiasticis, de suspensione, de excommunicatione* in the *Reformatio Legum Ecclesiasticarum*, in *Tudor Church Reform:*

legal offenses, including suspension and excommunication, within the realm's judicial processes under the monarch, serving the purposes of preserving the church's outward integrity as an evangelical and moral community and of assisting to restore offenders to the repentance of faith and amendment of life. To be an instrument of the spiritual restoration of offenders, however, the visible church must minister God's saving word in Jesus Christ and not only the condemning word of the public judicial process. If public judgment and punishment of offenders both express and overcome their separation from the visible company of believers brought about by their misdemeanors, pastoral care for them looks forward in hope to their spiritual communion with Christ's faithful people. Even the excommunicate is not to be denied the evangelical and pastoral ministrations of fellow Christians.[85]

A consistent thrust of Whitgift's orientation to ecclesiastical discipline was to emphasize that its faithful administration depends on generous, forbearing, forgiving, and sober relations among the church's members, who have taken to heart the teaching and example of Christ and his apostles, not only concerning love's humility in refraining from judging the neighbor;[86] but also concerning the inevitable preponderance of sinful conduct even among Christ's professed disciples.[87] At his theological best, Whitgift understands that only a congregation of the faithful that interprets and embraces its visible communion as of "word and sacrament," of evangelical practice, rather than of corporate holiness resting on discipline grasps the place of the juridical process as an occasional, variable, and quasi-extraneous aid to the church's ministries of nurturing living faith among its members.[88]

In the two decades following Whitgift's writings of the 1570s, episcopal defense of Elizabeth's church establishment made faltering and vacillating progress in

---

The Henrician Canon of 1535 and the "Reformatio Legum Ecclesasticarum," ed. Gerald Bray (Woodbridge: Boydell Press, 2000), 442–53, 462–75.

85. According to the *Reformatio Legum Ecclesiasticarum,* church members are not allowed amicable socializing with excommunicated persons but are allowed pastoral visits for the "godly work" of assisting their return to righteousness. Bray, *Tudor Church Reform,* 469.

86. Mt. 7:1-5; Lk. 6:37-8; Rom. 2:1-8, 14:1-13; 1 Cor. 4:4-5; 6:7-8; Jas 4:11-12, 5:9.

87. *Echoing* Augustine's anti-Donatist writings, Whitgift and his fellow conformists make much of Christ's parable about the householder patiently allowing the wheat and tares to grow together until the harvest (Mt. 13:24-30; Mk 4:26-29), and also of the gravity of the sins committed by members of the apostolic and subapostolic churches. *WJW,* 1:183–4, 382–8.

88. *WJW,* I:182–7; 2:98–100, 110–11. Significantly, Whitgift confines the church's ministries to those of "word and sacrament," presenting government as a remedial office and authority, or even a set of tasks and powers, that churches may structure differently. 2:91, 101.

building on Whitgift's strengths and rectifying his weaknesses,[89] culminating in the publication of the Books of Hooker's *Laws of Ecclesiastical Polity* between 1593 and 1661.[90] Hooker's achievement was to integrate within a coherent and comprehensive theoretical framework the conceptual distinctions upon which the defense of the Edwardian and Elizabethan church had relied. With considerable justification it has been hailed as fulfilling the potential of Tudor ecclesiological and political thought.

Hooker's framework—a Reformed, late scholastic reworking of Thomas's typology of law—provided the conceptual tools for harmonizing the action and authority of the church as a supernatural society of Christological grace and a natural political society. Within the terms of his harmonizing project, he mounted a thorough vindication of disputed Anglican liturgical practices, demonstrating, on the one hand, their conformity with the norms and paradigms of Israelite and apostolic worship revealed in Scripture; and on the other, their status as things not necessary to salvation, because nowhere required by explicit divine command. He showed how the invisible communion of God's predestined elect is built up over time through the visible, divine-human intercourse of worship, with its dual foci of preaching and the sacraments. On the disciplinary front, he showed that the Anglican hierarchy of episcopal church government, terminating in the royal supremacy, conformed to the governmental forms authorized by God for Israel and for the apostolic and post-apostolic church, and equally to the rational constitution of political society, on neither basis being permanently or exclusively established by divine law.

However, Hooker's harmonizing project introduced conceptual moves (many of which were anticipated in the preceding two decades) that reconfigured the legacy of Edwardian and earlier Elizabethan public theology, rendering it a less effective critique of the problematic aspects of both scholastic and late modern moral, ecclesiological and political thought.[91] Three moves are particularly relevant to the evangelical critique of scholastic thought.

First, in countering the literalistic and legalistic bent of Puritan biblical epistemology, Hooker systematically magnifies the epistemological scope and role of "natural knowledge" as the indispensable formal and substantive substratum of "supernatural" knowledge necessary to salvation. His argumentation is problematic on the evangelical grounds of not conveying adequately the captivity of natural

---

89. For example, in the writings of John Bridges, Thomas Bilson, and Matthew Sutcliffe. For overview of conformist writings in this period, see Lake, *Anglicans and Puritans?*, 88–145.

90. The Preface and Books I–IV were published in 1593, Book V in 1597, while Book VI and VIII appeared posthumously in 1648 followed by Book VII in 1661. For discussion of textual issues, especially connected with the last three books, *WRH*, vols 1–3.

91. Hooker's theological vindication of English church reform has long generated debates among scholarly interpreters about the consistency of his thought with the letter and spirit of the Cranmerian and continental magisterial reforming traditions.

reason to the interior logic of the biblical text, or the working of the Holy Spirit to disclose meaning and give certainty. Moreover, his assigning of primary authority to natural reason in the whole external realm of human moral action ruled by God's law given in creation and republished in the Decalogue, and in which the Spirit's sanctifying work takes place, echoes late scholastic overconfidence in the power of corrupted rationality to discern God's law of created nature apart from Christ's earthly example and commands.

Second, Hooker gives the ecclesiastical jurisdiction of bishops a higher profile than did earlier Cranmerian public theology, anchoring it in apostolic institution and divine ordination or authorization.[92] Crucially, he unifies the apostolic disciplines of coercive jurisdiction and penitence under the rubric of "apostolic regiment" or "keys of the kingdom," suggesting the seamless (continuous and harmonious, though not identical) operation of clerical judgment and correction in the church's internal and external *fora*.[93] Thus, he relates coercive jurisdiction to the Spirit's sanctifying work in a manner more congenial to Roman Catholic than to English evangelical ecclesiology.[94]

Third, Hooker gives theoretical priority to the natural purpose and corporative foundation of human jurisdiction, ecclesiastical and civil. While loosely concurring with Cranmerian public theology in presenting the purpose of coercive jurisdiction as external and remedial,[95] he departs from the former's wholly theocentric approach by constructing a conservative, corporative theory of "public regiment" in late scholastic fashion, on axioms of natural political reasoning, from the individual's permissive right of self-defense against assault, and his moral and practical incapacity to determine and maintain his right, to the rational necessity of individuals collectively consenting to a structure of binding communal judgment.[96]

---

92. Hooker, *Laws* 7.5: *WRH*, 3:159–70.

93. Hooker, *Laws* 6.3.6–6.4.1: *WRH*, 3:13–14. See Dean Kernan's instructive analysis of Hooker's incomplete account of ecclesiastical jurisdiction, "Jurisdiction and the Keys," in *A Companion to Richard Hooker*, ed. Torrance Kirby (Leiden and Boston: Brill, 2008), 435–79.

94. In so far as English Puritan ecclesiology follows Calvin, it denies that the church's "power of the keys," of "binding and loosing," entails "spiritual jurisdiction" as exercised in the Roman penitential discipline or in public coercive judgment and punishment. Rather, the church's "power of the keys" is always "the ministry of God's word" of redemption in Jesus Christ from the condemnation of sin, and its "spiritual jurisdiction" is that proclamatory ministry exercised in the pastoral disciplines of private admonitory correction and, finally, of public expulsion from the church of notorious, unrepentant sinners, and of reconciliation to the church of repentant sinners. Calvin, *Institutes* 4.11.1-5.

95. Hooker, *Laws* I.10.4: *WRH*, 1:98–100.

96. Hooker, *Laws* I.10.4. Paul Dominiak in "'All Thing Are Lawful': Adiaphora, Permissive Natural Law, Christian Freedom, and Defending the English Reformation" perspicaciously shows how exceptional among Tudor conformist argumentation was Hooker's rationalist,

Overcoming the Public Hegemony of Political and Technological Rule: The Publicity of Nonjuridical Practices and Authorities

As the defining practices of the visible church are practices of communicating God's saving word in Jesus Christ, so the defining authority of her vocational ministries is authority over and in these practices: exegetical, theological, catechetical, liturgical, sacramental, and pastoral. These ministries carry authority as instruments of the Holy Spirit in bringing sinful human beings to sure faith in Christ, seeking understanding and bearing fruit in practical judgment and action. They also carry authority as undertaken for the community and as validated by the community's judgments concerning ministerial preparation, appointment and testing for fitness, and related matters such as defining doctrine in accordance with Scripture and establishing or altering "indifferent" communal traditions. These judgments may be termed "public" on two time-honored theoretical grounds: they are given representatively for all the community's members, and they command willing acceptance or endorsement from all members. To understand the church's authority as public on these grounds is perfectly consistent with understanding it as a Christological endowment intrinsic to the church's evangelical mission and expressive of her members' spiritual unity.

However, English Reformation theology gives precedence to a third ground for designating the church's authority to judge as "public": that it includes the moral power of coercion intrinsic to political jurisdiction. And it presents the church's public jurisdictional authority as subject to, and even derivable from, the lay monarch's supreme jurisdiction. The theological strength of these moves is to distance the church's public jurisdiction from the Christological endowments intrinsic to her evangelical mission. The theological weakness is the tendency to obscure the public authority of the church's evangelical practices and ministries, through which Christ's universal rule renews disordered human community.

On all three grounds, the church's authority is public by virtue of *commanding* the beliefs, understandings, affections, and actions of its members. The church commands their belief and understanding by communicating God's revealed truth, their affections by communicating God's revealed goodness and glory, and their intentions and actions by communicating God's revealed will or law. But in commanding coercively, with threat of communal sanction, the church may elicit merely "outward" obedience from its members by appealing to their baser, self-protective fear of social condemnation and other punishment. Although coercive jurisdiction may be necessary to the stability and integrity of the visible church, it is, nonetheless, alien to the public authority of evangelical practices and ministries. For the practices of coercive jurisdiction do not communicate God's saving word of judgment spoken in Jesus Christ but, at most, serve it obliquely by protecting the church's outward order against corrupting and disordering forces.

scholastic use of permissive natural law in constructing his political argument for obedience to lay ecclesiastical supremacy. *Perichoresis* 20, no. 2 (2022): 73–103.

Thus, the visible church, in its multiple and diverse institutional arrangements, has the task of sustaining a theological and practical balance in which the alien public practices and authority of jurisdiction are peripheral to its essential public evangelical practices and authority. In different historical contexts, church authorities may pursue this task by taking on more or less public juridical responsibility, in more or in less dependence on civil juridical authorities. The church may fail in this task either by minimizing or denying its need of jurisdiction or by making jurisdiction a determinative element of its essential public authority and practices of communicating God's salvation in Jesus Christ. To the mainstream of English evangelical reformers, some radical Anabaptist movements exemplified the first failure, while the Roman papal tradition and, to a lesser degree, the Presbyterian church order exemplified the second. Regrettably, English reforming theology exemplified a third, if less conspicuous, failure, by identifying the church's public authority primarily with its coercive jurisdiction rather than with its essential ministries of evangelical proclamation.

In our late modern polities, the church in its various denominational divisions can too easily succumb to all three forms of failure, chiefly owing to its postwar theological absorption of the liberal, egalitarian, and pluralistic ethos and ethic of human rights. For the driving principle of maximizing the individual's freedom of self-disposal breeds aversion to the church's corporate striving for uniformity of doctrinal confession and common practice and to all disciplinary expressions of its epistemological and moral authority. At the same time, this ethos and ethic insinuates into the church's mission the endorsement and implementation of equal rights and social, moral, and religious plurality, and aided by governmental enforcement, overrides residual clerical and lay reservations. The resulting alignment of the church's public authority with the egalitarian-rights agenda of secular jurisdiction obscures the public claim of the redemptive rule of Jesus Christ over the whole of human society, and Christ's power through the Holy Spirit to liberate human institutions, the permanent spheres of cooperative social activity, from the present distortions of their divinely appointed purposes and modes of action. Corrupted by the political-juridical ethos and agenda of rights, the church's practices of proclamation inadequately communicate their own distinctive public authority and that of the other nonjuridical social institutions: of marriage and family, of acquiring and transmitting knowledge, of restoring and advancing physical, psychological, and social health and welfare, of artistic communication, and of economic production and exchange of goods and services. At the same time, the church's practices inadequately communicate the *extrinsic service* rendered by political jurisdiction to these essentially nonjuridical institutions.

At its liturgical and homiletic best, Tudor public theology presented coercive jurisdiction as extrinsically serving the nonjurisdictional practices and authorities composing human society by upholding their conformity to God's revealed right, justice, and law, in which their earthly stability and integrity resides. Primarily, it presented the incorporation in public law of aspects of the church's profession, practices, and ministries as an external, defensive undergirding of the communion of the faithful in the knowledge and love of Christ, reinforcing its authoritative outward expressions. Yet the Tudor reformers understood that the communal efficacy of legal enforcement was limited, uncertain, variable, and, most importantly, dependent on the prior spiritual efficacy of the churches evangelical practices.

The Tudor theological grasp of the dialectical tension and interdependence of the practices and authorities of proclamation and jurisdiction is instructive for our response to the disruption and distortion of institutional practices and authorities in contemporary society. It shows that theologians cannot adequately conceive the purpose and parameters of coercive jurisdiction without engaging with Christ's revelation of the created (natural) communicative goods, relationships, and practices of human society and their perfecting renewal through his resurrection victory over sin and death witnessed by the communicative relationships and practices of the post-resurrection community of faith. Only so can theologians conceptualize the moral priority and superiority of the natural and renewed orders of human society to its fallen order, and the corresponding subordination of political authority and practices to pre-political and supra-political authority and practices. But contemporary theologians must assert more robustly than did official Tudor theology the *intrinsically public character* of the divinely imparted authority of the church's evangelical practices and ministries. For recognition of the church's evangelical authority is instrumental to the renewal of individual and collective moral agency and action wrought by faith in Christ, on which truly good practice in every institutional and vocational sphere of social endeavor depends. One formal reflection of this dependence may be that authority in every nonjurisdictional sphere of common endeavor is intrinsically pedagogical and, at times, pastoral, coinciding with the church's ministerial paradigm.

Necessary to good practice in every (adult) vocational sphere is pedagogical preparation and, often, continuing transmission (and sometimes periodic testing) of knowledge, skills, and deliberative reasoning. Efficacious teaching goes beyond conveying practical rules, principles, requirements, and methods, whether technical or moral, to establishing a shared spiritual and emotional orientation to the field of practice, its challenges, and the means of progressing in it. Sharing in wisdom is the spiritual core of good practice in all spheres of common human service because it integrates practice, preventing it from becoming externalized and fragmentary; for sheer conformity to multiple, discrete regulations and formal objectives is frequently inadequate to the task and breeds despondency and corruption among practitioners. Moreover, sharing in wisdom prevents the spiraling of coercive regulation of practice by professional and governmental bureaucracies, which is the typical contemporary response to practical failures and corruption. It enables practitioners to acquire maturity of skills through experience in their practice and continually to test and establish on intrinsic grounds the goodness and efficacy of their vocational traditions of practice. Only in this sound vocational context does coercive regulation support rather than suppress good practice by curbing the more damaging and culpable deviations from it. To resist effectively the distortions of practice and corrosion of authority inflicted by inflated regulative and juridical control, practitioners in every cooperative endeavor need a coherent collegial understanding of the spiritual, moral, administrative, and technical aspects of their practices and authority. Such an understanding enables them to discern clearly when intrusive jurisdiction is substantially corrupting the intrinsic objectives and goods of their practices and their modes of pursuing them.

In addition, practitioners need to understand the public character of the authority belonging to their field of practice: its representative scope and contribution to the common welfare of society's members. The challenge of understanding and sustaining the public authority of social institutions and vocational spheres rooted in God's creating, sustaining, and renewing action is gargantuan in our late modern situation of extreme social fragmentation, uprootedness, subjectivism, and suspicion, on the one hand, and, on the other, the homogenizing juridical ideology and practice of liberal rights. Today, public authority, in the sense of public influence—that is, the power to command the beliefs, judgments, and actions of some members of society at large (the abstract "public")—has undergone massive proliferation within and across societies. Its innumerable agents range over an incalculable expanse of enterprises, organizations, associations, communities, social groups, and media platforms; and their authority demonstrates wide variation and asymmetry in regard to social scope, stability, credibility, and moral status. Such variation and nonalignment of the social, moral, and epistemic elements of *public authority as influence* correspond to the multiplicity of publics created and sustained by it. Diverse in size, composition, and internal relationships, as in moral, intellectual, religious, and cultural orientations, these have vastly multiplied by means of global internet communications.

Despite its variation and asymmetry, public influence affects political jurisdiction, shaping, sustaining, or undermining citizens' perceptions of the justice and legitimacy of governmental acts and authority. It is hardly surprising, then, that advanced liberal, pluralistic societies, having not merely accommodated, but encouraged and made culturally normative the multiplication of authorities, communities, and "publics," are now riddled with agitated debates over the common "values" and ideas needed to underpin stable, democratic, just, and limited government. Evidence is accumulating that these common "values" and ideas (or better, goods and truths) lie beyond the principles of egalitarian individualism and communal pluralism enshrined in the hybrid moral-juridical discourse of universal human rights and that their institutional embodiments currently lack the political recognition and protection proper to them.

Christian theologians are now as always called upon to entertain seriously the theoretical possibility that stable, representative, and just political jurisdiction requires underpinning by the common ethos and ethic embodied in the public authority and practices of the visible church. To be *the common social locus* of superjurisdictional authority and practice, the church cannot be construed as one among many "voluntary" religious associations formed by autonomous individuals. Nor can it be construed as a player in the market of rival religious allegiances competing for adherents on the "level playing-field" of equal civil and political rights. Indeed, this "playing field" is becoming a terrain of self-defensive inclusivity in which the hypersensitivity of religious organizations and communities to internal and external threats is accompanied by pressure to exercise missionary self-censorship: that is, to avoid invading the social-moral space of rivals.

Pari passu, Christian theologians are called upon to give more balanced critical and constructive consideration to past historical forms of intersection between the public authority of the church's practices and ministries and the public authority of coercive jurisdiction. In the Cranmerian tradition, it is in the church's political authority and practices of public judgment under the supreme lay magistrate that the rule of Christ's spirit renewing human moral agency and action intersects with secular jurisdiction protecting moral agency and action in the fallen human community. Undoubtedly, this form of intersection runs the danger of assimilating the church's public authority and action to an extrinsic jurisdiction, as do modern secularist forms. Nevertheless, this form may communicate effectively both the generic unity of public judgment as a divinely ordained social authority and practice and its ordering to God's saving renewal of the created goods of human moral community through the church's practices of proclamation.

While the history of fallen humanity has not exhibited, and cannot exhibit, the perfect form of intersection, or even the universally best form, given the shifting, irrational contingencies of sinful human existence, it is incumbent on Christian political thought to seek the best form of intersection in given societal circumstances. The crisis of late modernity shows plainly enough that, when coercive jurisdiction no longer defends the church's public authority of proclamation, it loses clear sight of its generic purpose of defending all common goods belonging to fallen and renewed human community, and particularly to the concrete historical community which it represents. It also loses sight of the divine basis of its communal representation, its subjection to divine law, and its intrinsic limitations and deficiencies.

All these aspects of political jurisdiction will be examined in the following critical exposition of the English Reformation's public theological account of it, and in the concluding appreciation of its contribution to formulating a Christian liberal political and legal alternative to the prevailing natural rights theory and, in some respects, to its scholastic antecedents.

Chapter 10

POLITICAL JURISDICTION UNDER GOD'S JUDGMENT

Throughout the Henrician, Edwardian, and Elizabethan phases of reform, the public theological account of political jurisdiction remained consistent in all significant respects, in part because the constitutional and other legal planks of Henrician reform, with their theological rationales, remained in force under Edward and were restored under Elizabeth. Over the three reigns, governmental proclamations, injunctions, and parliamentary enactments concerning reform of church polity played a leading role in the public theological elaboration of the purpose, source, structure, and limitations of coercive jurisdiction.

An apt starting point for exploring this theological elaboration is the preamble of the Henrician parliamentary Act of 1533 restraining judicial appeals to Rome, recognized by generations of historians to be a distillation of Tudor political theology.[1] This sets forth the ancient imperial status of the English realm as a sovereign body politic divided into "spirituality" and "temporality," governed by a monarch with "imperial" jurisdiction, that is, subject to no superior rule over both estates of the realm.[2] The supreme head is "institute" and "furnished" by God with "plenary ... power ... authority, prerogative and jurisdiction" to render "justice and final determination" to all residents and subjects of the realm "in all causes, matters, debates and contentions." Under the imperial crown, spiritual (ecclesiastical) authorities have always given judgment in cases involving "the law divine" or "spiritual learning," and temporal "judges and administers," likewise, "for trial of propriety of lands and goods," and for the "conservation of the people" in unity, peace, and security.

The Act's purpose of wholly domesticating judicial processes within the monarch's plenary jurisdiction, excluding papal jurisdiction, should not be read anachronistically, assuming the sharp distinction typically drawn in modern constitutional theory and practice between legislative, executive, and judicial

---

1. 1533: 24 Henry VIII, *c*. 12; *TC*, 353–4.

2. In late-medieval and Renaissance Roman jurisprudence (civil and canonist), the territorial monarch is said to be "emperor in his kingdom" (*rex imperator in regno suo*) when not subject to any superior authority within or outside his realm, such as the Holy Roman Emperor or the Pope. The act claims for the English king an imperial status of great historical longevity.

governmental offices, structures, and actions. For, as we shall see, the tendency in Tudor public political and legal formulations was to conceive the governing action of rulers in generic terms as "giving justice" or "giving judgment" in matters of actual and potential contention, conflict, offense, and injury: restoring the body politic to peace and unity when breaches had occurred and protecting the body politic against future breaches of peace and unity. Through promulgation of law, decree of policy, or court process, in person or by subordinate ecclesiastical and civil authorities, the ruler gave judgment in accordance with God's judgments (laws, commandments) revealed most plainly and comprehensively in the Scriptures and in accordance with existing laws of the realm recognized to be congruent with God's judgments. The Act's preface concisely conveys the symbiotic relationship in reformed Tudor public theology between the divine source and the divinely ordained purpose of political jurisdiction, which is the framework for the exposition to follow.

God's Ordination of Political Jurisdiction

A striking feature of the English Reformation's public treatment of political jurisdiction was its extensive dependence on the Scriptures. When setting out the purposes, authority, and limitations of political judgment, as well as the principles of communal right, justice, and obligation, the English reformers appealed to their revelation to God's chosen people: to the "Old Israel" by God's appointed giver and interpreters of His law, and to the "New Israel" by the example, commands, and judgments of Christ and his apostles.

A formidable achievement of their biblical treatment, indebted to their continental mentors, was to restore two New Testament texts to the commanding position they had occupied in the patristic and early medieval handling of the subject but had largely lost with the reception of Aristotle's political thought from the thirteenth century onward. For over a millennium, Rom. 13:1-7, supported by 1 Pet. 2:13-17, had been the foremost biblical *locus* for the Western church's theological understanding of human government and the duty of obedience owing to it. Appealing to these passages, the English framers of reformed public theology concurred with their Lutheran and Reformed colleagues, and with the Western patristic mainstream, that God had ordained the communal office of civil ruler to render binding public judgment concerning wrongdoing and well-doing within society, for the punishment, restraint, and correction of wrongdoing and the vindication and advancement of well-doing.

This concurrence is exhibited at length in three public sermons concerned with political jurisdiction and the duty of obedience: "An Exhortation concerning Good Order and Obedience to Rulers and Magistrates" published in the 1547 Edwardian collection, "A Sermon concerning the Time of Rebellion" preached by Cranmer in 1549,[3] and "A Homily against Disobedience and Wilful Rebellion" probably written

---

3. The sermon was a collaborative composition of Cranmer and the émigré theologian, Peter Martyr (Pietro Martire Vermigli). *MWL*, 190 n. 1; MacCulloch, *Thomas Cranmer*,

by Jewel published in 1570 and incorporated in 1571 into the Elizabethan collection. All three were episcopal responses to uprisings and rebellions within the realm on a large geographical and social scale, involving multiple groups of mobilized malcontents with grievances against evangelical church reform and spoliation or against unjust and oppressive economic and social conditions or both.[4]

The official homilies of 1547 and 1571, being set pieces for repeated liturgical use, rehearse in full the texts from Romans and 1 Peter and accord them a central role in developing the Scriptural argument for political obedience, for they are seen to consolidate the authoritative apostolic account of God's purposes in giving rulers to human society. The homilies agree that God "has set princes over particular kingdoms and dominions"[5] as supreme judges and law-givers in their territories, to sustain and advance a "godly order," protecting it against the "abuse," "carnal liberty," and "Babylonian confusion" bred by sin.[6] Both anchor coercive jurisdiction in the fallen condition of human society and construe it as the universal communal discipline ordained by God for the propensity of sinful human beings to violate his created and redeemed order of moral obedience. Both marshal supporting Old Testament texts to set forth the benefits bestowed or the damages inflicted on their polities by obedient or disobedient Israelite and non-Israelite monarchs. However, as a consequence of their preponderant concern with God's wrathful judgment on the collective disobedience of factional rebellion against his appointed rulers, the homilies pay less attention than does the apostle, Paul, to the communication of God's wrathful judgment in rulers' routine meeting out of public condemnation and punishment on evildoers, although the earlier homily does declare that God's pronouncement "*All vengeance is mine, and I will reward,*"[7] also pertains to the magistrates, who "exercise God's room" in judging and punishing "by good and godly laws here in earth."[8]

This lack of attention to routine judicial processes is more than compensated for in Cranmer's public sermon of 1549. Censoring the violent uprising of rebels to redress the agrarian injustice of land enclosures and oppressive rents, the sermon invokes Christ's testimony to God's exclusive ordination of kings and governors

---

435-6; For detailed discussion, W. J. Torrance Kirby, *The Zurich Connection and Tudor Political Theology* (Leiden: Brill, 2007), 121-80.

4. The Exhortation may have been responding to the Henrician rebellions of 1536—the Lincolnshire Rising and the Pilgrimage of Grace and their aftermath, as well as to the Anabaptist uprisings in Germany. The 1549 Sermon was responding to the recently quelled "Western Rebellion" centered on Cornwall and Devon, followed by "risings" in southern and eastern counties, and the 1570 Homily was responding to the 1569 Northern (Catholic) Rebellion. For an overview of these uprisings and rebellions see Anthony Fletcher and Diarmaid MacCulloch, *Tudor Rebellions*, 4th edn. (Harlow: Pearson Education Ltd., 1997).

5. *GH*, 553.
6. *GH*, 105.
7. Deut. 31.35.
8. *GH*, 107.

"to be common revengers, correctors, and reformers of all common and private things that be amiss,"[9] and, moreover, it adduces as a "special" cause of the popular rebellion that governing authorities under the Crown have been "too remiss" in punishing a variety of offenses, as "God's wrath against sin" dictates.[10] Confesses Cranmer:[11]

> We [i.e. civil and ecclesiastical authorities] have suffered perjury, blasphemy and adultery, slandering and lying, gluttony and drunkenness, vagabonds and idle persons, either lightly punished, or else not punished at all; either thinking this clemency for the time expedient for the commonwealth, or else not duly weighing how grievous those offences be in the sight of God. And whilst we lacked this right judgement of God's wrath against sin, lo! suddenly cometh upon us this scourge of sedition, the rod of God's wrath, to teach us how sore God hateth all wickedness, and is displeased with his ministers that wink thereat.

A pervasive theological theme in the Tudor laws and homilies is that all human offenses deserving of public condemnation, punishment, and correction, even if directly perpetrated against a single neighbor or set of neighbors, are also offenses against God, the ruler and the realm, as violating ordinances and laws given by God and by his appointed earthly governors for the ordering of human conduct and relations throughout the jurisdiction.

A related theological theme demonstrated by the passage and, more expansively, by the 1571 political homily, is the double moral logic of cause and effect at play in the historical vicissitudes of political society: on the one hand, the intrinsic outworking of virtuous or vicious actions on the part of ruler and ruled in beneficial or calamitous social outcomes, and, on the other, the extrinsic outworking of God's providential judgments of bountiful mercy or righteous wrath. Whereas the authorities' protection and preservation of "virtue and godliness" in the commonweal maintains God's blessings of material "wealth and prosperity," their overthrow of virtue and godliness, causing moral "decay" of the commonweal, elicits the communal scourges of God's wrath instead of his blessings.[12] In Cranmer's sermon, both the social prevalence of sinful conduct and the authorities' ill-judged sufferance of it are at work in bringing about the human vice and divine scourge of political sedition. Tudor public theology everywhere concurs with the Israelite and later Christian patristic insight that "the hearts of rulers are disposed [by God] according to their people's desserts."[13]

---

9. *MWL*, 193.

10. It adduces "sin, and under christian profession, unchristian living" as "the general cause of all these commotions."

11. *MWL*, 191.

12. *GH*, 553–4.

13. Gregory I (the Great) *Moralia* 25. 16. 35: *IG*, 202.

For Tudor reforming theologians, the practice of political judgment gives external social expression to the internal human encounter with God's address of command as the condemning law: the measure of righteous action that brings to light moral wrong, shame, and guilt.[14] In the conscience, God's law convicts human beings not only of sins already committed but, prospectively, of sins that will be committed, if they succumb to temptation. This prospective indictment is encapsulated in the admonishing mode of the divine prohibition: "Thou shalt not . . ." Public judgment, in its double form of adjudication and legislation, attends to both aspects of the command, entailing retrospective and prospective opprobrium for actual misdeeds and for their future repetition.

In the Tudor courts, as in courts today, judgment is a reaction to past wrongdoing, determining who has committed what offense, the degree of culpability, the appropriate punishment to be imposed, and the compensation to be required. Lawyers were then, as now, frequently involved in practices of establishing legal obligation, such as preparing contracts, personal wills and property deeds, for these, too, anticipate and seek to prevent the nonfulfillment of duties inhering in different kinds of social relationships. The anticipatory element of public justice was, and remains, greatest in work of legislation, which, although a response to past misdeeds of a particular type, primarily aims at deterring further commission of such misdeeds.

Thus, in Tudor theology and legal practice, the public judgments of rulers and governors, constituting a body of law over time, comprise an essentially negative ordering of the conduct and relations of those ruled by them. The judgments are typically concerned with defining specific deprivations of good, violations of right and of rights, harm and injury to individual and collective subjects, and degrees of culpability. They typically proceed by defining *derelictions of specific duties or obligations* binding on subjects within a jurisdiction, individually or collectively: duties owing to God, to rulers and governors, to one another as belonging to specific social estates or vocational groups and involved in specific contractual-proprietary and other structured social relationships. This restrictive logic, which has remained clearly visible in the English tradition of criminal and tort law, does not typically aim at *positively* defining and ordering various sets of human relationships, arranging and detailing the obligations within them, as in modern administrative law, and still less at bringing about the goods which these relationships embody. Tudor legal theology and practice broadly conformed to the theological view, closer to Augustine than to Thomas, that political judgment does not and should not aspire to bring about godly, righteous, virtuous, and just conduct by its own efficacy, but only to facilitate its growth remotely and

---

14. Illuminating the command as condemnation, the apostle Paul famously observed in his letter to the Roman church: "I had not known sin, but by the law: for I had not known lust, except the law had said, Thou shalt not covet. But sin, taking occasion by the commandment, wrought in me all manner of concupiscence. For without the law sin was dead." (Rom. 7:7-8, KJV, 1611).

externally, upholding and vindicating good conduct by proscribing and punishing those graver violations of God's law that seriously damage the welfare of human beings in society.[15]

The diverse aims of the magistrate's coercive judgment of legal offenses and the preacher's evangelical judgment of sins are thrown into relief in Cranmer's 1549 public sermon. For Cranmer's archiepiscopal exhortations and admonitions, injunctions and reprimands carry evangelical, prophetic, and pastoral authority, being directed not only against the sins of the seditious, poor, and oppressed farmers of the commons but also against the sins of their landed governors, the exploitative nobility and gentry who have deprived them of their livelihood. Above all, his judgments are directed against the sin of "worshipping riches," of "insatiable covetousness of worldly goods," afflicting "both the high and low" of the realm.[16] Their manifest purpose is to be an instrument of the Spirit's action in bringing about the inner repentance, faith, and moral amendment of offenders, whereas the aims of judicial censure and punishment are to pronounce communal and divine condemnation on wrongdoing, and to procure outward submission to the authority of governors and compliance with public policies and laws.

The Theological and Practical Insufficiency of Political Jurisdiction

English Reformation public theology recognizes that political jurisdiction, required by the restraining commands of God's law on human waywardness, does not represent God's law in its fullness but, more narrowly, his condemnation of human wrongdoing and merciful preservation of sinful society against intolerable assaults on common human goods. Even in respect of wrongdoing, as Cranmer's sermon shows, political judgments are under-determined by God's law as compared with prophetic, evangelical, and pastoral judgments. Nor does coercive jurisdiction represent the inner consensual agency of reconciled community, but only the external concurrence of wills in their subjection to a somewhat alien law. To fulfill their divinely ordained

---

15. Augustine in an influential passage in *De libero arbitrio* approves Evodius's defense of human law for not condemning and punishing all the vices and evildoing which divine providence condemns and punishes, for the reason that human law "deals with acts it must punish in order to keep peace among ignorant men, in so far as deeds can be governed by man" *IG*, 114. Aligning himself with this argument, Thomas Aquinas in *ST* I.2ae.96.2 says that, as human law is framed for "a great number of people, of which the majority are not perfect in virtue . . . it does not forbid all the vices from which the virtuous abstain, but only those grave ones from which the majority of men can abstain, and chiefly those vices that are harmful to others and must be prohibited for society to be maintained." (my translation). Thomas, however, affirms the aim and capacity of just human law to bring about human virtue, whereas Augustine affirms this aim, but does not grant the capacity of human law to fulfill it without the assistance of divine grace.

16. *MWL*, 192.

purpose, then, the practices of political judgment must presuppose a more extensive revelation of God's law than they, themselves, communicate.

They presuppose, first, the revelation of God's law in the intelligible structures of creaturely reality, the created order of human goods—physical, intellectual, and spiritual—and the relations entailed of human beings to God, to themselves, to one another, and to the nonhuman creation. They presuppose in all created human goods and relations a unity of love, right, and law: the free obedience by which human beings partake of these goods to satisfy their deepest needs and desires, and their irreducibly social character, involving an interpersonal communion of desire and obedience. Next, they presuppose revelation of the disjunction of love and law, desire and obedience, characterizing human moral failure and, with this, the diminution of common human freedom and ascendancy of personal isolation, the self-serving and ephemeral nature of the benefits sought in disordered relationships, and the injuries inflicted by the stronger on the weaker in their disordered pursuit. Finally, they presuppose God's ultimate revelation of the unity of love and law in Christ's obedient sacrifice on the Cross that fulfilled life-giving justice. They presuppose the community of repentant and lively faith in Christ in which the Spirit liberates sinners from blindness and disobedience, from the law's oppressive demands and condemnation, and imparts hope of a communion of persons in knowledge, love, and freedom. They presuppose the proleptic spiritual possession within this fellowship of the eternal Good, the Triune God, and creaturely goods in dependence on Him, which is the complete communication of divine and human right.

Thus, Tudor public theology understands juridical practices as dependent on, and ordered to, the practices of created and renewed community but also, as somewhat alien, even antagonistic, to them. For the goods, relationships, and practices of created and renewed human community interpenetrate, manifesting the unity of God's active word. The goods inhering in created human relationships and practices are received, attained, and sustained among human beings by the Spirit of the resurrected and ascended Son, and human enjoyment of them is a prelude and a pledge of the eschatological perfecting of the community of goods in God, the Good Himself. By contrast, the goods inhering in the relationships and practices of coercive jurisdiction, established by God's judgment on sinful disorder, relate to those of created and renewed human community in a more disruptive manner, entailing a degree of disunity, opposition, and contradiction.

The interpenetration of the goods, relationships, and practices of created and renewed human community, along with their disjunctive relationship to the political order, is conveyed, albeit unthematically, in three special Tudor liturgical and homiletic contexts: namely, those of "Rogation Days," the solemnizing of matrimony and a homily on matrimony. The homily for Rogation Days (possibly from Archbishop Matthew Parker),[17] "That All Good Things Cometh from God,"

---

17. The liturgical focus of the three Rogation Days, according to the 1559 royal Injunctions, was to praise and thank God for bestowing the fruits of the earth and to

expounds the cooperative action of the Father, Son, and Holy Spirit in giving, and in humanity's receiving and enjoying, God's abundant material and spiritual gifts in creation and salvation.[18] It teaches that the Father in his mercy imparts to created and fallen human creatures, by the mediation of Jesus Christ, the undeserved goods of nature and "fortune" (providence), enabling them, through the Spirit's inner working, to wait on these goods patiently and to use and enjoy them justly, for the benefit of their neighbors and themselves, in a perpetual litany of praise and thanksgiving to their Giver.[19] Continually receiving faith in Christ's reconciliation to God of themselves, their neighbors, and the whole creation, God's servants throughout their enjoyment and use of temporal goods are being conformed to Christ, "the clear image" of the Father.[20]

Completing the homily, the (anonymous) "Exhortation" to be delivered during the customary Rogation "perambulations" for overseeing the ancient "bounds and limits" of townships, does not merely urge townsmen to respect and "peaceably" preserve the inherited "liberties, franchises, bounds and limits of [their] town and country."[21] Beyond that, it admonishes them not to endanger their "heavenly inheritance" which Christ's "bloodshedding" has "bought" for each and all, by striving for their "rights and duties with the breach of love and charity . . . or the hurt of godly peace and quiet."[22] It includes "contentious suing" in defense of their "commodities and liberties" among the abuses for which litigators deserve to be deprived of them by "God's wrath," chiding with St. Paul: "Why rather suffer ye not wrong?,[23] and insists on the unity of God's commands of equity, righteousness, charity, and mercy in neighborly dealings.[24]

The adjacent homily "Of the State of Matrimony" pastorally expands the catechetical elements of the marriage service. Closely following the Latin tradition, the service opens by presenting "holy matrimony" as "instituted by God in the time of man's innocency, signifying unto us the mystical union that is betwixt Christ and his Church";[25] immediately connecting this institution of prelapsarian community to the spiritual communion of Christ and his faithful members, as an antecedent "sign." Accordingly, all three of the subsequently stated "causes" (purposes, goods) for which God ordained matrimony extend to the life of the church, in the ascending order of physical, moral, and spiritual: namely, "the procreation of children to be brought up in the fear and nurture of the Lord, and praise of God"; "a remedy against sin . . . that such persons as have not the gift of

supplicate him for their "increase and abundance."
18. *GH*, 471–2; Jas 1:17.
19. *GH*, 480–2.
20. *GH*, 485–6; Heb.1:3.
21. *GH*, 494–5.
22. *GH*, 495.
23. Ibid.; 1 Cor. 6:7 (Great Bible).
24. *GH*, 498–9.
25. *BCP*, 290.

continence might . . . keep themselves undefiled members of Christ's body"; and "the mutual society, help, and comfort that the one ought to have of the other."[26] A notable contribution of the homily is its diagnosis of the source of dissension destructive of the loving fellowship between spouses and its prescription of an efficacious preventive practice. The diagnosed source is the conceit of "self-love" in the spouses and their "stubborn will" to rule another, and never to "give over their right, as they esteem it," although their "right" is frequently "the wrong part."[27] The preventive practice is to pray continually for the Holy Spirit "so to rule their hearts and to knit their minds together"[28] that marital "concord, charity and sweet amity" does not give way to provocation, hatred, and conflict.[29] Only by God's continual forgiveness and assistance obtained through prayer do the spouses receive the blessings and fulfill the duties of marriage, "so to continue therein to a better life to come."[30]

Both homilies convey that juridical attitudes, relationships, and public practices are invariably disruptive of those of created and renewed human community by virtue of their contamination with the human evils that they seek to remedy, springing from the pride and covetousness of self-love. In that coercive jurisdiction necessarily entails relationships and practices of domination, condemnation, and punishment and necessarily establishes and protects morally ambiguous proprietary relationships and practices, it cannot be a *direct sign* of God's reconciling and renewing purposes, for these relations and practices will pass away with the *saeculum* at God's final judgment of demonic and human evil, and the universal revelation of Christ's rule.

To the greater part of English reformers, the church's faithful proclamation of reconciled community reveals the judgments of public law to be a shadowy mimesis of reconciling action in unreconciled community. Their displays of rationality and justice are ambiguous, determined as much by perennial moral limitations as by circumstantial factors, and infected with the disunity that they seek to overcome. Legislation and adjudication cannot achieve entire consistency over time because they are vulnerable to temporal contingencies, responding to shifting patterns of wrongdoing in society and shifting views about what types of wrongdoing warrant public censure. Moreover, the punishments and satisfactions assigned in public judgment are incapable of bringing about the reconciliation of formerly antagonistic wills which comes only through true contrition and forgiveness. No matter how wise, discerning, and compassionate political judgments may be, they cannot communicate the judgment of Christ's suffering and triumphant love that justifies and regenerates the repentant sinner and founds a community of forgiveness. They are no more than a remote instrument of the Spirit's saving

26. *BCP*, 290–1.
27. *GH*, 501–2.
28. *GH*, 501.
29. *GH*, 502–3.
30. *GH*, 514–15.

work, achieving peace as external order, the visible rectification of wrongdoing, and the outward reconciliation of antagonistic wills. Nevertheless, the reformers are persuaded that this external harmonization of human wills may create a social and psychological space for the Spirit's work of true reconciliation.

Thus, the mainstream of Tudor public theology portrays any tendency to legal perfectionism as encroaching primarily upon the renewed freedom of repentance and faith made available to sinful humanity through the church's ministry of gospel proclamation. An excessive and misdirected public legal pedagogy, whether in civil or ecclesiastical polity, assaults the freedom of the divine Spirit of Christ to reveal to repentant believers the fuller meaning and form of the natural obligations of love within the reconciled human community inaugurated by God's atoning and vindicating judgment of humankind. Accordingly, Elizabethan bishops resisted the aspiration of Puritan dissenters for corporate sanctification through legalistic and juridical ecclesiastical practices.

Political Authority and the Moral Priority of Obedience

The interdependence of political judgment and the church's proclamation of God's judgment was a dominant theological concern of the English reformers, acutely focused in the theological problematic of political obedience to the ruler's judgments: its grounds and limitations. For the crisis of ecclesiastical authority permeating the English Reformation was also a crisis of political authority and political obedience.

Generally, Tudor monarchs and their bishops were not theologically content with submission and conformity to public authority from motives of prudential social calculation, servile fear of temporal punishment, or spiritual terror of human and divine censure. True Christian obedience to earthly rulers, their judgments and laws "is not only for wrath, but also for conscience sake";[31] it is the well-doing of servants "for the sake of the Lord" of salvation,[32] the work of the Holy Spirit conforming Christ's faithful people to his royal law of love for fellow neighbors in the commonwealth and for God's appointed ruler. While often affirming the positive part in "civility" played by natural motivations of affection for land and people, reverence and adulation of regality, and inclinations to justice and peace, the English reformers advocate Christian civility, in which natural affections and inclinations are transformed by "faith working though love."[33]

It is because the Spirit trains the faithful in obedience to the reign of their risen Savior through the evangelical practices of the worshipping church that political jurisdiction extends over the church's polity, to establish and maintain the

---

31. Rom. 13:5, Great Bible.
32. 1 Pet. 2:13,15, Great Bible.
33. An influential statement of this transformation is in Thomas Starkey, *Exhortation to the People Instructing Them to Unity and Obedience* (London, 1536), 39a–40b.

corporate practices of obedience essential to the supervening of Christ's coming kingdom on the earthly commonweal. Rulers establish and maintain the church's evangelical practices by providing for and overseeing the building of churches, the training and appointment of clergy, and a territorial system of ecclesiastical jurisdiction. This continuing jurisdictional oversight is regularly affirmed in the Tudor church's petitionary prayer:[34]

> We beseech thee also to save and defend all Christian kings, princes, and governors, and specially thy servant Elizabeth our queen, that under her we may be godly and quietly governed: And grant unto her whole Council, and to all that be put in authority under her, that they may truly and indifferently minister justice, to the punishment of wickedness and vice, and to the maintenance of God's true religion and virtue.

For the ministration of justice to maintain the church's corporate practices, the sovereign ruler and subordinate governors must have effective coercive authority to suppress and correct offenses against their integrity. Thus, Queen Elizabeth restored in law the monarch's prerogative,[35] first enacted under Henry VIII[36]:

> to visit, reform, redress, order, correct, and amend all such errors, heresies, schisms, abuses, offences, contempts and enormities whatsoever, which by any manner [of] spiritual or ecclesiastical power, authority or jurisdiction can or may lawfully be reformed [etc.] ... to the pleasure of Almighty God, the increase of virtue and the conservation of the peace and unity of this realm.

The royal prerogative can fulfill its purpose only if the judgments of the monarch and subordinate judges are consistently informed by theological learning and practical wisdom in accordance with the Scriptures. Accordingly, Tudor law continued to vest judicial authority under the monarch in competent bishops and senior clergy, respecting cases of "the law divine" and "spiritual learning," as the Act of Appeals testifies. However, in both Tudor law and governmental practice, the jurisdictional authority of the senior clerical estate over the church was more limited than the Act's preamble would suggest. Administrative, legislative, and judicial determination of the church's practices (including the definition of doctrine) regularly issued from the monarch alone, or the monarch and Council, or the monarch-in-Parliament, at the expense of the senior clerics acting together in episcopal synods and provincial convocations. Although bishops sat on the

---

34. *BCP*, 254.
35. Act of Supremacy, 1559: 1 Elizabeth I, *c.* 1 (Section 8); *TC*, 374.
36. Act of Supremacy, 1534: 26 Henry VIII, *c.* 1; *TC*, 365.

monarch's Council[37] and in the parliamentary House of Lords,[38] their corporate governing authority lost ground over the course of Tudor church reform.

Behind the church's corporate loss of governing authority was its corporate loss of apostolic, ministerial authority, owing to the deep and bitter divisions among the learned, able, and powerful clergy over major soteriological and ecclesiological issues. Throughout Tudor church reform, intemperate clerical battles in the public theological and political arena inhibited an effective corporate reforming response from the higher clergy to diverse strata and factions of discontent, enhancing their vulnerability to the imposition of reforming measures from outside their ranks. While continuing parliamentary acknowledgment of the monarch's supreme jurisdiction in church affairs made possible the royal usurpation of corporate clerical judgment, constant quarreling and animosity within the clerical hierarchy gave occasion and justification for it, exposing the church to sweeping, intrusive, sometimes arbitrary and ill-judged, policies and judicial decisions that tended to impede rather than facilitate conciliatory clerical deliberations. Just as clerical conflict had abetted Henry VIII's revolutionary assumption of *imperium* over church ministries and property and his demoralizing policy vacillations over church doctrine and practice, likewise it abetted the iconoclastic excesses orchestrated by Edward VI's Council, and Elizabeth's high-handed suppression of preaching and inflexible opposition to modest Puritan-leaning innovations.

The persisting, if mutating, divisions within the church, even among reform-minded clergy and laity, reinforced the enduring conviction of episcopal reformers that open controversy over God's saving and commanding word is invariably a destructive manifestation of personal and communal sin, expressing contempt of peaceful social coexistence and the common spiritual welfare. Rulers are ordained by God not only to judge, punish, and correct violations of his law but also to quell and to prevent unruly and divisive disputes over his truth and law. The prolegomena of Tudor ecclesiastical statutes set forth the definitive settling and prevention of socially disruptive controversy as a principal justification for the monarch-in-Parliament's legislation of the church's doctrine and order of

---

37. As the Council members were chosen entirely at the monarch's discretion from the nobility, clergy, and gentry, the number of senior clergy fluctuated greatly and diminished under Elizabeth. Indeed, the number of councillors in total was reduced by over half during Henry VIII's reign, to produce the "Privy Council" with nineteen members. (Today, the most important standing committees of the Privy Council are the Cabinet composed of the Prime Minister and twenty-one senior government ministers and the Judicial Committee of senior judges that, among other legal and constitutional business, hears ecclesiastical appeals.)

38. With the removal of abbots from the House of Lords at the dissolution of the monasteries, the "spiritual peers," reduced by half to twenty-six bishops, lost their majority and were increasingly outnumbered by "temporal peers."

worship.[39] For the church's outward peace and unity of confession and practice, supporting the Spirit's unification of believers in faith, repentance, and love, is the bedrock of society's spiritual and moral unity in all domains of thought and practice, temporal as well as spiritual. God is displeased at every infringement of a "godly" order of social peace and unity, but especially at infringement of the church's "godly" order. Thus, Tudor theological jurisprudence from the 1530s onward displayed three complementary hallmarks: the coextension of the ruler's divine mandate of maintaining social peace and unity with the totality of his domestic jurisdictional powers (including his prerogative powers of appointing to the higher governing offices); the moral elevation of "concord, agreement and unity" as a primary work of charity in ecclesial and civil community;[40] and, correspondingly, the condemnation of every human crime, beyond its specific offense, as a violation of God's ordained order of communal peace and unity.

Precisely because the ruler's judgments in terminating controversies often cannot give equal satisfaction to the disputing parties, Tudor homilists exhorted faithful subjects to accept and obey all judgments of their governors "not repugnant" or "contrary" to God's "plain word written,"[41] no matter how otherwise unjust and deleterious they may appear. Reforming bishops regularly condemned public verbal dissent and overtly disobedient acts as "seditious," situating them on the slippery slope to rebellious or insurrectionary resistance to the monarch or to inferior governors, involving repudiation of their political authority, and worse, the threat or intention of violently harming, restraining, removing, or otherwise coercing them.[42] From the 1530s, English reformers uniformly adopted the position that political disobedience was seldom, if ever, justified by the Scriptural provisor that the faithful "must obey God rather than man."[43] Arguing this position often engaged, implicitly if not explicitly, the *adiaphoristic* argument that God's truths and laws necessary to salvation are *plainly and incontrovertibly* laid down in the Scriptures, whereas communal beliefs and practices not necessary to salvation (*adiaphora*) are arrived at by means of *uncertain, controvertible interpretation* of the Scriptures. As magisterial judgments, the argument ran, are occasioned by controversy or conflict (actual or threatened) over the congruence of certain beliefs and practices with God's revealed judgments, they cannot themselves be judged to contravene God's plain truth and laws necessary to salvation. Rather,

---

39. For example, Act abolishing Diversity in Opinions (Act of the Six Articles 1539: 31 Henry VIII, *c.* 14) and Act for the Uniformity of Service and Administration of the Sacraments (First Act of Uniformity 1549: 2 & 3 Edward VI, *c.* 1). *TC*, 399, 402–3.

40. Act abolishing Diversity in Opinions, *TC*, 399; also, Starkey, *Exhortation to the People*, especially 8a–14b.

41. Relevant are Articles V (VI), XXI (XX), XXIX (XXVIII), XXXIII (XXXIV).

42. In *English Evangelicals and Tudor Obedience* 1527–70 (Boston: Brill, 2013), Ryan Reeves argues that this stance on political disobedience dominated evangelical theology throughout the Tudor reigns.

43. Acts 5:29.

magisterial judgments are divinely ordained to give public interpretations and applications of God's truth and laws for which can be demonstrated only some degree of congruity with God's revealed judgments, or merely the absence of incongruity ("repugnance").[44]

This argument was logically implicit in the pervasive idea that the earthly church does not have a single uniform "common order" of belief and practice determined solely by God's truth and law revealed in the Scriptures, but multiple, diverse, and variable "common orders" determined by multiple political authorities in accordance with diverse, shifting historical exigencies, all under the universal requirement not to contravene God's "written word" (Article XXXIV). Although relatively uncontroversial in asserting the inevitable variability in territorial church orders, this notion was, nevertheless, a *petitio principii*, begging the question in the context of Tudor church battles. For many Catholic and some Reformed dissenters from the national church's common order were convinced that certain of its features did contravene beliefs and practices plainly given in Scripture as necessary to salvation and, consequently, that some form of disobedience to the common order was morally imperative. Against these dissenters, key reformers argued that the obedience of subjects to their sovereign lay rulers in all uncertain matters of Christian belief and practice was the *foremost practice* plainly commanded by God in the Scriptures as necessary to salvation, and moreover, that violent rebellion of subjects against their rulers was never justified, even by their rulers' incontrovertible contravention of God's law. The faithful response of subjects was to repent of those common sins deserving of God's communal punishment, to beseech God to convert the heart of the ruler from lawlessness to righteousness and to accept meekly the public punishment for any disobedience to human ordinance required by God's ordinance.

God's Appointment and Equipment of the Ruler

In making these arguments, Tudor reforming authorities appealed regularly to the portrayal in the Old Testament of the mediation of God's rule over Israel by rulers uniquely chosen and equipped by him. They drew chiefly on the books of Deuteronomy, Samuel, and kings, focusing attention on Moses' giving of God's law and the reigns of monarchs in the united and divided Israelite kingdoms prior to the Babylonian exile.[45] Their appeal to Israel's political history, to some extent,

---

44. This argument is most precisely and fully developed in Starkey's *Exhortation*, 1a–35b. For commentary, Daniel Eppley, *Defending Royal Supremacy and Discerning God's Will in Tudor England* (London: Routledge, 2007), 40–60.

45. Scholars today generally attribute the final compilation of the historical books of Joshua, Judges, 1 and 2 Samuel, and 1 and 2 Kings to an author or authors whose theological interpretation of Israelite history relates to the law code and accompanying speeches in the book of Deuteronomy, giving a degree of thematic consistency to the six books.

complemented their understanding of political authority informed by the Epistles and Gospels, but also introduced tensions arising from the centrality of political judgment and law to God's salvation of Israel and the corresponding elevation of kings as "God's anointed." Unsurprisingly, their appeal was somewhat selective and not always reflective of the internal theological dynamics of Israel's tradition but, rather, of a Christian history of interpretation of it, especially interpretation supporting royal imperial against papal imperial jurisdiction. We should not overlook the considerable thematic continuity of the Tudor appeal with western Frankish and eastern Frankish (Saxon) imperial theology from the sixth to the eleventh centuries. Although the English public appeal, like the Frankish, was made not only in theological prose but in the iconography of art, poetry, and other literary and cultural forms—the foci of much contemporary academic interest[46]— our concern is primarily with theological prose.

To begin with, in Tudor as in Frankish governmental circles, not only theologians and royal publicists identified their sovereigns with Israel's kings and their realms with God's elect people but the monarchs themselves made these identifications. Greatly enhancing the personal identification of Frankish and English monarchs with their elect Israelite predecessors were the biblical psalms and proverbs attributed to David and Solomon, which allowed Christian monarchs to appropriate to themselves in a privileged way both the interior and the public, the individual and the representative, relations of the Israelite ruler to God, to himself, and to his realm. These relations were given expression in the intimate and liturgical psalmic poetry of individual and communal faith, contrition, lament, petition, thanksgiving, praise, and exultation; and in the proverbial conveyance of parental wisdom in its theological, moral, psychological, and prudential compass. Although inevitably employed in flattery and propaganda, to feed royal narcissism and justify the royal supremacy, these public identifications were as often sincere, creditable, and effective attempts to educate the theological and moral self-understanding and conduct of monarchs and their office holders.

Central to the Tudor as to the Frankish conception of the king's supreme authority was the designation of "God's anointed," carrying all, or almost all, of the connotations given to the term by the Israelite (Deuteronomic) historians: connotations of God's continuous authorization, determination, equipment and defense of the king's personal rule, mediating God's own rule, and of the sacredness of the king's person by virtue of his divine elevation into an "office" and a "place" of mediation above his subjects, individually and corporately. One connotation

---

46. For example, John N. King, *English Reformation Literature: The Tudor Origins of the Protestant Tradition* (Princeton: Princeton University Press, 1982) and *Tudor Royal Iconography: Literature and Art in an Age of Religious Crisis* (Princeton: Princeton University Press, 1989); Kevin Sharpe, *Selling the Tudor Monarchy: Authority and Image in Sixteenth-Century England* (New Haven and London: Yale University Press, 2009); Roy Strong, *The Cult of Elizabeth: Elizabethan Portraiture and Pagentry* (London: Thames and Hudson, 1977).

that this designation did not carry for Cranmerian-minded reformers, unlike their Frankish predecessors, was the conferral of God's anointing through sacramental anointing. Rather, Cranmerian reformers regarded the priestly anointing as a public ceremonial showing forth of the monarch as God's anointed, in respect of his divinely ordained power, his personal election by God, and endowment with "the gifts of his Spirit" for "better ruling" his people.[47]

The monarch's mediation of God's rule was crucial to Israel's history of salvation, in which God's covenantal sanctification of his chosen people enabled them, individually and corporately, to live in obedience to the statutes delivered directly by Moses, his oracular mouthpiece. Israel's divinely given communal law was its unique and unrepeatable way of communal salvation, and Israel's kings were interpreters, implementers, and enforcers of the law, and, as well, military protectors of Israel and conquerors of her enemies. Therefore, the historic identification of Christian monarchs with the anointed Davidic kings sits ill with the reformers' more restrictive presentation of human coercive jurisdiction as an incomplete and insufficient mediation of God's condemning and preserving word of judgment. It sits ill with the tension in Tudor theology between God's word of condemnation and of salvation, Christ's rule in the commonwealth and in the church, the worldly order of peace and the spiritual communion of Christ's faithful.

On occasion, the Tudor identification of Christian with Israelite monarchs gave rise to the disturbing soteriological distortion in which the English monarch appears as the pivotal earthly embodiment of God's seamless, homogenous salvation in the histories of Israel and Christ. The iconographic apogee of this distortion may be Hans Holbein's title page for Miles Coverdale's 1535 English Bible. Crowned with the Hebrew Tetragrammaton representing the Trinity, the title page has two vertical "compartmentalized borders" containing corresponding law and gospel motifs, displaying in descending order: Moses atop Mount Sinai receiving the Tables of the Law across from Christ sending out his disciples to preach; Esdras expounding the law to the returned exiles in Jerusalem across from Peter and his fellow disciples proclaiming the good news of Christ's resurrection on the Day of Pentecost; King David with poised sword, playing on his harp (presumably composing psalms) across from the apostle, Paul, wielding the sword of God's word; and between the two is King Henry VIII enthroned with imperial regalia, handing down the vernacular Bible to kneeling bishops on his right with his left hand—an iconographic mannerism of Christ—flanked by kneeling lay magnates on his left.[48]

---

47. A document purported to be "The Archbishop's Speech at the Coronation of Edward VI" (February 20, 1547) is chiefly devoted to making this point. Despite uncertainty about its historical authenticity, it may be safely assumed to convey the view of Cranmer and evangelical associates. *MWL*, 126–7.

48. For commentary, Pamela Tudor-Craig, "Henry VIII and King David," in *Early Tudor England: Proceedings of the 1987 Harlaxton Symposium*, ed. Daniel Williams (Woodbridge: Boydell Press, 1989), 192–3.

This iconography is profitably understood against the backdrop of the intertwining in Frankish royal imperial theology of Israelite portraits of sacral kingship (whether Moses, David, Solomon, or the mysterious Melchizedek) with the Byzantine model of imperial rule, in which the emperor not merely foreshadows the heavenly rule of the Incarnate and glorified Christ but is Christ's living terrestrial image, imitation, and vicegerent. An outstanding Anglo-Norman elaboration of the Christocentric imperial model, intended to establish the superior jurisdiction of the royal over the priestly office (*c*. 1100),[49] argued that the king's anointing confers the sacramental image of Christ's divine kingship—of Christ creating, governing, and saving humanity in unity and equality with the Father, while the priest's anointing confers the sacramental image of Christ's human priesthood—of Christ redeeming humanity by his sacrificial offering from below to the Father. The ontological and soteriological priority of the royal to the priestly office of Christ is foreshadowed in the Israelite prototype of earthly monarchical rule over the entire body of favored people, ensuring the unity, outward order, and spiritual and corporeal welfare of the collective "temple of God."[50] This argument, which appears to have enjoyed some continuing influence in English ecclesiastical circles up to the Reformation,[51] gives theological intelligibility to the iconographic portrayal of Henry VIII's imperial rule as embodying the unity of law and gospel. As God's anointed, David's successor, and Christ's earthly vicar, King Henry is shown to mediate all God's judgments in human law, including God's saving judgment in Christ revealed in the Scriptures which he authoritatively delivers to his reverent and submissive episcopal and lay governors. Fortunately, the title page of the Great Bible, however adulating of royal authority, falls short of this extensive soteriological depiction.

Less alarming was the evangelical reformers' identification of King Edward in his minority with the youthful King Josiah, focused more narrowly on Josiah's campaign to cleanse Israel's piety and worship of superstition and idolatry. This use of Josiah as exemplar may indicate the influence of Zürich, particularly that of Heinrich Bullinger's celebrated sermon collection, *Sermonum Decades*, which achieved "quasi-canonical status" in the two English universities after Elizabeth's accession and was prescribed reading for the less well-educated clergy under

---

49. Among a collection of tracts attributed to the "Norman Anonymous," a clerk with apparent connections to York and Rouen, available in *Monumenta Germaniae Historica:Libelli de Lite imperatorum et Pontificum saeculis 11. Et 12 conscripti*, ed. Heinrich Böhmer, 3:642–78.

50. The relevant excerpt from Tract 24a, "The Consecration of Bishops and Kings," is translated in *IG*, 250–9.

51. Christological arguments of this structure turn up in the French historian, Hugh of Fleury's tract written for and dedicated to Henry I of England (*c*. 1100) and in John Wyclif's *Tractatus de officio regis* (1378); and more astonishing, the only extant manuscript today of the Norman Anonymous tracts was preserved in the library of Archbishop Matthew Parker.

Archbishop Whitgift.[52] In his seventh sermon, "Of the office of the magistrate" (the second on the Decalogue's sixth commandment), Bullinger argued that Israel's faithful kings are exemplars for Christian magistrates in carrying out the two divinely ordained tasks of "ordering" and "maintaining" true religion and of preserving "honesty, justice and common peace" in society.[53] In the first task Israel's faithful kings are exemplars because "they were Christians verily and indeed."[54] Anointed with the Spirit of God and of Christ,[55] they had faith in Christ and were "made partakers of Christ" in their sacraments; for "Paul affirmeth flatly, that we have the very same Spirit of faith"[56] and "doth moreover communicate our sacraments with them."[57] In both tasks they are exemplars because they knew and conformed to God's enduring truths and ordinances delivered to Moses, establishing the practices, parameters, and authority of the magisterial office. Two key examples are: that the worthy ruler is "the living law" if he "in his heart agree with the law, in his breast do write the law, and in his words and deeds express the law";[58] and that, in giving judgment, the ruler must not be partial, fearing man, because the judgment he gives is God's judgment.[59]

Bullinger shared with Zwingli and Pelican, his predecessors at Zürich, and with Bucer and Calvin at Strasbourg and Geneva, the concept of magistrates as occupying the elevated office of judging in God's place, their judgments being God's judgments, and the magistrates, in their office, "gods."[60] Concurring in this

---

52. W. J. Torrance Kirby, "The Civil Magistrate and the '*Cura Religionis*': Heinrich Bullinger's Prophetical Office and the English Reformation," *Animus* 9 (2004): 28. An English translation of *Sermonum Decades* (Zürich: Froschoverus, 1552) was issued in 1577. For Zürich influence, Kirby, *The Zürich Connection and Tudor Political Theology*; Reeves, *English Evangelicals and Tudor Obedience*.

53. *Fiftie godlie and learned sermons, divided into five decades* (London, 1577), repr. *The Decades of Heinrich Bullinger*, ed. T. Harding (Parker Society; Cambridge: Cambridge University Press, 1849), 2:323.

54. *Decades*, 2:326–7.

55. *Decades*, 2: 326, citing 1 Jn 2:20, 27.

56. *Decades*, 2:327, citing 2 Cor. 4:13 as referring to (David's) Psalm 116:10.

57. *Decades*, 2:327, citing 1 Cor. 10:2-4. Here, Bullinger implicitly asserts the covenantal unity of Israel and Christ's church, prominent in Swiss reforming theology.

58. *Decades*, 2:324–6, 339.

59. Second Decade, Sermon 6: *Decades*, 2:313–14, citing Exod. 22:28: "You shall not revile the gods, nor curse a ruler of thy people" and Deut. 1:17: "You shall not respect persons in judgement . . .; you shall not be afraid of the face of man; for the judgement is God's." (KJV); also 2 Chron. 19:6-7.

60. Interpreting Psalm 82 against the backdrop of Exod. 22:28, Pelican and Zwingli, followed by Bullinger, Bucer, and Calvin, took as referring to civil rulers the term "Elohim" in the opening verse of Psalm 82: v. 1. "God [Elohim] standeth in the congregation of the mighty: he judgeth among the Gods [Elohim]. v. 2. How long will ye judge unjustly and accept the persons of the wicked?"

portrayal, Tudor reforming theologians tended to underplay the unique status of Moses as prophetic mediator of God's law, above Israel's monarchs: Moses is simply the first among God's chosen rulers. This elevation of rulers, echoing the church's longer tradition of anointed kingship, reinforced the moral primacy of the subject's duty of obedience to the magistrate *as to God*. The 1571 "Homily Against Disobedience" elaborated a prominent view among English evangelical reformers that the human ruler's command of obedience mediates the creator's command of obedience to his rational creatures, so that the subject's duty of earthly political obedience is one with created humankind's generic duty of obedience to God.[61]

This view gives the political structure of command and conformity a purchase on the created social and moral order of human life, reflecting and supporting the cosmological vision of the hierarchy of human rule within the ontological order of creatures under God's sovereign rule—a salient theme of Israel's royal psalms.[62] It invests with permanence the English nation's highly stratified, social order of property and political power, still largely agrarian and feudal, meticulously laid out in Thomas Smith's *The Commonwealth of England* (*De republica Anglorum*, 1583).[63] Smith's descending order of social ranks is also an order of political ranks: from the greater and lesser landed nobility to the urban citizens and burgesses to the prosperous countryside yeomen, each with its level of administrative and juridical responsibility (in the Lords and Commons of Parliament, in the towns and the shires), from which a swath of population below them (poor farmers, day laborers, artisans, etc.) are excluded, left dependent on superiors to protect their interests.[64]

Nevertheless, the temptation of Tudor reformers to dignify sociopolitical hierarchy as an aspect of prelapsarian society, conspicuous in the 1547 homily on "Good Order and Obedience to Rulers,"[65] was far outweighed by their identification of political jurisdiction with the sinful disorder of postlapsarian society. Their concentration on the history of Israel's political rule from Moses to the Babylonian exile rather than on the primeval and patriarchal history of Genesis shows their disinclination to develop an Adamic-patriarchal political theology—especially unsuitable for the reigns of the minor, Edward VI, and the "Virgin Queen." Accordingly, Edwardian and Elizabethan public theology was relatively free from the Lutheran and Reformed extension of the Fifth Commandment ("Honour thy father and thy mother") to cover magisterial authority, blurring the distinction between paternal discipline and public jurisdiction.[66]

---

61. *GH*, 550–1.
62. For example, Psalms 18, 89, 132, 144.
63. The original printed text of *De republica Anglorum* (London, 1589) is available at quod.lib.umich.edu.
64. *De republica Anglorum*, 29–43.
65. *GH*, 105–6.
66. The 1571 "Homily Against Disobedience" lists the different types of divinely ordained obedience in society, but without drawing any analogies among them, not even

Also noteworthy is that Edwardian and Elizabethan homilies on political obedience predominantly present the monarch as God's (rather than Christ's) "vicegerent" and the royal judgments as God's (rather than Christ's) judgments.[67] In line with the Norman Anonymous, Marsilius of Padua, and John Wyclif, the homilists extol Jesus Christ's earthly rejection of "princely dominion" for himself, his apostles, and their "spiritual" successors, his example and teaching of submissive obedience to worldly governors[68] and of meek and patient suffering of the vexations and injuries inflicted by them, all in obedient surrender to his Father's saving will.[69] In this way the tension is sustained between the Incarnate Son's relations of equality with and subordination to the Father, and between God's penultimate work of preserving the fallen creation and his ultimate work of reconciling and renewing it.

It is chiefly on account of the god-like status of rulers that Tudor theologians construed the sin of "resisting" or "opposing" them as the unparalleled social defiance of God's sovereign "majesty." Apparently disregarding the spectrum from simple disobedience to violent opposition, they invested "resistance" per se with eschatological import, mindful of God's ferocious punishment of its various forms in Israel's history.[70] They interpreted Paul's phrase in Rom. 13:2, "οἱ δὲ ἀνθεστηκότεσ ἑαυτοισ κρίμα λήμψονται," as "they that resist shall receive to themselves damnation" (meaning "eternal punishment"), though the Greek "κριμα," like the Latin "damnatio" in the Vulgate, could equally well have been interpreted to mean merely "legal condemnation" or "negative judgement."[71] Throughout the Tudor reigns, the eschatological punishment envisaged for unrepented political resistance was anticipated in the severity of judicial punishments awarded to offenses of resistance, and in the wide scope given to the gravest offense of "treason."[72]

---

between the obedience required of slaves to masters and the obedience required of subjects to rulers. *GH*, 551–3.

67. Exemplifying this are Cranmer's political sermon and those in the official Tudor collections and the preached and published sermons discussed in Stephen Alford, *Kingship and Politics in the Reign of Edward VI* (Cambridge: Cambridge University Press, 2009), 51–6.

68. Cranmer's "Sermon concerning the Time of Rebellion," *MLW*, 192–3; "Concerning Good Order and Obedience," *GH*, 109–10; "Against Disobedience and Wilful Rebellion," *GH*, 568, 581, 585–6.

69. *MWL*, 192–3, 195–6; *GH*, 109, 568.

70. *GH*, 576–7, citing Num. 12:10, 16:46-49, 21:5-6; *GH*, 577–9; *MWL*, 199; citing 2 Samuel 13–18.

71. See H. G. Liddell, Robert Scott, and H. Stuart Jones, *A Greek-English Lexicon*, 9th edn. (Oxford: Clarendon Press, 1951), I:995; P. G. W. Glare, ed., *Oxford Latin Dictionary*, combined edn. (Oxford: Oxford University Press, 1982, repr. 1997), 483; Alexander Souter, *A Glossary of Later Latin to 600 A.D.* (Oxford: Clarendon Press, 1949, repr. 1997), 87.

72. In parliamentary acts, Henry VIII extended the existing statute law of treason to include treason "by words or writing" (preaching or publishing), to provide the legal

Nevertheless, Tudor evangelical reformers were not concerned with the defiance of God's sovereign majesty *in the abstract* when they portrayed human rebelliousness expressed in violent civil uprising as the root of the entire gamut of individual and social-moral disorders, but concerned with the sea of human misery issuing from civil rebellion. The 1571 "Homily Against Disobedience and Wilful Rebellion" meticulously analyzes the escalation over the course of rebellions, of vicious conduct, injury and injustice, wanton waste and destruction of natural resources, social deprivation, and damage to national security;[73] and it presents the escalation of evils committed as a compulsive dynamic of license and lawlessness engendered by the idolatrous, self-aggrandizing spirit of those who cast off the godly moral bonds of deference and respect that should constrain the conveyance of grievances and complaints to social superiors and governors. The pervasive conviction of Tudor reforming theology that God wills the speedy overthrow and punishment of all rebels against "their natural and lawful sovereign" and governors, whatever their "feigned pretence" of reforming social ills and redressing injustice, was grounded not only in historical accounts of rebellions by Scriptural and "profane" writers but in God's entire revelation of his merciful will to sustain the fragile moral and material goods of sinful human societies against the victory of Satanic forces of disorder and dissolution.[74]

The Human Constraints on Political Authority

Our critical exposition thus far has shown that Tudor political theology recognizes two kinds of theoretical limitations on the practice of public judgment: the teleological limitation, confining its purposes to giving social expression to God's judgment of sin and protectively sustaining the divinely bestowed goods of communal human life; and the epistemological limitation, confining its actions to those congruent with God's commands and prohibitions revealed in the Scriptures. We have also indicated the failures of consistency and coherence that weaken the Tudor public presentation and practical application of these two limitations. These failures relate to a third *apparent* weakness: an inadequate theological account of the communal limitations placed on the practice of "sovereign" public judgment

---

safeguards for each new wife and succession, and for his legislated supremacy and powers in the church. Although repealing the Henrician treason legislation, the Edwardian treason act of 1547 and subsequent acts of Edward, Mary and Elizabeth retained treason by "words, writing and printing" to give legal protection to the monarch's supremacy, marriage and succession, public religious settlement, life, and reign. Punishments for treason ranged from forfeiture of substantial property and a term of imprisonment for a first offense to forfeiture of the offender's life and entire estate to the Crown for the offense of "high treason." The treason acts are reproduced in *TC*, 61–80.

73. *GH*, 559, 569–75.
74. *GH*, 570–5.

by mechanisms of political representation and an inherited body of law. Our final expository task, then, is to examine the presentation and operation of these communal restraints in Tudor political thought and practice.

The most obvious restraint on the practice of Tudor monarchs was the legislating of their sovereign powers by the Parliament, in which every social rank of the realm with governing and administrative responsibility was represented. All the consequential legislation of *constitutional reform* in the Tudor period was by king-in-Parliament rather than by royal proclamation. In their prolegomena and elsewhere, various parliamentary Acts of religious reform vigorously assert God's ordination and appointment of the monarch's sovereign and supreme rule over his or her dominions, and simultaneously claim to be "enacted" by "the authority" of the assembled Parliament. In Tudor legal usage, the verb "enact" carries the senses both of "effect" (i.e., bring into being, "make") and of "validate" ("ratify," "confirm," formally "approve"). Consequently, the authority of "king-in-Parliament" constitutes the binding *communal authority* of public statute law on all subjects of the realm.

In enacting statute law, the representative authority of Lords and Commons was one of necessary ratifying or confirming assent, as well as of consultation, but their authority was not necessary for all law in the commonwealth on the following jurisprudential grounds: the monarch's supremacy over the commonwealth entailed the "prerogative" of promulgating authoritative law without commanding a meeting of Parliament; inherited custom, whether local or national, was authoritative law in the realm without statutory ratification of king-in-Parliament; adjudication of statute and customary law in the courts of the realm had its authority, formally, from the monarch's supreme jurisdiction. These grounds must, however, be qualified by the complex interrelations of royal, judicial, and parliamentary powers that were inherited and transformed by the Tudor reigns.

In Tudor jurisprudence, the divine foundation of the monarch's sovereign governance did not exclude definition of the royal "prerogatives" or privileges by common law and statute. Over the course of centuries, royal prerogatives originating in the monarch's feudal overlordship had been legally extended to additional political powers, so that Thomas Smith in 1565 can include within them: the absolute authority to wage war and sue for peace, to command and to punish (even mortally) in the field of battle, to dispense with existing law as required by equity, to appoint to the highest temporal and spiritual "offices or magistracies," to have all judicial "writs, executions, and commandments be done in [his] name," and to determine coinage "by his proclamation only."[75] In addition, the Tudor monarchs with their Councils had the common law prerogative of issuing "proclamations," that is, authoritative legislative orders, covering administrative, economic, social, and religious affairs.[76]

---

75. *De Republica Anglorum*, 58–62; *TC*, 19–20.

76. As Parliament met infrequently, its statutes often left to proclamations "the details and flexibility" of their legislative agenda.

However, these royal proclamations were hedged about by common law and statutory restrictions. Chiefly, although proclamations could create offenses with penalties, they could not create felonies and treasons involving forfeiture of life and property, as could parliamentary acts, nor anywise "touch" common law property rights.[77] Therefore, the monarch's freedom to give law without assent from the Lords and Commons was reduced by unavoidable juridical and fiscal necessities. Moreover, because proclamations were not enforceable in the "ordinary courts" of common law, as were statutes, their enforcement was "haphazard."[78] Finally, neither royal proclamation nor other prerogative action could "abrogate, repeal or suspend" statutes of Parliament, leaving Tudor monarchs with "very limited" means of evading or amending existing statutes. Confined to preventing the enactment of disagreeable legislation either by influencing and managing parliamentary business (routinely through their Councillors in Parliament) or by resorting to the less diplomatic royal veto,[79] Tudor monarchs chose to pursue their legislative agenda primarily by means of parliamentary statutes and proclamations enabled by statutes.

While the High Court of Parliament originated as the most eminent of the medieval royal courts, functioning as a curia of magnates for "dispensing the king's justice in doubtful, novel, or urgent cases," the vast bulk of dispensing justice was carried on in three courts of "common law" created by royal judicial reforms of the late twelfth and thirteenth centuries out of the monarch's entourage of itinerant judges. These were the Court of Common Pleas deciding civil disputes, the king's Bench originally deciding felonies (criminal cases) and cases affecting the king's person, and the Exchequer of Pleas deciding revenue cases.[80] The "common law" administered in these courts—a hybrid of older Saxon-Frankish customary law exposed to medieval civil law, with a Norman feudal core in the law of landed persons or land tenure—developed significantly through the practices and decisions in these royal courts.[81] Decisions gradually became precedents in which rules and principles inhered. Thus, the common law was national customary law, primarily as comprising a growing body of nationwide "forensic and judicial usage and learning,"[82] but also as comprising a procedural and substantive rationalization of the customary redressing of wrongs in the older manorial, shire, and local ("hundred") courts.[83]

---

77. *TC*, 22.
78. *TC*, 22–3.
79. *TC*, 21–2.
80. For the innovative reforms of procedural and substantive law entailed in the establishment of these courts, Berman, *Law and Revolution*, 440–59.
81. By the late fourteenth century all three were in Westminster Hall.
82. Norman Doe, *Fundamental Authority in Late Medieval English Law* (Cambridge: Cambridge University Press, 1990), 22.
83. For the earlier development of Frankish feudal customary law before 1050, Berman, *Law and Revolution*, 295–315.

The efficacy of the evolving law of "writs" and "remedies" administered in the royal courts, especially in Common Pleas, to protect specific liberties, land tenures, and other property "holdings" throughout the feudal hierarchy was enhanced by successive royal charters confirming, interpreting, and extending customary "concessions," "liberties," judicial practices, and principles. These included Henry I's Coronation Charter (1100), King John's Magna Carta (1215), reissued by Henry III in a definitive version (1225), and Edward I's confirmation by statute of the Great Charter as the common law of the realm (1301). The resulting eminence of the common law, reinforced by its purported antiquity, leant weight in English jurisprudence to the doctrine recognized in civilian and canonist jurisprudence, that the monarch rules "under the law" as well as "above the law." Its celebrated statement in the *magna summa* on English law traditionally attributed to Henry de Bracton (died 1268) runs: "The king must not be under man but under God and under the law, because law makes the king. [. . .] For there is no *rex* where will rules rather than *lex*."[84]

In this memorable maxim, "the law" refers ambiguously to the law of the realm and to the law of God (i.e., the "natural" or moral law),[85] an ambiguity typical of medieval English jurisprudence and justified a century earlier by John of Salisbury's reasoning that God's law is "equity" and "justice" and human law is their "interpreter," "in as much as law makes known the will of equity and justice."[86] Given that the cumulative law of the commonweal was, for both writers, an ongoing interpretation of God's law of equity, the king, in exercising the lawful prerogatives of the Crown, was morally and constitutionally bound to inform his judgments with the existing body of customary and statute law, primarily by consulting his learned judicial advisers and council of magnates.[87] However,

---

84. (My translation.) "Ipse autem rex non debet esse sub homine sed sub deo et sub lege, quia lex facit regem. [Attribuat igitur rex legi, quod lex attribuit ei, videlicet dominationem et potestatem.] Non est enim rex ubi dominatur voluntas et non lex." Brackets indicate suspected editorial interpolation into an earlier text. *Tractatus de legibus et consuetudinibus Anglie*, ed. George E. Woodbine (New Haven: Yale University Press, 1922–42); ed. and trans. Samuel E. Thorne (Cambridge, MA: Harvard University, 1968–77), 2:33. The bulk of the work is now thought to have been written and updated from the 1220s to the 1250s, the later additions probably attributable to Bracton, a clerical justice of the "coram rege" (later the king's Bench).

85. Parenthetically, Bracton compares the king as God's vicar to Christ who chose to redeem the human race according to the maxim of justice, by willingly placing himself under the judgment of Roman law.

86. John of Salisbury, *Policraticus*, ed. and trans. Cary J. Nederman (Cambridge: Cambridge University Press, 1990), 30.

87. The moral and constitutional relationship of the monarch's prerogative rule to the common law is summed up in the introduction to *De legibus*: "It will not be absurd to call English laws *leges*, though they are unwritten, since whatever has been rightly decided and approved with the counsel and consent of the magnates and the general agreement of the

the monarch was neither legally nor even morally bound always to observe and uphold existing laws, as his person and estate were above the law,[88] and he had to be free to disregard, amend, or remove laws antipathetic to God's law and the common utility (with parliamentary assent when required).

The English common law tradition, then, acquired authority concurrent with that of the commonwealth, so that even after Parliament had arrived at its representative scope and status as the assenting chambers of Lords and Commons, the statutes of king-in-Parliament continued to be presented as confirming, interpreting, codifying, extending, supplementing, or restoring customs and laws of the realm that were approved by use and observed and defined in past judicial proceedings and decisions, royal proclamations, and parliamentary statutes. Many of the radical Tudor reforming statutes exemplify just this presentation.[89] Nevertheless, over several centuries, the relation of monarch and Parliament to the common law was somewhat nuanced by two developments which gained momentum during the Tudor reforming reigns: namely, the addition of royal courts in Westminster to remedy the deficiencies of the common law courts in giving justice and the expansion of parliamentary enactments in number, scope, and authority.

The first development strengthened the control of the monarch and his councillors over the administration of justice in the realm, with councillors sitting in three of the four additional courts, two of which—the conciliar courts of Star Chamber and Requests—were definitively reestablished under Henry VIII. These courts made available to plaintiffs speedier and more equitable relief than the common law and older feudal courts provided, or relief lying outside their compass. The courts of Chancery and Requests were both "courts of equity," applying principles of "natural justice" and common fairness, and treating cases on their particular merits, while Requests attended to "poor petitioners, seeking relief in small matters."[90] All three courts adopted procedures of the

---

res publica, the authority of the king or prince having first been added thereunto, has the force of law." Thorne, Woodbine, *De Legibus*, 2:19. https//amesfoundation.law.harvard.edu/Bracton/Framed/mframe.htm

88. The maxim "breve non currat contra inpsum [regem]" is quoted, *De legibus*, 2:33.

89. For example, the prologue of the Act for the termination of exactions paid to the see of Rome recalls that "this your Grace's realm, recognizing no superior under God but only your Grace, hath been and is free from subjection to any man's laws but only to such as have been devised, made and ordained within this realm for the wealth of the same, or to such other as by sufferance of your Grace and your progenitors, the people of this your realm have taken at their free liberty by their own consent to be used amongst them, and have bound themselves by long use and custom to the observance of the same." (1534: 25 Henry VIII, *c.* 21) *TC*, 360–1.

90. *TC*, 187. Here, the term "equity" more narrowly refers to the juridical application of principles of natural justice and fairness in cases of injustice not falling within the procedural and formal constraints of the common law system of writs and remedies. The equity courts

civil law allowing for more flexible petition, fuller investigation of cases, and more trustworthy evidence on which to base decisions; but unlike the other two, the Court of Star Chamber, dealing with criminal breaches of the monarch's peace,[91] breaches of royal proclamations, and offenses against law enforcement in every other court,[92] administered the common and statute law throughout. Among their accomplishments, these additional royal courts in Westminster, supplemented by regional conciliar courts,[93] made the monarch's justice available to all subjects of the realm, giving respite from sometimes oppressive manorial and local justice.

The expansion of parliamentary enactments coincided with the expansion of communal representation in the Parliaments beyond the monarch's "Great Council" of secular nobility and senior ecclesiastics to include elected landed gentry: knights from the shires and burgesses from the boroughs. Originally summoned by monarchs in the thirteenth century to give broader social consent to royal taxation and to bring communal grievances before the councillors, "the Commons" became over three centuries a permanent, separate lower chamber of the composite assembly, equal to the upper chamber in its assenting authority and competence. During the Tudor reigns, membership of the Commons increased vastly,[94] the majority of bills and all money grants originated in this chamber, and many "great matters" of state were first debated there. The political scope of parliamentary statute law was extended to include all constitutional aspects, and many substantive aspects, of ecclesiastical reform. Freedom of speech in deliberations and debates was customarily conceded by the Tudor monarchs to

---

adopted different forensic procedures, gave decisions not bound by legal precedent, and awarded remedies other than the "damages" awarded in the common law courts.

91. For example, cases of riotous conduct, assaults on persons extending to libel and slander, and on peaceful possession of land and chattels.

92. For example, contempt of court and corruptions of justice by perjury, false jury verdicts, conspiracy, suborning of witnesses, etc. *TC*, 174.

93. To strengthen royal jurisdiction over the realm, regional councils with military, administrative, and judicial powers were set up in the insecure and turbulent border areas of the Welsh marches and the northern shires, drawing on powerful local feudatories. The continuing threat to the monarch's national jurisdiction posed by the entrenched military and governing authority of these local magnates cum councillors was finally addressed effectively when Cromwell, in Wolsey's footsteps, reconstituted the Council of the North and the Council in the Marches of Wales as formal, permanent conciliar courts, composed of royally appointed administrators and judges, with jurisdiction derived from royal commissions covering the civil and criminal matters decided in the common law and equity courts of Westminster. Both councils significantly contributed to eliminating the semi-independent franchises and jurisdictions of rival regional lords. *TC*, 199–217.

94. Always more numerous than similar institutions in more populous continental countries, membership in the Commons grew under the Tudors from 296 to 462, owing mainly to "the enfranchisement (new or restored) of English boroughs." *TC*, 248.

members of both Houses, although leave to discuss a contentious matter was not always given. Inevitably, the Crown and Council exerted influence on the activity of the Parliaments, mainly through management of their proceedings.[95] However, evidence that management of the Houses did not amount to "dictation or coercion"[96] is that the divisions and alignments of members of the Councillors, Lords, and Commons ran vertically as well as horizontally, and on occasion, all three stood opposed to royal policy.[97]

Through these developments the Crown-in-Parliament was emerging as the supreme law-giving authority, in which the royal head and all subjects of the realm were represented. Even Henry VIII concurred with his judges that "we at no time stand so highly in our estate royal as in the time of Parliament, wherein we as head and you as members are conjoined and knit together into one body politic."[98] There was a broad understanding that the supreme authority of the monarch was intrinsically bound up with the authority of the community of the realm embodied in the customary law of the courts and the enactments of the Parliaments.

A Theological Alternative to the Western Natural Rights Political Tradition

Our exposition of the presentation of political jurisdiction in English Reformation public theology has attempted to show how its employment of the controlling biblical loci, under multiple historical influences, composes a complicated weave of both sound and unsound theological threads. The concluding task is to argue that the sound threads, disentangled from the unsound, vitally contribute to a coherent account of political jurisdiction capable of overcoming the damaging contradictions vitiating the Western tradition of liberal natural rights.

The Purposes and Practices of Coercive Judgment

The controlling conception of English Reformation political theology, that of political rule as the communal discipline of coercive public judgment, keeps in view the multiplicity of active relationships among God, the ruler, the community, and its members, without allowing the eclipse of the divine by the human or vice versa. Its lynchpin is the understanding that binding public judgment for the restraint, punishment, and correction of wrongdoing and vindication of well-doing in

---

95. The avenues of management were "the maintenance of a government front bench" of Councillors, charged with "a specific legislative programme" and responsible for preparing parliamentary business and guiding debate, and employment of the Speaker to control the Commons. *TC*, 294.

96. *TC*, 290.

97. Elton's overview and selected documents show the complexity of intraparliamentary conflicts and alignments throughout the Tudor period. *TC*, 307–26.

98. Ferrer's Case, 1542: Holinshed, III, 824–6 in *TC*, 277.

society is required by the restraint imposed by God's law on human waywardness, and serves his condemnation of antihuman conduct and merciful preservation of human goods against sin's corrosive disorder. The ordering of human life together by practices of public judgment is, therefore, both an obligation of sinful human beings under God's disciplinary law and an intrinsic necessity of human moral and material welfare. In the reformers' view, moral and material welfare are inseparable in both the extrinsic outworking of God's just and merciful dealings with peoples and their rulers and the intrinsic consequences of the judgments and actions of rulers and ruled for their common enjoyment of spiritual and material goods. Focused on objective moral right and the ordering of moral and political judgment and action by the laws of God and the commonweal, Tudor public theology seeks to unify the political agency of ruler and subjects, individually and corporately, within common bonds of obligation and obedience.

Political jurisdiction is never portrayed as serving *purely immanent* human goods, individual or collective, whether self-preservation, property, civil peace, or social freedom. For these are human goods in so far as they serve, however, inadequately, to channel human love toward God, the eternal Good, above all else, and from him toward fellow creatures and every temporal good. Most centrally, civil and ecclesiastical freedom are individual and collective goods in so far as they serve the universal and comprehensive good of evangelical freedom, which is willing obedience to God's commanding love. In theologically mapping the moral terrain of human social and political life, the evangelical reformers dismiss the concept of a freedom apart from obedience that would deflect attention away from the conformity to the revealed Truth and Good at which human agency aims. Their perspective does not allow that political jurisdiction should have as its primary purpose to protect and advance an original, universal, and comprehensive human moral right of freedom, conceived as the agent's proprietary power of self-disposing acts of choice, along with a "natural" right of self-preservation and protection effective against all other agents. The Scriptures witness that human beings are created *in* and *for* a fellowship of obedient knowledge and love with their creator and with one another, the fellowship of marriage and family being a paradigm of created human communion and a symbol of its spiritual renewal in the ecclesial fellowship of faith.

Thus, Tudor public theology affirms the ontological and soteriological priority of an obedient human community of goods under the creator's beneficent rule to the conflictual society of disordered humanity subjected by God to coercive discipline. Moreover, at its best it portrays human moral community as originally and perennially comprising a sharing by persons in material and spiritual goods, contrary to its rationalist reduction to axioms of practical reasoning in the natural rights tradition. To the English reformers, moral knowledge and reasoning are inseparable from the divine and human love that constitutes human relationships, renewed in Jesus Christ, so that the created goods of individual life and freedom are not immanent human rights held defensively against fellow humans, but continuous gifts of God in which inhere the obligations of loving God, our neighbors and ourselves. The *telos* of these gifts is human beings' rational service of praise and thanksgiving to God for creating the worldly mirror of his inestimable perfection. The immeasurable value of human and nonhuman creatures in their ordered relationships under God's governance and care places human agents under duties of appropriate care and consideration for all creatures, and sinful human community under the obligation of restraining, punishing, and correcting derelictions of these duties. Therefore, Tudor public theology affirms the comprehensive scope of communal political obligation, there being no spheres of transitive human action that, in principle, lie outside it. Rather, the limits of political obligation are set by its purpose as a response to grave derelictions of moral duties: duties of individuals to one another and to the whole of society, duties of the whole of society to the individuals and communities within it, and duties of each and all to God.

This limitation of political obligation is seriously undermined in late modern egalitarian-rights society, where the idol of self-creating and self-owning human freedom has eclipsed the theological matrix of relational goods and duties; for when human equality as a political principle is wedded to the single good of the agent's proprietary freedom, the ensuing rights-claims and the scope of communal political obligation are potentially unlimited, bounded only by fiscal and scientific-technological limitations. Missing in a society devoted to maximizing and equalizing individual and collective freedom and derivative rights is a shared recognition that the strength of social-moral relations is inversely related to the volume of coercive law and litigation, the former diminishing as the latter expands. To recognize this inverse relationship depends on understanding coercive communal law as protecting the just communication in society of nonproprietary, nonjuridical, nonquantifiable, and common spiritual goods, in which the strength of moral relations mainly consists.

Against the backdrop of Tudor reforming theology, the political tradition of liberal natural rights can be seen as deviating in contradictory ways from the scope of human moral and political obligations revealed in the Scriptures. In *reducing* the scope of individual and communal care owed to our fellow creatures to observance and protection of the equal rights of free, self-disposing subjects, the tradition *inflates* the scope of communal political responsibility for defining, protecting, and advancing juridical goods among the governed. Without a widespread concurrence of governors and governed on the true pre-juridical and trans-juridical, communicative and participatory goods of human community, no apparatus of democratic accountability and influence will reverse the extension of jurisdiction through scientific techniques of control, because the democratic apparatus has been co-opted to serve the suppression of moral unity and freedom, on the one hand, and, on the other, the escalation of arbitrary, irrational rights.

If then, created social relationships and practices are renewed and unified through the ecclesial relationships and practices of communicating faith, protecting the latter from outward degradation is a central obligation of political order. The modern tradition of liberal natural rights fundamentally denies this political obligation, but it is not alone. From the sixteenth century, the obligation has been denied on the evangelical ground that political protection of faith and its practices violates the freedom intrinsic to faith. On this ground, many Christians today object to the public provision of one or more historical orders of church practice and ministry in a political jurisdiction, even when objectors have ample exemptions and alternatives. Contemporary defenders of some form of church establishment concur with objectors that the freedom of faith dictates a large measure of political freedom in the sphere of religious adherence and practice, but disagree over the distance between political order and church membership required. Defenders favor sustaining and advancing an "arms-length" relation of governmental oversight and support of the church's public practice and ministry that does not compromise its independent, institutional authority and integrity by imposing political priorities on it. The pressing issue is whether this relationship can be defended as desirable and realistic in the present circumstances.

Granting that the Tudor reforming authorities were not misguided in regarding as a central political obligation protection of the church's practices and ministries, they may be faulted for requiring an excessive degree of uniformity, imposing excessive compulsion on clergy and laity and employing excessive sanctions against dissent. Inevitably, contemporary argument against political church establishment remains freighted with communal memories of the wars within and among the Protestant and Catholic territories of Europe in the sixteenth and seventeenth centuries, uniquely in the British Isles involving Protestant communities fighting each other. Compounding revulsion at past religious persecution and conflict is revulsion at its current forms in reactionary Islamic and secular totalitarian regimes. Nevertheless, it is historically and theologically unjustified either to regard such political evils as necessarily entailed in the political protection of the institutional foundation of society's moral and spiritual unity or to summarily to dismiss historical attempts to manage that protection more justly, charitably, and peaceably. In any case, theologians cannot evade the challenge to consider how politically to uphold the public integrity, authority, and unifying power of the church's witness to Christ's reign over society, while protecting the freedom of religious belief and practice for all individuals and communities within it. The alternative is to concede that communal faith in Christ can have no political (governmental and legal) expression.

To meet this challenge, theologians must be realistic about the contemporary religious, social, and political conditions averse to the church's public witness, while at the same time, resisting egalitarian pressure to equate *just* political protection of the religious freedom of all individuals and communities with *identical* political protection. The foremost imperative is to distinguish clearly between the factual *plurality* of religious (and irreligious) professions and communities in society and the ideological norm of religious *pluralism*, which makes plurality of religious/irreligious professions and communities a requisite of individual and communal religious freedom. Pluralism, like secularism, is an offshoot of the liberal natural rights' requirement that the strict equality of agents' natural rights of religious freedom be mirrored in a strict equality of legal rights. Whereas secularism pursues this strict equality by legally excluding all religious beliefs and practices from the public (political) realm, pluralism may pursue it by including all religious beliefs and practices on an equal legal footing, irrespective of long-standing communal religious tradition. From a deficient understanding of human equality and freedom comes a deficient understanding of their juridical protection and advancement. When equality and freedom are understood to be the free participation of individual and communal agents in the divinely ordered, objective, communicable goods and duties of society, some legal inequality may be justified in their political protection and advancement.

The ideology of rights-egalitarianism suppresses the political insight that equality of regard for each person's welfare may indicate identical or nonidentical legal treatment, depending on the specific good under consideration: on its substantive meaning and constitution and on the available means of protecting or advancing access to it. A governmental norm of scientific neutrality in determining these matters is illusory. With respect to the protection of innocent life and physical integrity, security of property and contract, due process before the civil and criminal law, and public provision of basic material and social necessities, equal treatment and nondiscrimination among society's members are morally required and practically achievable in many societies. But the good of religious freedom, like that of political representation, may require more complex legal discriminations among society's members dependent on historical circumstances.[99] In this context, a government may be justified in imposing on one or more church organization an obligation of public ministry and practice not imposed uniformly on all religious (or nonreligious) organizations. It may expose all members of the political community to some form(s) of that public ministry while still defending the principle that adherence to any or no religious belief must be free of inducement or coercion. In these discriminations a government may properly be guided by traditional conceptions of religious freedom and social unity shaped by centuries of Christian thought and practice. Ignorance or disregard of long-continuing and widely respected indigenous tradition(s) breeds political incoherence.

In various countries with Reformation traditions, legal enforcement of modest Christian duties connected with "mild church establishment" has included Sunday closing laws prohibiting business and work practices incompatible with the fulfillment of individual and corporate Christian observances, laws requiring church catechesis and worship in schools, and legal enforcement of church tithing. With the decline of active adherence to national and other churches, the rise of widespread unbelief and irreligion, and increasing affiliation with non-Christian religious communities, governments have reassessed the service of such laws to the common benefit, reforming them either in a secularist or religious pluralist direction. Such reassessment is obviously a political imperative, whatever the wisdom or unwisdom of the resulting reforms, because a law serves the common benefit only as it benefits all of society's members in important respects, including

---

99. A nonelected chamber of a national parliamentary assembly, such as the British House of Lords, may embody these more complex discriminations in political representation.

those dissenting from it. A law enforcing Christian duties will benefit dissenters only if it does not place an excessive burden or inhibition on them, causing justified resentment and deterring their free embrace of the goods of Christian practice.

Throughout most of the twentieth century, English religious law managed to support the unified institutional witness of Anglican establishment to Christ's rule over society while coherently accommodating other Christian churches, non-Christian religious communities, and the nonreligious population. This accommodation, largely in ministries in state-run or state-subsidized organizations such as schools and colleges, the armed forces, prisons, hospitals, and orphanages, and in privately run educational and charitable enterprises, has required discriminating appraisal of the greater burden placed by restrictive provision of ministry on members of other religious bodies as compared to individuals with no religious belief or affiliation, owing to the encompassing claim of long-shared religious beliefs and practices on communal adherents and their profound penetration of moral, social, and cultural experience. In their orientation to non-Christian religions, Christians have throughout the past been instructed by the tension in the apostle Paul's writings between a missionary urgency to make the gospel heard, dispelling idolatrous distortions, and a readiness to engage with non-Christian forms of participating in God's good creation, redolent of what lies beyond it and inviting dialogue. British Christians have, similarly, been open to the removal of restrictive religious burdens as part of a renegotiated hospitality in a traditionally Christian, but now religiously plural, society. In this context, to give justice to non-Christian religious minorities is to protect the freedom of their ministries and practices to the fullest extent compatible with protecting the primacy of the church's faith and practice informing the communal political enterprise. It is not to impose ideological measures which impede the communication of religious belief and the practice of worship not harmful to the religious freedom of others: that is to suppress *the* universal human good and right.

One condition which will and should carry weight in determining the direction of religious law is the profile of religious belief and practice in the population. For giving justice requires some consonance of government and people as to the goods to be protected and evils to be suppressed, and this consonance appears to be seriously lacking at present in Britain regarding the political protection of public Christian (or non-Christian) religious ministry and practice. According to one survey of the population in Britain from 1983 to 2018,[100] the proportion of people identifying as affiliated to the Church of England or Anglican church decreased from 40 percent to 12 percent, and the proportion identifying as Christian decreased from 66 percent to 38 percent, while the proportion identifying as having non-Christian (primarily Muslim) religious affiliation increased from 2 percent to 9 percent, and the proportion having no religious affiliation rose from 32 percent

---

100. https://www.bsa.natcen.ac.uk/media/39293/1_bsa36_religion.pdf

to 52 percent of the population.[101] Other figures evidence the steep generational decline in Christian adherence. If these statistics primarily focus attention on the failings of Christian ministries in Britain over the last forty years, they also focus attention on the longer crisis of political authority occasioned by the eclipse of the historic theological moorings of the British polity. Contributing to both has been the theoretical elaboration and juridical implementation of liberal natural rights, which has not only nourished and consolidated the culture of secular humanism, moral voluntarism, egalitarian pluralism, and atheistic scientism but has produced an inflation of governmental policy and law, accompanied by a deflation of governmental authority. The latter has resulted from the inevitable disparity between the popular demand to maximize freedom and dignity for all society's members through legal rights provisions, and the dispiriting outcomes of these provisions in ineffectual bureaucratic regimentation, ideological homogeneity and conflict, institutional degradation, and rising inequality.

The practical ambiguities of public judgments and the deep divisions in society they arouse constantly threaten the secular liberal democratic ideal of grounding political authority entirely on the consent of the ruled, chiefly acted out in the periodic ritual of popular elections, in which the governed pass judgment on their governing representatives, replacing or retaining them. In liberal modernity, it is inevitable that the claim of this periodic ritual to express the teleological ordering of political authority and practice to the autonomous freedom and self-government of individuals and their contracted associations will continue to lose credibility. As the longer Christian political tradition knows well, the consent of the governed to those who govern, determining the stability and quality of their service to the commonweal, must be consent to divine rule before human rule. This priority is affirmed in the traditional theological doctrine, central to the English Reformation, that both subjects and their rulers are placed under the obligation of consent and obedience to God's sovereign governance. This shared obligation remains key to contemporary theological efforts to improve upon the inadequate and contradictory formulations in the liberal natural rights tradition of the moral relations of the political community to its members and its government.

The Structure of Political Judgment

The structure of political judgment is determined by its dual service to human society and to God: in serving human society by restraining, punishing, and correcting human wrongdoing and vindicating well-doing, it serves God by communicating his efficacious condemnation of sin and protection of common

---

101. By 2018, only 11 percent of the British population reported weekly attendance at religious services (apart from weddings, funerals, and other special rites), with the majority of Christians in all denominations (led by Anglicans) attending services occasionally or very occasionally rather than regularly, contrasting with the higher rates of attendance in non-Christian religious communities.

human goods from sin's assault. This dual service implies a dual representation. On the one hand, political judgment represents the concurrence of a population on the need for collective discipline and on its administrative structure and guiding principles. This representation both exhibits concurrence and constructs concurrence, for political judgment would not be necessary were people not everywhere divided as well as united in their practical judgments. Political judgment exhibits concurrence by attending to the traditional, concrete forms of common goods that have defined society, and to the history of customary and statutory laws protecting them. It constructs concurrence by interpreting and assessing these social and legal realities in the light of present and emerging challenges. In the Tudor period, both the exhibition and the construction of the people's concurrence by the representative practices of public judgment are articulated primarily in jurisprudential writings and the prolegomena of statute laws, being summarized in the jurisprudential maxim that the ruler is both under the law and over the law. The ruler's subjection to the law is embodied in the definition of the royal prerogative by common and statute law and in the primacy of forensic and judicial precedent in the common law courts. The law's subjection to the ruler is embodied in the appeal to natural "equity" in the royal courts and in the jurisdictional scope of parliamentary enactment, extending to constitutional law, and the repeal of past statutes.

Concomitantly, in Tudor theological jurisprudence public judgment represents God's sovereign judgment, and this representation is crucial to its validity and stability. Crucially, the representation of God's judgment follows a different logic from the representation of popular judgment. Public judgment may exhibit a popular concurrence in laws lying anywhere on the moral spectrum, in evil and unjust laws as well as in good and just laws; but it can only exhibit God's judgment in exhibiting his true, good, and just laws revealed in nature and Scripture. This exhibition is never more than an indirect, dim, and partial disclosure; for the truth, goodness, justice, and unity of God's laws are fully revealed only in the rule of Jesus Christ in human hearts through his Holy Spirit. Furthermore, unlike the representation of the people's concurrence, representation of God's judgment never stands over God's revealed law, as over existing human law, but always under it. In attending to the claim made by God's law, rulers retain no such critical distance and freedom to deal with his law, as with human law, in the light of prevailing circumstances and demands. Instead, their aim is reflectively to discern and to obey its concrete demand in the present situation.

Our discussion of the English reformers' appropriation of Israelite and Christological models of human rule has examined at some length the models' problematic aspects for representing God's rule. This enables us to draw certain parallels between idolatrous tendencies in English Reformation formulations and in subsequent liberal rights formulations of the purpose and authority of human political rule. In appropriating these models, English reformers occasionally gave human government and law a central place within God's rule as creator, redeemer, and perfecter of human society, suppressing the differences between human mediations of God's condemning and saving word of judgment, between Christ's rule over civil society and his rule over and in the church. The tendency to exult human jurisdiction as a complete representation of God's rule invested the human ruler, along with the structure and practices of rule, with a singular semidivine status above human society and a pivotal participation in God's creative and saving action. In an analogous manner, the modern tradition of liberal natural rights has elevated the realization of human proprietary freedom through the political, juridical, and cultural/institutional advancement of human rights into the pivotal creative, reforming and perfecting action in civil society. The governmental agent of the rule of rights, as well as its forms and practices, represents the unified will, the dignity, and the highest good and right of "the people," designating not only a territorial population but all persons everywhere or universal humanity. In the modern rights tradition, the rule of juridical humanity has taken the place of God's rule in political representation.

A related idolatrous tendency in English Reformation political theology, deriving from the identification of the Tudor kingdom with Israel, was to render God's providential rule superficially transparent or scrutable. Interpreting the contemporary history and vicissitudes of the Tudor kingdom according to the Deuteronomic dynamic of national disobedience and divine punishment, national repentance and divine deliverance, national reform and divine blessing, Tudor theologians gave communal events a facile moral transparency, often serving to magnify royal authority and encourage popular compliance with governmental policies, propelling public theology toward an ideology of political control. Similarly, the tradition of liberal natural rights has made the history of political freedom and rule superficially scrutable by constructing a quasi-historical genealogy of representative, accountable government by law. Locating its origin in the rights of freedom and self-preservation belonging to human individuals by nature, the narrative has explicated its historical emergence by positing a voluntary compact of individuals creating communal political authority, and simultaneously or subsequently, establishing the structure and processes of government, and the governors themselves. Thus, the narrative has conferred a facile moral transparency on the historical ascendance of representative government by law in the emerging economic and political empires of the West. In late modernity, the liberal natural rights tradition continues to construe Western political history as a rational vindication of the liberal rights law state and its persisting political and economic power and influence on the global stage.

Obviously, the decisive difference between the idolatrous tendencies of the English Reformation and the modern liberal natural rights tradition is that the former were offset and largely overcome by more discriminating theological treatment of the inherited models of political rulership and rule, closely controlled by the apostolic perspectives. In contrast to modern natural rights thinkers, Tudor theologians had the decisive advantage of detailed, far-ranging, and devoted engagement with the Scriptural writings. For the most part, official and influential Tudor sermons and writings extolled the reforming Israelite monarchs as models of faithful and obedient rule while safeguarding the disciplinary purpose and parameters of coercive jurisdiction, the incompleteness of its mediation of God's judgment, and its distance from Christ's saving rule in the church's proclamation. Less frequently, they presented rulers as Christ's rather than God's vicegerents but without inflating their mediation of Christ's rule. Similarly, in adopting the moral dynamic of Israel's history to interpret the historical vicissitudes of the Tudor kingdom, the orientation of English reformers was often as prophetic as it was political, concerned to encourage a self-critical, repentant response of the whole nation, monarch and subjects, to communal adversity, each estate examining its own failings in serving God and the commonweal rather than projecting failings and culpability onto the others.

To some extent, scholastic developments of natural rights were also restrained by their biblical theological inheritance. It is hardly surprising that English Reformation theologians, more broadly, were influenced by such thinkers as Marsilius, Ockham, and Wyclif in explicating the intersection of divine and human authority and action in political jurisdiction. Yet the considerable divergence of moral and political conceptuality between scholastic natural rights and Tudor public theology reveals the extent and depth of the reformers' theological departure from the scholastic treatment of anthropology, soteriology, ecclesiology, and epistemology, in which the development of rights theory was embedded. In assessing the usefulness of scholastic natural rights for elaborating a theological corrective to modern liberal natural rights, contemporary theologians could profitably pay more attention to this broader scope of theological divergence and, as well, to the unresolved theoretical issues internal to the natural rights models of political rule.

Chapter 4 presented these issues as largely arising from the controlling and defensive character of the individual's natural rights of freedom and self-preservation, intrinsically connected with the assimilation of created natural right/law (*ius naturale*) to the proprietary and political right/law of fallen human beings (*ius gentium, ius civile*). This assimilation produced monistic juridical models of communally integrated or harmonized rights-bearing individuals and associations which suppressed the dual character of communal integration by secular jurisdiction, on the one hand, and by nonjuridical and nonproprietary church ministries, on the other. Moreover, these models produced unresolvable theoretical contradictions in respect of the several loci of rights: individuals, the civil association, and the ruler. The most glaring contradiction is that the foundational moral rights of freedom and self-preservation inhering in an individual subject are rationally and voluntarily transferable or alienable to a collective subject, and again, from the civil corporation to the magistracy (or directly from the individuals to the magistracy), for "inherent" rights are, as such, inalienable. The contradiction is not overcome by separating the inherent rights from their social exercise, for rights are, as such, socially active, as many rights theorists well understood. Nor is it overcome by distinguishing alienable from inalienable rights, for this sets up an untenable competition among the inalienable rights of individual, collective, and governing subjects. While a corporation model of political rule could abandon the contradictory idea of transferring natural rights and, instead, ground the unity and perpetuity of individual and communal natural rights in corporate mechanisms of participation and representation, this immanent unification of rights is vulnerable to two serious criticisms. It underestimates the complications of morally harmonizing individual and communal natural rights and, as importantly, it undermines the authority of government by conceiving it as merely "delegated" by the civil association and wholly subject to its shifting demands.

To avoid the stubborn issues encountered in constructions of political rule from natural rights should be for contemporary, as for past, theologians a weighty benefit. The apologetic argument of this chapter is that English Reformation public theology offers this benefit by providing an account of political rule devoid of the conceptuality of original, natural, and universal human rights. Rather, the controlling theological conceptuality of its homiletical, liturgical, juristic, and legal sources is that of God's institution and continuing authorization of human political authority, of God's righteousness and law, giving objective content to human right and law; of human freedom as faithful obedience to God's will revealed in creation and salvation, and of the unity of ruler and ruled within the common bonds of obedience.

This controlling conceptuality places fundamental limitations on the ruler's *dominium* (right of rule) not by deriving it from, hedging it by, or assimilating it to, a prior individual or communal *dominium*, but by subordinating it to the authoritative disclosure in the Scriptures of the creaturely goods and right relationships which God ordained it to serve, the purpose and forms of its service, the principles and laws ordering its action, and the requisite spiritual equipment to be entreated of God. At the same time, the theocentric conceptuality upholds the political authority of human communities and their members by placing them under the obligation to assent to a form of rule and to rulers, to be subject to rule as a faithful, reflective moral practice, and to provide rulers with the material, moral, and intellectual resources required for their service to the concrete common good. Prominent among the moral and intellectual resources is legal wisdom: the customary tradition(s) of judicial usage, learning, and jurisprudence, of which the community remains the guardian. It is not disingenuous to conclude this chapter and this study by proposing that English Reformation public theology, critically appropriated, offers an alternative political tradition of freedom to that of natural rights, as timely as it is perennial.

BIBLIOGRAPHY

Church of England Service Books and Liturgies

The Book of the Common Prayer and Administration of the Sacraments, and Other Rites and Ceremonies of the Church after the Use of the Church of England. London: Edward Whitchurch, 1549.

The Book of Common Prayer and Administration of the Sacraments and other Rites and Ceremonies in the Church of England. London: Edward Whitchurch, 1552.

The First and Second Prayer Books of Edward VI. Introduction by Douglas Harrison. London: Dent, 1910, repr. 1968.

The Form and Manner of Making and Consecrating of Archbishops, Bishops, Priests and Deacons 1550, . . . *Bishops, Priests and Deacons* 1552. In *The First and Second Prayer Books of Edward VI.* Introduction by Douglas Harrison, 291–317, 437–63. London: Dent, 1910, repr. 1968.

The Book of Common Prayer 1559: The Elizabethan Prayer Book. Edited by John E. Booty. The Folger Shakespeare Library. Charlottesville and London: The University of Virginia Press, 1976.

Lambeth 1988 Statement on Liturgy, Section 168: Flexibility in Rites. In *Lambeth and Liturgy 1988.* Grove Worship 106. Edited with introduction and commentary, by Colin Buchanan. Nottingham: Grove Books, 1988.

Patterns for Worship: A Report by the Liturgical Commission of the General Synod of the Church of England. London: Church House Publishing, 1989.

The Collect in Anglican Liturgy: Texts and Sources 1549–1989. Alcuin Club Collection, no. 72. Compiled and edited by Martin R. Dudley. Collegeville: The Liturgical Press, 1994.

Lyman, Warren J. *Patterns for Worship.* London: Church House Publishing, 1995.

The Book of Common Prayer: 1662 Version. Introduction by Diarmaid MacCulloch. London: Everyman's Library, 1999.

The Alternative Service Book 1980. With Index, 1984. Cambridge: Cambridge University Press (and other publishers).

Common Worship: Services and Prayers for the Church of England. London: Church House Publishing, 2000.

Writings, Sermons, and Notes of Thomas Cranmer

Cranmer, Thomas. *Miscellaneous Writings and Letters of Thomas Cranmer.* Edited by John Edmund Cox for The Parker Society. Cambridge: University Press, 1846. Contents include:

"Corrections of the Institution by Henry VIII with Cranmer's Annotations," 83–114.

A Confutation of Unwritten Verities (1547?), 1–67.

"Speech at the Coronation of Edward VI. Feb. 20, 1547" (attribution uncertain), 126–7.

"Homily of Salvation," 128–34.

"A Short Declaration of the True, Lively, and Christian Faith," 135–41.
"Homily or Sermon of Good Works Annexed unto Faith," 141–9.
"Notes for a Homily against Rebellion," 188–9.
"A Sermon Concerning the Time of Rebellion" (with Peter Martyr), 188–202.
Cranmer, Thomas. "A Fruitful Exhortation to the Reading and Knowledge of Holy Scripture" (attribution probable). In *The Two Books of Homilies Appointed to be Read in Churches*. Edited by John Griffiths, 7–15. Oxford: Oxford University Press, 1859.
Cranmer, Thomas. "Preface to the *Book of Common Prayer* and 'Of Ceremonies, Why Some Be Abolished and Some Retained.'" In *The First and Second Prayer Books of Edward VI*. Introduction by Douglas Harrison, 3–5, 286–9. London: Dent, 1910, repr. 1968.
Cranmer, Thomas. *Answer unto A Crafty and Sophistical Cavillation Devised by Stephen Gardiner Against the True and Godly Doctrine of the Most Holy Sacrament of the Body and Blood of our Saviour Jesus Christ*. London: John Daye, 1580. In *Writings and Disputations of Thomas Cranmer Relative to the Sacrament of the Lord's Supper*. Edited by John Edmund Cox for The Parker Society, 1–367. Cambridge: Cambridge University Press, 1844.
Cranmer, Thomas. *Defence of the True and Catholic Doctrine of the Body and Blood of Our Saviour Christ* (1550). References to the *Defence* in *Writings and Disputations* are taken from Cranmer's *Answer* or from *The Remains of Thomas Cranmer D.D.* Edited by Henry Jenkyns. Vol. 2. Oxford: Oxford University Press, 1833.

Church Fathers

Ambrose of Milan (Ambrosius Mediolanensis). *De officiis ministrorum*. PL 16: 23–184.
Ambrose of Milan. *De Nabuthae*. PL 14: 731–56.
Ambrose of Milan. *Expositio de Psalmo cxviii*. PL 15: 1197–526.
Ambrosiaster. *Comm. in 2 Cor*. PG 17: 275–338.
Augustine of Hippo (Augustinus Hipponensis). *Ennaratio in Psalmum cxlvii*. PL 37: 1913–37.
Augustine of Hippo. *Contra Faustum*. PL 42: 207–518.
Augustine of Hippo. *De civitate Dei*. PL 41: 13–804.
Augustine of Hippo. *De Doctrina Christiana*. Edited with translation by R. P. H. Green. Oxford: Clarendon Press, 1995.
Augustine of Hippo. *De libero arbitrio*. PL 32: 1221–310.
Augustine of Hippo. *Epis*. 153. PL 33: 653–65.
Augustine of Hippo. *Tractatus VI in Evangelium Ioannis*. PL 35: 1425–37.
Basil the Great (Basilius Magnus Caesariensis). *Homilia in illud: Destruam horrea mea*. PG 31: 261–77.
Clement of Alexandria (Clemens Alexandrinus). *Paidagogus*. PG 8: 249–684.
Clement of Alexandria. *Quis dives saluetur*. PG 9: 603–52.
Chrysostom (Chrysostomus, Johannes). *De Lazaro*. PG 48: 963–1054.
Gregory the Great (Gregorius Magnus). *Moralia*. PL 75: 509–1162.
Gregory the Great. *Regula pastoralis*. PL 77: 13–128.
Migne, J. P., ed. *Patrologia cursus completa . . . Series graeca*. 166 vols. Paris: Petit-Montrouge, 1857–83.
Migne, J. P., ed. *Patrologia cursus completes Series prima [Latina]*. 221 vols. Paris: J. P. Migne, 1844–65.

Other Primary Works

Almain, Jacques. *Libellus de auctoritate ecclesiae*. Paris, 1512. *A Book Concerning the Authority of the Church*. In *Conciliarism and Papalism*. Edited and translated by J. H. Burns and Thomas M. Izbicki, 134–200. Cambridge: Cambridge University Press, 1997.
Alvarus Pelagius. *De planctu Ecclesiae*. Edited by J. T. Rocaberti. *Bibliotheca Maxima Pontifica* 3: 23–266. Rome 1698.
Anselm of Canterbury. *Cur Deus Homo: Why the God-Man*. Translated by Jasper Hopkins and Herbert Richardson. Minneapolis: Arthur J. Banning Press, 2000.
Aquinas, Thomas. *De perfectione spiritualis vitae*. In *Opera Omnia iussu Leonis XIII, edita*. 41: Part B, 67–122. Rome, 1970.
Aquinas, Thomas. *Summa Theologiae*. Blackfriars Edition. Edited by Thomas Gilby and T. C. O'Brien. New York: McGraw-Hill and London: Eyre and Spottiswoode, 1964–76.
Augustinus Triumphus. *Summa de potestate ecclesiastica* 1326. Rome, 1584.
Bellarmine, Robert. *De potestate summi pontificis*. Rome, 1610.
Bonaventure. *Apologia Pauperum*. *Opera Omnia* 8. Florence: Quaracchi, 1898. *Defense of the Mendicants*. Translated by Jose de Vinck and Robert J. Karris. Saint Bonaventure: Franciscan Institute Publications, 2010.
Bond, Ronald B., ed. *Certain Sermons or Homilies (1547) and A Homily against Disobedience and Wilful Rebellion (1570): A Critical Edition*. Toronto: University of Toronto Press, 1987.
Bracton, Henry de (attributed). *Tractatus de legibus et consuetudinibus Anglie*. Edited by George E. Woodbine. New Haven: Yale University Press, 1922–42. *Bracton on the Laws and Customs of England*. Translated with commentary by Samuel E. Thorne. Cambridge, MA: Harvard University, 1968–77.
Bray, Gerald, ed. *Tudor Church Reform: The Henrician Canon of 1535 and the "Reformatio Legum Ecclesasticarum."* Woodbridge: Boydell Press, 2000.
Brightman, Frank Edward. *The English Rite: Being a Synopsis of the Sources and Revisions of the Book of Common Prayer*. 2 vols. London: Rivingtons, 1915.
Brownlie, Ian, ed. *Basic Documents on Human Rights*. 2nd edn. Oxford: Oxford University Press, 1981.
Bucer, Martin. *Censura*. In Edward Charles Whitaker, *Martin Bucer and the Book of Common Prayer*, 9–174. Alcuin Club. Great Awakening: Mayhew-McCrimmon, 1974.
Bucer, Martin. *De ordinatione legitima ministrorum ecclesiae revocanda*. In *Scripta Anglicana*. Edited by Konrad Hubert, 238–59. Basel, 1577. *Concerning the Restoration of the Lawful Ordination of the Church's Ministries*. In Edward Charles Whitaker, *Martin Bucer and the Book of Common Prayer*, 176–83. Alcuin Club. Great Awakening: Mayhew-McCrimmon, 1974.
Bullinger, J. Heinrich. *De Origine Erroris in Divorum et Simulacrorum Cultu*. Basel: Thomas Wolff, 1529.
Bullinger, J. Heinrich. *Fifty Godly and Learned Sermons Divided into Five Decades*. Translated by H. I. London: Ralph Newberry, 1577. Repr. *The Decades of Heinrich Bullinger*. Edited by Thomas Harding. Parker Society. Cambridge: Cambridge University Press, 1849.
Cajetan, Tommaso de Vio. *Auctoritas papae et concilii sive ecclesiae comparata*. Rome, 15ll. *On the Comparison of the Authority of Pope and Council*. In *Conciliarism and*

Papalism. Edited by J. H. Burns and Thomas M. Izbicki, 1–133. Cambridge: Cambridge University Press, 1997.

Calvin, John. *Institutio Christianae Religionis* (1559). Edited by Wilhelm Baum, Edward Cunitz, and Edward Reuss. Halle, 1864. *Institutes of the Christian Religion* 1559. Translated by Henry Beveridge 1845. 2 vols. London: J. Clark, 1962.

The Canons and Dogmatic Decrees of the Council of Trent. Translated by J. Waterworth. In *Creeds of Christendom*. 3 vols. Edited by Philip Schaff, 2: 77–206. Repr. Grand Rapids: Baker Book House, 1977.

Cartwright, Thomas. *The Second Reply of Thomas Cartwright against Master Doctor Whitgift's Second Answer, Touching The Church Discipline*. Heidelberg: Michael Schirat/London, 1575.

Elton, G. R. *The Tudor Constitution: Documents and Commentary*. 2nd edn. Cambridge: Cambridge University Press, 1982.

Forty Two Articles (1553) and Thirty Nine Articles (1571). In Oliver O'Donovan, *On the Thirty-Nine Articles: A Conversation with Tudor Christianity*. 2nd edn. Appendix 1, 134–57. London: SCM Press, 2001.

Frere, Walter Howard and C. E. Douglas, eds. *Puritan Manifestoes: A Study of the Origin of the Puritan Revolt*. London: SPCK/New York: E. S. Gorham, 1907.

Frere, Walter Howard and William Paul McClure Kennedy, eds. *Visitation Articles and Injunctions of the Period of the Reformation*. 3 vols. London: Longmans, Green, 1910.

Gardiner, Stephen. *Explication and Assertion of the Catholic Faith Touching the most Blessed Sacrament of the Alter*. 1551.

Gee, Henry and William John Hardy, eds. *Documents Illustrative of English Church History*. London: Macmillan, 1896.

Gerson, Jean. *De potestate ecclesiastica*. *Oeuvres completes*. Edited by Palémon Glorieux, 6: 210–50. Paris: Desclée, 1965.

Gerson, Jean. *De vita spirituali animae*. In *Oeuvres completes*. Edited by Palémon Glorieux, 3: 113–202. Paris: Desclée, 1965.

Giles of Rome (Aegidius Romanus). *De ecclesiastica potestate*. Edited by Richard Scholz. Weimar: H. Böhlaus Nachfolger, 1929. Giles of Rome *on Ecclesiastical Power: The De ecclesiastica potestate of Aegidius Romanus*. Translated by R. W. Dyson. Woodbridge, Suffolk: Boydell Press, 1986.

The Great Bible. London: Richard Grafton and Edward Whitchurch, 1540.

Griffiths, John, ed. *The Two Books of Homilies Appointed to be Read in Churches*. Oxford: Oxford University Press, 1859.

Hill, Mark. *Ecclesiastical Law*. 2nd edn. Oxford: Oxford University Press, 2001.

Hobbes, Thomas. *Leviathan*. Edited and introduced by J. C. A. Gaskin. Oxford: Oxford University Press, 1996.

The Holie Bible: Conteynyng the Olde Testament and the Newe (Bishops' Bible). Edited by Matthew Parker and William Alley. London: Richard Jugge, 1568.

The Holy Scriptures of the Olde and Newe Testamente with the Apocripha, 1535. Translated by Miles Coverdale. London, 1847.

Hooker, Richard. *Of the Laws of Ecclesiastical Polity. The Folger Library Edition of the Works of Richard Hooker*. 6 vols. Edited by W. Speed Hill. Cambridge: Belknap Press of Harvard University Press, 1977–93.

Huguccio. *Summa Decretorum*. Admont, Stiftsbibliotek, MS 7.

Jewel, John. *Apologia Ecclesiae Anglicanae*. London, 1562. *An Apology or Answer in Defence of the Church of England*. Translated by Anne Becon. London, 1564. In

The Works of John Jewel. Edited by John Ayre, 5–108. Parker Society. Cambridge: Cambridge University Press, 1848.
John of Paris (Jean Quidort). *De potestate regia et papali* 1301. On Royal and Papal Power. Translated by J. A. Watt. Toronto: Pontifical Institute of Mediaeval Studies, 1971.
John of Salisbury. *Policraticus.* Edited and translated by Cary J. Nederman. Cambridge: Cambridge University Press, 1990.
Krueger, Paul, ed. *Institutiones Justiniani.* Berlin: Berolini apud Weidmannos, 1893. *Corpus Iuris Civili.* 3 vols. Edited by Theodor Mommsen, Paul Krueger, et al. Berlin: Berolini apud Weidmannos, 1872–95.
Kuttner, Stephan. *Repertorium der Kanonistik, 1140–1234.* Vatican City: Biblioteca apostolica vaticana, 1937.
Locke, John. *The Second Treatise of Government.* In *Two Treatises of Government.* Edited by Peter Laslett. Cambridge: Cambridge University Press, 1988.
Mair, John. "A Disputation Concerning the Authority of the Council over the Supreme Pontiff" (on Mt. 18.15, 16.19). In *Conciliarism and Papalism.* Edited and translated by J. H. Burns and Thomas M. Izbicki. Cambridge: Cambridge University Press, 1997.
Mansi, Giovanni Domenico, ed. *Sacrorum conciliorum nova et amplissima collectio.* 31 vols. Venice and Florence, 1759–98.
Marsilius of Padua. *Defensor Pacis.* Translated by Alan Gewirth. Toronto: Medieval Academy of America, 1980.
May, Herbert G. and Bruce M. Metzger, eds. *The Oxford Annotated Bible, Revised Standard Version.* Oxford: Oxford University Press, 1962.
Melanchthon, Philip. *Loci Communes Theologici* (1521). In *Corpus Reformatorum*, 21: 1–230. Translated by Lowell J. Satre. In *Melancthon and Bucer.* Edited by Wilhelm Pauck. Philadelphia: The Westminster Press, 1969.
Melanchthon, Philip. *Loci Communes Theologici* (1535). In *Corpus Reformatorum*, 21: 230–560. Edited by Heinrich Ernst Bindseil. 1854.
Mommsen, Theodore and Paul Krueger, eds. *Digesta Justiniani.* Berlin: Berolini apud Weidmannos, 1895. *The Digest of Justian.* 4 vols. Translation edited by Alan Watson. Philadelphia: University of Pennsylvania Press, 2011.
A Necessary Doctrine and Erudition for Any Christian Man. Set Forth by the King's Majesty of England &c. The King's Book, 1543. Introduction by T. A. Lacey. London: R. Browning, 1895.
Norman Anonymous. "The Consecration of Bishops and Kings." Tractatus Eboracenses (York Tracts) 24a. Edited by Heinrich Böhmer. In *Monumenta Germaniae Historica: Libelli de Lite imperatorum et Pontificum saeculis 11 et 12 conscripti.* 3: 642–78.
O'Brian, David J. and Thomas A. Shannon, eds. *Catholic Social Teaching: The Documentary Heritage.* 2nd edn. Maryknoll: Orbis Books, 1992.
O'Donovan, Oliver and Joan Lockwood O'Donovan, eds. *From Irenaeus to Grotius: A Sourcebook in Christian Political Thought.* Grand Rapids: Eerdmans, 1999.
Paine, Thomas. *The Rights of Man, Being an Answer to Mr. Burke's Attack on the French Revolution.* London: J. Watson, 1848.
Quitslund, Beth and Nicholas Temperley, eds. *Whole Book of Psalms Collected into English Metre by Thomas Sternhold, John Hopkins, and Others: A Critical Edition of the Texts and Tunes.* Renaissance English Text Society, 7th Series, vols 36, 37. Tempa: Arizona Centre for Medieval and Renaissance Studies, 2018. Smith, Thomas. *The Commonwealth of England* (*De republica Anglorum*) 1583. London, 1589.
Singer, Heinrich. *Die Summa Decretorum des Magister Rufinus.* Paderborn: Schöningh, 1902.

Soto, Domingo de. *De iustitia et iure libri decem*. Salamanca, 1556.
Starkey, Thomas. *Exhortation to the People Instructing Them to Unity and Obedience*. London, 1536.
Suárez, Francisco. *Defensio fidei Catholicae et apostolicae adversus Anglicanae sectae errores*. Conimbricae: Didacum Gomez de Loureyro, 1613.
Summenhart, Conrad. *Septipertitum opus de contractibus pro foro conscientiae atque theologico*. Hagenau: Heinrici Gran, 1515.
Taverner, Richard. *Postils on the Epistles and Gospels* 1540. Edited by Edward Cardwell. Oxford: Oxford University Press, 1841.
Travers, Walter. *A Full and Plain Declaration of Ecclesiastical Discipline Out of the Word of God*. Heidelberg: Michael Schirat/ London, 1574.
Tyndale, William. *The Obedience of a Christian Man*, 1527-8. In *Doctrinal Treatises and Introductions to Different Portions of the Holy Scriptures by William Tyndale*. Edited by Henry Walker, 127-344. Parker Society. Cambridge: Cambridge University Press, 1848.
Tyndale, William. "A Pathway into the Holy Scripture" 1527-8. In *Doctrinal Treatises and Introductions to Different Portions of the Holy Scriptures*, 1-28. 1848.
Tyndale, William. "Preface to the Five Books of Moses." In *Doctrinal Treatises and Introductions to Different Portions of the Holy Scriptures*, 392-7. 1848.
Vázquez de Menchaca, Fernando. *Controversiarum illustrious usuque frequentium libri tres*. 1564. Reprinted Frankfurt, 1572.
Vitoria, Francisco de. *De Indis (On the American Indians)*. In *Francisco de Vitoria, Political Writings*. Edited and translated by Anthony Pagden and Jeremy Lawrance, 231-92. Cambridge: Cambridge University Press, 1991.
Vitoria, Francisco de. *De potestate civili (On Civil Power)*. In *Francisco de Vitoria, Political Writings*. Edited and translated by Anthony Pagden and Jeremy Lawrance, 1-44. Cambridge: Cambridge University Press, 1991.
Vitoria, Francisco de. *De potestate ecclesiae (On the Power of the Church)*. Relectio 1 and 2. In *Francisco de Vitoria, Political Writings*. Edited and translated by Anthony Pagden and Jeremy Lawrance, 45-152. Cambridge: Cambridge University Press, 1991.
Vitoria, Francisco de. *On Homicide and Commentary on Summa theologiae 2a 2ae Q. 64*. Translated and introduced by John P. Doyle. Milwaukee: Markquette University Press, 1997.
Whitgift, John. *The Works of John Whitgift*. 3 vols. Edited by John Ayre. Parker Society. Cambridge: Cambridge University Press, 1851-3.
William of Ockham. *Breviloquium de principatu tyrannico*. In *Wilhelm von Ockham als politischer Denker und sein Breviloquiium de principatu tyrannico*. Edited by Richard Scholtz and William Hiersemann. Stuttgart: Anton Hiersemann Verlag, 1952. *A Short Discourse on Tyrannical Government*. Edited by Arthur Stephen McGrade, translated by John Kilcullen. Cambridge: Cambridge University Press, 1992.
William of Ockham. *Dialogus*. In *Monarchia S. Romani imperii*. Edited by M. Goldast, 2: 392-976. Frankfurt, 1614.
William of Ockham. *Octo quaestiones de potestate papae*. In *Opera Politica*. 2nd revised edn. 3 vols. Edited by H. S. Offler, 1: 1-217. Manchester: Manchester University Press, 1974.
William of Ockham. *Opus nonaginta dierum*. In *Opera Politica*. Edited by H. S. Offler, 1-2: 287-858. Manchester: Manchester University Press, 1963-74. *A Translation of William of Ockham's Work of Ninety Days*. John Kilcullen and John Scott, 2 vols. Lewiston: Edwin Mellen Press, 2001-2.

William of Ockham: A Letter to the Friars Minor and Other Writings. Edited by Arthur Stephen McGrade and John Kilcullen. Translated by John Kilcullen. Cambridge: Cambridge University Press, 1995.
Wyclif, John. *De civili dominio*. 4 vols. Edited by Johann Loserth. Wyclif Society. London: Trübner, 1885–1904.

Secondary Works

Alford, Stephen. *Kingship and Politics in the Reign of Edward VI*. Cambridge: Cambridge University Press, 2009.
Armitage, Frederick. *A History of the Collects*. London: Weare & Co., 1919.
Averbeck, Richard E. "'Offerings and Sacrifices' and '*kpr*.'" In *New International Dictionary of Old Testament Theology and Exegesis*. 5 vols. Edited by Willem A. VanGemeren, 4: 996–1022. Carlisle: Paternoster, 1997.
Avis, Paul. *Church, State and Establishment*. London: SPCK, 2001.
Ayris, Paul and David G. Selwyn. *Thomas Cranmer: Scholar and Churchman*. Woodbridge: Boydell Press, 1993.
Beckford, James A. and Sophie Gilliat. *Religion in Prisons: "Equal Rites" in a Multi-Faith Society*. Cambridge: Cambridge University Press, 1998.
Berman, Harold J. *Law and Revolution: The Formation of the Western Legal Tradition* Cambridge, MA: Harvard University Press, 1983.
Bicknell, Edward John. *A Theological Introduction to the Thirty-Nine Articles of the Church of England*. 3rd edn., revised by H. J. Carpenter. London: Longmans, Green, 1955.
Biggar, Nigel. *What's Wrong with Rights?* Oxford: Oxford University Press, 2020.
Black, Anthony. *Guilds and Civil Society in European Political Thought from the Twelfth Century to the Present*. Ithaca: Cornell University Press, 1984.
Bray, Gerald. *The Faith We Profess: An Exposition of the Thirty-Nine Articles*. London: Latimer Trust, 2009.
Bretherton, Luke. *Christ and the Common Life: Political Theology and the Case for Democracy*. Grand Rapids: Eerdmans, 2019.
Bretherton, Luke. *Christianity and Contemporary Politics: The Conditions and Possibilities of Faithful Witness*. Chichester: Wiley-Blackwell, 2010.
Brett, Annabel. *Liberty, Right and Nature: Individual Rights in Later Scholastic Thought*. Cambridge: Cambridge University Press, 1997.
Brown, Francis. "Influencing the House of Lords: The Role of the Lords Spiritual 1979–1987." *Political Studies* 42, no. 1 (1993): 110–14.
Buchanan, Colin. *Cut the Connexion: Disestablishment and the Church of England*. London: Darton, Longman and Todd, 1994.
Buchanan, Colin. *Ordination Rites in Common Worship*. Grove Worship 186. Cambridge: Grove Books, 2006.
Carlyle, R. W. and A. J. Carlyle. *A History of Mediaeval Political Theory in the West*, 5th impression, 6 vols. Vol. 1: A. J. Carlyle, *The Second Century to the Ninth*. Edinburgh and London: William Blackwood, 1962.
Chan, Cathy. "The Advancement of Religion as a Charitable Purpose in an Age of Religious Neutrality." *Oxford Journal of Law and Religion* 6, no. 1 (2017): 112–36.
Chaplin, Jonathan. *Faith in Democracy: Framing a Politics of Deep Diversity*. London: SCM Press, 2021.

Clarke, Kenneth, et al. *Reforming the House of Lords: Breaking the Deadlock*. London: University College, The Constitution Unit, 2005.
Collinson, Patrick. *Archbishop Grindal 1519–1583: The Struggle for a Reformed Church*. London: Jonathan Cape, 1979.
Collinson, Patrick. *The Elizabethan Puritan Movement*. London: Routledge, 1967.
Coolidge, John S. *The Pauline Renaissance in England: Puritanism and the Bible*. Oxford: Clarendon Press, 1970.
Cuming, Geoffrey J. *A History of Anglican Liturgy*. London: Macmillan, 1969.
Daalder, Hans. "Trends and Dangers of Increased Bureaucracy in Higher Education: A View from Below." *International Journal of Institutional Management in Higher Education* 9, no. 1 (1985): 35–43.
Daniell, David. *The Bible in English*. New Haven and London: Yale University Press, 2003.
Davie, Martin. "Calvin's Influence on the Theology of the English Reformation." *Ecclesiology* 6, no. 3 (2010): 315–41.
Davies, Horton. *Worship and Theology in England: From Cranmer to Baxter and Fox, 1534–1690*. Combined edn. Grand Rapids: Eerdmans, 1996.
Dix, Gregory. *The Shape of the Liturgy*. London: A & C Black, 1945.
Doe, Norman. *The Legal Framework of the Church of England: A Critical Study in a Comparative Context*. 2nd edn. Oxford: Oxford University Press, 1996.
Dominiak, Paul. "'All Things are Lawful': Adiaphora, Permissive Natural Law, Christian Freedom, and Defending the English Reformation." *Perichoresis* 20, no. 2 (2022): 73–103.
Donahue, Charles Jr. "*Ius* in Roman Law." In *Christianity and Human Rights: An Introduction*. Edited by John Witte, Jr. and Frank S. Alexander, 64–80. Cambridge: Cambridge University Press, 2010.
Drewry, Gavin and Jenny Brock. "Prelates in Parliament." *Parliamentary Affairs* 24, no. 3 (1971): 222–4.
Elton, G. R. *The Parliament of England 1559–1581*. Cambridge: Cambridge University Press, 1986.
Eppley, Daniel. *Defending Royal Supremacy and Discerning God's Will in Tudor England*. London: Routledge, 2007.
Evans, G. R. (Gillian Rosemary). *The Language and Logic of the Bible: The Road to Reformation*. Cambridge: Cambridge University Press, 1985.
Fletcher, Anthony and Diarmaid MacCulloch. *Tudor Rebellions*. 4th edn. Harlow: Pearson Education Ltd., 1997.
Fletcher, Jeremy. *Communion in Common Worship: The Shape of Orders One and Two*. Grove Worship Series 159. Cambridge: Grove Books, 2000.
Gant, Andrew. *Sing unto the Lord: A History of English Church Music*. London: Profile, 2015.
Gibson, C. S. Edgar. *The Thirty-Nine Articles of the Church of England*. 5th edn. London: Routledge, 1906.
Grant, George. "Knowing and Making" (1975). In *The George Grant Reader*. Edited by William Christian and Sheila Grant, 407–17. Toronto: University of Toronto Press, 1998.
Hammond, Gerald. *The Making of the English Bible*. Manchester: Carcanet Press, 1982.
Harlow, Anna, Frank Cranmer, and Norman Doe. "Bishops in the House of Lords: A Critical Analysis." *Public Law* (Autumn 2008): 490–509.
Heal, Felicity. *Reformation in Britain and Ireland*. Oxford: Oxford University Press, 2003.

Heidegger, Martin. "The Question Concerning Technology." In *The Question Concerning Technology and Other Essays*. Translated by William Lovitt, 3–35. New York: Harper and Row, 1977.

Hollenbach, David. *Claims in Conflict: Retrieving and Renewing the Catholic Human Rights Tradition*. New York: Paulist Press International, 1999.

Hopf, Constantin. *Martin Bucer and the English Reformation*. Oxford: Blackwell, 1946.

Hudson, Winthrop S. *The Cambridge Connection and the Elizabethan Settlement of 1559*. Durham: Duke University Press, 1980.

Ishiguro, Kazuo. *The Unconsoled*. London: Faber and Faber, 1995.

Jacobs, Alan. *The Book of Common Prayer: A Biography*. Princeton: Princeton University Press, 2019.

Jeanes, Gordon P. *Signs of God's Promise: Thomas Cranmer's Sacramental Theology and the Book of Common Prayer*. London: T&T Clark, 2008.

Jonas, Hans. *The Phenomenon of Life: Toward a Philosophical Biology*. Evanston: Northwestern University Press, 2001.

Jones, Norman L. *Faith by Statute: Parliament and the Settlement of Religion 1559*. London: Royal Historical Society, 1982.

Kantorowicz, Ernst H. *The King's Two Bodies: A Study in Medieval Political Theology*. Princeton: Princeton University Press, 1957.

Kelly, J. N. D. (John Norman Davidson). *Early Christian Creeds*. 3rd edn. London: Longman, 1972.

King, John N. *Tudor Royal Iconography: Literature and Art in an Age of Religious Crisis*. Princeton: Princeton University Press, 1989.

Kirby, W. J. Torrance. "The Civil Magistrate and the '*Cura Religionis*': Heinrich Bullinger's Prophetical Office and the English Reformation." *Animus* 9 (2004): 25–36.

Kirby, W. J. Torrance. *The Zurich Connection and Tudor Political Theology*. Leiden: Brill, 2007.

Lake, Peter. *Anglicans and Puritans? Presbyterian and English Conformist Thought from Whitgift to Hooker*. London: Routledge, 1988.

Langholm, Odd. *Economics in the Medieval Schools: Wealth, Exchange Value, Money and Usury according to the Paris Theological Tradition, 1200–1350*. Leiden: Brill, 1992.

Le Huray, Peter. *Music and the Reformation in England 1549–1660*. Repr. with corrections. Cambridge: Cambridge University Press, 1978.

Leigh, Ian. "Balancing Religious Autonomy and Other Human Rights under the European Convention." *Oxford Journal of Law and Religion* 1, no. 1 (2012): 109–26.

Leigh, Ian. "Freedom of Religion: Public/Private, Rights/Wrongs." In *Religious Liberty and Human Rights*. Edited by Mark Hill, 137–9. Cardiff: University of Wales Press, 2002.

Lester, Antony and Paola Uccellari. "Extending the Equality Duty to Religion, Conscience and Belief: Proceed with Caution." *European Human Rights Law Review* 5 (2008): 567–73.

MacCulloch, Diarmaid. *Thomas Cranmer*. New Haven and London: Yale University Press, 1996.

MacCulloch, Diarmaid. *Thomas Cromwell: A Life*. London: Penguin Random House, 2018.

MacIntyre, Alasdair. *A Short History of Ethics: A History of Moral Philosophy from the Homeric Age to the Twentieth Century*. London: Routledge, 1966.

MacLure, Millar. *The Paul's Cross Sermons 1534–1642*. Toronto: University of Toronto Press, 1958.

Macpherson, C. B. *The Political Theory of Possessive Individualism: Hobbes to Locke*. Oxford: Oxford University Press, 1962.

Manschreck, Clyde L. *The Role of Melanchthon in the Adiaphora Controversy*. New York: Penguin Random House, 1967.

Mawson, Michael. "Introduction." In *The Freedom of a Christian Ethicist: The Future of a Reformation Legacy*. Edited by Brian Brock and Michael Mawson. London: T&T Clark, 2016.

McCrudden, Christopher. "The *Gay Cake* Case: What the Supreme Court Did, and Didn't, Decide in *Ashers*." *Oxford Journal of Law and Religion* 9, no. 2 (2020): 238–70.

McGrath, Alister E. *Iustitia Dei: A History of the Christian Doctrine of Justification*. Cambridge: Cambridge University Press, 1986.

Milbank, John and Adrian Pabst. *The Politics of Virtue: Post Liberalism and the Human Future*. London and New York: Rowman and Littlefield, 2016.

Minnerath, Roland. "The Position of the Catholic Church Regarding Concordats from a Doctrinal and Pragmatic Perspective." *Catholic University Law Review* 47, no. 2 (1998): 467–76.

Modood, Tariq, ed. *Church, State and Religious Minorities*. London: Policy Studies Institute, 1997.

Modood, Tariq. "Establishment, Multiculturalism and British Citizenship." *The Political Quarterly* 65, no. 1 (1994): 53–73.

Modood, Tariq. "Religious Pluralism in the United States and Britain: Its Implications for Muslims and Nationhood." *Social Compass* 62, no. 4 (2015): 526–40.

Morris, Robert M., ed. *Church and State in 21st Century Britain: The Future of Church Establishment*. London: University College, The Constitution Unit, 2009.

Nozick, Robert. *Anarchy, State and Utopia*. Oxford: Blackwell, 1974.

Nozick, Robert. *Philosophical Explanations*. Cambridge, MA: Harvard University Press, 1981.

Null, Ashley. *Thomas Cranmer's Doctrine of Repentance: Renewing the Power to Love*. Oxford: Oxford University Press, 2000.

O'Donovan, Joan Lockwood. "Historical Prolegomena to a Theological Review of 'Human Rights.'" *Studies in Christian Ethics* 9, no. 2 (1996): 52–65.

O'Donovan, Joan Lockwood. "Understanding Law and Constitutionalism in Modernity: The Critical Contribution of English Reformation Public Theology." In *Christianity and Constitutionalism*. Edited by Nicholas Aroney and Ian Leigh, 149–72. Oxford: Oxford University Press, 2022.

O'Donovan, Oliver. *The Problem of Self-Love in St. Augustine*. New Haven: Yale University Press, 1980.

O'Donovan, Oliver and Joan Lockwood O'Donovan. *Bonds of Imperfection: Christian Politics Past and Present*. Grand Rapids: Eerdmans, 2003.

Oliva, Javier Garcia and Helen Hall. "Same-Sex Marriage: An Inevitable Challenge to Religious Liberty and Establishment." *Oxford Journal of Law and Religion* 3, no. 1 (2014): 25–56.

Ong, Walter J. *The Presence of the Word: Some Prolegomena for Cultural and Religious History*. New Haven: Yale University Press, 1967.

O'Sullivan, Orlaith, ed. *The Bible as Book: The Reformation*. London: British Library and New Castle: Oak Knoll Press, 2000.

Partington, Andrew and Paul Bickley. *Coming Off the Bench: The Past, Present and Future of Religious Representation in the House of Lords*. London: Theos, 2007.

Patterson, Dennis, ed. *A Companion to Philosophy of Law and Legal Theory*, Part 2. Oxford: Blackwell, 1999.

Peterson, David. "Atonement in the Old Testament." In *Where Wrath and Mercy Meet: Proclaiming the Atonement Today*. Edited by David Peterson. Milton Keynes: Paternoster, 2001.

Pitt, Valerie. "The Protection of Faith?" In *Church, State and Religious Minorities*. Edited by Tariq Modood, 36-9. London: Policy Studies Institute, 1997.

Poschmann, Bernhard. *Busse und Letzte Ölung, Handbuch der Dogmengeschichte*. Band 4, Faszikel 3. Freiburg: Herder, 1951. *Penance and the Anointing of the Sick*. Translated and revised by F. Courtney. London: Burns and Oats 1964.

Reeves, Ryan. *English Evangelicals and Tudor Obedience 1527-70*. Boston: Brill, 2013.

Rivers, Julian. *The Law of Organised Religions: Between Establishment and Secularism*. Oxford: Oxford University Press, 2010.

Rivers, Julian. "Promoting Religious Equality." *Oxford Journal of Law and Religion* 1, no. 2 (2012): 386-401.

Robinson, Ian. *The Establishment of Modern English Prose in the Reformation and the Enlightenment*. Cambridge: Cambridge University Press, 1998.

Robinson, I. S. "Church and Papacy." In *The Cambridge History of Medieval Political Thought c. 350-c. 1450*. Edited by J. H. Burns, 252-305. Cambridge: Cambridge University Press, 1988.

Rosenthal, Alexander S. *Crown under Law: Richard Hooker, John Locke and the Ascent of Modern Constitutionalism*. Langham: Lexington Books, 2008.

Sacks, Jonathan. *The Persistence of Faith: Religion, Morality and Society in a Secular Age*. London: Bloomsbury Continuum, 1991.

Shapiro, Ian. *The Evolution of Rights in Liberal Theory*. Cambridge: Cambridge University, 1986.

Sharpe, Kevin. *Selling the Tudor Monarchy: Authority and Image in Sixteenth-Century England*. New Haven and London: Yale University Press, 2009.

Simpson, George. "Bureaucracy, Standardization, and the Liberal Arts: Evidence of Mass Production in Higher Education." *The Journal of Higher Education* 50, no. 4 (1979): 504-13.

Skinner, Quentin. *The Foundations of Modern Political Thought 2: The Age of Reformation*. Cambridge: Cambridge University Press, 1978.

Swift, Christopher. *Hospital Chaplaincy in the Twenty-First Century: The Crisis of Spiritual Care on the NHS*. London: Routledge, 2009.

Tentler, Thomas. *Sin and Confession on the Eve of the Reformation*. Princeton: Princeton University Press, 1977.

Tierney, Brian. *Foundations of the Conciliar Theory: The Contribution of the Medieval Canonists from Gratian to the Great Schism*. Cambridge: Cambridge University Press, 1955.

Tierney, Brian. *The Idea of Natural Rights: Studies on Natural Rights, Natural Law and Church Law 1150-1625*. Atlanta: Scholars Press, 1997.

Tierney, Brian. *Liberty and Law: The Idea of Permissive Natural Law 1100-1800*. Washington, D.C.: Catholic University of America Press, 2014.

Trinterud, Leonard J. *Elizabethan Puritanism*. New York Oxford University Press, 1971.

Tudor-Craig, Pamela. "Henry VIII and King David." In *Early Tudor England: Proceedings of the 1987 Harlaxton Symposium*. Edited by Daniel Williams, 183-205. Woodbridge: Boydell Press, 1989.

Tully, James. *A Discourse on Property: John Locke and His Adversaries*. Cambridge: Cambridge University Press, 1980.

Verhey, Allen. "Manager and Therapist as Tragic Heroes: Some Observations of a Theologian at a Psychiatric Hospital." *Studies in Christian Ethics* 21, no. 1 (2008): 7–25.

Verkamp, Bernard J. *The Indifferent Mean: Adiaphorism in the English Reformation to 1554*. Athens: Ohio University Press, 1977.

Verkamp, Bernard J. "The Limits upon Adiaphoristic Freedom: Martin Luther and Philip Melanchthon." *Theological Studies* 36, no. 1 (1975): 52–76.

Verkamp, Bernard J. "The Zwinglians and Adiaphorism." *Church History* 42, no. 4 (1973): 486–504.

Vickers, Lucy. *Religious Freedom, Religious Discrimination and the Workplace*. Oxford: Hart Publishing, 2008. Revised and updated edition, 2016.

Voegelin, Eric. *History of Political Ideas, Vol. IV: Renaissance and Reformation*. The Collected Works of Eric Voegelin, vol. 22. Columbia: University of Missouri Press, 1998.

Wannenwetsch, Bernd. *Political Worship: Ethics for Christian Citizens*. Translated by Margaret Kohl. Oxford: Oxford University Press, 2004.

Watkins, Oscar D. *A History of Penance*. 2 vols. New York: Burt and Franklin, 1961.

Whitgift, John. *The Works of John Whitgift*. Edited by John Ayre. 3 vols. Parker Society. Cambridge: Cambridge University Press, 1851–3.

Wilks, Michael. *The Problem of Sovereignty in the Later Middle Ages: The Papal Monarchy with Augustus Triumphus and the Publicists*. Cambridge: Cambridge University Press, 1963.

Witte, John Jr. *God's Joust, God's Justice: Law and Religion in the Western Tradition*. Grand Rapids: Eerdmans, 2006.

Witte, John Jr. *The Reformation of Rights: Religion and Human Rights in Early Modern Calvinism*. Cambridge: Cambridge University Press, 2008.

Witte, John Jr . *Religion and the American Constitutional Experiment: Essential Rights and Liberties*. Boulder: Westview Press and New York: Perseus Books, 2000. Revised and expanded 4th edn., co-authored with Joel A. Nichols. New York: Oxford University Press, 2016.

Wolin, Sheldon S. *Politics and Vision: Continuity and Innovation in Western Political Thought*. Princeton: Princeton University Press, 1960, expanded edition 2004.

Wurzburger, W. S. "Atonement: Jewish Concepts." In *Encyclopedia of Religion*. 2nd edn. Edited by Lindsay Jones, I: 593–4. Detroit and London: Macmillan Reference, 2005.

INDEX

adiaphora 239, 244–5, 267
Almain, Jacques 127, 130, 136, 230 n.28, 231 n.30
Althusius, Johannes 105
Alvarus Pelagius 228 n.17
Ambrose, Bishop of Milan 110 n.14
Ambrosiaster 110 nn.13–14
Anselm, Archbishop of Canterbury 121 n.61, 143, 143 n.9, 147
anthropology
    English Reformation 9–10, 83–4, 133–7, 154–7
    imago Dei 9, 104, 139–41, 151–4, 157, 262
    modern liberal 8, 83–94, 154–5 (*see also* liberalism)
Aquinas, Thomas 105, 113, 119, 121, 124–5, 127–9, 132, 162, 248, 259, 260 n.15
    Thomism 2, 91 n.13, 105, 124, 127, 131, 161–3, 230 n.28
Aristotle 124, 256
    Aristotelian 2, 83, 105, 116, 119, 124, 132, 162
Augustine, Bishop of Hippo 109–10, 116, 143 n.9, 159, 170 n.42, 184–5, 205, 218 n.84, 259, 260 n.15
Augustinus Triumphus 114, 228 n.17, 203 n.27
Avis, Paul 61 n.20, 73 n.50

Bacon, Francis 97
Barnes, Robert 170
Basil of Caesarea 110 nn.13–14
Baxter, Richard 41 n.94
Beckwith, Roger 59 n.16, 60 n.17
Becon, Thomas 44
Bellah, Robert 65 n.28
Bellarmine, Robert 230 n.28

Berman, Harold 111 n.19, 116 n.35, 277 n.80, 277 n.83
Beza, Theodore 105, 240
Bicknell, E. 49 n.119
Biggar, Nigel 96, 106, 121 n.66
Bishops' Book (King's Book) 21, 42
Black, Anthony 116 n.35
Bonaventure (Franciscan Cardinal) 116–17, 121
Boniface VIII, Pope 114
Bonner, Edmond 43
Book of Common Prayer 1559 38–41, 167–8, 195–6, 202, 204–5, 207–14, 237, 239, 262–5
de Bracton, Henry 278
Bray, Gerald 59 n.16, 247 n.85
Brennan, Patrick 65 n.28
Bretherton, Luke 70 n.42
Brett, Annabel 124 n.82, 128 n.97, 130 n.107
Brightman, Frederick 34 n.62
Bucer, Martin 27, 31 n.49, 34, 35 n.67, 141, 159, 184, 239, 272
Buchanan, Colin 55 n.9, 56 n.10, 62 n.22
Bullinger, Heinrich 13, 46, 48, 184, 217, 218 n.84, 239, 271–2
bureaucracy, *see under* science, modern

Cajetan, Tommaso de Vio 230 n.28, 231 n.30
Calvin, John 48, 151, 159, 171, 184, 239, 243, 249 n.94, 272
Carlyle, A. J. 108 n.6
Carlyle, R. W. 108 n.6
Cartwright, Thomas 240–3
church, *see* ecclesiology
Church of England, historical foundations 17–18, *see also* English Reformation ecclesiology; law; Scripture; worship

doctrinal articles   17–18, 22, 43,
    48–50, 58–60, 150, 166, 173–4,
    179–86, 195, 206, 218 n.85, 221,
    223–5, 244–5, 267–8
  laws   18–23, 255, 259, 265, 267 n.39,
    276–81, 288
  official homilies   17–18, 41–7,
    148–54, 160–1, 164–73, 182,
    186 n.18, 188 n.24, 194–5, 202–3,
    212, 217–18, 226–7, 232–8, 256–8,
    261–4, 273–5
  prayer books, liturgies   17–18, 21,
    27–41, 194–215, 265
  vernacular Bibles   17–18, 23–7, 57–8,
    180, 183, 187–9
Church of England, late modern
    crisis   7–9, 51–82, 284–7
  ecclesiastical   51–60
  of establishment   61–81
  legal   51–2, 66–9, 78–81
  in political discourse   51–2, 62–6, 82
Clement of Alexandria   110 nn.13–14,
    218 n.84
Collinson, Patrick   241 n.65, 243 n.73
common good   95, 102, 131, 134, 136,
    156, 253, 266, 288
common possession   91 n.13, 110,
    112–13, 117–18, 123 n.73, 283,
    see also under society
conciliarism   115, 125, 127, 130, 230–1
contractarianism   88–94, 98, 137
Coolidge, John   241 n.67
corporation
  legal (public and private)   68, 73, 105,
    114–15, 125, 130–1, 229, 231, 290
  natural civil   122–3, 130–2, 134, 136,
    249, 290
Coverdale, Miles   24–5, 187, 270
Cranmer, Thomas, Archbishop of
    Canterbury   7, 17–18, 22, 40 n.90,
    149, 159, 161, 163, 181–4, 208–9,
    212, 226 n.12
  Forty-Two Articles   17–18, 43, 48–9,
    142–8, 150, 169, 173
  Great Bible   17–18, 24–6, 271
  homilies and sermons   10, 17–18,
    42–5, 142–8, 153, 160–1, 164–73,
    256–60, 274
  ordinals   34–5, 232–8

prayer books, liturgies (1549,
    1552)   17–18, 27–39, 166–8, 204
creation, God the creator   136, 144–5,
    150, 153, 177–8, 211, see also under
    society
  order of   110, 169, 177, 211, 260–2,
    283
Cromwell, Thomas   20, 25, 279

D'Ailly, Pierre   230 n.28
Daniell, David   24 nn.18–19, 26 n.24,
    27 n.30, 41 n.92
Davie, Martin   36 n.70, 222 n.1
Davies, Horton   40 n.88, 201 n.26
democracy, democratic polity   8, 52, 63,
    65, 81, 85–7, 96, 102–3, 105, 225,
    283, 287, see also under society
Descartes, René   97
Dix, Dom Gregory   54
Doe, Norman   67 n.31, 277 n.82
Dominiak, Paul   249 n.96
Donahue, Charles   108 n.5
Douglas, C.   241 n.65
Duns Scotus, John   163
Durham, W. C.   65 n.28

ecclesiology, see also Church of England;
    sacraments; Scripture; worship
  corporatist ecclesiology   113–15, 125,
    130–2, 134, 249
  English Reformation ecclesiology (see
    ecclesiology, English Reformation)
  papal scholastic ecclesiology   113–16,
    134, 227–32, 251
  presbyterian ecclesiology   239–43,
    249 n.94, 241, 251
ecclesiology, English Reformation   134–5,
    see also under Church of England
  authority   221–54
  corporate worship   29–30, 135,
    193–220
  episcopacy   21–2, 34–5, 222, 235–7,
    249
  eschatological community   3–4, 54,
    135, 156, 168, 191, 203, 209, 221
  historical community   3–4, 189–92
    (see also under Church of England)
  jurisdiction   13–15, 21–2, 66–70, 135,
    224–7, 236–8, 243–54, 265–7

ministry, ministerial orders 13–14, 34–5, 135, 221–2, 226–7, 232–9
  proclamation 13–15, 135, 225–7, 237, 246, 250–1, 260, 263
  rule of Scripture 11–12, 30–1, 135, 179–92, 204–5, 210–12
economics, *see also* Locke, John
  libertarian 92, 94, 95 n.27
  modern liberal market 87, 90–2, 94–5, 99
  scholastic 110 n.12
  welfare capitalism 92, 94
education 71–2, 101, 252–3
Edward VI, King of England 4, 17–18, 21–2, 26, 29, 39 n.81, 42, 195, 239 n.60, 266, 271, 273, 275 n.72, 278
Elizabeth I, Queen of England 4, 17, 22, 26, 38–41, 45, 195, 239–43, 247, 265–6, 271, 275
Ellul, Jacques 100 n.34
Elton, G. R. 241 n.65
empire, imperial rule 5, 52
  papal 113–16, 127, 134, 229–30, 269 (*see also* papacy)
  Roman 108–9, 114 n.29, 132, 255 n.2
  royal 19–22, 225, 229, 255, 266, 269–71 (*see also* kingship, monarchy)
equality, *see also* democracy; pluralism
  created 91, 109–10, 112
  political, social 64, 65 n.28, 70, 71 n.43, 73–80, 86–94, 283–5
  restored in Christ 110, 221
Erasmus 24, 184
European Union 75–81
Evans, G. R. 184 n.14, 185 n.15

faith 159–78, *see also* church; Holy Spirit; hope; Jesus Christ; justification; law
  active and receptive 11, 175
  certainty, assurance 11, 160, 171–5
  good works 11, 84, 141, 160, 166, 169–72
  hope 11, 165, 169, 175
  liveliness 11, 160, 165–9
  love 11, 165, 169, 176–7
  obedience (*see* obedience)

single object 11, 160–5
worship 203–4, 215 (*see also* worship)
First Amendment (American) 63–4
FitzRalph, Richard, Archbishop of Armagh 122
Fletcher, Jeremy 54 n.6
Frankfurt School 100 n.34
freedom 127, 133, 136–7, 244, 280, 282
  Christological 13, 104, 134–5, 155, 191, 204–5, 212, 219, 221, 264, 284, 291
  created 9, 84, 88–94, 109–11, 120, 129–30, 133, 135, 139–41, 154, 192, 282 (*see also under* society)
  evangelical 121–2, 282, 284
  liberal, autonomous 8, 12, 61, 95–9, 102–4, 220, 251, 284–5 (*see also under* anthropology)
  loss of, contradictions of 8, 85–7, 261, 287, 290
  natural right of 84, 88–94, 111, 120, 129–30, 133, 135, 139–40, 282, 290
  religious 63–5, 73–4, 76, 80, 96–9, 284–6
  self-ownership, control 88–94, 101, 120–6, 129–30, 140, 154–5, 174, 283, 289
Frere, W. 241 n.65
Frith, John 170

Gant, Andrew 40 n.89, 41 n.92, 56 n.11
Gardiner, Stephen 24, 35
Gerson, Jean Charlier de 124–5, 130, 230 n.28, 231 n.30
Gibson, C. S. Edgar 170 nn.53–4, 170 n.56
Giles of Rome 114
Gilson, Étienne 105
Gottfried, Paul Edward 100 n.34
Grant, George 83, 98 n.31
Gregory I (the Great, *Magnus*), Pope 110 n.14, 218 n.84, 258 n.13
Gregory VII, Pope (Hildebrand) 113
Griffiths, John 44 n.102, 45–6
Grosseteste, Robert, Bishop of Lincoln 170
Gwalther, Rudolf 46 n.112

Hammond, Gerald   26 n.27
Harpsfield, John   43, 167
Heal, Felicity   20 n.4, 38 n.80
Heidegger, Martin   98 n.32
Henry VIII, King of England   4, 17–26, 48, 165–6, 255 n.1, 265–7, 270–1, 274 n.72, 279, 281
Hobbes, Thomas   8, 83, 88–90, 92–3, 98–9, 129–30, 137
Hobson, Theo   62 n.22
Holbein, Hans   270
Hollenbach, David   65 n.28, 105 n.41
Holy Spirit, person and work   140, 148, 153, 173, 263–4, *see also* sanctification
  in the church   197, 204–7, 212–14, 216
  in Scripture   12, 179, 184, 189, 192
Hooker, Richard   105, 196, 198 n.11, 198 n.13, 199 n.15, 201, 248–9, 250 n.96
hope   11, 149–50, 160, 165–9, 175, 184–5, 203, 215, 247, 261, *see also* faith
Hopf, Constantin   34 n.62
Hudson, Winthrop   38 n.80
Huguccio (Decretist)   111–13, 119

iconoclasm   13, 22, 38, 46–7, 216–20
idolatry   13, 17, 37, 39, 46, 194, 216–20, 271, 288–9
Ishiguro, Kazuo   215 n.76

Jacobs, Alan   55 n.8
James I, King of England and VI of Scotland   41, 45
James of Viterbo   114
Jeanes, Gordon   205 n.40
Jesus Christ, *see also* justification; law; revelation; salvation
  history of   9, 140, 154, 182–4, 202
  rule in the church   121, 203–5, 216, 221, 226, 243–4
  rule in the commonwealth   270, 284, 286
  two natures   149, 152
  unity of God's work   134, 152, 156, 184, 211, 216, 260
Jewel, John, Bishop of Salisbury   45–7, 148, 153, 194, 217, 238, 257

John XXII, Pope   117–18
John Chrysostom   47 n.115, 110 n.14, 189 n.26
John of Paris   115, 227 n.14
John of Salisbury   279
Jonas, Hans   98 n.31
Jones, Norman   38 n.80
justice, injustice   128, 275, *see also under* law; law courts; right; rights
  divine   10, 110, 123–5, 141, 143–6, 155–6, 160–1, 164–5, 175, 251, 261, 288
  equity   94, 243, 276, 278–9, 288
  legal   92, 105, 117, 119, 126, 136, 252–3, 255–6, 259–60, 263, 277, 280, 286
justification   141–3, 153, 159–75

Kant, Immanuel   83
Kantorowicz, E. H.   115 n.34, 229 n.24
Kernan, Dean   249 n.93
kingship, monarchy   115, 122, 131–2, 136, 225, 229, *see also under* Jesus Christ
  Byzantine (Christocentric)   225, 229, 271
  English   14–15, 17–22, 25, 50, 66–7, 70, 135, 225–6, 233, 244–5, 247, 255, 265–81, 289
  Frankish   269–70
  Israelite   15, 257, 268–73, 289
Kirby, Torrance   239 n.61, 256–7 n.3, 272 n.52
Knox, David Broughton   59–60 n.17
Knox, John   240 n.62
Kuttner, S.   112 n.23

Lactantius   218 n.84
Lake, Peter   241 n.67
Langholm, Odd   110 n.12
Latimer, Hugh, Bishop   44
Laud, William, Archbishop of Canterbury   41 n.94
law, *see also under* Church of England; empire, imperial rule; right
  canon (contemporary Anglican, traditional Catholic)   8, 14, 18 n.1, 19, 21 n.10, 22 n.11, 48–9, 59 n.15, 60–1, 66–7, 73, 79, 84, 105, 107–15, 133, 227, 229, 244, 255 n.2, 278

civil, *ius civile*   15–16, 89, 107, 109,
    111–13, 126, 276–81, 290
Decalogue   36, 39 n.85, 47, 111,
    161 n.7, 170, 211, 217, 243, 249,
    272–3
divine, *ius divinum* and
    commandments   13, 15, 84,
    110–12, 118–22, 128, 131, 133, 137,
    142, 154, 160, 166, 169–72, 177,
    188, 204–5, 211–12, 216–17, 226,
    242, 244–5, 248, 256–61, 278, 288
English, British   6, 18–20, 67, 69–72,
    77–81, 276–81, 288
international, contemporary   63, 69,
    75–82, 104–5 (*see also* European
    Union)
natural, *ius naturale*   84, 89–91, 101,
    106–13, 118–37, 188, 290
of peoples, *ius gentium*   107, 109,
    111–13, 120, 122, 126, 129–30, 290
Roman   108–9, 114 n.29, 132,
    255 n.2, 278 n.85
law courts   18–19, 64, 95–6, 119, 126, 256
    English ecclesiastical   18–21, 66,
        78, 227 (*see also under* Church of
        England)
    English secular, ancient and
        conciliar   17–20, 66–7, 80–1, 259,
        276–81, 288
    High Court of Parliament   21–2,
        66–7, 69–70, 276–81
    international, contemporary   75–81
        (*see also under* European Union,
        law)
le Huray, Peter   40 n.89
Leo I, Pope   114 n.30
Leo XIII, Pope   105
Levy, E.   108 n.3
liberalism (egalitarian, pluralistic)   6–8,
    12–16, 52, 65, 74, 81–2, 87, 94–102,
    104, 176, 191–2, 251–4, 283–7, 289,
    see also pluralism
Locke, John   8, 83, 88, 90–3, 97–9, 101
lordship, *dominium*
    Adamic, created   117–19, 123, 125, 128
    legal   108, 114, 117–21, 123–37, 177,
        291
love   11, 164, 169, 176–7, 261, 264, 282
Luther, Martin   27, 159, 171, 184, 239

MacCulloch, Diarmaid   25 n.23, 33 n.60,
    48 n.118, 239 n.61, 256–7 n.3
McGrath, Alister   159 n.1, 162 nn.9–10,
    163 n.15
MacIntyre, Alasdair   2 n.2, 214 n.75,
    215 n.78
MacLure, Millar   45 n.109
MacPherson, C. B.   83, 88
Madood, Tariq   73 n.51, 74 n.52
Mair, John   230 n.28
Manschreck, Clyde   239 n.61
Maritain, Jacques   105
marriage   33, 60, 79–80, 111 n.19,
    111 n.21, 251, 262–3, 282
Marsilius of Padua   115–17, 119–23, 131,
    226, 274, 290
Mary I, Queen of England   18, 275 n.72
media, communications   86–7, 102–3,
    220, 253
Melanchthon, Philip   48, 142, 159, 171,
    184, 239, 243
Milbank, John   2 n.2
Minnerath, R.   75 n.55
moral action   133, 203–16, *see also*
    obedience
moral agency   133, 154–5, 204, 209–10,
    see also ecclesiology; faith; freedom;
    Holy Spirit
    renewal of   13–14, 104, 134–5, 168,
        175–8, 252
More, Thomas   24
Mouw, Richard   65 n.28

nature   85–6, 97–9
    human (*see* anthropology)
    nonhuman   98, 127–8, 135–6, 177–8,
        209, 283 (*see also* creation)
Neuhas, Richard   65 n.28
Nicholas of Cusa   231 n.30
Norman Anonymous   271 n.49, 274
Nozick, Robert   83, 92 n.19, 95 n.27
Null, Ashley   161 n.8, 162 n.13,
    163 nn.15–16

obedience, *see also under* worship
    to God, Christ   121, 133, 137, 142,
        148, 154, 160, 165–6, 169–71, 182,
        184, 204, 212, 216, 237, 246, 261,
        264, 270, 273–5, 282, 287, 291

(*see also* faith; moral action; moral agency)
  to political authorities   15, 246, 250, 256–7, 264–8, 273–5, 283
O'Donovan, Joan Lockwood   1 n.1, 105 n.39, 116 n.36
O'Donovan, Oliver   59 n.16, 117 n.39, 150 n.25, 174
O'Neill, Onora   100 n.35
Ong, Walter   185 n.16, 193 n.1
Origen of Alexandria   147 n.16
Osiander, Andreas   27
Overton, Richard   83, 88

Pabst, Adrian   2 n.2
Packer, J. I.   59 n.16, 60 n.17
Paine, Thomas   93–4
papacy   113–14, 125, 127, 134, 228–32, *see also under* empire, imperial rule; political jurisdiction
Parker, Matthew, Archbishop of Canterbury   26, 49, 187, 271 n.51
Pelican, Konrad   272
Philip IV, King of France   114
Pitt, Valerie   62 n.22
Pius XI, Pope   104
pluralism   52, 70–4, 87, 96, 105, 251, 253, 284–6
political (coercive) jurisdiction, *see also* justice; law
  in modern liberal natural rights theory   92–7, 101
  in papalist theology   113–15, 121, 134
  in patristic theology   109–10, 134
  in scholastic natural rights theory   84, 107, 121–5, 129–37
political jurisdiction, English Reformation public theology   5, 18, 155–6, 250–2, 255–91
  authority   13, 15, 224–7
  ecclesiastical (*see* ecclesiology; English Reformation; Church of England)
  judgment   15, 84, 225–7, 256–64, 267–8, 287–91
  limitations   10, 15, 155–6, 260–4, 275–81
  punishment   13, 257–8, 275
  purpose   15, 249, 256–60, 281–91
  representation   276, 281, 288–9

Poschmann, B.   161 n.8, 162 n.9, 163 nn.13–15, 227 n.16, 227 n.18
poverty, evangelical   116, 119–20, 134
predestination   173–5
property   88–9, 107–8, 110, 112, 116–20, 125, 133–5
prophecy, prophet, prophetic   62, 153, 290
Ptolemy of Lucca   114
public theology   1–2, 132–7, *see also* Church of England
  English Reformation, crisis of   1–2, 7–9, 60–82, 281–2

Rawls, John   64 n.28, 83, 92 n.19
reason, rationality
  instrumental, technological   94, 98–101, 192
  rationalist, rationalism   8, 84, 118, 124, 133, 154–5, 249–50 n.96, 282
  and revelation   118–20, 177, 248–9
  and will   89, 98
Reeves, Ryan   267 n.42, 272 n.5
repentance   11, 32, 46, 46 n.112, 146, 157, 161, 163 n.16, 164–8, 170, 175, 215, 237–8, 246–7, 260, 264, 289
  penance   84, 141, 161–4, 227–32
representation
  political (*see under* political jurisdiction, English Reformation public theology)
  soteriological   145–7, 152
republicanism   115, 131
revelation   137, 260–1, *see also* divine; law; Scripture
  in Christ   12, 152–3, 164, 169–71, 182–4, 188–9, 261
  through the Scriptures   12, 139, 179–92, 204–5, 210–12
right
  divine   8, 104, 106–7, 110, 115, 117, 131–4, 137, 155, 256, 287, 291
  (*see also under* law)
  legal (*see under* justice, injustice)
  meanings   108–11, 124–6
  natural   107, 109–11, 129, 133
  (*see also under* law)
  objective   107, 119, 133, 137
rights (subjective)   107–8, 111, 117, 124–5, 290–1

human   75–8, 94–6, 104
   and human dignity   9, 104–5, 140, 154
   modern development of   9, 74–6, 87–96, 103–10
   premodern, proto-modern development of   8–9, 84, 105–37, 290
rights, legal (and constitutional)   8, 16, 63–5, 69, 74–82, 93–7, 101–2, 115–17, 122, 127, 241–2, 255, 276, 278, 288, *see also* lordship, *dominium*
ius civile   89–90, 94–9, 102, 107–19, 126–30, 137
ius gentium   107, 126, 129–30
ownership, property   89–90, 92–4, 108–10, 108–13, 116–17, 119–20, 123, 125 (*see also under* corporation)
rights, natural (individual and communal)   124, 129, 290–1, *see also* lordship, *dominium*
   freedom   84, 88–92, 120, 133, 135, 282, 289
   permissive   107, 112, 118, 128, 133
   proprietary paradigm   8, 88–94, 290
   self-defense   128–32, 136, 249, 282
   self-preservation   89–93, 128–9, 133, 135–7, 282, 289
Rivers, Julian   69 n.40, 76 n.58, 79 n.68, 80
Robinson, Ian   26 n.25
Rogers, John   24–5
Rosenthal, Alexander   106 n.42
Rousseau, Jean Jacques   83
Rufinus (Decretist)   111–13, 119, 134

Sacks, Jonathan   73 n.51
sacraments   195, 202–3, 205–6, 236
   baptism   32–3, 37–8, 210, 212
   communion (eucharist)   13, 31–2, 36–8, 47, 55, 206–14
salvation completed in Christ   139–52
   atonement   10, 143, 145–7, 149, 207–9
   judicial paradigm   141–2, 156
   rescue, ransom   147, 149
   resurrection   148–50
   sacrifice   32, 36–7, 145–7, 207–9

salvation ongoing   155, 171–3, *see also* faith
sanctification   153–4, 159–60, 173, 240–3, 246, 264
science, modern   97–101
   bureaucracy   70, 86, 95, 99, 100, 100 nn.34–5, 101, 103, 287 (*see also under* society)
   social science   97, 99
   technology   12, 85–6, 97–101
Scrawley, James   33 n.61
Scripture, *see also under* Church of England; revelation
   authority and sufficiency   3, 11–12, 179–84, 188–92
   divine and human genesis   184–92
   interpretation   23, 25, 182–9
   rule in the church (*see under* ecclesiology; English Reformation ecclesiology)
   scholarship   23–4, 57–8, 180, 184–7
   tradition of   12, 189–92, 214–16
   translation of   23, 57–8, 187–9
   in worship (*see under* worship)
Shapiro, Ian   83, 91 n.13, 92 n.17, 95 n.27, 99
sin   144–5, 151–2, 164, 166–7, 175–6, 261
Skillen, James   64–5 n.28
Skinner, Quentin   2 n.2, 83
Smith, Thomas   273, 276
society
   created, Adamic   117–19, 134, 151, 261–2, 273
   ecclesial (*see under* ecclesiology, English Reformation ecclesiology)
   eschatological community (*see under* English Reformation ecclesiology)
   fallen, postlapsarian   9, 14, 112–13, 119, 125, 135, 155, 191, 252, 254, 257, 273, 290
   modern, late modern   8, 52, 74, 82–7, 95–7, 176, 253–4, 283–7, 289 (*see also* liberalism)
   nonproprietary   9, 118–19, 123, 134, 155, 283
   restored, perfected   11, 110, 155, 201, 261–2
   technological   85–6, 97–101, 219–20

de Soto, Domingo   128–9, 132, 136
Starkey, Thomas   264 n.33, 267 n.40, 268 n.44
Strauss, Leo   83
Suárez, Francisco   230 n.28
Summenhart, Conrad   125–7
supererogation, works of   121

Taverner, Richard   42 n.96, 46 n.110, 149
Tentler, Thomas   161 n.6, 163 n.15
Tierney, Brian   8 n.4, 107 n.1, 111–12, 121 n.66, 127 n.92, 244 n.76
tradition   12, 189–92, 214–16
   of Roman Catholic social teaching   105
   of Scripture (*see under* Scripture)
   Western, of natural rights (*see under* rights, natural)
Travers, Walter   240–3
Trinterud, Leonard   240 n.63
Tuck, Richard   108 n.3, 126 n.89
Tully, James   91 n.13
Tyndale, William   24, 170–1, 185–6, 226 n.12

Universal Declaration of Human Rights   104

Vázquez, Fernando (de Menchaca)   129–30, 136–7
Verhey, Allen   102 n.37
Verkamp, Bernard   239 n.61, 242 n.7, 245 n.78
Vermigli, Peter Martyr   31 n.49, 35 n.67, 239, 256 n.3

virtue   215, 260 n.15, *see also* faith; Holy Spirit; MacIntyre, Alasdair; tradition
de Vitoria, Francisco   127–32, 136, 230 n.28, 231 n.30
Voegelin, Eric   2 n.2, 83

Wannenwetsch, Bernd   203 n.34
Watkins, Oscar   161 n.8, 227 n.13
Weber, Max   99
Whitaker, Edward   34 n.62, 35 n.67
Whitgift, John, Archbishop of Canterbury   245–7, 272
Wilks, Michael   229 n.24
William of Ockham   115–22, 124–5, 131, 230 n.28, 290
Witte, John, Jr.   63–4, 106 n.42, 108 n.4
Wolin, Sheldon   2 n.2, 83
Wolterstorff, Nicholas   65 n.28
worship   193–220, *see also under* Church of England; English Reformation ecclesiology; faith; sacraments; Scripture
   archetype of faithful action   12–13, 203–16
   corporate, common (*see under* church)
   images in   216–20
   music, song   39–41, 56, 198–201
   prayer   47, 197–203
   preaching   196–7, 222
   Scripture in   12–13, 195–201
Wright, N. T.   184 n.13
Wyclif, John   123–4, 170, 185 n.14, 226, 274, 290

Zwingli, Huldrych   184, 242 n.71, 272

www.ingramcontent.com/pod-product-compliance
Lightning Source LLC
Chambersburg PA
CBHW071232230426
43668CB00011B/1395